Tomorrow's Cities, Tomorrow's Suburbs

By

William H. Lucy
and
David L. Phillips

PLANNERS PRESS
AMERICAN PLANNING ASSOCIATION
Chicago, Illinois
Washington, DC

ISBN (paperback edition): 1-932364-14-5
ISBN (hardbound edition): 1-932364-15-3
Library of Congress Control Number 2005930924

Printed in the United States of America

Interior composition and copyediting by Joanne Shwed, Backspace Ink
Cover design by Susan Deegan

Contents

Preface

After more than 30 years of feeling pessimistic about central cities' prospects in the United States, it is a pleasure to be optimistic for the first time. Until recently, we have been resigned to the success of suburbs at cities' expense. During the 1980s, we believed that suburban patterns that required motor vehicles for routine daily activities would lead to frustration and eventual suburban decline, but we did not expect that clear signs of suburban decline would be apparent across the nation by the 1990 and 2000 censuses.

This emerging reversal of fortunes between cities and suburbs generates two conflicting attitudes. Given the smugness among many suburban politicians and residents that central cities are not needed anymore, seeing some suburbs decline and other suburbs plummet arouses a certain sense of justice being done. At the same time, we dread the emerging rearrangement of spatial assets and liabilities that will produce many suburbs more stressed than the central cities whose travails suburbanites have criticized.

The worst suburbs will be similar to the worst city neighborhoods—filled with abandoned buildings and vacant lots, debris and junk cars scattered about, a few homeless persons in vacant buildings, high crime and drug abuse, low morale, and little hope. Some suburbs already have those characteristics.

However, cities had, and still have, business, cultural, institutional, government, and residential assets—significant buildings and important activities around which economic elites and neighborhood activists could rally. Evidence of progress in reviving central cities can be found across the U.S., inspired by these assets and the commitment of people to sustain them. Progress is uneven to be sure, and usually decline continues in parts of cities as other parts revive. The problem of small suburbs is that they lack most valued assets, other than the houses and retail shops that are falling into disrepair amid neglect and inability to compete with newer and older areas. Most of the suburbs that will be hardest to sustain and revive are the middle-aged suburbs created between 1945 and 1970, which are filled with small houses with little variation, rather than the older suburbs, which have more housing diversity, public transportation, and proximity to central cities.

Problems in middle-aged suburbs will lead to two effects in older areas and on the metropolitan fringe. More people who prefer walking, convenience, and density will gravitate to central cities and some older suburbs adjacent to cities and contribute to reviving them. More people who favor low density and accept the inconvenience that goes with it will move even farther from metropolitan centers.

Prospects of middle-aged suburbs also can be affected by natural disasters radically transforming settlement patterns, as occurred in August 2005 in the New Orleans metropolitan area in the aftermath of Hurricane Katrina.

It seems likely that New Orleans, when rebuilt, will have less land area and fewer residents than before Katrina. Psychological attachments will motivate some returns, but physical constraints, plus variation in business and government service capacity, will favor some neighborhoods over others. More buildable land above sea level could be created by dredging some parts of the city for parks and marshes. These low areas would create visual and recreational amenities and aid stormwater management.

The lowest parts of New Orleans will be the last areas chosen for rebuilding by private developers; some areas may never be rebuilt. Public housing has not been built in the U.S. in recent years. Little, if any, will be built in New Orleans. Private developers of projects with Low Income Housing Tax Credits may not have projects approved in low-lying areas. Because the better-off neighborhoods survived the hurricane with little damage, much of the restored housing, as well as new housing, will be more suitable for middle- and upper-income households than for lower-income households. High demand for housing during the rebuilding stage will lead to high prices and higher incomes in neighborhoods with larger and higher-quality housing.

Where will the poor go? Many have left the region and will never return. Other low-income workers will return to the suburbs, often occupying small, middle-aged, post-World War II housing. Doubling up will be common. Low-cost manufactured housing will be provided inland, farther from the coast, where flooding is less likely but where travel access to work will be difficult. Expanded public bus service, much of it funded by the federal government, will be featured in the early stages of rebuilding; sustaining this service may be problematic.

The suburbs of New Orleans were declining before Katrina. From 1960 to 1990, six of New Orleans' nine suburbs large enough to be in the 1960 census declined by more than 10 percent in relative median family income, while two of the nine suburbs declined faster than the City of New Orleans. After Katrina, New Orleans' suburbs will continue to diverge from each other, with some suburbs absorbing numerous low-income residents

The new metropolitan pattern after rebuilding will feature the City of New Orleans with less poverty than before Katrina as well as a smaller population. The entertainment district in New Orleans is likely to attract more creative young adults with higher incomes to locate in the city. Consequently, the rebuilt city will be much better off in residents' income relative to its suburbs than before Katrina.

Other metropolitan areas are apt to see an influx of Katrina migrants settling in middle-aged suburbs, just as a majority of immigrants from other nations settled in suburbs during the 1990s. With more than 100,000 evacuees relocating to the Houston area immediately after Katrina, the City of Houston and its suburbs could experience long-term increases in responsibilities and burdens. During the 1990s, Houston declined at a modest rate in income relative to metropolitan income levels. Forty percent of Houston's suburbs declined faster than the central city in relative income. Seven of Houston's suburbs were worse off in relative income in 2000 than Detroit, the city suffering the most extreme income disparity relative to its metropolitan norms. Thus, a large increase in Houston area residents without a corresponding increase in jobs could have drastic negative effects on the City of Houston and several of its suburbs that were distressed before Katrina.

Providing theories and trend data that support these predictions for New Orleans and Houston are major themes in this book. New Orleans, however, was not one of the metropolitan areas that we emphasized in our research.

Effects of widespread suburban decline will make many old cities stronger and increase sprawling outer suburban areas. Coping with middle-aged suburban decline will be one of the major challenges confronting the U.S. This prediction assumes that conditions driving recent city and suburban trends remain roughly the same. If conditions change drastically, such as by gasoline prices doubling or tripling, then middle-aged suburbs could revive.

Acknowledgements

While most of the research and writing in this book occurred from 2001 to 2005, glimmerings of concepts and partial drafts of current chapters emerged over many years. Because of that evolution, many contributors of ideas may have disappeared from memory or may have been submerged beneath an exaggerated belief in our own creativity.

Certain assistance remains clear. Financial support from The Brookings Institution Center on Urban and Metropolitan Policy enabled us to extend research in Chapters 5, 6, and 7 to a national scale. We thank Bruce Katz, Amy Liu, Robert Puentes, Alan Berube, and Audrey Singer of The Brookings Institution for their advice, critiques, and support. Research about suburban decline was launched previously in the context of Virginia suburbs with financial support from Katherine Imhoff, executive director of the Virginia Commission on Population Growth and Development; Michael Pratt, director of the Center for Urban Development of Virginia Commonwealth University; and James Oliver and Neal Barber, board member and staff director, respectively, of the Partnership for Urban Virginia. Financial support from the Pew Cities Partnership, Suzanne Morse, executive director, and Jacqueline Dugery, research director, facilitated research about successful revitalization of Charlottesville's downtown in Virginia.

We would like to thank readers of all or part of the manuscript, and discussants of various ideas, especially Carolyn Adams, Timothy Beatley, William Morrish, E.M. Risse, Reid Ewing, Neal Barber, Donna Shalala, William H. Hudnut III, and Jaquelin Robertson. Numerous able students at the University of Virginia contributed to our research: Thomas Brockenbrough, Matthew Dalby, Jeffrey Driscoll, Michael Fenner, Steven Golden, Jana Lynott, Lara Mathes, Kristin Mitchell, Michelle O'Hare, Christine Piwonka, Raphael Rabalais, Matthew Robbie, Rebecca Ross, Lori Savron, Douglas Stanford, Steven Tredennick, and Angie Williamson. We also thank Bettie Hall for occasional typing and consistent ability to retrieve selected tables from large files.

Our spouses and children at home have supported and tolerated our work. For that, we thank Sherry and Carole, Rachel, Zachary, and Cathleen.

We appreciate the editorial judgment and support of Sylvia Lewis, director of publications of the American Planning Association, and the insights of her editorial staff. During production, it has been a pleasure working with Joanne Shwed of Backspace Ink who was remarkable in the thoroughness of copyediting, layout, and design.

William H. Lucy
David L. Phillips

List of Figures

List of Tables

List of Maps

List of Acronyms

AHS	average household size
APHA	American Public Health Association
CDC	community development corporation
CDP	Census Designated Place
CMSA	Consolidated Metropolitan Statistical Area
DPZS	Andres Duany, Elizabeth Plater-Zyberk, and Jeff Speck
FBI	Federal Bureau of Investigation
FHA	Federal Housing Administration
HUD	[U.S. Department of] Housing and Urban Development
ITE	Institute of Transportation Engineers
MSA	Metropolitan Statistical Area
NAR	National Association of Realtors
PMSA	Primary Metropolitan Statistical Area
SCORE	Suburban Core Opportunity, Restoration, and Enhancement [Act of 2005]
SUV	sports utility vehicle
ULI	Urban Land Institute

Themes and
Policy Approaches

1

Is the Past Prologue for Change?

In this book, we examine four themes. Exploring them led to surprising optimism about prospects for coping with persistent central city ills, but we also feel deep anxiety about certain suburban trends. The first theme we examine is mainly descriptive. What are some important growth, decline, and revival trends in all the cities in all 50 states, in all the suburban places in 35 large metropolitan areas, and in all the census tracts in six major metropolitan areas? We explore a large number of cities, suburbs, and neighborhoods so that we can be confident we are capturing several dimensions of the diversity and complexity of metropolitan America.

The second theme involves trying to explain the diverse variety of improvements and declines in cities, suburbs, and neighborhoods (census tracts). This theme is that housing stock characteristics are important in interpreting differences in conditions and trends in cities, suburbs, and neighborhoods. The housing stock and physical aspects of neighborhoods are more important as causes of decline, we argue in Chapter 2, than 10 recent authors of books about metropolitan conditions have emphasized in their work.

Third, common beliefs about cities, suburbs, and neighborhoods have powerful influences on residential location trends and on the vitality of local government jurisdictions. Some beliefs about which areas are safe, for example, are myths—partially accurate but significantly distorted interpretations of reality that influence decisions. Results of location preferences—which we refer to as mega-decisions because of their sweeping impact on society—create spatial inequalities. Influences on location preferences are important subjects for separate inquiry—our third theme.

Interactions between location preferences, housing supply, and neighborhood characteristics influence which policies will be effective in achieving public goals, as well as which households can be effective in achieving their private goals. The new regionalists, to be discussed in Chapter 2, are correct in their arguments about how regional reforms, especially by state governments, would help reduce spatial inequalities and their adverse effects. Our emphasis, however, leads to a supplementary opinion. We believe that progress has been made by individuals, developers, and local public officials on the central problems of cities and suburbs without regional reforms. Location decisions, development projects, and place-making efforts by local public officials can have useful results, even if regional reforms do not occur—our fourth theme.

The net effect of these themes is that we are optimistic about the future of most central cities. Trends since the 2000 census are consistent with our optimistic perspective. Some central cities, however, confront ongoing disinvestment and face Herculean struggles. In addition, our pessimism about the future of many suburbs, which began to emerge when we worked on our previous book, *Confronting Suburban Decline*,[1] accelerated as we worked on these four themes. Still, even in badly deteriorated suburbs, a "can do" spirit and insightful policies can lead to useful actions.

DISPARITIES IN RELATIVE INCOME

Spatial patterns of residents' income distribution in metropolitan areas in the United States have changed dramatically. Some suburbs, often thought of as uniformly thriving, already have fallen to astonishingly low income levels compared to metropolitan income norms. Income disparities between central cities and suburbs usually have been exceeded by income gaps between suburbs.

Searching for explanations of increasing intersuburban income disparities, we turn more to housing markets, individuals' beliefs, and spatial patterns resulting from residential location decisions, and less to effects of federal public policies—policies that often have been blamed for suburban expansion and central city decline. Effects of public policies, either federal or state, have not necessarily been neutral in their spatial impacts or blameless for suburbanization, but beliefs and decisions that lead to residential location patterns probably have had greater effects.

If this is not so, then how can one explain trends, which we describe in Chapters 3 through 8, that modify the trickle-down theory of neighborhood change—a theory which every perspective on metropolitan evolution has accepted explicitly or implicitly? Several theories of metropolitan evolution will be discussed in Chapter 2. The most familiar conceptual model of neighborhood change is the filtering or trickle-down process, which predicts a neighborhood housing stock of a particular vintage will transition successively to lower-income groups as it depreciates with advancing age. We find considerable evidence that neighborhood changes became more complex in the 1980s and 1990s.

Our conclusion, jumping ahead, is that typical outcomes of housing filtering processes, which we usually refer to as the trickle-down process of neighborhood change,[2] dominated socioeconomic trends in neighborhoods and local governments from 1950 through 1980. However, trends changed substantially in the 1990s, after being foreshadowed in the 1980s. From 1980 to 2000, our analysis reveals that the trickle-down process was modified. Older areas did better, especially in the 1990s. Middle-aged areas faded more than they did earlier. The reason why this shift occurred is a puzzle we begin to explore.

We conducted neighborhood scale (census tract) analyses of income trends in six metropolitan areas—Atlanta, Chicago, Los Angeles, Philadelphia, Richmond, and Washington, D.C. In each metropolitan area, the trickle-down process—in which housing and neighborhoods are occupied by lower-income residents as housing ages—clearly was interrupted in the 1990s, after a more modest change in the 1980s. The coast-to-coast distribution of these metropolitan areas, as well as their economic, demographic, and social diversity, leads us to hypothesize that this phenomenon occurred nationwide.

The absence of any probable public policy cause emanating from the federal government for altering neighborhood change outcomes is curious and significant. No changes occurred in federal policies in the 1980s and 1990s that were remotely as sweeping as new housing policies in the 1930s and 1940s or new highway policies in the 1950s—policies often credited with leading to subsequent rapid suburbanization.[3] Because relative income improvements have occurred in neighborhoods at every income level, federal policies aimed at poverty neighborhoods also cannot explain most neighborhood changes.

Consequently, we think it is promising to explore causes that are rooted in individuals' beliefs, expressed in households' residential location decisions, and revealed in spatial residential patterns. Most of the first half of this book is about spatial patterns, with patterns often measured by the income of residents in cities and suburbs. In the second half, we examine some influences on location decisions, especially beliefs about safety. We consider whether changes in beliefs about safety could have meaningful future effects on residential location patterns—in addition to the effects that already have occurred. We also examine the influence of small, post-World War II houses, many of them in suburbs, on residential location trends. Avoidance by the middle class of small, middle-aged houses is contributing significantly, we believe, to altering the trickle-down process of neighborhood change.

Large spatial income disparities are an outcome of sprawl on the suburban fringe,[4] concentrated poverty in central cities,[5] too little reinvestment in old and middle-aged housing,[6] and excessive inequalities in local governments' revenue capacity and tax burdens.[7] High-density development can also lead to income segregation, unless mixed housing types are included in neighborhoods.[8] Three interacting factors have led to extensive and diverse spatial income inequalities: individuals' beliefs, housing markets, and public policies. Federal and state policies are relevant, but here we emphasize beliefs, spatial disparities, and local policies that affect "place" characteristics. The shared task of citizens and public officials is to understand the respective influences of beliefs, markets, and public policies and to find ways to improve results by altering each arena as needed. Attitudes of consumers and voters may matter more than public policies, partly because they contribute support for policies, but also because attitudes are expressed every day through market choices.

Dramatic transformations have been routine in cities and suburbs through the 20th century. Conditions and trends at the beginning of the 21st century foreshadow additional upheavals. Some of the 20th-century losers will become 21st-century winners—especially some central cities. Some of the previous winners, which now are middle-aged suburbs, will continue their recent descent, often to perilous conditions—a peril to which some suburbs already have descended. Sprawl on the metropolitan fringe will threaten some but not all older jurisdictions. Some jurisdictions—both central cities and some suburbs—will benefit from sprawl by offering welcome alternatives to sprawl's stresses. Choices by individuals, households, businesses, and governments will make a difference. Transformation in cities and suburbs is shaped partially by voluntary human decisions. Significant changes in location decisions took root in the 1990s and will continue during the next decade.

GROWTH, SPRAWL, AND DISPARITIES

The 50 years from 1950 to 2000 were dominated by the decline of large central cities, combined with suburban growth and prosperity. By the 1990s, however, conflicting trends had emerged, including some notable central city revival and considerable suburban decline, while outer suburban sprawl accelerated.

Briefly, here are a few of the metropolitan trends that will be elaborated in subsequent chapters:

• Between 1950 and 2000, metropolitan areas' share of the United States' population increased from 55 to 80 percent. Most of the growth occurred outside central cities.

• By 2000, 62 percent of metropolitan population was outside central cities compared with 42 percent in 1950. Population decline was common in large central cities. Baltimore, and St. Louis were two extreme cases, losing 31 and 59 percent of their population, respectively, between 1950 and 2000. Socioeconomic status of central city residents also was falling.

• By 1990, median family income in 15 of the 40 central cities in the 35 most populous metropolitan areas was below 70 percent of suburban income. David Rusk had referred to such central cities as having fallen below the "point of no return," meaning that their self-renewal capacity had been exhausted.[9] During the 1990s, however, 28 of these 40 central cities were stable or increased in relative per capita income. Relative income increases occurred most often in neighborhoods that specialized in housing built before 1940.

• In the late 20th century, population decline and relative income decline also were common in many suburbs. Twenty-seven percent of 2,586 suburbs in 35 large metropolitan areas lost population between 1990 and 2000. Approximately half of the 2,586 suburbs declined in relative income during that decade.

• In 1990, 121 suburbs had fallen below 60 percent of metropolitan per capita income. By 2000, 155 suburbs were below 60 percent of metropolitan per capita income. Relative income is the income of residents in any jurisdiction or census tract relative to median family income or per capita income of residents for the entire metropolitan area. These decline trends were fueled by sprawl development on the metropolitan fringe.

• In 1950, America's cities were the least dense in the modern developed world. By 2000, they were even less dense, and suburbs had become much less convenient territories in which to move around in each successive decade. Suburban and exurban sprawl settlement patterns had become ever more extensive geographically and more controversial politically.

• By 2000, opposition to sprawl growth patterns had become a prominent political issue in many outer metropolitan counties.[10] In a quality-of-life survey, 57 percent of respondents said that sprawl is a very important (30 percent) or somewhat important (27 percent) problem.[11] In November 2000, referenda passed in more than 200 metropolitan areas to acquire land for parks and permit conservation easements, and to adopt other development limitations.[12]

Population and socioeconomic decline in many central cities and suburbs reflect the spatial manifestation of citizen attitudes toward space and place, and the public policies that support those dominant, low-density, sprawling spatial patterns. Ironically, considerable suburban decline reflects the success of public policies to achieve private preferences, as Anthony Downs emphasized in his introduction to *New Visions for Metropolitan America*: "For half a century America has had one dominant vision of how its metropolitan areas ought to grow and develop. It is best described as unlimited low-density sprawl. This vision encompasses personal and social goals—a home in the suburbs, a car, good schools, and responsive local government—that most Americans cherish."[13] While these outcomes are cherished by many, others believe excessive inconvenience and stress have accompanied sprawl development.

As attitudes about spatial patterns change, they affect outcomes. Because the dominant citizen attitudes toward space and place have altered, a diverse variety of neighborhoods in central cities and inner suburbs has rebounded. Compared with previous decades, more people sought alternatives to driving, sometimes for commuting to work and sometimes for errands and entertainment.

Income polarization between concentrated poverty districts near the center and middle- and upper-income subdivisions in a low-density sprawl pattern on the edges has been the norm since 1960.[14] Income disparities are deeply rooted in social and economic conditions and trends and in public policies that have facilitated suburbanization. Income disparities also are the outcome of residents, businesses, and developers' location decisions. Influences on location decisions shifted at least moderately, we believe, during the 1990s, partly because of reduced expectations of dangers from crime. They may shift more, because some individuals' residential location decisions are based partially on myths about safety related to exaggerating crime dangers and underestimating traffic risks.[15]

Location decisions are decentralized. More than 30 million people decide each year where to move. If a modest proportion of those decisions lead to destinations that reduce rather than increase income polarization between cities and suburbs or among suburbs, that is the most effective means by which sprawl and perhaps even concentrated poverty can be reduced. The key question is: Can such a change in individuals' decisions occur?

Some changes in information, urban design, and politics may strengthen cities and some inner suburbs. More accurate information and more persuasive arguments may shift location decisions that have been based on misinformation, miscalculation, and shallow beliefs. Explicit attention and skillful design may enhance public and private places, where many people want to spend some social and civic time. More effective local public policies can reduce some disincentives put in the path of people who would prefer to stay in or move to cities and older suburbs.

In addition, we have argued elsewhere[16] that obstacles to creating more satisfying places should be reduced. These include, in particular, the obstacles imposed by federal highway and housing policies, state policies concerning annexation and education finance, and excessive local government fragmentation and financial inequities. Reducing these obstacles is important but very difficult. Success, so far, has been rare. Success probably will continue to be rare, even though interest in regionalism and its reform agenda has increased.[17] Consequently, avenues to influence location decisions should be pursued in addition to proposing regional reform policies.

HOUSING MARKETS, MOBILITY, AND FEDERAL POLICIES

In metropolitan areas in the U.S., politics and markets reinforce each other. Markets are systems in which people make choices about the value of goods and services. In a federal system, politics is a set of interlocking national, state, and local systems in which people exert influence on government decisions. In markets, money purchases goods and services. In politics, votes and interest group activities (letters, petitions, arguments, protests, and campaign contributions) are the usual currency of influence.

However, in the United States, where the national average was 90 local governments per metropolitan area in 1987, residential mobility is the currency with which the greatest political influence is exerted. Purchasing a residence, either temporarily through rent or for a longer period through ownership, garners political values by choosing among local governments. Residential location decisions purchase physical safety, investment security, access to daily needs and wants, education opportunities for children, and aesthetic and cultural amenities—much of the pantheon of elements that determine one's quality of life. Location decisions also purchase the right to vote and organize politically within one or more of the 90 average local governments.

High potential for income disparities within metropolitan areas is embedded in Americans' mobility propensities. About 45 to 50 percent of metropolitan residents move within five years. This finding has been consistent for the five years before each of the recent national censuses from 1960 through 2000. After eight years, 50 percent of metropolitan home owners, who are much more rooted than renters, have moved. High mobility rates carry the seeds but not the necessity of neighborhood instability. Residential movers could relocate to places with density similar to the places from which they moved, as well as to housing of similar tenure, size, and age, and to jurisdictions similarly positioned with respect to metropolitan centers and edges. Some have done so, and others have moved to smaller housing units, switched from owner to renter status, and chosen more central locations. The dominant trend resulting in sprawl, however, has been the opposite: More residents have chosen larger and newer dwellings with more land closer to metropolitan edges. Why?

An often-cited reason is that federal programs expanded home ownership opportunities. Federal guarantees of mortgages with low down payments and deductions of mortgage interest and local property taxes from federal income taxes increased the percentage of the population for whom home ownership has been feasible and attractive. In addition, to avoid federal capital gains taxes, house sellers were required before the law changed in 1997 to purchase replacement housing as expensive as the property that was sold. Expansion of capital available for housing loans through federally supported secondary mortgage markets also helped increase the proportion of home owners.

Before World War II, home ownership rates were in the 40 to 45 percent range. After World War II, the home ownership rate climbed to 62 percent in 1960. In 2000, the home ownership rate was 67 percent. The federal Interstate Highway Program, which dedicated the federal gasoline tax to highway construction, and favorable terms which provided 90 percent of federal funds for state-sponsored projects, expanded the metropolitan territory within which commuting to work was feasible. It also expanded the potential locations for employment centers, extending the commuting territory within which residential settlements could be developed.

These opportunities have largely been seized, because rising affluence made practical the desire for control of more private space. More space can be reached in less time by those with automobiles. Most people have made that choice. Once a car has been purchased, the marginal use of the car often is less expensive than public transit as well as more flexible. However, when too many car drivers are following similar routes during similar periods of the day, more time is required to reach destinations. Hence, control of more space in far-flung locations leads easily to more cars using the same routes, with severe problems of sprawl and congestion ensuing.

CONSUMERISM AND CAREERISM

Consumerism and careerism encourage car use. Consumerism is the propensity to buy goods frequently and to look for "good deals" in making purchases. Most good deals depend on mass marketing. Good deals are more likely to be found in large display rooms with massive storage areas and immense parking lots. Businesses in such locations have opted for control of more space. They form an alliance with consumers invested in being smart, even frugal, consumers. Consumers control more residential space for their "stuff." Businesses control more space to offer more goods for sale. The desire by consumers and businesses to control more privately owned space leads to more sprawl.

Whereas consumerism is expressed by controlling more space and filling it with acquisitions, careerism treats one's lifetime as a commodity. A lifetime is composed of childhood, preparation for a career, the career launch, the decision to move in pursuit of career opportunities—several times for some people—and the decision to move for a desirable retirement setting with high amenities and moderate taxes, often where one has not lived previously. Viewed in this way, the residence is an investment. In most of these residential stops, a good housing investment is one of the main financial aspects of career choices. A good investment appreciates in value.

Predictability supports security of investments. Most people believe they can better predict the short-term future of new housing than old housing. They have more confidence in the settings where new housing exists, usually being surrounded by other new housing and by people who can afford new housing. Thus, people who move, or want to have the flexibility to move, prefer housing that fits their image of a good commodity for sale, especially if they are in-movers from outside the metropolitan area. More people with these priorities have chosen residential locations toward the edge than toward the center. Thus, careerism nurtures sprawl, and increases poverty concentrations in areas left behind, even though it is not directly related to these results.

The construction period of housing and neighborhoods impacts income disparities among neighborhoods and suburbs for another reason. Each decade, purchasers of new residences have controlled more space. In 1950, the median-size, single-family, detached new house contained 1,100 square feet. In 1970, its median size had increased to 1,375 feet. In 2000, the median-size new house was 2,000 square feet.[18] When these new houses were purchased, several elements were included in the price: the dwelling, nearby dwellings, the neighborhood, the jurisdiction, and accessible distances to various settings where goods, services, and facilities were located. To the extent that control of more space was the purchasers' goal in 2000, they would be unlikely to consider buying the 1,100-square-foot house built in 1950, unless the settings of the small houses greatly exceed the appeal of large house settings farther toward the metropolitan edge.

From these size data, one can see the potential for sprawl to be induced by purchasers buying larger houses. How much sprawl is induced depends on where the new, large houses are built. They could be built as replacements for smaller houses and built on the same sites where small houses were demolished or expanded. It is more likely that they will be built on undeveloped land, so-called greenfield sites, close to the metropolitan fringe. Why?

LOCAL GOVERNMENT DEVELOPMENT DECISIONS

It may seem obvious that the fringe sites will be preferred because the sites will be less expensive, lacking other buildings requiring removal or expansion, but that depends on two minimum conditions. The first condition is that local governments permit, facilitate, or do not unduly impede the development of these fringe sites. The second condition is that local governments of jurisdictions with small houses do not sufficiently facilitate redevelopment or expansion to make these closer-in sites equally or more attractive.

Here, the perverse quality of preferences for local governance comes into play in two respects. The first perverse quality is that local governments, where small houses are located, rarely facilitate replacing them with greater density. They also may be reluctant to encourage expanding small houses. Neighbors of potential expansion, replacement, and infill sites generally protest proposals to increase density, either by an increase in land coverage or an increase in housing units. Increased density usually brings to mind more cars, more congestion, and perhaps more residents with lower socioeconomic status. More land coverage brings to mind fewer trees and open space. This litany of argument is common at zone change and site plan hearings and receives considerable press attention.

Local government legislators usually are elected from districts within the larger jurisdiction. Other local legislators tend to defer to the legislator in whose district the project in contention is located. The district legislator in turn tends to give considerable weight to the views of neighboring constituents. As a consequence, a small minority of voters usually has political influence disproportionate to their number. They have this influence in part because the potential beneficiaries of the new or expanded housing usually are not current constituents. Consequently, the contest is between those with a few votes who feel strongly and those with potentially as many or more votes who are anonymous, not yet aware of who they are.

Developers recognize these situations. They are interpreted as "trouble" and tie up money and time. The outcome is likely to be uncertain and delays are highly likely. Developers with options usually choose other alternatives because they are driven by the search for adequate profit and limited risks, rather than by the goal of enhancing particular neighborhoods.

Local government officials with jurisdiction over greenfield sites have other political dynamics in play. One political dynamic is that developers and other real estate interests often are among the largest financial contributors to election campaigns of local officials. While that may seem an obvious path to political influence, successful political advocacy by developers depends on two other conditions. One condition is that population growth is in the interest of many local businesses. In addition, many citizens associate growth with progress. They begin with a positive attitude toward it. Hence, they are good prospects to support pro-growth candidates in elections. In this way, developers' political contributions sometimes facilitate greenfield development.

The second condition is that population growth strains local budgets, primarily because public school costs per pupil are much higher than the annual taxes generated by typical new residences. This condition is particularly problematic because county governments and independent school districts are heavily dependent on local real property tax revenues. Except in instances in which a large office building or manufacturing plant is located in outer suburban or rural locations, or a regional shopping center captures a location where major highways intersect, residential development precedes most business development on the metropolitan fringe. Consequently, jurisdictions experience fiscal stress where residential development predominates. Many local businesses and voters argue that business development is needed to diminish property tax pressure on residents. Counterarguments are likely that more business growth will lead to more residential growth. The next counterargument is that more residential growth will occur regardless of whether businesses increase. The net effect of these arguments is that most local governments do little to impede fringe development, and some actively support it.

TYRANNY OF EASY DEVELOPMENT DECISIONS

Local government passivity usually is sufficient for development to occur because private property rights give owners rights to sell. Most land is zoned for densities at which development can be profitable. Even if some fringe governments resist development, other fringe governments usually welcome development or are neutral toward it. Thus, private property rights prevail and development proceeds.[19] In addition, less citizen opposition will occur if development is proposed some distance from existing settlements. Hopscotch sprawl development in small leaps becomes common. Contiguous development is not required. Rarely do local governments construct roads, sewers, water, and schools in advance of development. Advance construction of public facilities would constitute major inducements to developers to build in well-served locations; however, local taxpayers and public officials usually lack a clear vision about where development should occur. They are not willing to make expensive advance public investments. Even "smart growth" policies rarely emphasize infrastructure investments prior to development to guide new construction to preferred locations.

The net effect of these conditions is what we call the tyranny of easy development decisions. Most developers prefer to build where land is available, opposition is limited, and market demand is adequate. Many greenfield sites provide these ingredients; few brownfield or grayfield sites do. Brownfield sites have environmental contamination, often in unspecified amounts that may be difficult to predict, even after careful investigation. Grayfield sites are developed sites where redevelopment occurs through combinations of expansion, adaptation, demolition, and new construction. These adaptive projects require more skill, patience, and resources by developers than projects on greenfield sites. Partnerships with local governments often are needed to solve infrastructure deficiencies—another potential source of uncertainty and delay. Adaptive projects also involve more risk due to probable opposition from neighbors. Hence, fewer developers and lenders are interested in these projects.

Easy development alternatives usually are chosen, levying a sort of tyranny over the development of entire regions. Tyranny implies that actions are taken without citizens or elected representatives having a say. This description is partially accurate in that fringe development is agreed to by a small proportion of metropolitan residents and elected officials. On the other hand, neighborhood opposition to redevelopment and infill development is so common that, in a sense, many inner and mid-range metropolitan residents forfeit their potential influence on fringe development by opposing development in inner- and central metropolitan locations. One outcome is that there is a mismatch between the small scale of most development decisions and cumulative regional impacts of these small development increments. In the process, a vote never occurs by anyone for or against the regional development pattern that emerges from these processes. This is another sense in which development processes are tyrannical—carried out without popular consent or meaningful regional deliberations. Portland, Oregon, is the only metropolitan area in which democratic processes avoid these metropolitan outcomes.

The tyranny of easy development decisions has been an obstacle to redevelopment in cities, but cities have some sites crying out for redevelopment—shrunken downtowns, abandoned warehouses, transit station areas, unused rail yards, demolished housing, and clearly deteriorated but not yet abandoned neighborhoods. These sites typically are easily accessible to public transportation and may have attractive adjacent areas. Local elected officials usually agree that many of these sites should be redeveloped and are willing to invest public resources in renewal plans.

In middle-aged suburbs, except for abandoned shopping centers, the imminent need for redevelopment is less apparent and potential gains from major reinvestment are less obvious. Local elected officials in suburbs are less likely to agree on which sites should be redeveloped, and they are more likely to doubt that public resources should be invested in them. They may be coping with capital costs for schools, which linger in 30-year bond issues after the student bubble has burst and demand for schools has receded. These are reasons why the tyranny of easy development decisions may prove more debilitating to middle-aged suburbs than to older central cities.

BELIEFS AND PUBLIC POLICIES

The general remedy for income disparities between central cities and suburbs is to modify both individual behavior and public policies. That is the tack taken here. The extent and significance of income disparities is discussed by several authors whose views we examine in Chapter 2. Reducing income disparities among suburbs is more complicated than reducing city-suburb disparities, and requires addressing "the small house problem" that we focus on in Chapter 12. Policies that influence metropolitan form should be changed, as should policies that distribute public and private resources unequally and inequitably throughout metropolitan areas, as the new regionalists argue.[20] Individuals also should change their behavior and, to some extent, behavior changes have been occurring.

If behavior does change, it will be reflected in residential location decisions, transportation choices, and consumption trends. If more people want places that are walkable, more such places will be created and adapted. Markets are experimental.

Products are introduced and buyers render judgment. Results often are not predicted. Housing markets are complex and outcomes sometimes are difficult to interpret. With place making, the geographic reach of positive results also is in doubt. Does successful downtown redevelopment influence redevelopment of adjacent gray areas? Do positive effects of transit-oriented development extend beyond the immediate development envelope? In Chapter 13, we point briefly at examples of the relationships between making places and empirical information about effects and benefits. More would be accomplished by integrated public policies that address sprawl on the fringe, concentrated poverty near the center, and place making in cities and suburbs. We will consider whether place making can accomplish some positive results, even if it is not supported directly by limits on sprawl and remedial action in poverty areas. Puncturing some popular myths that encourage sprawl may help with this process.

In these emphases, we point attention toward the influential role of beliefs on actions and results. In the simplest terms, beliefs influence actions, which shape results and impacts on society, which then return or feed back to influence beliefs:

$$\text{Beliefs} \rightarrow \text{Actions} \rightarrow \text{Results} \rightarrow \text{Impacts} \rightarrow \text{Feedback} \rightarrow \text{Beliefs}$$

In this study, our work is focused on results described most often with income characteristics of residents. Because we see results (spatial patterns) following from actions—mainly residential location decisions—we infer that beliefs influence location decisions. More survey research has addressed why people move from origins than why they choose certain destinations. Moreover, survey research has been fragmentary, has employed shifting questions and categories, and has not been linked systematically to location results, as we illustrate in Chapters 3 and 9. These relationships can be explored in future research, which should be conducted within different metropolitan areas and linked to changes in location patterns in those metropolitan areas, in addition to tracking national trends in beliefs that influence location choices.

In a private market system, housing supply is influenced by beliefs about preferred housing tenure, styles, quality, cost, and locations. However, as indicated in our discussion of the tyranny of easy development decisions, locations of new housing also are influenced by organizational and political dynamics. Organizational and political contributions to housing supply characteristics, therefore, limit housing choices, especially location choices. In addition, location choices are limited by the preexisting supply of housing. With more than 100 million housing units in the U.S., only one to two million new units are built annually. Locations of new housing are influenced by developers' assessment of political and financial risks and opportunities. Housing locations are not necessarily based on developers' judgments about buyers' location preferences, although buyers' preferences are considered.

Beliefs about housing preferences can be inferred better from changes in housing values and the location of persons of different incomes than from the location of new housing. We assume that the income trends we describe for residents of cities, suburbs, and census tracts reflect evolving beliefs about housing and location characteristics rather than being random occurrences.

ORDER OF CHAPTERS

This book is organized into three parts:

- In Part I, "Themes and Policy Approaches," themes are introduced in Chapter 1 and policy approaches are described in Chapter 2.
- In Part II, "Cities and Suburbs: Trends and Interpretations" (Chapters 3 through 8), growth, decline, and revival in central cities and suburbs are described and interpreted.
- In Part III, "Beliefs and Places" (Chapters 9 through 14), some causes of these outcomes are explored, including misguided beliefs about advantages and disadvantages of types of residential locations, and useful public policies are suggested.

Ten perspectives on the roles of markets and public policies in shaping current metropolitan conditions and problems constitute Chapter 2. Theses of Anthony Downs,[21] David Rusk,[22] Myron Orfield,[23] Bruce Katz,[24] Paul Grogan and Tony Proscio,[25] Peter Dreier, John Mollenkopf, and Todd Swanstrom,[26] Andres Duany, Elizabeth Plater-Zyberk, and Jeff Speck,[27] Peter Calthorpe and William Fulton,[28] William H. Hudnut III,[29] and William Lucy and David Phillips[30] are summarized and critiqued. These critiques set the stage for extensions of, and departures from, their theses that follow in succeeding chapters.

In Chapters 3 and 4, we focus on central cities. Although many central cities, especially northern cities with industrial economies, faded dramatically between 1950 and 2000, many other central cities were doing well. One puzzle, therefore, is why there has been so much variety in central cities' fates. This variety provides clues about reasons for the rise, fall, and revival of parts of metropolitan areas. We provide evidence that central cities in numerous states have done well, from which we infer that state policies made a difference. Moreover, we discovered that demand for housing increased in many central cities, and home ownership also increased, even as population decreased. This is a second puzzle to interpret.

In addition, while many central cities fell behind suburbs in the median and average incomes of their residents, three countertrends occurred. First, many cities stabilized or improved in relative income during the 1990s. Second, many cities were significantly better off when income was measured per person rather than per family. Third, surprisingly, incomes of whites in some cities were higher per capita than incomes of whites in suburbs. Evidence of improvement in relative income in central cities continued after the 2000 census, as was discovered in the *American Community Survey* of city and metropolitan conditions in 2003.

Suburbs' variety also has been given too little attention. In aggregate, suburbs were in ascendancy from 1950 to 2000, growing in population, relative income, and political influence, and supplanting central cities as the dominant sector in most metropolitan areas. Cracks in this apparent uniform dominance appeared in the 1970s. Suburban vulnerability increased in frequency and extent in the 1980s and again in the 1990s. The decline of many suburbs in population, occupied housing, and relative income is documented in Chapters 5 and 6. Numerous suburbs declined faster than their central cities despite more concentrated poverty in central cities. Per capita income levels in more than 100 suburbs declined below 60 percent of metropolitan income. Why did these declines occur in some suburbs but not in most? We suggest that housing characteristics have received too little attention in explaining suburbs' problems as well as central cities' problems.

Growth in outer suburbs continued at spectacular and disconcerting rates in the 1990s. Extreme suburban sprawl patterns emerged at much lower population densities than had previously. Costs of sprawl became a potent issue in local and regional politics, often becoming the dominant political conflict. Images to describe sprawl evolved from edge cities[31] to edgeless cities.[32] Outer locations for manufacturing and wholesale distribution continued to be popular and to grow in scale. On one hand, these trends raised the specter of even more residential sprawl in response to remote job locations. On the other hand, the low wage character of many of these jobs suggested that sprawl was segmented by income and class differences. Some sprawl occurred in the favored quarter, as described by Christopher Leinberger.[33] Sprawl also occurred in modest housing, often manufactured, where land and housing costs were low.[34] As roads became more congested and travel delays increased, and as school construction lagged behind the increase in families, demand for inner residential locations in cities and suburbs also increased. The geographic gainers and losers became more diffuse.

While decline was common and sometimes quite severe, many suburbs have stabilized or revived after declining. We explore why stability and revival have occurred in suburbs, and compare these explanations to conditions of revival in central cities. In Chapter 7, we describe how suburbs with substantial proportions of pre-1940 housing were more likely to increase in relative income than suburbs with substantial proportions of housing constructed during any decade between 1940 and 1990. A multivariate analysis buttresses the interpretation. In Chapter 8, we describe similar trends for neighborhoods in cities and suburbs in the Atlanta, Chicago, Los Angeles, Philadelphia, Richmond, and Washington, D.C., metropolitan areas. These findings indicate the trickle-down process of neighborhood change, which dominated residential income transitions from 1950 to 1980, was altered in the 1990s and, to a lesser extent in the 1980s, as neighborhoods with pre-1940 housing tended to outperform middle-aged neighborhoods. These modifications of the trickle-down process indicate that significant revival of central cities and older suburbs is possible.

BELIEFS AND PLACES

In Part III, "Beliefs and Places," myths about safety on cul-de-sacs and in outer suburbs, and potential for public policies that focus on housing and enhancing place characteristics, are explored. The role of small houses in suburban decline is examined, and public policy reforms that can facilitate balanced market calculations by households are proposed.

Beliefs about these settings and structures influence residential location patterns. We argue that beliefs, habits, institutions, public policies, demographic characteristics, and current location patterns were sufficiently different by the 1990s compared with the 1950s and intervening decades that different results should not be surprising. The filtering process of trickle-down neighborhood change was not operating in the same way in the 1990s as in previous decades. Beliefs about race, neighborhoods, crime, and traffic safety have changed and will change again. Dissatisfaction by some residents with current residential location patterns has altered some beliefs. In Chapter 9, these relationships are sketched, setting the stage for attention to myths, small house effects, and place making that are discussed in succeeding chapters.

In Chapter 10, we examine effects of the myth of cul-de-sac safety on development patterns. Automobiles created opportunities for settlement of larger territories than had been accessed by commuter rail and street cars. They also created a safety problem in cities because they were dangerous to drivers and pedestrians. Small children walking and playing were seen as the people most in need of protection from cars. The planning and development solution that emerged was to prevent through traffic by terminating streets in dead ends, usually in a cul-de-sac mode that facilitated reversing direction by driving forward in a circle. Cul-de-sacs were promoted by the Federal Housing Administration as good planning, with considerable persuasive effects, during the late 1930s and 1940s. Cul-de-sacs and single-use, residential subdivisions soon typified development in much of the nation.

We challenge the claim that cul-de-sacs lead to safety for pedestrians, drivers, and passengers. We argue that the transportation network and transportation mode preferences that emerge when cul-de-sacs dominate residential street patterns may be more dangerous than grid networks. Furthermore, obstacles to walking in cul-de-sac neighborhoods contribute to increases in overweight children and adults, resulting in numerous dangers to health.

The mantra of suburban developers has gone like this: If suburban cul-de-sacs are not safe and remote enough for you, try the outer suburbs where large houses beckon on 2- to 10-acre lots and in gated subdivisions. In contrast, we provide data that traffic fatalities and serious injuries are more likely in exurbia (another word for the outer suburbs) than murders and aggravated assaults by strangers are in cities. Most homicides are committed by people who know their victims, often intimately. Traffic fatalities at the hands (or motor vehicles) of a stranger (or oneself) are 13 times more likely than being a homicide victim of a stranger. The myth of exurban safety, which we examine in Chapter 11, has complemented the myth of cul-de-sac safety, driving sprawl ever outward.

In Chapters 7 and 8, we explored our belief that many neighborhoods in central cities and suburbs, but especially in suburbs, became relatively unattractive to middle-income households in the 1990s because of their typical small size and inconvenient locations. In Chapter 12, we return to this theme by examining relative income trends in the City of Richmond, Virginia, and its surrounding counties of Henrico and Chesterfield. We explain decision-making hurdles faced by the owners and buyers of small houses who may consider expanding them rather than moving to larger houses.

If our diagnosis of causes of trends in cities and suburbs has some merit, reasons for optimism and pessimism about the futures of cities and suburbs depart from the norm. In both cities and suburbs, greater attention to place making and reinvesting in small houses is needed. Whereas cities and older suburbs, for all their apparent problems, have numerous assets on which to ground place making and reinvestment policies, middle-aged suburbs have fewer assets and therefore less promising futures. In Chapter 13, we argue for the importance of pedestrian-friendly downtowns, the potential for transit-oriented development, the means of combining housing preservation with rehabilitation finance, public-private collaborations facilitating small house reinvestment, and a variety of local and state measures to ease redevelopment of abandoned and deteriorated properties. Each of these policies is distinguished by potential for individual local governments to make progress on their own, although in numerous instances, assistance from state governments or alliances with other local governments would be useful.

In Chapter 14, we conclude by revisiting our theme that transformation of cities and suburbs takes many forms, evolving through interactions between decisions by people acting in housing and other investment markets and through patterns influenced by public policies. Housing characteristics have the greatest influence on the fate of local government jurisdictions and neighborhoods because of housing's central role in households' residential location decisions. Beliefs about characteristics of good dwellings, streets, neighborhoods, and communities influence location decisions. Beliefs are subject to persuasion, evolution, realization of previous misperceptions, and faddish transitions. Because some current preferences are based on apparent misperceptions and mistaken calculations, such as those involving safety of streets and outer suburbs within metropolitan territories, location preferences might change rapidly.

Signs that local preferences shifted significantly during the 1990s have been revealed in downtown population increases, reductions in poverty concentrations, stability in some poor suburbs, revival in neighborhoods featuring pre-1940 housing, frequent relative income declines in middle-aged neighborhoods, rising property values near some downtowns and transit stations, and racial dispersion and intermixing. Public policies that encourage more housing for middle-income residents in poor areas, encourage mixed-use walkable districts, and promote income and racial integration may accelerate these trends.

NOTES

1. William H. Lucy and David L. Phillips, *Confronting Suburban Decline* (Washington, DC: Island Press, 2000).
2. Anthony Downs, *Opening Up the Suburbs* (New Haven, CT: Yale University Press, 1973); Anthony Downs, *Neighborhoods and Urban Development* (Washington, DC: The Brookings Institution, 1981).
3. Robert Fishman, "The American Metropolis at Century's End: Past and Future Influences," *Housing Policy Debate* 11 (2000), pp. 199-213.
4. Gregory Squires, ed., *Urban Sprawl* (Washington, DC: Urban Institute Press, 2002).
5. Peter Dreier, John Mollenkopf, and Todd Swanstrom, *Place Matters* (Lawrence: University Press of Kansas, 2001).
6. William H. Lucy and David L. Phillips, *Confronting Suburban Decline* (Washington, DC: Island Press, 2000).
7. Myron Orfield, *American Metropolitics* (Washington, DC: The Brookings Institution, 2002).
8. Rolf Pendall, *Exploring Connections between Density, Sprawl, and Segregation by Race and Income in U.S. Metropolitan Areas, 1980-1990* (Cambridge, MA: Lincoln Institute of Land Policy, 2001).
9. David Rusk, *Cities Without Suburbs* (Baltimore: Johns Hopkins University Press, 1993).
10. "Position Statements of the Presidential Candidates on Federal Role in Dealing with Sprawl," *Planning Commissioners Journal*, posted September 7, 2000.
11. Penn, Schoen, and Berland Associates, *Why Voters Care About the Quality of Life Survey* (Storrs, CT: The Roper Center for Public Opinion Research, University of Connecticut, June 2000).
12. Phyllis Myers and Robert Puentes, *Growth at the Ballot Box: Electing the Shape of Communities in November 2000* (Washington, DC: The Brookings Institution, 2001).
13. Anthony Downs, *New Visions for Metropolitan America* (Washington, DC: The Brookings Institution, 1994), p. 3.
14. Rolf Pendall, *Exploring Connections between Density, Sprawl, and Segregation by Race and Income in U.S. Metropolitan Areas, 1980-1990* (Cambridge, MA: Lincoln Institute of Land Policy, 2001); Todd Swanstrom, Colleen Casey, Robert Flack, and Peter Dreier, *Pulling Apart:*

Economic Segregation among Suburbs and Central Cities in Major Metropolitan Areas (Washington, DC: The Brookings Institution, 2004).

15. William H. Lucy, "Mortality Risk Associated With Leaving Home: Recognizing the Relevance of the Built Environment," *American Journal of Public Health* 93, no. 9 (2003), pp. 1564-1569.

16. William H. Lucy and David L. Phillips, *Confronting Suburban Decline* (Washington, DC: Island Press, 2000).

17. Bruce Katz, ed., *Reflections on Regionalism* (Washington, DC: The Brookings Institution, 2000); Myron Orfield, *American Metropolitics* (Washington, DC: The Brookings Institution, 2002); David Rusk, *Inside Game Outside Game: Winning Strategies for Saving Urban America* (Washington, DC: The Brookings Institution, 1999).

18. National Association of Home Builders, *Housing Facts, Figures, and Trends* (Washington, DC: National Association of Home Builders, 2001).

19. Pillsung Byun and Adrian X. Esparza, "A Revisionist Model of Suburbanization and Sprawl: The Role of Political Fragmentation," *Journal of Planning Education and Research* 24, no. 3 (Spring 2005), pp. 252-264.

20. Bruce Katz, ed., *Reflections on Regionalism* (Washington, DC: The Brookings Institution, 2000); Myron Orfield, *American Metropolitics* (Washington, DC: The Brookings Institution, 2002); David Rusk, *Inside Game Outside Game: Winning Strategies for Saving Urban America* (Washington, DC: The Brookings Institution, 1999).

21. Anthony Downs, *New Visions for Metropolitan America* (Washington, DC: The Brookings Institution, 1994).

22. David Rusk, *Inside Game Outside Game: Winning Strategies for Saving Urban America* (Washington, DC: The Brookings Institution, 1999).

23. Myron Orfield, *Metropolitics* (Washington, DC: The Brookings Institution, 1997); Myron Orfield, *American Metropolitics* (Washington, DC: The Brookings Institution, 2002).

24. Bruce Katz, ed., *Reflections on Regionalism* (Washington, DC: The Brookings Institution, 2000).

25. Paul Grogan and Tony Proscio, *Comeback Cities* (Boulder, CO: Westview Press, 2000).

26. Peter Dreier, John Mollenkopf, and Todd Swanstrom, *Place Matters* (Lawrence: University Press of Kansas, 2001).

27. Andres Duany, Elizabeth Plater-Zyberk, and Jeff Speck, *Suburban Nation* (New York: North Point Press, 2000).

28. Peter Calthorpe and William Fulton, *The Regional City* (Washington, DC: Island Press, 2001).

29. William H. Hudnut III, *Halfway to Everywhere* (Washington, DC: Urban Land Institute, 2003).

30. William H. Lucy and David L. Phillips, *Confronting Suburban Decline* (Washington, DC: Island Press, 2000).

31. Joel Garreau, *Edge City: Life on the New Frontier* (New York: Doubleday, 1991).

32. Robert E. Lang, *Edgeless Cities: Exploring the Elusive Metropolis* (Washington, DC: The Brookings Institution, 2003).

33. Christopher Leinberger, "The Beginning of the End of Sprawl," *Urban Land* (January 2000).

34. Myron Orfield, *American Metropolitics* (Washington, DC: The Brookings Institution, 2002).

2

Too Little Housing in Policy Critiques

Analysts of metropolitan problems agree that sprawl, interjurisdictional disparities, and concentrated poverty are serious problems. Most agree that each aggravates the other. Therefore, these problems should be attacked together. Several analysts argue that attacking concentrated poverty effectively depends upon limiting sprawl. A few analysts believe that concentrated poverty can be inhibited or eroded by place-making policies, either directed at social problems or through physical changes guided by urban design principles. In this chapter, we describe the views of 10 individual, or teams of, policy critics.

Each of these critiques contains useful interpretations and proposals. Each critique is also interesting for a policy dimension that is given little emphasis—characteristics of housing and how the supply of housing influences residential location decisions and the spatial distribution of affluence, poverty, and middle-income households. In this book, in contrast, housing supply characteristics and their implications are emphasized.

The main approach by several analysts to cope with system effects on sprawl, interjurisdictional disparities, and concentrated poverty calls for reorganizing metropolitan governance by reformed federal government policies, more sensitive state policies, and new regional institutions. One pair of analysts places more faith in reformed service delivery by nongovernmental, local organizations that are committed to improving their own neighborhoods. Two critical books emphasize local and neighborhood changes in community design, while also calling for change in regional patterns. Each of these approaches is important. When combined, they may be sufficient in the policy dimension, except that none of them wrestle significantly with the role of public schools, which generally are considered intractable obstacles to reviving poverty neighborhoods. While being aware that mobility of residents influences spatial patterns, most of the writers pay insufficient explicit attention to how location decisions are made and how changes in location decisions and their effects may be achieved.

Each approach aspires to change social outcomes by changing government policies. Changes in public policies should be attempted. Realistically, however, it is difficult to change some government policies without changing the beliefs that led to, or
accompanied, the government policies that need to be changed. A chicken-and-egg
situation occurs. Which come first: public policies or the beliefs that support them? If
public policies should be changed, can that occur without confronting the beliefs that
contributed to the old policies? This connection between beliefs and public policies is
one of the puzzles facing practical politicians as well as analysts.

Connections between beliefs and public policies are influenced by roles of interest
groups, campaign contributions, and lobbying. Policy makers are least stressed when
dominant interest groups and popular beliefs are aligned. Motor vehicle manufactur-
ers, road builders, truckers, land developers, builders, lenders, and Realtors enjoyed
several decades of compatibility with popular sentiment after World War II. Stresses
have emerged in that alignment reacting to results of it, including issues about spatial patterns. Outcomes, which include sprawl, concentrated poverty, and disinvestment, have become contentious and controversial. Individuals' decisions in private,
regulated markets have contributed to these results. To some extent, we argue, these
individual market decisions have been based on beliefs that are partially mistaken
factually and have miscalculated future effects on one's own household.

We think inaccurate beliefs contribute to and support some public policies.
Attempts should be made to alter these beliefs, which is no small task. Other beliefs
embody values that have dysfunctional effects for society and also for the individuals who hold them. Sounder beliefs would support public policies that could lead to
better results—another major challenge. Inspiration from achievements by some
states and localities in the U.S., and examples from other nations, may help. In addition, local governments could be more assertive about creating places that people
value if public officials and citizens had clearer beliefs about gains that could occur
with such an emphasis. Evidence about successful policies and places can contribute
to clarifying beliefs about potential gains.

These two problems—inaccurate beliefs, which we sometimes describe as adher-
ence to myths; and insufficient commitment by local governments and citizens to create valued places—are discussed in the remainder of this book, along with modest
attention to regional reforms. Now we turn to a brief description of the two main
dimensions and three pervasive consequences of metropolitan spatial patterns. Then
we examine 10 analysts' recommendations and present our own suggestions for overcoming these problems and the metropolitan consequences that accompany them.

LAND CONSUMPTION

Metropolitan polarization is expressed spatially by most population growth occurring through development at and beyond the fringes of previous settlements. Developers, like Gary Garczynski of the National Association of Home Builders, often
claim that "demand is still predominantly for single-family detached homes," which
are easier to build on the fringes of metropolitan areas.[1] The alternatives are for population growth to occur by filling in existing undeveloped spaces within established
development areas, refilling previously developed spaces where population has
declined, and increasing the density of currently developed spaces. Many such
developments occur, but they have been a small part of development trends. One

result of sprawl development at the metropolitan fringe is that overall metropolitan densities have declined each decade since World War II. "Between 1982 and 1997," according to William Fulton and his colleagues, "the amount of urbanized land in the United States increased by 47 percent, from approximately 51 million acres in 1982 to approximately 76 million acres in 1997. During this same period, the nation's population grew by only 17 percent. Of the 281 metropolitan areas included in this report, only 17 (6 percent) became more dense."[2]

Continuing, Fulton and his associates said: "In 1997, ten of the 15 densest metropolitan areas in the nation were located in California, Nevada, and Arizona. The South is accommodating a great deal of population growth but is urbanizing a large amount of previously nonurban land to do so, while in the Northeast and Midwest, slow-growing metropolitan areas have consumed extremely large amounts of land for urbanization in order to accommodate very small quantities of population growth ... Regions that were very dense in 1982 tended to urbanize more land in relation to population growth."[3]

Many problems accompany sprawl development: high infrastructure costs, longer commuting distances, more time spent in motor vehicles, less developmental autonomy for children, and more fiscal stress in metropolitan fringe counties and municipalities. One of the most serious consequences is how sprawl increases poverty concentrations in inner and central parts of metropolitan areas, because most fringe development is for middle-income households and relatively little low-cost housing development occurs there.[4] In addition, more land consumption was associated from 1982 to 1997 with more local government fragmentation and greater reliance on local revenue for schools, both of which are associated with greater fiscal inequalities.[5]

POVERTY CONCENTRATIONS

Spatial configurations are not primary causes of poverty, although they may have some effects by creating obstacles for some residents to commute from home to potential work sites. However, concentrations exacerbate the consequences of poverty. Therefore, they contribute to transferring poverty to the next generation of people who grow up in high-poverty ghettos. Where poverty is concentrated, adverse health and crime conditions accumulate. Students' performance in schools deteriorates. Social capital through which residents support neighborhood organizations and help each other is reduced because, in single-parent households, time is scarce and networks are inadequate between poverty area residents and potential employers.[6] Paul Jargowsky found those poverty concentrations in which more than 40 percent of households were below the poverty level increased from a little over 2,000 in 1980 and 3,417 in 1990. By 2000, high-poverty census tracts decreased to 2,510.[7] This reduction is another puzzle that will be discussed in Chapter 4.

TAXABLE RESOURCE INEQUALITIES

In 1997, metropolitan areas included the following average number of governments per 100,000 by region of the nation: 12.5 in the South, 14.7 in the West, 19.9 in the Northeast, and 27.2 in the Midwest.[8] They are not mere service delivery instruments. Most have revenue-raising responsibilities. Most revenue capacity depends on resources within each local government's boundaries. Local revenues mainly depend on taxation of real property or retail sales. In a few instances, interlocal revenue sharing has mitigated differences in local revenue capacity, but these instances—such as in Minneapolis–St. Paul, Minnesota; Hackensack, New Jersey; and Charlottesville–Albemarle, Virginia—have been rare.

Revenue problems in central cities are well known. For that reason, the federal government and some states have adopted aid formulas, which have provided more aid per capita in central cities than in suburbs. Federal aid, however, is a modest proportion of local revenues, especially for public schools for which it has provided 5 to 8 percent of total revenues since the 1960s. State aid formulas, with exceptions, have done little to reduce local revenue inequalities.[9]

Most local governments are suburbs. Myron Orfield has documented that taxable resource inequalities among local governments are large and have increased. Moreover, some suburbs are worse off than central cities. In an analysis of socioeconomic, fiscal, and social indicator disparities in the Philadelphia region, Orfield generalized his findings: "It is important to note that in older metropolitan areas of the country, as poverty and social instability crossed city/suburban lines or began to grow in old towns and cities overrun by urban sprawl, [disparities] actually began to accelerate and intensify. Many older transitioning suburbs on the south side of Philadelphia and in communities such as Camden, New Jersey, Compton, California, and East St. Louis, Missouri suffer much more severe segregation, deprivation, and intense levels of crime than the cities they adjoin."[10] Similar conditions are found in smaller suburbs, like Centreville and Wellston, in the St. Louis metropolitan area; Highland Park, in the Detroit area; Harvey, near Chicago; East Cleveland, outside Cleveland; Braddock and McKees Rocks, near Pittsburgh; Chester, southwest of Philadelphia; College Park and Hapeville, outside Atlanta; and many others.

RACIAL SEGREGATION IN SUBURBS

Some central cities are populated mainly by minority residents, especially by African-Americans in cities in the Northeast, Midwest, and South, and by Hispanics in the West. This growing minority presence in cities in the 1960s and 1970s was accompanied by suburbs that continue to be segregated white bastions, leading to a sense of urgency about opening up the suburbs to increase opportunities for residential desegregation, more fairly distribute local tax resources, and reduce inequalities in public services.[11] In the 1980s, suburban movement of minorities into suburbs increased. Segregation was only slightly reduced because many suburbs repeated the segregation pattern of central cities.[12]

In the 1990s, suburbanization of minorities accelerated but racial integration increased only slightly.[13] Many suburbs became predominantly minority (Compton and Santa Ana, near Los Angeles; Highland Park and Benton Harbor, near Detroit; Camden and Chester, near Philadelphia; and Hapeville and Chamblee, near Atlanta). Frequently, these suburbs had as much concentrated poverty as poor neighborhoods in central cities. Some suburbs had worse prospects than cities because suburbs' poverty matched central cities' poverty but they lacked the cities' resources, such as centers of business, government, education, and culture.

MARKET TESTS AND SPATIAL INEQUALITIES

Decline has become a suburban as well as a central city phenomenon. Local government jurisdictions are vulnerable, whatever their current circumstances. Because of the fragmented governance of metropolitan areas, each local jurisdiction is subject to housing and commercial market tests.[14] The financial and political strength of each jurisdiction depends upon the mix of its resident population, private investment, and public institutions. Because of large fiscal responsibilities, local government officials are concerned about their revenue capacity relative to constituents' service demands. In addition to concerns about taxes, local residents worry about the security of their housing investments, the safety of their surroundings, the quality of public education for their children, and other aspects of the quality of their setting and associations.

Two conditions make all local jurisdictions vulnerable: First, nearly all housing in the United States is allocated in private markets based on ability and willingness of consumers to pay what is asked for it. Second, housing and labor markets are regional in scale, fueled by auto technology, household affluence, and elaborate highway infrastructure. For several decades, labor markets and housing markets have exceeded the geographic scope of any single local government.[15] Middle- and upper-income residents can afford many locations. These affordable locations usually are in many different local government jurisdictions. The economic status of each local jurisdiction is persistently in jeopardy. With an average metropolitan residential mobility rate in five years of 45 to 50 percent between 1995 and 2000, as well as from 1985 to 1990 and from 1975 to 1980, the character and quality of local jurisdictions can change substantially within a decade or less. Each local government, therefore, is subject to market tests about its attractiveness to movers and stayers in a highly mobile society.

High residential mobility and substantial vulnerability of local governments influence prospects for making places that will attract in-movers who have capacities similar to the capacities of out-movers and residents who die. Many people in the U.S. prefer low-density residential settings. The tendency for metropolitan areas to sprawl at low densities into exurban rural territories, consuming farmland at a rapid pace, is well documented.[16] Additional survey evidence indicates that low-density, suburban, small-town, and even rural residences have been preferred by a majority of Americans.[17] Thus, efforts to construct and sustain more compact communities may fail the market tests that confront every private development and public jurisdiction, although relative income trends in the 1990s indicate that preferences for older neighborhoods have increased and should be taken into account by developers. These characteristics of regional housing markets affect suburbs as well as central cities.

Based on theories of metropolitan evolution, substantial suburban decline is not surprising. Several approaches to describing metropolitan socioeconomic patterns and trends suggest that older, denser parts of cities will be occupied by lower-income people and newer, less dense parts of cities and metropolitan areas will tend to be occupied by middle- and upper-income residents. These circumferential ring analyses,[18] sector theories,[19] sector and nodal descriptions,[20] transportation cost housing and space trade-off approaches,[21] and their descendants and refinements[22] all point toward older, inner areas declining in socioeconomic status of residents while newer areas tend to be occupied by people of higher status.

The major exception to this analytic norm has been the suburban-persistence approach,[23] in which the argument was made that the initial socioeconomic characteristics of residents tend to persist in the same suburbs for several decades. Against this suburban-persistence perspective, others have argued that, while there is considerable continuity in comparing the same set of suburbs with each other, when older suburbs arc compared with additional newer ones, the tendency for older areas to decline relative to newer ones still applies.[24] The main thrust of theories of metropolitan and suburban evolution and of survey research about location preferences leads one to expect older suburbs to decline. Neither stability in, nor revival of, older inner suburbs would be a typical outcome. Some sites, either through depreciation or abandonment, may attract reinvestment, but often such sites sit empty or derelict for years, as the federal urban renewal program amply demonstrated.

On the other hand, research findings in Part II of this book describe how, in the 1990s, these trickle-down processes changed, still applying to middle-aged neighborhoods but more often not applying to pre-1940 neighborhoods, which were more likely to increase in relative income than all but neighborhoods constructed in the 1990s. Some older suburbs have been stable in relative income and their housing values have risen relative to other parts of metropolitan areas. They have matched or exceeded the persistence of their socioeconomic status. They provide clues about conditions and policies that could help other suburbs and cities succeed in market tests of attracting sufficient reinvestment and replacement in-movers.

PROPOSED REMEDIES

The causes of sprawl and concentrated poverty are complex, as are the remedies proposed by several analysts whose themes will be summarized here. Several analysts have proposed remedies in recent years. We will examine the perspectives of 10 authors and author teams here: Anthony Downs in *New Visions for Metropolitan America*; David Rusk in *Inside Game Outside Game*; Bruce Katz, editor of *Reflections on Regionalism;* Myron Orfield in *Metropolitics* and *American Metropolitics*; Peter Drier, John Mollenkopf, and Todd Swanstrom in *Place Matters*; Paul Grogan and Tony Proscio in *Comeback Cities*; Andres Duany, Elizabeth Plater-Zyberk, and Jeff Speck in *Suburban Nation*; Peter Calthorpe and William Fulton in *The Regional City* William H. Hudnut III in *Halfway to Everywhere*; and William H. Lucy and David L. Phillips in *Confronting Suburban Decline.*[25]

Anthony Downs, *New Visions for Metropolitan America*

Anthony Downs in *New Visions for Metropolitan America* argues that public policies reflect voter preferences. Sprawl and concentrated poverty are the norm, in his view, because most middle- and upper-income Americans prefer low-density, single-family, detached housing, often accessible only by automobiles, located in small suburban governments. Public policies support this widely shared vision.

New visions are needed, he argues, that recognize the collective deficiencies that have emerged from Americans' emphasis on freedom, accumulation, and pursuit of individual opportunities. Although he believes that government and public policy reform are needed in many dimensions, he argues that citizens must change their own visions of the good life as an indispensable part of the social change process.[26]

The dominant vision, according to Downs, has five elements[27]: ownership of detached, single-family homes; ownership of automotive vehicles; employment in low-rise workplaces in park-like settings with free parking; small communities with strong local governments; and communities without signs of poverty. Downs has the dominant American vision clearly sighted, in our opinion, except for the third element. We agree that free parking is important, but park-like settings are less common than isolated buildings surrounded by parking. Most of these work settings are more a product of the tyranny of easy development decisions rather than employee preferences.

Downs observes that the down side of success in achieving this five-part vision contains the possibility of altering direction. "Ironically," he said, "the underlying cause of recent hostility toward growth has been the overwhelmingly successful realization of Americans' common vision of how growth ought to occur."[28]

Turning to new visions, Downs focuses on what central cities need, especially poor parts of large cities[29]: ". . . America must create a new coherent, and comprehensive response to urban decline . . . The highest priority should be to reduce personal insecurity in inner cities. Insecurity paralyzes local initiatives and poisons the quality of life. . . . The second priority should be to improve the care of poor children. Failure to do this will generate enormous future social costs. The third priority should be to improve job opportunities for inner-city residents . . . [E]fforts should focus on retaining and expanding businesses and activities already there."

Each of Downs' priorities has much to commend it. These proposals, however, have three limitations. First, they do not emphasize a vision that would improve the lives of middle-income households whose pursuit of the dominant vision has led indirectly to the present problems in low-income parts of central cities. Downs may believe the dominant vision has worked better for the winners in the residential location game than we do. Second, Downs' proposals do not address conditions that led to a continuing cycle of decline by moderate- and middle-income neighborhoods and eventually to poverty concentration status. Downs has addressed the "trickle-down neighborhood change process" elsewhere by which most housing for poor people is provided in the United States.[30] Third, and somewhat surprisingly, given Downs' other writings, these priorities do not address housing preferences, housing investments and reinvestments, and developers' decisions that drive the location patterns that emerge from individuals' decisions about where to live. These location decisions and the beliefs that drive them should be addressed directly through housing and development policies, rather than only indirectly through attention to crime, jobs, and education.

Perhaps Downs believes that housing policies are even more difficult to change usefully than policies applicable to security, child poverty, employment, and public education. However, housing market outcomes have been changing. In subsequent chapters, we speculate that market results partially reflect changes in citizens' visions and buyers' preferences that occurred during the 1980s and 1990s. Building on Downs' emphasis on individuals' preferences, we suggest how some questionable beliefs—we call them myths—that have influenced location destinations may change in the future.

David Rusk, *Inside Game Outside Game*

David Rusk's work is a mixture of moral exhortation and data-rich analysis. Rusk's policy prescriptions call for regional action. While paying respect to the intentions of those playing what he calls the "inside game," Rusk argues that the "outside game" is more important in helping central cities in the Northeast and Midwest, which are his target jurisdictions. "My answer is a three-pronged agenda: . . . require regional land use planning . . . ensure that all suburbs have their fair share of low- and moderate-income housing . . . implement regional revenue sharing."[31]

The "inside game"—composed for 30 years of community action, model cities, community development block grants, urban development action grants, empowerment, and enterprise zones—is a "losing strategy," Rusk argues.

Rusk reached this opinion after analyzing population, income, and poverty trends in neighborhoods served by community development corporations (CDCs), the very CDCs that Paul Grogan and Tony Proscio (see below) extol for their achievements.

Rusk concluded: ". . . a handful of [34] target areas have experienced some economic improvement . . . Family poverty rates, individual poverty rates, or both, stabilized or declined slightly in only seven target areas."[32] Average household incomes declined in 30 of 34 areas relative to metropolitan incomes, while population and the number of households declined in nearly all.

While it may be argued that conditions would be even worse without CDC's efforts, Rusk concluded that by 1999 they had not succeeded in improving their neighborhoods, using data for population, income, and poverty as indicators. Instead of focusing only on what he calls the inside game, as exemplified by CDCs, Rusk argues that metropolitan policies that increase racially integrated, geographically dispersed affordable housing are the key to reducing the prevalence of concentrated poverty ghettoes. Moreover, growth boundaries and other means of limiting sprawl are necessary because unrestrained sprawl has secondary effects that contribute to the increase in the number and severity of poverty concentrations.

Rusk did not expect. major improvements from federal policy changes, however, instead pointing policy makers in another direction—toward state governments—because "state legislatures set the rules for local governments' land use planning power (that is, potential antisprawl controls), zoning powers (potential mixed-income housing mandates), and intergovernmental agreements (potential revenue or tax base-sharing agreements)."[33]

Rusk touches on residential location decisions in arguing that avoidance by whites of racial mixing with minorities, especially African-Americans, has driven suburbanization, and the pattern of much racial segregation has been repeated in the suburbs. However, he does not examine whether whites were more likely to stay when African-Americans move nearby in the 1990s than in previous decades, nor whether whites were more likely to move to an area that has more than an "appropriate" percentage of minorities in the 1990s. He also does not examine the role that housing size, ownership, quality, and reinvestment opportunities may play in residents' location decisions.

In Chapters 3 through 8, we describe relative income increases in many low-income neighborhoods with pre-1940 housing, as well as numerous cities where the number of housing units increased even though population decreased. These findings indicate that the types of neighborhoods where CDCs were active experienced increases in housing and relative income in the 1990s, although we know of no evidence to indicate that CDCs were mainly responsible for these improvements.

Bruce Katz, *Reflections on Regionalism*

Reflections on Regionalism is a collection of essays edited by Bruce Katz,[34] director of the Center on Urban and Metropolitan Policy at The Brookings Institution. Katz summarized the views of regionalists in his introductory essay as follows: "Regionalists ... argue that many pressing environmental, social, and governance problems cannot be solved by independent jurisdictions acting alone ... urban decline increases development pressure on the suburban fringe; and government policies that facilitate fringe development ... make it more difficult for cities to maintain their social and economic health ... cross-jurisdictional problems demand cross-jurisdictional solutions."[35]

The essays in *Reflections on Regionalism* are mainly about the structures and processes that can enhance regional policy approaches to coping with problems of sprawl and concentrated poverty. The politics of building regional coalitions is emphasized. The final essay, by Paul R. Dimond, argues that families will "vote with their feet," and public policies should avoid augmenting the market advantages that subsidies have given to sprawl.[36] Regionalists emphasize reducing inequalities in tax burdens among local jurisdictions—another market impetus to sprawl. Housing characteristics are not given much attention in these essays, however, other than the goal of constructing some affordable housing in suburbs. Place making—the focus of new urbanists—is not regarded in these essays as having much potential to combat forces stimulating sprawl. Residents generally are thought to make calculations of personal gain, using local government fragments to accumulate advantages for themselves. John A. Powell, on the other hand, citing Myron Orfield, states that "most whites do not economically benefit from a fragmented, sprawling region; only about one-quarter—the favored quarter—of a region's population benefit from this arrangement."[37] In this limited sense, Powell raises the possibility that education about who benefits and loses from sprawl might lead to different preferences and market choices by suburban whites, a theme elaborated by Myron Orfield.

Myron Orfield, *Metropolitics* and *American Metropolitics*

Myron Orfield shares Rusk's perspective that state governments are crucial. As a state legislator, Orfield worked through the 1990s constructing coalitions to try to change state policies in Minnesota. He also took his coalition-building campaign nationwide. In his books, *Metropolitics* and *American Metropolitics*, Orfield argues that state policy reforms are needed to aid struggling central cities and suburbs alike. His emphasis on struggling suburbs and his analyses, which have demonstrated similarities in problems of central cities and many suburbs, has brought national attention to Orfield's arguments.

In *Metropolitics* and *American Metropolitics*, Orfield describes fiscal and socioeconomic disparities between cities and well-off suburbs, but he also emphasizes that moderate-income suburbs share interests more with central cities than with wealthier suburban neighbors.

He focuses on three themes.[38] First, central cities and low and moderate tax-base suburbs have much in common. Second, central cities and similarly situated suburbs should form alliances in seeking public policies that will treat them more equitably, will distribute public resources more fairly, and will reduce disparities between rich and poor local government jurisdictions. Third, the main target of their alliance should be state governments. Compared with the federal government, states wield more powers, distribute more funds, and construct or determine locations of more facilities that impact the well-being of people in low- and moderate-income cities and suburbs.

Like Rusk, Orfield finds the heart of the metropolitan problem in concentrations of poverty, usually in central cities. In *Metropolitics*, he wrote ". . . the forces of polarization must be broken. Reforms are needed in several closely related areas: housing and reinvestment, property tax-base sharing, schools, land use and infrastructure planning, transportation and transit, and welfare."[39] He adds, hopefully, "A small amount of pull in terms of affordable housing continually achieved at the edge of a metropolitan area can make a huge difference."[40]

Some more affordable housing on the metropolitan fringe may help slightly, but metropolitan areas have seen a substantial amount of affordable, or at least modest, housing built on much of their metropolitan fringe through the 1980s and 1990s. It has become a common and accurate image that high-value residences are built on only a portion of the ever-expanding metropolitan fringe. Christopher Leinberger calls this "the favored quarter."[41] Metropolitan regions have become so enormous that there are not enough wealthy and upper-middle-income households to capture them. Most fringe housing is middle income and some is moderate income. The modest quality housing often is concentrated in certain counties, towns, and villages, as Orfield's own research demonstrates. Therefore, Orfield advocates some form of regional revenue sharing: ". . . breaking the mismatch between social needs and property tax base resources; . . ."[42]

In *American Metropolitics*, Orfield expanded on these themes, buttressing his arguments with analyses of polarization patterns in 25 metropolitan areas. Besides the central cities, which contained 28 percent of the metropolitan population, Orfield divided the suburbs into three categories: at-risk suburbs (40 percent), bedroom-developing suburbs (26 percent), and affluent job centers (7 percent).[43]

Orfield's policy agenda in *American Metropolitics* is similar to the one he described in *Metropolitics* and promoted in the Minnesota state legislature from 1990 on. Orfield advocated: ". . . increased fiscal equity among local governments, with an emphasis on reinvestment in central cities and older suburbs; coordinated regional land-use planning, with a strong emphasis on affordable housing; and improved governance and leadership at the regional level, to help facilitate the development of policies that benefit all types of communities."[44]

In a further variation on this theme, Robert Puentes and Orfield focus on what they term "first suburbs" in a booklet entitled *Valuing America's First Suburbs: A Policy Agenda for Older Suburbs in the Midwest*. Acknowledging the ambiguity of the "first suburbs" term, Puentes and Orfield argue that these generally inner suburbs "are caught in a policy blindspot . . . they are not poor enough to qualify for many federal and state reinvestment programs and not large enough to receive federal and state funds directly . . . they are ill suited to federal and state programs that focus on building new infrastructure and housing rather than maintaining, preserving and renovating what is already built."[45]

Orfield sees the fate of the metropolitan core and the metropolitan fringe linked symbiotically. If the fringe continues to expand, the core must decline. Certainly, the core has declined as the fringe has expanded. The question is: Are these paired trends of fringe expansion and core decline inevitable, or do they result from underlying attitudes of individuals, policies that nurture and reward these attitudes, and disastrous social and economic conditions in parts of the core that add impetus to the attitudes?

On the other hand, other results are apparent in Europe, Canada, and Australia. Polarization is less, poverty concentrations are less onerous, the cores are home to many affluent and middle-income households, the fringe is more diverse, and clean edges between the urban edge and farmland are typical. Attitudes and policies also are different in these nations; therefore, fringe development is not inevitable for the rich nor is core deterioration inevitable for the poor. Can attitudes in the United States change? Have they been changing? Can policies change? Must attitude changes come first? Can the institutions that nurture both attitudes and policies change? The options are more numerous than Orfield's analysis makes apparent. The future also is less certain.

We believe that there are necessary complements to regional, state, and federal policy reforms, namely actions by individuals through residential location decisions, private investments by developers pursuing altered visions of good neighborhoods, and public investments by public officials to encourage attractive, walkable, land-use combinations. Moreover, individuals, developers, and public officials can make a difference without regional policy reforms.

Peter Dreier, John Mollenkopf, and Todd Swanstrom, *Place Matters*

The three authors of *Place Matters* skillfully present arguments and findings pertinent to their "simple theme: place matters. Where we live makes a big difference in the quality of our lives . . . Place becomes more important as one moves down the economic ladder . . . Place affects our access to jobs and public services (especially education), our access to shopping and culture, our level of personal security, the availability of medical services, and even the air we breathe."[46]

Dreier, Mollenkopf, and Swanstrom also are fairly optimistic about the potential for coalitions of city voters and some suburban voters. "The evidence [from presidential elections] shows," they wrote, "that where suburbs are experiencing decline, suburbanites are more likely to vote like urban dwellers, except where that decline is perceived to emanate from adjacent central city neighborhoods."[47]

In the foregoing views, we are in close synchronization with Dreier, Mollenkopf, and Swanstrom. Where we differ most is in the importance we attribute to housing stock characteristics in projecting potential trends in cities, suburbs, and neighborhoods, and the potential reordering effects of changes in housing and neighborhood preferences.

Paul Grogan and Tony Proscio, *Comeback Cities*

In *Comeback Cities*, Paul Grogan and Tony Proscio have a more optimistic view of cities. They do not discuss suburbs. For that reason, the policy changes they propose are less ambitious than those proposed by the authors discussed above. They argue that the efforts of more than 2,000 CDCs created since the late 1960s have led the way in rejuvenating many of the most destitute neighborhoods in large central cities. They also attribute advances in poverty areas to innovations in community policing, welfare reform and, to a lesser extent, public education reform.[48] They do not present data that demonstrate neighborhood progress over time, limiting their persuasiveness.

Many changes in neighborhoods have occurred, but it was not apparent in 2000 that the neighborhoods they cite had made measurable progress, or that the number and percentage of neighborhoods suffering the effects of concentrated poverty had been reduced. Subsequently, studies published by The Brookings Institution[49] and the Urban Institute[50] confirmed that extreme poverty concentrations diminished between 1990 and 2000. However, these studies did not link spatial poverty decreases to activities in those census tracts by CDCs or other neighborhood-focused public policies. While acknowledging the temporary lack of supporting data, Grogan and Proscio were confident they were on to important trends other analysts had missed.

Grogan and Proscio begin optimistically: "The American inner city is rebounding ... It is the result of a ... palpable change in both the economics and the politics of poor urban neighborhoods."[51] Grogan and Proscio criticize Rusk and Orfield for being starry-eyed utopians. Metropolitan solutions, however desirable, are much less likely in their view than self-help efforts supported by targeted outside assistance focused on low-income areas. David Rusk and Myron Orfield, they wrote, "feel that the only hope for an urban turn-around lies in changing municipal boundaries to capture the wealthier tax base of the suburbs ... this school of thought embraces an even more complex and ambitious vision: harmonizing the politics and economics of the whole, fractious metropolitan regions."[52]

Rather than pursue regional strategies they consider utopian, Grogan and Proscio see four trends—activities of neighborhood nonprofit organizations, private market recovery, less crime, and less stifling public bureaucracy—as having already made many poor parts of cities more livable with brighter prospects ahead.[53]

They praise the federal Community Reinvestment Act, originally passed in 1977, for helping redirect credit to low-income neighborhoods, thereby reinvigorating local commerce: "... leaving the [Community Reinvestment] act [of 1999] alone ...," they said, "would by itself represent a significant federal reinforcement of the credit revolution now under way."[54]

Of the six analysts whose views have been described, Downs, Rusk, Katz, Orfield, and Drier, Mollenkopf, and Swanstrom emphasize intraregional interdependence. Only Grogan and Proscio argue that central cities and central city neighborhoods can substantially go it alone, with some federal government help and with considerable assistance from foundations, but with little attention from states and from regional coalitions. They reject regional strategies because they are not practical and lack voter support.

In our analysis, we find support for their conclusion that many poor neighborhoods have stabilized or turned around. We are skeptical of their interpretation of causes. We believe changes in location preferences, variation in housing stock, and quality of governance—perhaps including some of their policy emphases—have been important. Differentiating among reasons for successful and less successful revival in neighborhoods is an important research challenge.

Andres Duany, Elizabeth Plater-Zyberk, and Jeff Speck, *Suburban Nation*

In *Suburban Nation*, Andres Duany, Elizabeth Plater-Zyberk, and Jeff Speck (hereafter referred to as DPZS) decry the pattern of suburban development. As with other critics, they deplore the fate of cities since World War II, but they argue that the promise of suburbia also has been fatally damaged.[55] This creates a puzzle. If suburbs are horrendous, why have they damaged cities? The partial answer is that suburbs serve cars and people love cars. Developers have built single-family, detached houses where cars are served. People buy the houses, even though many people don't like the metropolitan landscape that results. Another answer is that because people also love traditional neighborhoods, some cities and older suburbs have prospered—and potentially far more will in the future. DPZS's goal is to chart the path by which far more cities and suburbs can prosper by becoming or remaining in places where people want to be.

This auto-dependent form and character was caused by federal policy, local zoning, and the automobile, according to DPZS.[56] They identify the federal policy culprits mainly as the Interstate Highway System and federal support for low down-payment, guaranteed housing loans by the Federal Housing Administration and Veterans Housing Administration. However, they aim most of their criticism at local zoning, other technical regulations, and environments that serve the automobile. Sprawl, DPZS argue, "is the direct outcome of regulations governing modern engineering and development practice. Every detail . . . comes straight from technical manuals."[57]

In this respect—that is, the problems with sprawl are an unintended consequence of aspects of the vision of single-family, detached dwellings accessed with automobiles—DPZS share the perspective of Anthony Downs. Whereas Downs interprets residents' choices as significantly reflecting a desire to capture advantages of sprawl while being indifferent to the damage done by concentrating poverty, DPZS are more inclined to hope that education of citizens and key actors in the development process can obtain a more balanced and humane pattern filled with more traditional neighborhoods.

The traditional neighborhood, DPZS wrote, "was built following six fundamental rules . . .: 1. Each neighborhood has a clear center. . . . 2. A local resident is rarely more than a five-minute walk from the ordinary needs of daily life. . . . 3. Because the street pattern takes the form of a continuous web . . . numerous paths connect one location to another. . . . 4. . . . each street can be small. . . . 5. . . . almost all . . . blocks are of mixed use, as are many of the buildings. . . . 6. . . . traditional neighborhoods devote unique sites to civic buildings, . . ."[58]

Because the problem with sprawl involves the absence of these detailed elements, special blame falls on development professions. Codes and practices can be changed. The burden comes back to citizens and those who can influence developers and buyers' beliefs and actions.

Why, one wonders, have the nonplaces in suburbs that DPZS decry grown exponentially, while cities and older suburbs have languished, despite having qualities that were praiseworthy? Part of the answer lies in the seductive power of the car for individuals and for professionals who designed the elements of sprawl to accommodate the car. Another part of the answer lies in well-intentioned but misguided efforts to change traditional towns to make them more modern, hence reducing their mixed-use, walkable qualities and eroding their attractive power. Where traditional qualities were apparent and of a high order—Alexandria, Annapolis, Coral Gables, Santa Fe, and many others—traditional towns flourished, just as have many traditional neighborhoods in large central cities.

DPZS are not arguing that every place should be a traditional neighborhood or town. Instead, they emphasize that far more places with these characteristics should be available so that people can choose them.

From these arguments, it follows that one way for central cities or older suburbs to thrive is for them to rediscover and renew their traditional neighborhood qualities. Enhance them, don't obscure them. That course of action has numerous virtues. In particular, it is within reach of influence by individuals, families, businesses, developers, architects, engineers, planners, lawyers, elected officials, and politicians. Decisions that enhance traditional neighborhood qualities are decentralized. Codes can be rewritten. Project plans can be redesigned. Investments can be targeted. Small steps may suffice. Additional steps can be taken as needed. Local governments can act. Neighborhood associations can influence. Planning commissions can propose. Rehabilitation is useful. Infill projects should fit in aesthetically. Most business proposals that add street life should be welcome.

Action does not need to wait on federal legislation, state budget increases, or the creation of regional government processes. Coalitions can be within reach rather than encompass scores of local governments. Changes can be made within any neighborhood, not only in those favored by developers.

However, there are limits. Given current conditions—too much sprawl, too many poverty concentrations, and too little reinvestment—what will tip the net amount of effort, whether more skillfully applied or not, toward the parts of metropolitan areas that have been in decline rather than toward the parts that have been ascendant? Perhaps two conditions. First, the ascendant, sprawling parts of metropolitan areas have become more difficult to live in. Their virtues have been sullied by success. They have become more inconvenient, too inconvenient for a growing percentage of the population. Second, aspirations may have been altered. Advocates of new urbanism—another name for promoters of traditional towns and neighborhoods—like DPZS, have designed enough projects, written enough books and articles, and gotten enough hearings in universities, professional meetings, and civic assemblies that the public image of good communities has changed. More people probably agree now than 10 or 20 years ago that the traditional patterns of towns and neighborhoods are better than sprawl. If so, then older cities and suburbs, which retained those traditional patterns, may be rediscovered. Behavior follows beliefs. If old neighborhoods are valued more today than 40, 30, 20, or 10 years ago, then these value preferences should be reflected in income and housing value trends, and perhaps in population trends. Those are empirical matters that can be researched. Evidence about them will be examined in Chapters 3 through 8.

Peter Calthorpe and William Fulton, *The Regional City*

Like other authors whose works are described here, Peter Calthorpe and William Fulton attack the twin problems of sprawl and concentrated poverty. They see sprawl in the lead role, causing concentrated poverty. While some may benefit from sprawl, as Calthorpe and Fulton see recent events, the beneficiaries of sprawl have been reduced substantially and the number of victims has increased.[59] In their interpretation of sprawl's net effects on the middle class, Calthorpe and Fulton seem closer to Orfield's skepticism that sprawl produced benefits for the supposed beneficiaries than to Downs' belief that middle-class self-interest as expressed through sprawl has run amuck, damaging others even as the middle class benefits.

Sprawl, Calthorpe and Fulton say, ". . . was a postwar strategy to house a growing middle class in low-density places knitted together by the car . . . Now homes are distant and more expensive, crime spreads, open space recedes, and cars are stuck in traffic."[60]

Calthorpe and Fulton in one sense seek an even more utopian solution than do the regionalists. They seek a positive regional network of compact livable communities. They see most national and local reform efforts as being misdirected, avoiding the main problem. Solving the main problem—an unworkable metropolitan form—requires a positive image of how the region should function, not just a positive image of how neighborhoods should function, as DPZS emphasize, and not mainly a level playing field among jurisdictions that pursues spatial fairness, as one might say that Rusk, Katz, and Orfield emphasize. Yet, utopian as Calthorpe and Fulton's goal may seem, it has the virtue of facilitating small project planning and site plan review in light of a metropolitan image, as well as focusing attention on the importance of metropolitan planning and action.

Calthorpe and Fulton wrote that because policy makers "operate at the wrong scale, they persist in treating symptoms rather than addressing root causes. As a result, . . . they control air pollution with tailpipe emissions, fuel consumption with efficiency standards, and congestion with more freeways, rather than making cities and towns that are less automobile dependent."[61]

The regional policies advocated by Calthorpe and Fulton are similar to the ones advocated by other analysts: regional limits on sprawl, equalized tax structures, redirecting development, fair housing, regional transit systems, and more accessible preschool and after-school programs.[62] In addition, Calthorpe and Fulton[63] advocate coping with the maturation, and incipient decline, of older suburbs, which, they argue, is surprisingly easy: "This maturation can be largely accomplished through rebuilding the suburb's strip commercial areas, . . . Inserting urban places—walkable and diverse—into these auto zones may seem radical, but it is, ironically, quite practical."[64]

It is striking that Calthorpe and Fulton emphasize regional patterns and neighborhood design, and the network that unifies or divides them, but pay little attention to the makers of most decisions: individuals, households, families, and investors. We find little disagreement with Calthorpe and Fulton, but we believe that essential elements are left out or are given too little attention, namely influences on decision making and effects of housing characteristics in neighborhoods and jurisdictions.

William H. Hudnut III, *Halfway to Everywhere*

As a four-term mayor of Indianapolis, William Hudnut is familiar with the crucial role leadership and community involvement play in achieving constructive action. In *Halfway to Everywhere*—about first-tier suburbs in large metropolitan areas—Hudnut tells the stories, relying on his travels, observations, and interviews with key local participants, of first-ring, built-out suburbs, most of which had peaked by 1970. In Hudnut's view, "The first tier is now experiencing declining population and tax base, deteriorating infrastructure, rapid ethnic change, increasing poverty, and poorer school performance . . . these locales need to be placed on the policy and political radar screens, where currently they are not. The challenges they face differ from either central cities or new suburbs farther out primarily because they lack the tax base and fiscal capacity of their neighbors."[65]

Although Hudnut's interpretation is valid, as far as it goes, it leaves out the distinctions we emphasize here. These special characteristics are that these suburbs usually have too much middle-aged, small, single-family, detached housing for which the market in the late 20th and early 21st centuries is limited, substantially being ignored by middle-income households. In addition, they are less convenient, lack ambiance, and are not conducive to walking to nearby diverse activities compared with many parts of central cities. To the extent that they have larger houses and more convenience, their potential for overcoming their fiscal limitations is considerably greater, in our view.

Still, Hudnut's prescriptions are useful, inclusive as they are of many important actions. Perhaps they are too inclusive, requiring leaders to select the most important problems and opportunities from among his recommendations. The recommendations also do not focus on the small, post-World War II house problem, although they do pay considerable heed to inadequate convenience, unsatisfactory ambiance, and too little walking. Hudnut's prescriptions reflect his travels and interviews, as well as workshops at the Urban Land Institute, and, of course, his vast experience. While his prescriptions incorporate the vision of the new regionalists, they emphasize local public and private actions.

Hudnut's 10 Principles for Revitalizing Inner-Ring Suburbs[66]
1. Empower Local Leadership
2. Be Competitive
3. Find a Niche/Attraction/Market or Purpose
4. Create Opportunity, Stability, and Diversity
5. Strengthen Schools to Achieve Balance
6. Incentivize the Private Sector
7. Maintain and Strengthen Infrastructure
8. Embrace Smart Growth Principles
9. Think and Act Regionally
10. Be Results Oriented

Like the former mayor he is, Hudnut established an ambitious work agenda. Federal and state help will be useful. Regional institutions and processes should be encouraged. The local public and private sectors have much to do, however, regardless of whether federal, state, and regional collaboration can be energized.

Most of Hudnut's book describes aggressive actions by local governments, civic organizations, and private businesses aimed at revitalizing first-tier suburbs. Many of these actions may have been useful. Most trend data for relative income changes between 1990 and 2000, however, reveal that these suburbs continued to decline relative to their metropolitan areas. The effectiveness of the policies and actions described in these case studies, therefore, is uncertain despite their potential.

William H. Lucy and David L. Phillips, *Confronting Suburban Decline*

In *Confronting Suburban Decline,*[67] we argue that many suburbs face a future as bleak as or bleaker than many poverty neighborhoods in central cities. That future, which we predict will be widespread and intractable, was already present in some suburbs in 1990, with more suburbs reaching crisis conditions by 2000.[68]

We attributed much of suburban decline to housing and neighborhood conditions, but with a different twist than most analyses. We arrived at this hypothesis by inference from research findings. In an analysis of 554 suburbs in 24 large metropolitan areas, we discovered that 405 declined in median family income relative to their metropolitan median family income from 1960 to 1990.[69] Moreover, 112 of these suburbs declined in relative median family income faster than their central cities. Surprisingly, age of housing in these suburbs showed no statistical association with income decline. This negative finding was the opposite from what previous theories of neighborhood change had claimed. The common prediction has been that, as housing ages in the trickle-down process of neighborhood change, housing is likely to be inhabited gradually and increasingly by lower-income occupants until the housing deteriorates to the time at which it is demolished.[70]

In this current book, we increase the study areas to 2,586 suburbs in 35 large metropolitan areas and emphasize changes between 1990 and 2000. We also conduct a factor analysis that classifies suburbs by type, and a correlation analysis that distinguishes more and less important influences on conditions and trends in suburbs (Chapters 5 and 6).

In an analysis of 770 census tracts in the Richmond, Hampton Roads, and Northern Virginia metropolitan areas (part of the Washington, D.C., metropolitan area), we found that a majority of suburban census tracts declined in relative median family income from 1980 to 1990.[71] In these metropolitan areas, the most likely census tracts to decline in relative median family income were the ones in which much of the housing was constructed in the 1950s and 1960s. Conversely, a majority of census tracts dominated by housing built before 1940 went up in relative median family income in each of the three metropolitan areas. Most of this older housing was in the central cities of Richmond, Norfolk, and Portsmouth, and some was in Alexandria and Arlington in northern Virginia, where relative median family income increased in each census tract where pre-1940 housing was prominent (40 percent or more of total housing units). Why would these income trends occur, contrary to traditional theories of neighborhood change? In this current book, we expand neighborhood analyses to 8,471 census tracts in the central cities and suburbs of Atlanta, Chicago, Los Angeles, and Philadelphia, in addition to Richmond and Washington, D.C., to provide firmer ground for concluding that these trends persisted, were pervasive, and are important to interpret (Chapters 7 and 8).

In *Confronting Suburban Decline,* we suggested that housing size and quality made 1950s and 1960s neighborhoods vulnerable to being left behind by housing preferences reflecting greater affluence. Not only are 1950s houses far from mint condition in 1990, 2000, and beyond, they are in neighborhoods with questionable characteristics.[72]

Because the challenges to suburbs are as, or more, pervasive than the challenges to cities, the burden for major changes in public policies is even greater, as we see the future, than follows from the perspectives of Downs, Rusk, Katz, Orfield, and Grogan/Proscio. By the same token, the potential for city/suburban coalitions is greater than others foresee, not because well-placed suburbanites are likely to turn benevolent toward central cities, as Grogan and Proscio scornfully imagine that Rusk and Orfield must anticipate, but because a much smaller proportion of suburbanites and suburbs will be well placed and separated from traditional central city problems. Our view in that regard is closer to arguments expressed by Dreier, Mollenkopf, and Swanstrom in *Place Matters*.

Which steps are practical will vary with political and policy cultures. Los Angeles is not the same as San Francisco. Cities in Iowa are not struggling nearly as much as cities in New Jersey. Charlottesville is not like Utica. Minneapolis–St. Paul and Portland are not the same as Atlanta and Houston. These comparisons should remind us not only that economic characteristics vary, but so do the ideological, resource, and attitudinal mindsets of people who are active politically. This diversity suggests that mindsets can and do change. We contend that changing mindsets is one of the tasks for analysts to consider, along with proposals for changing public policies.

MEGA-DECISIONS AND DAILY LIFE

For public policies to be effective in combating polarization—too much sprawl, too much poverty concentration, too little reinvestment—a range of local, regional, state, and federal policies are needed. Public policies, however, are not enough, because they need political, market, and residential location decision support. The support is not only for more useful public policies. The support needed occurs in realms of daily life and occasional mega-decisions that have far-reaching effects on social outcomes. The decisions of daily life concern where to shop and eat and recreate. The mega-decisions are decisions with far-reaching and long-lasting effects—decisions about going to college, getting married, having children, deciding on what work to pursue, and choosing where to live. The decision about choosing where to live is the one with the most apparent spatial consequences and the one with the most political significance, but the other mega-decisions (college, marriage, children, and work) interact to influence residential location decisions. Thus, we argue that policies and public and private actions that influence location decisions and reinvestment are of great importance in shaping the past, present, and future of cities and suburbs.

DECISIONS AND SMALL-SCALE POLICIES

Metropolitan policies as suggested by David Rusk (revenue sharing, affordable housing in new developments, and regional land-use planning) are useful, although very difficult and unusual. They involve two problems. First, they will rarely occur, because they threaten well-established habits and vested interests in preserving location advantages. Second, if they occur, they will not accomplish much. More regional land-use planning will not hurt, but planning without implementation will not help. Interlocal revenue sharing, where it has occurred (Minneapolis–St. Paul, Hackensack, and Charlottesville–Albemarle), has reduced fiscal disparities, which is important, but it has not limited sprawl or reduced poverty concentrations. Affordable housing in new developments would need to be a substantial percentage of new housing for many years to have much impact on concentrated poverty.

Downs emphasizes the need for a revised vision of the good community, and metropolitan area, based mainly on an informed altruism. We agree, but we will argue that more realism is needed. Altruism will not hurt but, with the passage of more time and increased understanding, more realism may be sufficient to create a close contest between family-centered aggrandizement and realistic planning for short-term safety and security.

Orfield has shown how geographic analyses of social conditions, mapped skillfully and supplemented by fiscal characteristics, can demonstrate tangible political self-interests that could encourage many suburbs to ally with central cities. His legislative program has demonstrated how city and suburban coalitions can garner legislative majorities. However, the obstacles imposed by a governor in Minnesota firmly in opposition also demonstrate the difficulties faced even by skillfully organized legislative majorities.

Grogan/Proscio remind us that the metropolitan dimension is not sufficient, even if it was easy rather than difficult. Stimulating private investment, supportive skill-building by residents, and nurturing place-based organizations focused on revitalization in poverty and other low- and moderate-income areas also are important. However, such an emphasis, though necessary, is not sufficient, even if it is combined with regional successes.

Two questions arise: What is needed for middle- and moderate-income neighborhoods to be stable or thrive, as well as to revive poverty neighborhoods? Whatever is needed, is it useful and important enough to have some impact if none of the metropolitan reorganization efforts, as proposed by Rusk and Orfield, succeed?

A variety of policies that make attractive, self-renewing places are needed. Some of these are small scale, potentially affordable locally (street trees and tree reclamation and adopt-a-park efforts). Some are large scale (brownfield clean-up, sewer line replacements, mass transit investments) and require major state and federal (and/or regional) roles. Hudnut, DPZS, and Calthorpe and Fulton each have useful contributions on these subjects.

However, better public policies are not enough. Everyday decisions are needed. Investment decisions by residents, landlords, and businesses are sought that stabilize and revive neighborhoods, downtowns, and neighborhood commercial districts, based on hundreds or thousands of decisions by individuals, families, and investors that places merit investments. These everyday decisions can be encouraged by public policies, but they also need to be motivated by opinions that 80 years of suburbanization have gone astray and become too inconvenient and annoying, with reminders every day about bizarre daily coping with long errand and commuting distances. In addition, a new vision, or a revived old vision, of the good neighborhood, the good community, and the good life must complement everyday growing annoyance about indignities associated with sprawling suburbia and exurbia.

Survey results provide modest evidence, which we will examine later, that visions of good neighborhoods have shifted. Survey responses, however, do not describe behavior and are not necessarily linked causally to behavior. The most useful evidence, therefore, are results of location decisions over time. One can infer that beliefs and preferences probably have had some bearing on changes in results. We describe and explain results of location decisions in Chapters 3 through 8.

Motivations to invest and reinvest are influenced by underlying beliefs about the current desirability and the future prospects of different kinds of sectors and neighborhoods. Investment decisions, like all decisions, emerge from social constructions or interpretations of real contexts, evaluating decisions in terms of desires to be related to real contexts and participating in them. Thus, if enough of these decisions are positive, reorganizing metropolitan governance will be useful, but its absence will not prevent some progress. It may be treated as the icing in and on the cake, rather than the flour without which no cake would be possible.

NOTES

1. Peter Grant, "Sprawl Thins Populations of Older Suburbs," *The Wall Street Journal*, July 9, 2001.
2. William Fulton, Rolf Pendall, Mai Nguyen, and Alicia Harrison, *Who Sprawls Most? How Growth Patterns Differ Across the U.S.* (Washington, DC: The Brookings Institution, 2001), p. 1.
3. Ibid.
4. Gregory Squires, ed., *Urban Sprawl* (Washington, DC: Urban Institute Press, 2002).
5. William Fulton, Rolf Pendall, Mai Nguyen, and Alicia Harrison, *Who Sprawls Most? How Growth Patterns Differ Across the U.S.* (Washington, DC: The Brookings Institution, 2001), p. 13.
6. William T. Dickens, "Rebuilding Urban Labor Markets: What Community Development Can Accomplish," in Ronald F. Ferguson and William T. Dickens, eds., *Urban Problems and Community Development* (Washington, DC: The Brookings Institution, 1999).
7. Paul A. Jargowsky, *Stunning Progress, Hidden Problems: The Dramatic Decline of Concentrated Poverty in the 1990s* (Washington, DC: The Brookings Institution, 2003).
8. Ingrid Gould Ellen, "Spatial Stratification Within U.S. Metropolitan Areas," in Alan Altschuler, William Morrill, Harold Wolman, and Faith Mitchell, eds., *Governance and Opportunity in Metropolitan America* (Washington, DC: National Academies Press, 1999), p. 201.
9. Myron Orfield, *American Metropolitics* (Washington, DC: The Brookings Institution, 2002).
10. Delaware Valley Regional Planning Commission, *The Future of First Generation Suburbs in the Delaware Valley Region* (Philadelphia: Delaware Valley Regional Planning Commission, December 1998), p. 73.
11. Anthony Downs, *Opening Up the Suburbs* (New Haven, CT: Yale University Press, 1973); Anthony Downs, *New Visions for Metropolitan America* (Washington, DC: The Brookings Institution, 1994).
12. William H. Frey, "The New Geography of Population Shifts: Trends Toward Balkanization," in Reynolds Farley, ed., *State of the Union: America in the 1990s, Vol. 2* (New York: Russell Sage Foundation, 1995).
13. William H. Frey, *Melting Pot Suburbs: A Census 2000 Study of Suburban Diversity* (Washington, DC: The Brookings Institution, 2001).
14. Paul E. Peterson, *City Limits* (Chicago: University of Chicago Press, 1981); Charles M. Tiebout, "A Pure Theory of Local Expenditures," *Journal of Political Economy* 64 (October 1956), pp. 416-424.
15. William R. Barnes and Larry C. Ledebur, *Local Economies: The U.S. Common Market of Local Economic Regions* (Washington, DC: National League of Cities, 1994); Committee for Economic Development, *Reshaping Government in Metropolitan Areas* (New York: Committee for Economic Development, 1970); Gerald E. Frug, "Beyond Regional Government," *Harvard Law Review* 115, no. 7 (May 2002), pp. 1766-1836; William H. Lucy, "Metropolitan Dynamics: A Cross-National Framework for Evaluating Public Policy Impacts in

Metropolitan Areas," *Urban Affairs Quarterly* 11, no. 2 (1975), pp. 155-185; David Rusk, *Cities Without Suburbs* (Baltimore: Johns Hopkins University Press, 1993).

16. Arthur C. Nelson, "Characterizing Exurbia," *Journal of Planning Literature* 6, no. 4 (May 1992), pp. 350-368.
17. Ivonne Audirac, Anne H. Shermyen, and Marc T. Smith, "Ideal Urban Form and Visions of the Good Life: Florida's Growth Management Dilemma," *Journal of the American Planning Association* 56, no. 4 (Autumn 1990), pp. 470-482; Judy S. Davis, Arthur C. Nelson, and Kenneth J. Dueker, "The New 'Burbs: The Exurbs and Their Implications for Planning Policy," *Journal of the American Planning Association* 60, no. 1 (Winter 1994), pp. 45-59; Charles Levin and Jonathan H. Mark, "Revealed Preferences for Neighborhood Characteristics," *Urban Studies* 14 (1977), pp. 147-159.
18. Ernest W. Burgess, "The Growth of the City," in Robert E. Park, Ernest W. Burgess, and Roderick D. McKenzie, eds., *The City* (Chicago: University of Chicago Press, 1925).
19. Homer Hoyt, *The Structure and Growth of Residential Neighborhoods in American Cities* (Washington, DC: Federal Housing Administration, 1939).
20. Chauncy D. Harris and Edward L. Ullman, "The Nature of Cities," *Annals of the American Academy of Political and Social Science* 242 (1945), pp. 7-17.
21. William Alonso, *Location and Land Use* (Cambridge, MA: Harvard University Press, 1964).
22. John S. Adams, *Housing America in the 1980s* (New York: Russell Sage Foundation, 1987); John R. Logan, "Industrialization and the Stratification of Cities in Suburban Regions," *American Journal of Sociology* 82, no. 2 (1976), pp. 333-348; Harry W. Richardson, "On the Possibility of Positive Rent Gradients," *Journal of Urban Economics* 4, no. 1 (1977), pp. 60-68; Leo F. Schnore, *Class and Race in Cities and Suburbs* (Chicago: Markham, 1972).
23. Reynolds Farley, "Suburban Persistence," *American Sociological Review* 29, no.1 (1964), pp. 38-47.
24. Harvey M. Choldin, Claudine Hanson, and Robert Bohrer, "Suburban Status Instability," *American Sociological Review* 45 (December 1980), pp. 972-983; Avery M. Guest, "Suburban Social Status: Persistence or Evolution?" *American Sociological Review* 43 (April 1978), pp. 251-264.
25. Anthony Downs, *New Visions for Metropolitan America* (Washington, DC: The Brookings Institution, 1994); David Rusk, *Inside Game Outside Game: Winning Strategies for Saving Urban America* (Washington, DC: The Brookings Institution, 1999); Bruce Katz, ed., *Reflections on Regionalism* (Washington, DC: The Brookings Institution, 2000); Myron Orfield, *Metropolitics* (Washington, DC: The Brookings Institution, 1997); Myron Orfield, *American Metropolitics* (Washington, DC: The Brookings Institution, 2002); Peter Dreier, John Mollenkopf, and Todd Swanstrom, *Place Matters* (Lawrence: University Press of Kansas, 2001); Paul Grogan and Tony Proscio, *Comeback Cities* (Boulder, CO: Westview Press, 2000); Peter Calthorpe and William Fulton, *The Regional City* (Washington, DC: Island Press, 2001); Andres Duany, Elizabeth Plater-Zyberk, and Jeff Speck, *Suburban Nation* (New York: North Point Press, 2000); William H. Hudnut III, *Halfway to Everywhere* (Washington, DC: Urban Land Institute, 2003); William H. Lucy and David L. Phillips, *Confronting Suburban Decline: Strategic Planning for Metropolitan Renewal* (Washington, DC: Island Press, 2000).
26. Anthony Downs, *New Visions for Metropolitan America* (Washington, DC: The Brookings Institution, 1994).
27. Ibid., p 6.
28. Ibid., p. 5.
29. Ibid., pp. 96, 119-120.
30. Anthony Downs, *Opening Up the Suburbs* (New Haven: Yale University Press, 1973); Anthony Downs, *Neighborhoods and Urban Development* (Washington, DC: The Brookings Institution, 1985); Anthony Downs, *New Visions for Metropolitan America* (Washington, DC: The Brookings Institution, 1994).

31. David Rusk, *Inside Game Outside Game: Winning Strategies for Saving Urban America* (Washington, DC: The Brookings Institution, 1999), pp. 11-13.

32. Ibid., pp. 49-51.

33. Ibid., p. 325.

34. Bruce Katz, ed., *Reflections on Regionalism* (Washington, DC: The Brookings Institution, 2000).

35. Ibid., p. 3.

36. Bruce Katz, ed., *Reflections on Regionalism* (Washington, DC: The Brookings Institution, 2000).

37. Ibid., p. 228.

38. Myron Orfield, *Metropolitics* (Washington, DC: The Brookings Institution, 1997); Myron Orfield, *American Metropolitics* (Washington, DC: The Brookings Institution, 2002).

39. Myron Orfield, *Metropolitics* (Washington, DC: The Brookings Institution, 1997), p. 76.

40. Ibid., p. 79.

41. Christopher Leinberger, "The Beginning of the End of Sprawl," *Urban Land* (January 2000), pp. 74-78.

42. Myron Orfield, *Metropolitics* (Washington, DC: The Brookings Institution, 1997), pp. 84-85.

43. Myron Orfield, *American Metropolitics* (Washington, DC: The Brookings Institution, 2002), pp. 2-3.

44. Ibid., p. 3.

45. Robert Puentes and Myron Orfield, *Valuing America's First Suburbs: A Policy Agenda for Older Suburbs in the Midwest* (Washington, DC: The Brookings Institution, 2002), p. 3.

46. Peter Dreier, John Mollenkopf, and Todd Swanstrom, *Place Matters* (Lawrence: University Press of Kansas, 2001), pp. 1-3.

47. Ibid., p. 232.

48. Paul Grogan and Tony Proscio, *Comeback Cities* (Boulder, CO: Westview Press, 2000).

49. Paul A. Jargowsky, *Stunning Progress, Hidden Problems: The Dramatic Decline of Concentrated Poverty in the 1990s* (Washington, DC: The Brookings Institution, 2003).

50. G. Thomas Kingsley and Kathryn L.S. Pettit, *Concentrated Poverty: A Change in Course* (Washington, DC: Urban Institute, 2003).

51. Paul Grogan and Tony Proscio, *Comeback Cities* (Boulder, CO: Westview Press, 2000), p. 1-2.

52. Ibid., p. 3.

53. Ibid., pp. 3-7.

54. Ibid., p. 258.

55. Andres Duany, Elizabeth Plater-Zyberk, and Jeff Speck, *Suburban Nation* (New York: North Point Press, 2000).

56. Ibid., p. xiii.

57. Ibid., p. 13.

58. Ibid., pp. 15-17.

59. Peter Calthorpe and William Fulton, *The Regional City* (Washington, DC: Island Press, 2001).

60. Ibid., p. 2.

61. Ibid., pp. 4-5.

62. Ibid., p. 8.

63. Ibid., p. 6.

64. Ibid., pp. 7-8.

65. William H. Hudnut III, *Halfway to Everywhere* (Washington, DC: Urban Land Institute, 2003), p. xiii.

66. Ibid., pp. 468-471.

67. William H. Lucy and David L. Phillips, *Confronting Suburban Decline: Strategic Planning for Metropolitan Renewal* (Washington, DC: Island Press, 2000).

68. William H. Lucy and David L. Phillips, "Suburbs: Patterns of Growth and Decline," in Bruce Katz and Robert E. Lang, eds., *Redefining Urban and Suburban America: Evidence from Census 2000* (Washington, DC: The Brookings Institution, 2002).
69. David L. Phillips and William H. Lucy, "Suburban Decline Described and Interpreted, 1960 to 1990, 554 Suburbs in 24 Largest Urbanized Areas." Report to the Center for Urban Development (Richmond: Virginia Commonwealth University, 1996).
70. Anthony Downs, *Neighborhoods and Urban Development* (Washington, DC: The Brookings Institution, 1981).
71. William H. Lucy and David L. Phillips, *Confronting Suburban Decline: Strategic Planning for Metropolitan Renewal* (Washington, DC: Island Press, 2000).
72. Ibid., p. 214.

Cities and Suburbs:
Trends and Interpretations

3

Exaggerating City Population Decline

Everyone knows central cities have declined, some of them precipitously and disastrously. There is considerable truth in this image of city decline, but it is an exaggeration. City conditions and trends have been diverse. Here we emphasize the diversity, deemphasizing the uniformity in city decline.

Some cities have resisted decline. In some states, little city decline has occurred. Even where city decline seems to have been extreme—as indicated by major losses of population—the decline image typically is exaggerated; it can be brought into clearer focus with other indicators, such as changes in occupied housing units. Income changes are the clearest indicator of meaningful socioeconomic changes. With income, exaggeration has been less common, but which income measure is used—median family income or per capita income—can yield large differences in image and reality. We examine income and poverty changes in Chapter 4.

As hints to what follows in this chapter, and for readers who may want to skip the details, we provide this summary of findings:

• Most central cities increased in population during the 1970s, 1980s, and 1990s. Small- and medium-size cities were more likely to increase in population than large cities. Population increases occurred more frequently in the 1990s than in preceding decades, especially in large cities.

• Occupied housing changes are a more accurate indicator of demand for residences than are population changes. Population declines are influenced by the reduction in average household size (AHS) from 3.14 in 1970 to 2.59 in 2000. Occupied housing increased in most cities in the 1970s, 1980s, and 1990s. Occupied housing even increased in two-thirds of large cities in the 1970s, when population declines were most prevalent.

• Population in downtowns increased in most large cities during the 1990s, even in cities that declined in population.

• Housing segregation of blacks decreased slightly in the 1990s, continuing a trend of slight decreases in black segregation in the 1980s. In some cities, black segregation declined more substantially, such as in Detroit where black segregation declined to the lowest level since 1950.

• The foreign-born population increased by 57 percent in the United States in the 1990s. Immigration contributed significantly to population increases in many large central cities.

• A majority of respondents to surveys continued to say in the 1990s that they preferred living in small towns and rural areas to cities and suburbs. This preference may be reflected in continuing sprawl into outer suburban and exurban areas in the 1990s, but it does not account for cities increasing in population and occupied housing.

• In surveys, respondents reported less fear of crime in the 1990s than previously. Large central cities, as the areas of highest crime rates, might benefit most from lower anxiety among residents and potential residents about their prospects for becoming crime victims.

Overall, population and housing in most central cities have increased, downtowns are attracting more residents, residential segregation has decreased slightly, immigration is up, and negative perceptions of cities' crime rates have decreased.

TWENTIETH-CENTURY TRENDS

Through the first half of the 20th century, central cities generally were growing and prosperous. Central cities, as used here, follow the definition of U.S. Census Bureau reports.[1] The population of central cities increased each decade from 1900 to 1950, a total increase of more than 36 million, which is four times more city residents in 1950 than in 1900. Even from 1940 to 1950, the period when suburban expansion bloomed after World War II's end in 1945, central cities' population increased 14 percent (Table 3.1).

Central cities' population also exceeded the population outside central cities within metropolitan areas each decade from 1900, when central cities contained 79 percent of population in 25 metropolitan areas, through 1950, when they held 58 percent of population in 168 metropolitan areas (Table 3.1). Metropolitan areas' share of national population increased from 21 percent in 1900 to 56 percent in 1950—the first census year when a majority of the United States' population lived in metropolitan areas.

Political strength flowed from population. In presidential elections, the number of central city voters exceeded voters in suburbs outside cities until 1964. This numerical and voting prominence was reflected in the greater attention presidents and members of congress paid to city policy issues during the 1960s and earlier—attention that diminished in the 1970s and in subsequent decades.

Urban expressways through central cities were included in the Interstate Highway Act of 1956 at the demand of the U.S. Conference of Mayors. The mayors believed downtown businesses needed fast highway access to the growing suburbs in order to maintain their economic, especially retail, dominance within their metropolitan areas.[2] The irony is that construction of interstate highways, especially from cities to suburbs, usually is blamed in retrospect as being one of the two most important causes of cities' decline.[3] The population, voting, and income strength of cities enabled them to command attention of the federal government in the 1950s as their strength ebbed. However, cities did not always spend their waning political capital wisely, as indicated by interpretations of effects of interstate highways.

Table 3.1
Central Cities' Share of Metropolitan Population 1900 to 1960

Year	Number of Metro-politan Areas	Central Cities	Percent of Metro-politan Total	Outside Central Cities	Percent of Metro-politan Total	Metro-politan	Percent of Conti-nental U.S. Total	Total of Conti-nental U.S.
						Population		
1900	25	12,833,201	79	3,489,599	21	16,322,300	21	75,994,575
1910	25	17,099,904	77	4,988,427	23	22,083,331	24	91,972,266
1920	29	22,111,380	76	7,127,202	24	29,238,582	28	105,710,620
1930	140	40,343,442	70	17,259,423	30	57,602,865	47	122,775,046
1940	140	42,706,170	68	20,169,603	32	62,965,773	48	131,669,275
1940	168	42,391,718	63	25,887,957	37	69,279,675	53	131,669,275
1950	168	49,412,792	58	35,087,888	42	84,500,680	56	150,697,361
1940	212	45,552,383	63	27,182,085	37	72,834,468	55	131,669,275
1950	212	52,385,642	59	36,931,261	41	89,316,903	59	150,697,361
1960	212	58,004,334	51	54,880,844	49	112,885,178	63	178,464,236

Sources: U.S. Census Bureau, *Number of Inhabitants, U.S. Summary 1960 (1950, 1940, 1930, 1920 and 1910)* (Washington, DC: U.S. Government Printing Office).

Much of the image of decline of central cities comes from the diminished share cities have of metropolitan population and of total voter shares in national and state elections. The 1970 census was the first decennial census to reveal that a majority of metropolitan residents—54 percent—lived outside central cities. In 1960, central cities still contained 51 percent of metropolitan population (Table 3.1). Outside central cities' share increased steadily thereafter, by 2000 containing 62 percent of metropolitan population. This suburban population had grown even more dramatically in national importance because metropolitan areas contained 80 percent of national population by 2000. In 1992, a majority of presidential voters were suburbanites.[4] By 1996, suburbanites cast 52 percent of total votes in the presidential election.[5]

The image of city decline also comes from many large cities losing population after 1950. Some large cities continued to lose population through 2000. As Jordan Rappaport emphasizes, however, the image of population decline by large cities needs refinement. After examining trends in cities that had 200,000 residents in 1950 or thereafter, Rappaport suggests it is more accurate to distinguish cities that declined consistently from cities that grew consistently, and cities that declined and then revived.[6] ". . . cities that declined continuously tended to be in the Northeast and Midwest . . .," Rappaport said. "Cities that grew continuously tended to be in the South and West . . . Cities that reversed population declines were scattered throughout the country."[7] Cities that reversed from population declines to increases tended to be high quality-of-life cities with numerous entertainment amenities, such as New York, San Francisco, Portland, Seattle, and Denver.[8]

Population declines typically are inferred to be signs of deterioration, in severe cases even trauma, based either on regional economic transformations or significantly diminished interest in living in cities. William H. Frey, from the vantage point of the mid-1990s, wrote: "Since central city declines are exacerbated when the entire metropolitan area is undergoing an economic downturn, it is not surprising that all large central cities in the older Northeast and Midwest regions lost population back in the 1970s."[9] In documenting a population turnaround in large industrial cities in the 1990s, Patrick A. Simmons and Robert E. Lang recalled the 1970s as a particularly grim period for central cities: "The postwar years were not kind to America's older industrial cities. Most endured substantial population decline—particularly in the 1970s . . . Many older industrial cities have rebounded considerably from the traumatic population losses of the 1970s. During the 1970s, all of the thirty-six cities in this study lost population, and twenty-nine experienced their worst decade of the postwar period."[10]

POPULATION AND OCCUPIED HOUSING CHANGES

Data for occupied housing reveal an altered image of central city decline. Old industrial cities experienced their largest population declines in the 1970s, but even in this group, demand for housing did not diminish as much as did population. In fact, occupied housing units actually increased, usually by small numbers, in 17 of these 36 cities in the 1970s (Atlanta, Birmingham, Boston, Denver, Kansas City, Milwaukee, Minneapolis, New Orleans, Norfolk, Oakland, Portland, Richmond, San Francisco, Seattle, St. Paul, Toledo, and Worcester).

Interest in city living is measured better with change in the number of occupied housing units than by population changes. In the 35 most populous metropolitan areas in 2000, for example, only 15 of their 40 central cities gained population between 1970 and 1980. In 1980, however, 28 of these 40 central cities actually had more occupied housing units than in 1970. Only 12 lost housing units, principally in the Northeast and Midwest.

In subsequent decades, population increases in these 40 cities were more common, with 24 gaining population and 26 increasing in occupied housing units in the 1980s. In the 1990s, 29 of 40 cities increased in both population and occupied housing. Twenty-three of 40 cities increased in population and 28 had more occupied housing units in 2000 than in 1970 (Table 3.2). A similar sequence for central city population and household changes in the 1970s, 1980s, and 1990s for the 102 largest metropolitan areas was discovered by William H. Frey and Alan Berube.[11] These population trends themselves contrast substantially with the image that most large central cities lost population in the last few decades of the 20th century. The data for occupied housing units in central cities contrast with the popular myth of central cities emptying all but the poor and minorities in the 1970s.

Why have these differences occurred between trends in population and occupied housing units? The main reason is that the number of persons per household has diminished. In 1950, the national AHS was 3.37. Most of the subsequent decline occurred after 1960, when AHS was 3.33. By 2000, it was 2.59—not much less than the 1990 level, 2.63, but it was 22 percent less than in 1960. The biggest drop occurred in the 1970s, from 3.14 in 1970 to 2.76 in 1980, a decline of 12 percent.

Table 3.2
Population and Occupied Housing Unit Changes
in 40 Central Cities in 35 Large Metropolitan Areas 1970 to 2000

40 Central Cities	1970-1980	1980-1990	1990-2000	1970-2000
Less Population and Less Occupied Housing	12	14	11	12
Less Population and More Occupied Housing	13	2		5
More Population and More Occupied Housing	15	24	29	23

Sources: U.S. Census Bureau, *Census of Population and Housing 2000* and *Census of Housing 1990 (1980 and 1970)* (Washington, DC: U.S. Government Printing Office).

This decline in AHS accounts for the large discrepancy between population and occupied housing changes in the 1970s—25 cities among the 40 central cities in the largest 35 metropolitan areas (in 2000) lost population, but only 12 declined in occupied housing units. With an average 17.5 percent decline in AHS in these 40 central cities from 1970 to 2000, an increase of 17.5 percent in occupied housing units was needed to compensate for AHS decline just for cities to stay even in total population.

CITIES' EVOLUTION FROM 1950 TO 1970

Failure to distinguish between population loss, reductions in AHS, and occupied housing changes also is evident in analyses of the period after 1950. William H. Frey and Alden Speare, Jr., explained that suburbanization in the 1950s and 1960s "contributed to an 'emptying out' of older metropolitan areas' central cities whose pre-World War II populations were still highly concentrated within compact legal boundaries."[12] David Rusk in *Cities Without Suburbs* argued that only low-density cities increased in population and all high-density cities (10,000 or more persons per square mile) declined in population density between 1950 and 1990.[13] However, Frey, Speare, and Rusk did not examine occupied housing data.

Because most cities added land area in the 1950s or 1960s, we examined 16 older cities with little land area change between 1950 and 1970. These were our findings: 11 of 16 cities declined in population, two stayed the same, and three increased (Gary, Miami, and New Orleans), but 13 of 16 cities increased in occupied housing from 0.6 percent (Cincinnati) to 53 percent (Miami). Two cities where urban renewal had been prominent (Boston and New Haven) decreased slightly in occupied housing. Only Detroit had a noticeable occupied housing decline (2.8 percent). Boston lost 20 percent of its population despite its occupied housing going down only 0.2 percent.

The significance of these findings is that demand for city locations still was increasing in the 1950s and 1960s, even in cities that were heavily industrial and had most of their housing built before 1940. Cities have not been avoided, and "emptied out," as thoroughly in the past as the standard interpretation has held. Surprise at recent demand for central city housing has been greater, because avoidance of cities in general, rather than avoidance of specific cities, has been exaggerated in previous interpretations.

Table 3.3
20 Most Populous Cities in 1930

		Peak Population	Year 2000 Population is Lower Than	Percent Change Population 1990-2000	Percent Change Downtown 1990-2000
1.	New York	2000		9.4	-0.6
2.	Chicago	1950	1930	4.0	34.4
3.	Philadelphia	1950	1910	-4.3	8.8
4.	Detroit	1950	1920	-7.5	2.9
5.	Los Angeles	2000		6.0	8.5
6.	Cleveland	1950	1910	-5.4	51.0
7.	St. Louis	1950	1880	-12.2	4.2
8.	Baltimore	1950	1920	-11.5	3.3
9.	Boston	1950	1910	2.6	29.0
10.	Pittsburgh	1950	1910	-9.5	38.0
11.	San Francisco	2000		7.3	21.6
12.	Milwaukee	1960	1950	-5.0	21.2
13.	Buffalo	1950	1900	-10.8	34.7
14.	Washington, D.C.	1950	1940	-5.7	17.7
15.	Minneapolis	1950	1930	3.9	20.1
16.	New Orleans	1960	1940	-2.5	15.5
17.	Cincinnati	1950	1910	-9.0	-16.9
18.	Newark	1930	1910	-0.6	-11.4
19.	Kansas City	1970	1950	1.5	-13.1
20.	Seattle	2000		9.1	43.6

Sources: U.S. Census Bureau, *Statistical Abstract of the U.S. 2000* (Washington, DC: U.S. Government Printing Office); Alan Berube and Benjamin Forman, "Patchwork Cities: Patterns of Urban Population Growth in the 1990s," in Bruce Katz and Robert E. Lang, eds., *Redefining Urban & Suburban America* (Washington, DC: The Brookings Institution, 2002).

DOWNTOWN POPULATION CHANGES

Much of cities' image of decline comes from cities that were large before World War II. The 20 most populous cities in 1930 (Table 3.3) illustrate this observation. A majority (12) of these 20 peaked in population in 1950. Two others (Milwaukee and New Orleans) peaked in 1960, Kansas City did so in 1970, and Newark reached its zenith in 1930. By 2000, most of these cities had fewer residents than in 1940 or earlier, with St. Louis having fallen from the earliest peak population year—1880.

On the other hand, four of these 20 largest cities in 1930 (New York, Los Angeles, San Francisco, and Seattle) reached their population peak in 2000, with population increases between 6.0 (Los Angeles) and 9.4 percent (New York) in the 1990s. In addition, eight of these cities increased in population in the 1990s (Chicago, Boston, Minneapolis, and Kansas City, in addition to the previously mentioned four cities).

Within cities, downtowns were important growth centers. Population increased in 15 of these 20 downtowns. Only five downtowns (New York, Los Angeles, Cincinnati, Newark, and Kansas City) lost population (Table 3.3).[14] Using data for New York's two downtowns, Eugenie Birch[15] found a 10.9 percent increase in downtown residents, rather than the 0.6 percent reduction in the Berube and Forman study. Downtown population change data were described for 11 of these 20 downtowns by Rebecca Sohmer and Robert Lang.[16] Their calculations were different for some downtowns, indicating that methodology matters. Sohmer and Lang's general findings were similar, however, since population increased in nine of 11 downtowns in their study.

Increases in residents downtown also increase population density. The norm since 1950 has been for residential development to occur at lower densities than in preceding decades. The cities that have been most likely to increase in population have had expansive boundaries permitting low-density development. Annexation by cities of territory nearby has been a key aspect of cities' opportunity to develop at low densities.

Within cities, most population growth has occurred in low-density census tracts. As Alan Berube and Benjamin Forman discovered, "the bulk of central city population growth occurred at the suburban edge, with many Midwestern and Southern cities experiencing extensive population decentralization within their own borders. While downtowns grew in most of the 100 largest cities, even in cities that experienced population declines, they often represented islands of population growth within a larger sea of population loss in the urban core."[17] Elaborating, Berube and Forman wrote: ". . . the inner core of central city census tracts . . . increased in population by only 2.7 percent overall. The middle ring grew at a little more than twice that rate (6.2 percent), while the outer ring boomed in population (15.1 percent growth)."[18]

On the other hand, dense neighborhoods and high-poverty neighborhoods did not inevitably lose residents, although often they did. High-poverty tracts (30 percent or more below poverty level) had a median population loss of 5 percent compared with a median 5 percent population increase where less than 10 percent of residents experienced poverty, according to G. Thomas Kingsley and Kathryn L.S. Pettit.[19] They reported that, in the central cities of the 100 largest metropolitan areas, "there was a nontrivial number of high-poverty neighborhoods whose populations grew significantly (by 5 percent or more) in the 1990s. They are important because they demonstrate that it is possible to attract growth to some high-poverty environments. These neighborhoods made up 29 percent of all high-poverty tracts in the 100 cities . . ."[20]

RACIAL CHANGE

Minority populations increased in central cities in the 1990s, but at a slower pace than in the 1980s. Neighborhood racial segregation declined in the 1990s, continuing a trend observed in the 1980s. We describe results of two studies about the 1990s, and then note the contrast with studies about the 1970s and 1980s.

The nation's 100 largest cities, which were majority white by a small margin in 1990 (52 percent white), became majority minority cities by 2000, with whites constituting only 44 percent of their residents. By 2000, only 52 of the top 100 cities had white majorities, down from 70 in 1990.[21] Even so, the black percentage of residents in these cities declined slightly, from 24.7 percent in 1990 to 24.1 percent in 2000, as the Hispanic share of their population increased by 5 percent.[22] The median black population decline in predominantly (60 percent of more) black census tracts was 7 percent in the 1990s, less than the 11 percent black population decline in similar tracts in the 1980s.[23]

Neighborhood racial patterns continued to change slowly in the 1990s. In a study of 291 metropolitan areas, racial segregation of blacks declined an average 5.5 percent. Some decline in racial segregation occurred in 272 of these 291 metropolitan areas. Most of the decline occurred from more blacks residing in formerly all-white census tracts. The number of tracts where 80 percent or more of residents were black remained the same in 2000 compared with 1990. Most of the reduction in metropolitan racial segregation occurred in the West and South.[24] Segregation remained high in the Northeast and Midwest. However, even in the most segregated cities, segregation of blacks diminished in the 1990s, falling in Detroit (the most segregated city) to the lowest level since 1950 and in Milwaukee (the second most segregated) to the lowest level since 1920.[25]

Based on data for the 1970s, mainly for larger cities in the Northeast and Midwest, Douglas Massey and Nancy Denton argued that little change in segregation of blacks from whites had occurred, despite the civil rights revolution in the 1960s.[26] Roderick J. Harrison and Claudette E. Bennett concluded that "no matter how segregation is measured, blacks were the most segregated group in both 1980 and 1990, usually by a substantial margin . . . Second, all forms of residential segregation either remained stable or declined modestly [10 percent or less] for blacks during the decade (1980s)."[27] William H. Frey agreed that black segregation was highest among racial groups in 1990, as in previous decades: "What is not consistent with the past," Frey added, "is the pervasive decrease [in the 1980s] in the black segregation score among nearly nine-tenths of metropolitan areas . . ., while the majority of metros with minimal Hispanic and Asian populations showed segregation increases for those groups."[28] In 331 metropolitan areas nationwide, there was a 5 percent decline in black segregation in the 1980s, followed by a 4 percent decline in the 1990s.

These studies found black segregation remained high in 2000, but it had been diminishing for 20 years. Even highly segregated Detroit and Milwaukee were significantly less segregated in 2000. These findings raise the possibility that the role of race in influencing residential location patterns in metropolitan areas was less pervasive in 1990 and 2000 than previously. If so, other influences on location patterns may have had greater influence by 2000 than previously.

POPULATION AND HOUSING IN 50 STATES

Considering all 326[29] metropolitan areas with their 542 cities in 50 states, an image of city growth and decline emerges that differs markedly from a narrow focus on large metropolitan areas and large cities. From our perspective, the past should be reinterpreted and a more promising future for cities can be foreseen.

For 539 cities, population increased in 60 percent in the 1970s. In the 1980s, population increased in 67 percent. In the 1990s, population increased in 72 percent (Table 3.4). occupied housing units were even more likely than population to increase, but the progression by decade was reversed compared with population trends. In the 1970s, 88 percent of 542 cities increased in occupied housing units. Between 1980 and 1990, 80 percent increased in occupied housing units, as did 80 percent from 1990 to 2000 (Table 3.4).

Between 1970 and 1980, the average population increase in cities was 13.9 percent, followed by 14.4 percent in the 1980s, and 11.8 percent in the 1990s. Occupied housing increased more than population each decade—a very large 30.6 percent average in the 1970s, followed by 18.1 percent in the 1980s, and 13.1 percent in the 1990s. During the 1990s, the difference between population and occupied housing increases narrowed, probably because little change in AHS occurred during the 1990s.

The role of AHS influencing population change was evident in the 1970s. Its role becomes most apparent in specific cases. To illustrate, there were 156 of 539 cities (three were not cities in 1970) where there was a decline in population and an increase in occupied housing units in the 1970s.

A 50-state perspective also is revealing. During the 1970s, cities on average increased in population in 37 states, decreasing in 13. In the 1980s, cities increased in population in 36 states, decreasing in 14. In the 1990s, population on average increased in cities in 42 states, decreasing in only eight.

Occupied housing again revealed greater demand for city locations than was revealed in population data. This difference was most pronounced during the 1970s, when occupied housing on average increased in cities in all 50 states. Occupied housing increased in cities in 47 states in the 1980s (exceptions were New Jersey, Pennsylvania, and West Virginia), and 46 states in the 1990s (exceptions were Michigan, New York, Pennsylvania, and West Virginia).

These trends presumably influenced national and state politics. The image of central city crisis, which diminished as the urban riots of the 1960s subsided in the 1970s, was further diminished by population and housing trends, which were contrary to the impression that people were suburbanizing and abandoning cities. Suburbanization did occur at a rapid pace, but many cities also were growing.

Table 3.4
Increases in Population or Occupied Housing Units
By Size of 542 Cities in 326 Metropolitan Areas 1970 to 2000

City Population Size	Percent of Cities Increasing in Population or Occupied Housing Units					
	1970[1]-1980		1980-1990		1990-2000	
	Population	Occupied Housing	Population	Occupied Housing	Population	Occupied Housing
Less than 25,000	85.4	97.8	85.9	92.2	65.0	75.0
25,000-49,999	65.3	94.2	68.3	84.7	71.2	81.4
50,000-99,999	55.4	89.2	61.2	76.9	72.8	82.2
100,000-350,000	46.9	81.6	63.9	81.5	73.4	76.1
More than 350,000	32.5	67.5	55.0	55.0	76.6	78.7
Total	60.0	88.7	66.6	80.6	72.1	79.9

[1]In 1970, there were valid data for 539 cities.

Source: U.S. Department of Housing and Urban Development, *HUD User: State of the Cities Data System* (2003), http://socds.huduser.org.

VARIATION BY SIZE AND REGION

The standard image of central cities being places of population decline stems from trends in well-known, large cities like Detroit, Cleveland, and St. Louis. The trends described above indicate that the standard city decline image is distorted. Even for large cities, however, including cities in the Northeast and Midwest, the image of city population decline has been exaggerated. For the largest population group of cities (350,000 and up), 33 percent increased in population from 1970 to 1980. However, in more recent decades, a majority of these large cities increased in population—55 percent in the 1980s and 77 percent in the 1990s. Note that the number of cities in each size group changed with population increases. Moreover, substantial proportions of these large cities grew in occupied housing units—68 percent in the 1970s, 55 percent in the 1980s, and 79 percent in the 1990s (Table 3.4).

Stronger growth tendencies occurred in the second most populous group—cities between 100,000 and 350,000 residents. Occupied housing increased more than population in these cities (Table 3.5). Growth was more frequent in cities with less than 100,000 residents. In the 25,000 to 50,000 residents category, population increased 65 percent from 1970 to 1980, 68 percent from 1980 to 1990, and 71 percent from 1990 to 2000. Occupied housing growth was stronger than population growth, but these two indicators were converging by the 1990s toward similar growth tendencies (Table 3.4).

Large variations occurred among regions. The West was twice as likely than the Northeast to have cities increasing in population and occupied housing. However, during the 1970s—the decade of population growth in the fewest cities—occupied housing increased in a majority of cities, even in the Northeast. In the South, high growth frequencies occurred each decade. In the Midwest, population growth frequencies increased each decade, and most cities increased in occupied housing (Table 3.5).

Differences in metropolitan growth rates and differences in building permits relative to changes in numbers of households may have affected regional variations in cities losing and gaining population. Thomas Bier and Charlie Post concluded in a study of 74 metropolitan areas that "when metropolitan building permits outpace household growth, it generally comes at the expense of the central city and possibly older, inner-ring suburbs. All but one of the 27 cities that lost households in the 1990s had a small share (less than 10 percent) of their area's building permits."[30] The differences between building permits and household increases from 1980 to 2000 were greatest in the Midwest (35 percent) and Northeast (30 percent) and were considerably lower in the South (17 percent) and West (7 percent).[31] These gaps corresponded broadly to regional differences in tendencies for central cities to lose population during the 1980s and 1990s. Variation among metropolitan areas were much larger than these regional differences. The San Francisco area, for example, had 29 percent fewer building permits than increase in households during the 1990s, while the Buffalo area had nearly three times more building permits than household increases. One consequence was that housing abandonment increased in the City of Buffalo but not in the City of San Francisco.[32]

When demand by households exceeds housing supply, housing prices increase, as in San Francisco, where median value of owner-occupied housing was $396,400 in

Table 3.5
Increases in Population or Occupied Housing Units
by Region of 542 Cities in 326 Metropolitan Areas 1970 to 2000

Region	Number of Cities	Percent of Cities Increasing in Population or Occupied Housing Units					
		1970[1]-1980		1980-1990		1990-2000	
		Population	Occupied Housing	Population	Occupied Housing	Population	Occupied Housing
Northeast	95	22.1	55.8	54.7	53.7	44.2	52.6
Midwest	131	36.6	77.9	48.1	53.4	62.6	72.5
South	201	77.6	94.5	69.7	76.1	77.6	86.6
West	115	87.0	95.7	92.2	93.0	96.5	99.1
Total	542	60.0	88.7	66.6	80.6	72.1	79.9

[1]In 1970, there were valid data for 539 cities.

Source: U.S. Department of Housing and Urban Development, *HUD User: State of the Cities Data System* (2003), http://socds.huduser.org.

2000. In Buffalo, where housing supply exceeded demand, housing prices were restrained, and median value of owner-occupied housing was only $59,300 in 2000.[33]

Although central cities' share of metropolitan employment declined in the post-World War II period through 2000, metropolitan manufacturing employment remained more concentrated than metropolitan population in cities. In 24 large metropolitan areas, for example, central cities' share of metropolitan population declined from 56 percent in 1950 to 39 percent in 1970. In 1948, these central cities had an 18 percent larger share of metropolitan manufacturing payroll than metropolitan population. By 1968, these central cities had a 21 percent larger share of metropolitan manufacturing payroll than metropolitan population.[34] During the 1980s, private sector employment of all types increased by 29,000 in Richmond, but population declined. By 1990, Richmond contained 46 percent of metropolitan private sector employment, but only 23 percent of metropolitan population.[35] As these examples indicate, households were not choosing suburban locations primarily to be closer to work.

IMMIGRATION

U.S. foreign-born population increased by 57.4 percent in the 1990s, from 19.8 million in 1990 to 31.1 million in 2000. Ninety-four percent of immigrants lived in metropolitan areas in 2000, of which 48 percent lived in central cities.[36] Immigrants, therefore, played a significant role in population increases in cities during the 1990s.

The role of immigrants was noteworthy in four cities, discussed above, which were among the 20 most populous cities in the 1930s but which reached their population peaks in 2000. New York City's foreign-born population increased by 38 percent in the 1990s, Los Angeles increased 14 percent, San Francisco rose 16 percent, and Seattle went up 54 percent. In each of these cities, the foreign-born population increased faster than total population shown in Table 3.3.

While the increase of foreign-born population in central cities was significant in the 1990s, changes in the distribution of foreign-born population between cities and suburbs was even more striking. In 1970, for example, 54 percent of immigrants to gateway metropolitan areas lived in central cities; in 2000, only 43 percent did. Consequently, immigrants contributed increasingly to population growth in suburbs, as well as diversifying the racial and ethnic mixes in both central cities and suburbs. In addition, "recent arrivals . . . are poorer than the native-born population,"[37] limiting the contribution immigrants made to central city revitalization in the 1990s.

BELIEFS AND PREFERENCES

In Chapters 1 and 2, we discussed briefly the potential importance of beliefs about conditions and location preferences as influences on the evolution of cities and suburbs. At a superficial level, this seems self-evident, but behavior and results of behavior can change without beliefs and preferences being fully conscious and motivating. Further, stated preferences in surveys may not reveal actual preferences. Preferences as stated in surveys are likely to occur in response to questions that are much simpler than real-world decisions. We have referred to location decisions, for example, as mega-decisions. They are not as sweeping in their impacts as decisions about marriage, children, and higher education, but location decisions are significant, especially when purchasing a residence. A residence is the most valuable possession for most households. The residences' setting, including schools, peers, activities, and routine travel distances, may have effects on children and adults that can last for decades. Consequently, general survey results about types of preferred locations for residences, even if the surveys are administered systematically over time, are not likely to provide reliable evidence about reasons for changes in city and suburban location patterns.

Still, surveys have been conducted, with similar questions asked over time, that may provide some clues about location trends that have occurred. One of the most frequent surveys has inquired about whether respondents would prefer to live in cities, suburbs, small towns, or rural areas. Unfortunately, even this simple array of options has varied considerably, and definitions of these terms have not been provided, contributing to the ambiguity of responses.

In February 1965, a Gallup poll asked: "Suppose you could have the same standard of living and the same educational opportunities for your children—where would you prefer to live—in the city or in the suburbs of a city?" Twenty-one percent said city and 69 percent answered suburbs.[38] In the 1970s, the most extensive survey of beliefs about conditions in cities and suburbs and about location preferences was reported by Louis Harris to the U.S. Department of Housing and Urban Development: "Almost half of Americans—47%—express a preference to live in a rural area or in a small city, town, or village not in the suburbs. In addition, more than 1 in 4—27%—selected a medium-size city, small city, town or village in the suburbs, while only 16% would prefer a large city (over 250,000 population) as their 'very first choice.'"[39] These response categories are extremely ambiguous. Each of them contains the word "city" at least once. Small cities are lumped in with rural areas in one category. Medium-size and small cities are combined with suburbs in another category. Population growth in small cities, which we have tracked from 1970 to 2000, may reflect these preferences.

In the Harris survey, another set of ambiguous responses occurred in answer to a question about whether people planned to move in the next few years. Forty-seven percent of city residents who planned to move said they would relocate within the same city or another city. Among suburbanites intending to move, 43 percent said they would move to another suburban location, with 13 percent preferring cities and 37 percent choosing small towns or rural areas. Seventy-one percent of small-town and rural residents intended to move to similar areas, with 12 percent preferring large cities and 13 percent suburban destinations.[40] While these responses seem to forecast more sprawl to outer locations in metropolitan areas, it seems questionable whether their intended destinations should be counted as rural areas or as suburban subdivisions in low-density areas. Moreover, suburban residents seemed slightly more likely than city residents to seek different types of locations, and rural/small-town residents were no more likely to prefer suburban than large city destinations. Consequently, one can imagine problems for post-World War II suburbs lurking in these preference data as much or more than problems for large cities.

Three surveys from 1991 to 2001 had similar findings, by our interpretation, and none of them were encouraging for either cities or suburbs. Peter Hart Research Associates conducted a survey for NBC News and *Newsweek* in July 1991. They asked: "If you could live anywhere in the United States that you wanted to, would you prefer a city, suburban area, small town, or farm?" The responses were 13 percent city, 25 percent suburban area, 37 percent small town, and 24 percent farm.[41] Cities and suburbs contained nearly 80 percent of total population, if one counts residents of metropolitan areas as living in cities or suburbs. Respondents, of course, may have thought that the outside city areas of metropolitan areas contained suburbs, small towns, and farms. The real world of destinations would have 3 percent or less of residents living on real farms. Which sort of mythical farms these respondents had in mind, one cannot know, but these responses do suggest some yearning for low-density, perhaps less stressful, residential settings. These responses may foreshadow the low-density sprawl that continued through the 1980s and 1990s.

In 1998, the Gallup Organization asked this same question: "If you could live anywhere in the United States that you wanted to, would you prefer a city, suburban area, small town, or farm?" The responses were similar: 15 percent city, 25 percent suburban area, 36 percent small town, and 24 percent farm.[42]

In 2001, the Gallup Organization conducted a similar poll, expanding the categories, for CNN and *USA Today*. They asked: "If you could live anywhere you wished, where would you prefer to live—in a big city, small city, suburb of a big city, suburb of a small city, town, or rural area?" The answers: 8 percent big city, 15 percent small city, 20 percent suburb of a big city, 9 percent suburb of a small city, 12 percent town, and 35 percent rural area.[43] It appears that the appeal of towns fell from 36 percent in 1998 to 12 percent in 2001. However, if one combines town, small city, and suburb of a small city, the percentage was 36 percent, about the same as in 1998 and 1991. In this 2001 survey, the rural focus seems to have increased to 35 percent, but we suspect the terms "farm" and "rural area" conjure up different images of destinations by the respondents.

A more useful image of perceptions of cities and suburbs emerged from the Harris survey, when the strengths and weaknesses of each setting were probed. Harris reported[44]: "Large cities are clearly the top choice of most Americans when asked to rate which type of area—large city, medium-size city, suburban communities, or town and rural areas—offers the best shopping (mentioned by 49%), the best employment opportunities (60%), the best health care (61%), the best colleges and universities (53%), the best public transportation (75%), the best restaurants (69%), the best selection of movies (72%) and the best plays and cultural activities (87%). Suburbs and rural areas receive scant mention as best in any of these areas.

"However, the city's image today as a place to live and raise children is overwhelmingly negative. . . . Americans are almost unanimous (82%) in rating large cities as the 'worst place to raise children.' Also, 62% rate large city public schools 'worst;' [sic] 62% attribute the worst housing to the large city; 54% say the highest taxes are in the large city. . . . A near-unanimous 91% point to large cities as having the highest crime rates."

Several caveats are warranted about these findings. First, which of these subjects is salient in motivating decisions to move and in selecting destinations? When respondents have been asked that question, they usually indicate that the lead influence on their location decisions has been the interaction between life cycle evolution (marriage, children, divorce, children leaving home, death of a spouse, and income changes) and housing desires (space, quality, tenure, affordability). Housing characteristics, therefore, may be more important than other beliefs referred to above. Second, these concerns vary with household circumstances. As fewer households have children, an evolution that occurred in the 1980s and 1990s, opinions about the importance of cities and suburbs as places to raise children may have diminished in motivating location choices. Third, opinions on some of these subjects may have changed both as to issue salience and as to locations relevant to the issue.

Crime is one subject that has changed in both salience and location interpretations. According to the National Advisory Commission on Civil Disorders, about 70 percent of residents in riot and nonriot cities considered control of crime a very serious problem, the highest percentage for any problem. Ranking next as very serious problems were preventing violence and other civil disorder, 55 percent, and race relations, 52 percent, respectively.[45]

In 1993, a *Time*/CNN/Yankelovich Partners poll asked: "Five years ago [in 1988], do you think that people who lived in small towns and suburban areas were more likely, less likely, or about as likely to be victims of crimes as people who live in big cities?" The responses were: 5 percent more likely, 84 percent less likely, 9 percent about as likely. When respondents were asked the same question concerning conditions in 1993, they said: 6 percent more likely, 69 percent less likely, and 23 percent about as likely.[46] Whereas the 1988 responses to Yankelovich were similar to the responses to Harris in 1978, conditions in big cities were seen as moving closer to conditions in small towns and suburbs in 1993.

Then, in 2001, the Gallup Organization reported the following: ". . . Americans are feeling safer from crime than they have at any other point in over 30 years. National crime rates have steadily declined over the past decade, and, despite the shock of the Sept. 11 terrorist attacks, Americans increasingly recognize this positive trend. Most are confident about the safety of their local area, and most major U.S. cities—including New York and Washington—are increasingly seen as safe to live in and visit."[47]

Crime barely registered as a concern in national surveys of the most serious problems facing the United States. Moreover, cities where crime had been perceived as very serious in the 1960s, 1970s, and 1980s were considerably more likely to be seen as safe, more like suburbs and small towns than previously. Such beliefs could have contributed to slowing central city decline in the 1990s, as well as helping some cities and many city neighborhoods revive.

DEMAND INCREASED

How to evaluate central city population and occupied housing increases in the 1990s is a puzzle. Some revival in central city population also occurred in the 1980s. Considering these increases in his analysis of the 1980s, William H. Frey concluded: ". . ., none of these central city rebounds should be misinterpreted as city revival. City population gains that draw from particular economic niches or immigrant waves displacing long-gone suburbanites will not bring back the grander, more dominant central city that shaped urban America during most of its history. Rather than causing a revival, these trends merely buy a continued survival of central cities in what has become a suburban-dominated society."[48] This seems a balanced assessment of the 1980s, but is it sufficient for the 1990s?

Growth tendencies for population and occupied housing are summarized in Tables 3.4 and 3.5. Several trends stand out. First, population growth became more common in the 1990s compared with preceding decades. Second, occupied housing growth exceeded population growth each decade for each size of cities. Third, as household size changes diminished from 1980 to 2000, the difference between population and occupied housing changes in cities narrowed.

Population and occupied housing trends indicate that demand for central city residential locations was stronger in the period of rapid suburban population increases than is commonly believed. Recognizing that central city decline has been considerable, although varied, have some changes in its extent and causes occurred in the 1990s? Has the role played by housing supply characteristics changed in the 1990s compared with previous decades? Has dissatisfaction with the quality of life found in ever more sprawling suburbs reshaped demand for housing and neighborhoods in the 1990s? We will begin to explore these subjects in Chapters 6, 7, and 8.

NOTES

1. Each metropolitan statistical area (MSA) must have at least one urbanized area of 50,000 or more inhabitants. The standards for defining metropolitan areas were issued in 1949 and modified in 1958, 1971, 1975, 1980, 1990, and 2000. As of June 6, 2000, there were 362 MSAs. Some of these were parts of Primary Metropolitan Statistical Areas and Consolidated Metropolitan Statistical Areas. The U.S. Department of Housing and Urban Development data series used in this chapter has 326 metropolitan units of analysis (www.census.gov/population/www/estimates/masrp.html). The term "central city" in this chapter and book is used in the same way as by the U.S. Census Bureau. "Suburb" is an informal term that applies to areas outside of central cities that are within metropolitan areas. Both the central city and suburb terms encompass wide diversity by history, function, size, and housing. Although the downtowns of central cities lack the employment and tax base significance of previous decades, they continue to be important. Sometimes the downtowns are near the center of central cities. In other instances, such as Washington, D.C., the downtown is near one edge of the city. Effects of proximity can be expected to be different for suburbs close to being adjacent to the central city downtown than if they are located more traditionally at several miles away from the centers of large cities. Suburbs

that originated as mill towns in the 1800s, which later were engulfed by development, are different from suburbs that originated as bedroom suburbs on commuter railroads in the 1920s, which are also are different from bedroom suburbs that developed after World War II in the era of single-use zoning (residential-only development) in large subdivisions. Census data are available for "places," some of which are central cities and most of which are relatively small suburban jurisdictions with governmental powers or are census-designated places that lack local government powers. However, census data are not classified by the percentage of a metropolitan area that is contained within a central city, nor is it classified based on the origins of a suburban place.

2. Pietro Nivola, *Laws of the Landscape* (Washington, DC: The Brookings Institution, 1999), p. 14.

3. Robert Fishman, "American Metropolis at Century's End," *Housing Policy Debate* 11 (2002), p. 200; Pietro Nivola, *Laws of the Landscape* (Washington, DC: The Brookings Institution, 1999), pp. 14, 22.

4. Peter Dreier, John Mollenkopf, and Todd Swanstrom, *Place Matters* (Lawrence: University Press of Kansas, 2001), p. 234.

5. Robert Fishman, "American Metropolis at Century's End," *Housing Policy Debate* 11 (2002), pp. 199-213.

6. Jordan Rappaport, "U.S. Urban Decline and Growth, 1950 to 2000," *Federal Reserve Bank of Kansas City Economic Review* 88, no. 3 (2003), pp. 15-44.

7. Ibid., p. 34.

8. Edward L. Glaeser, Jed Kolko, and Albert Saiz, *Consumer City Journal of Economic Geography* 1 (January 2001), pp. 27-50.

9. William H. Frey, "The New Geography of Population Shifts: Trends Toward Balkanization," in Reynolds Farley, ed., *State of the Union: America in the 1990s, Vol. 2* (New York: Russell Sage Foundation, 1995), p. 311.

10. Patrick A. Simmons and Robert E. Lang, "The Urban Turnaround," in Bruce Katz and Robert E. Lang, eds., *Redefining Urban & Suburban America* (Washington, DC: The Brookings Institution, 2003), p. 51.

11. William H. Frey, and Alan Berube, "City Families and Suburban Singles: An Emerging Household Story," in Bruce Katz and Robert E. Lang, eds., *Redefining Urban & Suburban America* (Washington, DC: The Brookings Institution, 2003), p. 264.

12. William H. Frey and Alden Speare, Jr., *Regional and Metropolitan Growth and Decline in the United States* (New York: Russell Sage Foundation, 1988), pp. 176-177.

13. David Rusk, *Cities Without Suburbs* (Baltimore: Johns Hopkins University Press, 1993), p. 8.

14. Alan Berube and Benjamin Forman, "Patchwork Cities: Patterns of Urban Population Growth in the 1990s," in Bruce Katz and Robert E. Lang, eds., *Redefining Urban & Suburban America* (Washington, DC: The Brookings Institution, 2003), pp. 96-99.

15. Eugenie Ladner Birch, "Having a Longer View on Downtown Living," *Journal of the American Planning Association* 68, no. 1 (2002), p. 6.

16. Rebecca R. Sohmer and Robert E. Lang, "Downtown Rebound," in Bruce Katz and Robert E. Lang, eds., *Redefining Urban & Suburban America* (Washington, DC: The Brookings Institution, 2003).

17. Alan Berube and Benjamin Forman, "Patchwork Cities: Patterns of Urban Population Growth in the 1990s," in Bruce Katz and Robert E. Lang, eds., *Redefining Urban & Suburban America* (Washington, DC: The Brookings Institution, 2003), p. 76.

18. Ibid., p. 83.

19. G. Thomas Kingsley and Kathryn L.S. Pettit, *Population Growth and Decline in City Neighborhoods* (Washington, DC: Urban Institute, 2002), p. 1.

20. Ibid.

21. Alan Berube, "Racial and Ethnic Change in the Nation's Largest Cities," in Bruce Katz and Robert E. Lang, eds., *Redefining Urban & Suburban America* (Washington, DC: The Brookings Institution, 2003), p. 140.
22. Ibid., pp. 144-145.
23. G. Thomas Kingsley and Kathryn L.S. Pettit, *Population Growth and Decline in City Neighborhoods* (Washington, DC: Urban Institute, 2002), p. 1.
24. Edward L. Glaeser and Jacob L. Vigdor, "Racial Segregation Promising News," in Bruce Katz and Robert E. Lang, eds., *Redefining Urban & Suburban America* (Washington, DC: The Brookings Institution, 2003), p. 218.
25. Ibid., p. 225.
26. Douglas Massey and Nancy Denton, *American Apartheid* (Cambridge, MA: Harvard University Press, 1993).
27. Roderick J. Harrison and Claudette E. Bennett, "Racial and Ethnic Diversity," in Reynolds Farley, ed., *State of the Union: America in the 1990s, Vol. 2* (New York: Russell Sage Foundation, 1995), p. 161.
28. William H. Frey, "The New Geography of Population Shifts: Trends Toward Balkanization," in Reynolds Farley, ed., *State of the Union: America in the 1990s, Vol. 2* (New York: Russell Sage Foundation, 1995), p. 328.
29. U.S. Department of Housing and Urban Development, *HUD User: State of the Cities Data System* (2003), http://socds.huduser.org.
30. Thomas Bier and Charlie Post, *Vacating the City: An Analysis of New Homes vs. Household Growth* (Washington, DC: The Brookings Institution, 2003), p. 1.
31. Ibid., p. 4.
32. Ibid., p. 5.
33. U.S. Census Bureau, *Census of Population and Housing 2000*, American FactFinder, Data Sets, Census 2000 Summary File 3 (SF3)–Sample Data, Detailed Tables.
34. U.S. Census Bureau, *Census of Manufacturing 1948* (Washington, DC: U.S. Government Printing Office, 1950); U.S. Census Bureau, *Census of Manufacturing 1968* (Washington, DC: U.S. Government Printing Office, 1970).
35. William H. Lucy and David L. Phillips, *Confronting Suburban Decline* (Washington, DC: Island Press, 2000).
36. Audrey Singer, *The Rise of New Immigrant Gateways* (Washington, DC: The Brookings Institution, 2004), pp. 3, 10.
37. Ibid., pp. 1, 10.
38. Gallup Organization, Gallup poll (Storrs, CT: The Roper Center for Public Opinion Research, University of Connecticut, 1965).
39. Louis Harris, A *Survey of Citizen Views and Concerns about Urban Life, Final Report* (Washington, DC: U.S. Department of Housing and Urban Development, 1978), p. 17.
40. Ibid., p. 18.
41. Peter Hart Research Associates, *Survey for NBC and Newsweek* (Storrs, CT: The Roper Center for Public Opinion Research, University of Connecticut, July 1991).
42. Gallup Organization, Gallup poll (Storrs, CT: The Roper Center for Public Opinion Research, University of Connecticut, 1998).
43. Gallup Organization, Gallup poll, survey for CNN and *USA Today* (Storrs, CT: The Roper Center for Public Opinion Research, University of Connecticut, 2001).
44. Louis Harris, *A Survey of Citizen Views and Concerns about Urban Life, Final Report* (Washington, DC: U.S. Department of Housing and Urban Development, 1978), p. 5.
45. Otto Kerner, Chair, *Supplemental Studies for the National Advisory Commission on Civil Disorders* (Washington, DC: U.S. Government Printing Office, 1968), p. 84.
46. Yankelovitch Partners, survey for CNN and *Time* (Storrs, CT: The Roper Center for Public Opinion Research, University of Connecticut, 1993).

47. Gallup Organization, Gallup poll (Storrs, CT: The Roper Center for Public Opinion Research, University of Connecticut, 2001).
48. William H. Frey, "The New Geography of Population Shifts: Trends Toward Balkanization," in Reynolds Farley, ed., *State of the Union: America in the 1990s, Vol. 2* (New York: Russell Sage Foundation, 1995), p. 314.

4

Housing and
Cities' Prospects

Central cities did better in the 1990s than in previous decades. Some cities improved in relative income citywide and many neighborhoods improved in the 1990s. Concentrated poverty neighborhoods also were less numerous in 2000 than in 1990. Each of these conditions contains seeds of hope for many cities. Despite these promising conditions, the trend continued to be an overall decline in relative median family income in central cities during the 1990s. The challenges for cities remain great, the remedies needed are numerous, and the paths that may prove useful are diverse.

In this chapter, we will explore dimensions of central city diversity with measures of relative income and poverty, comparing recent decades, discerning trends, and probing for explanations. We begin by researching 542 cities in 326 metropolitan areas in 50 states. We study 40 cities in the largest 35 metropolitan areas in more detail. Shifting scale, we examine relative income changes in more than 8,000 census tracts in six metropolitan areas (Atlanta, Chicago, Los Angeles, Philadelphia, Richmond, and Washington, D.C.). Then we draw on analyses of changes in concentrated poverty by Paul Jargowsky and the Urban Institute to compare the 1990s with the 1980s.

One of our themes is that housing stock characteristics influence city and suburban prospects by interacting with individuals' housing and neighborhood preferences. Beliefs about conditions and trends, and preferences for various types of housing, affect location decisions and then influence jurisdictions' prospects. In this chapter, we begin to explore how cities' housing stock may have affected late 20th-century income trends in cities and suburbs.

In Chapters 7 and 8, we examine relative income trends in suburbs and in census tracts in cities and suburbs. There we discover that relative income often increased in neighborhoods (census tracts) with substantial amounts of pre-1940 housing. Based on our hypotheses about explanations for our findings, we expected the trend of revival in old neighborhoods to continue between 2000 and the 2010 census. If the trend was strong enough, then it might appear in citywide data trends rather than mainly in old neighborhoods.

The *American Community Survey* is a new activity of the U.S. Census Bureau that provides periodic data for large cities and metropolitan areas before the next full census in 2010. Examining data for 20 of the 40 central cities (the only data available at this time for our sample) in 35 metropolitan areas on which we focus in Chapters 3 through 6, we were able to track relative income trends from 2000 to 2003. The trend results are strikingly consistent with our hypothesis. For the first time, these data trends show that substantial majorities of these 20 large central cities increased in relative per capita income ratios and, more surprising, a majority increased in relative median family income ratios.

SUMMARY OF FINDINGS

As a guide to this data-rich chapter, we provide this summary of findings:

• Despite overall relative income declines in each decade from 1970 through 2000, cities in 21 states still had incomes of at least 95 percent of metropolitan incomes in 2000.

• Incomes in smaller cities had held up better than in larger cities.

• Cities were more likely to make relative income gains in the 1990s than in previous decades, and relative income gains were particularly evident in large cities in comparison with the 1970s.

• Surprisingly, per capita incomes of central city whites on average were higher than whites' incomes in suburbs of metropolitan areas in 2000, up slightly from 1990. Relative income decline in large cities was attributable to more minorities being present, in most instances, rather than to avoidance of cities by middle- and upper-income whites.

• Average family income increases in central city neighborhoods were considerably more frequent in the 1990s than in the 1980s.

• Extreme concentrated poverty declined substantially in the 1990s, after increasing rapidly in the 1980s.

• Composition of cities' housing stock influenced relative income trends. Opportunities to increase owner occupancy were one key to maintaining incomes in cities relative to suburbs.

• Cities that were able to build substantial amounts of housing in the 1980s and 1990s did well in maintaining their relative income standing.

• In dense cities, construction of, or conversion to, condominiums contributed to maintaining relative incomes.

• Perhaps most significantly, 15 of 20 large central cities increased in relative per capita income (four decreased and one remained the same), and 11 of 20 increased (seven decreased and two remained the same) in relative median family income from 2000 to 2003. This post-2000 upward trend at citywide scale is the most surprising finding. It may signal that a major turnaround in fortunes of central cities is underway.

THE RELATIVE INCOME MEASURE

In this and subsequent chapters, we use relative income as a measure of attractive and retentive power of cities and suburbs. Most often, we use median family income and per capita income, although occasionally we use average family income and median household income. Relative income measures the difference between the incomes of residents of a city, suburb, or census tract relative to the income of all residents of their metropolitan area.

For a given census year, such as 2000, the relative median family income or per capita income of a city, suburb, or census tract measures the operational preferences of people to live in that place versus the numerous other places in the metropolitan area in which they could choose to live. Households with more income, or wealth, have more choices open to them. Because approximately 98 percent of noninstitutional housing is provided in the U.S. through private markets, spatial patterns reflect choices in which middle- and upper-income households have the leading roles because they have more options. The median family and per capita income of a city, suburb, or census tract relative to metropolitan income in a given year reflects the current and accumulated attractive and retentive power of that place versus the other places in the metropolitan area. Relative income can be tracked over time, from one census decade to another, revealing how the attractive and retentive power of locations has changed. Relative income conditions in a given year, and changes in income trends from decade to decade, reveal whether a city, suburb, or neighborhood (census tract) is stable, declining, or improving.

Relative income data provide information that is useful for its implications for public policies—some places have high-need populations and low resources to tax for public services, for example. Relative income data also are useful for interpreting effects of previous public policies and anticipating effects of present and future public policies concerning transportation, land use, state and local public finance, elementary and secondary education, public safety, land development and redevelopment, and housing.

Relative income is calculated as follows: If a city, suburb, or census tract has income of $28,000 per family, household, or person, and the metropolitan income for that category is $35,000, then the city, suburb, or census tract's relative income is .80 (80 percent) of metropolitan income. If 10 years earlier, the city, suburb, or census tract's income had been $27,000 and the metropolitan income was $30,000, their relative income would have been .90 (90 percent) of metropolitan income. The difference in relative income would have been .10 or 10 percent, which, adjusted for the .90 relationship in the base year of 1990, would be .10 divided by .90 = .11 (the rate of decline).

We use median family income as the best available indicator of housing location decisions of families, which in the census constituted 70.2 percent of households in 1990 and 68.1 percent in 2000.[1] We use per capita income to infer more about the preferences of unrelated individuals, who constitute a substantial portion of the population. Historically, central cities have fared better on relative per capita income than on the relative median family income indicator. We generally avoid using median household income, except when it is the only available alternative, because it combines aspects of median family income and per capita income; hence, it disguises the sometimes large differences between these indicators. The largest difference we have found is in Atlanta, where in 2000 the City of Atlanta scored only .63 on relative median family income, but its score on relative per capita income was 1.03—40 percent higher than its relative median family income. Unfortunately, per capita income data were not available in the U.S. Department of Housing and Urban Development (HUD) data set we relied upon for the analysis of 326 metropolitan areas in 50 states.

DISPARITIES BETWEEN CITIES AND SUBURBS

Focusing on inequalities in 1990, William H. Frey found that per capita income in U.S. central cities was 16.2 percent lower than per capita income in suburbs—$13,840 to $16,507. The largest gap was in the Midwest, 24.2 percent, and the smallest was in the West, 7.8 percent, with the Northeast (21.2 percent) and South (11.4 percent) between them. Population size was another distinguishing feature, as per capita income of central cities in large metropolitan areas was 19.0 percent lower than in their suburbs, with gaps of 13.3 percent in medium-size metropolitan areas and 1.1 percent in small metropolitan areas.[2]

City-suburb income and poverty inequalities increased through 2000. Measured by per capita income, city residents' income was 8 percent lower than suburban residents' income in 1970, 12 percent lower in 1980, and 16 percent lower in 1990. Measured by median family income, city residents' income was 11 percent lower than the suburbs in 1960, 15 percent lower in 1970, 19 percent lower in 1980, and 23 percent lower in 1990. A similar trend to the disadvantage of cities occurred for family poverty, which was higher in cities than in suburbs by a 1.52 ratio in 1960, 1.75 in 1970, 2.08 in 1980, and 2.35 in 1990.[3] This trend continued in the 1990s. As noted below, however, a 50-state perspective provides an additional useful window on interpreting city-suburb disparities.

542 CITIES

City-versus-suburb disparities can be measured either by comparing one to the other or by comparing each to metropolitan medians and means. We have chosen the latter, which tends to understate differences. Many analysts have chosen the former, as in the paragraphs above, which may overstate differences. Whichever method is used, variations in city-to-suburb relationships are large, including when compared for regions of the nation, sizes of cities, and states.

In 2000, central cities in five states with small populations (Arizona, Wyoming, North Dakota, New Mexico, and Alaska) had higher incomes than their suburbs. More significantly, 16 additional states had average median family income ratios of .95 or more for their cities. Nearly all of these states were in the South, West, or Great Plains. Several of these states had numerous central cities: California, 59; Texas, 44; Florida, 30; and North Carolina, 21. These state averages mean that in 42 percent of the states, central cities were faring quite well in attracting and retaining families with means sufficient to live anywhere in their metropolitan areas. Findings for median owner-occupied housing value were similar. In 22 states in 2000, median housing value averages in cities were .95 or more of metropolitan housing values. Given that central city houses, on average, are smaller than suburban houses, these housing values are additional evidence of the continuing appeal of living in many cities.

This relative prosperity and strength was bound to be reflected in state politics and in the outlooks of their selected representatives in the U.S. House of Representatives and the U.S. Senate. After 50 years of supposed deterioration of central cities since 1950, in these 21 states a large majority of central cities were doing well. That is one clear indicator of the diversity of conditions in central cities. It raises the possibility that state policies concerning annexation, municipal incorporation, finance, land use, transportation, and education may make a difference in how well cities have performed.

Median family income averages in some states, however, were at .80 or below, indicating widespread problems in attracting and retaining middle-income and affluent families. These states were in the Northeast and Midwest, except for Maryland and Utah (Table 4.1). Behind the average lies the range. In the case of Connecticut with 11 cities, the lowest state with a .72 ratio in 2000, only one city was above .85, and Hartford, at .43, was competing for the lowest central city score in the United States.

While diversity may be a more accurate single label than decimation for central cities, state averages for median family income ratios revealed a worrisome downward trend from 1970 to 2000. As recently as 1970, 43 states had median family income averages that were .95 or higher relative to their metropolitan areas. Only Connecticut (.89), Georgia (.92), Massachusetts (.94), Michigan (.94), New Jersey (.89), New York (.93), and Ohio (.93) had average incomes in cities less than .95 of metropolitan incomes in 1970. Since 1970, the descent in state averages has been steady—34 states had income ratios of .95 and above in 1980, 27 in 1990, and 21 in 2000. The rate of change in cities' median family income ratios has been modest and has diminished over time—a reduction of 4.7 percent from 1970 to 1980, 3.0 percent from 1980 to 1990, and 2.5 percent from 1990 to 2000.

Table 4.1
States with 10 Lowest Average Central City
Median Family Income Ratios in 2000

Rank	State	Number of Cities	Average of Cities' Median Family Income Ratios	Percent Change 1970 to 2000	Percent Change 1990 to 2000
1	Connecticut	11	.72	-18.6	-8.3
2	Pennsylvania	18	.78	-18.2	-7.3
2	New Jersey	10	.78	-12.2	-5.1
4	Rhode Island	4	.79	-17.6	-10.6
4	Michigan	18	.79	-15.8	-2.0
4	Ohio	24	.79	-15.0	-1.9
7	Utah	5	.80	-15.4	-7.2
8	New York	19	.81	-13.3	-6.0
8	Maryland	5	.81	-11.3	0.1
8	Vermont	1	.81	-15.4	-5.9
	Average		.79	-15.3	-5.4

Source: U.S. Department of Housing and Urban Development, *HUD User: State of the Cities Data System* (2003), http://socds.huduser.org.

REGION AND POPULATION

Comparing the number of cities that were 10 percent above or 10 percent below the metropolitan median family income provides a clear picture of change from decade to decade. In 1970, 76 of 539 cities were above and 99 were below the 10 percent difference from metropolitan median family income. In 2000, 45 were above and 257 were below a 10 percent difference from the metropolitan median family income (Table 4.2), almost six times more below than above this 10 percent benchmark. While cities continued to decline in the 1990s, their rate of decline slowed.

Differences among regions were dramatic. In 1970, only 14 cities in the Northeast and Midwest were 10 percent or more above their metropolitan median family income, while 62 were above it in the South and West. By 2000, the Northeast and Midwest had not changed greatly, still with 11 cities above the 10 percent benchmark, but the number above that level in the South and West had plummeted to 34. In each region, the number of cities below 10 percent of their metropolitan median family income had grown substantially larger.

Population size also produced clear differences in cities' income standing relative to metropolitan income norms. In 1970, no cities larger than 350,000 exceeded the benchmark of city income 10 percent above the metropolitan median family income, whereas 18 of 40 cities were 10 percent or more below the metropolitan median (Table 4.3). By 2000, 26 of 48 cities were below this 10 percent benchmark; again, no cities were 10 percent or more above the metropolitan median. Small cities (25,000 to 50,000) were quite different—33 were 10 percent or more above their metropolitan median family income in 1970, with 21 that were 10 percent or more below that standard. By 2000, however, only 16 were 10 percent above and 78 were 10 percent or more below their metropolitan median family income.

Table 4.2
Cities Above and Below Metropolitan
Median Incomes 1970 to 2000

542 Cities	Median Family Income: Central City Relative to Metropolitan Area				
	10% or More Below	2.5% to 9.9% Below	2.49% Above to 2.49% Below	2.5% to 9.9% Above	10% or More Above
1970[1]	99	134	115	115	76
1980	177	139	91	78	57
1990	237	104	74	73	54
2000	257	113	73	54	45

[1]In 1970, there were valid data for 539 cities.

Source: U.S. Department of Housing and Urban Development, *HUD User: State of the Cities Data System* (2003), http://socds.huduser.org.

Table 4.3
Cities Above and Below Metropolitan Median
Family Income by Population Size 1970 to 2000

542 Cities	Relative to Metropolitan Median Family Income					
	10% or More Below	2.5% to 9.9% Below	2.49% Above to 2.49% Below	2.5% to 9.9% Above	10% or More Above	Total
1970[1]						
Less than 25,000	14	21	15	20	19	89
25,000 to 49,999	21	39	38	42	33	173
50,000 to 99,999	24	36	31	32	16	139
100,000 to 350,000	22	25	24	19	8	98
More than 350,000	18	13	7	2	0	40
1980						
Less than 25,000	16	13	9	13	13	64
25,000 to 49,999	55	47	23	32	26	183
50,000 to 99,999	42	43	30	20	12	147
100,000 to 350,000	40	28	21	13	6	108
More than 350,000	24	8	8	0	0	40
1990						
Less than 25,000	15	5	6	7	7	40
25,000 to 99,999	79	30	21	24	23	177
50,000 to 99,999	63	43	21	27	15	169
100,000 to 350,000	51	15	23	12	8	109
More than 350,000	29	11	3	3	1	47
2000						
Less than 25,000	15	9	3	3	4	34
25,000 to 49,999	78	25	16	16	16	151
50,000 to 99,999	72	40	31	18	18	179
100,000 to 350,000	66	25	20	12	7	130
More than 350,000	26	14	3	5	0	48

[1]In 1970, there were valid data for 539 cities.

Source: U.S. Department of Housing and Urban Development, *HUD User: State of the Cities Data System* (2003), http://socds.huduser.org.

Table 4.4
Changes in Incomes of Cities Relative
to Metropolitan Income 1970 to 2000

	Median Family Income: Changes of Cities Relative to Metropolitan Area					
	Declined by 2.5% or More		Stable: Less than 2.5% Change		Increased by 2.5% or More	
542 Cities	**Number**	**Percent**	**Number**	**Percent**	**Number**	**Percent**
1970 to 1980[1]	356	66.0	135	25.0	48	8.9
1980 to 1990	279	51.5	185	34.1	78	14.4
1990 to 2000	288	53.1	172	31.7	82	15.1

[1]In 1970, there were valid data for 539 cities.

Source: U.S. Department of Housing and Urban Development, *HUD User: State of the Cities Data System* (2003), http://socds.huduser.org.

NONSTABLE CITIES

Trends for 542 cities in all 326 metropolitan areas in the *HUD User: State of the Cities Data System* confirm that the 1970s witnessed more relative income decline in central cities than subsequent decades. For this analysis, we identified a category of stable cities with relative income increases or decreases of 2.5 percent or less. When the increasing and stable cities were combined, they totaled 263 of 542 (49 percent) from 1980 to 1990, and 254 (47 percent) from 1990 to 2000 (Table 4.4). Trends for median household income changes show slightly better performance by cities (Table 4.4). This large number of stable and improving cities indicates again that diversity is common, but the trend overall has been that cities' ability to attract and retain middle- and upper-income families has continued to diminish.

Considerable variation is discernible by population size of cities. This variation, as we see later, may contain some clues about why some cities have been more successful than others at attracting and retaining middle-class families.

Most of the 48 cities that increased in relative average family income in the 1970s had fewer than 25,000 residents (26) or between 25,000 and 50,000 residents (12). No city of more than 350,000 improved, and only three improved in the 100,000 to 350,000 category. Between 1980 and 1990, somewhat larger cities enjoyed more success. Thirty-one cities between 25,000 and 50,000 population increased in relative income, as did 25 in the 50,000 to 100,000 group. Large cities did slightly better in the 1980s than in the 1970s, but still struggled. More stable cities in the large city categories was the most noticeable characteristic of the 1980s. Small- and modest-size cities again fared best in the 1990s but, for the first time, several large cities also improved in relative income, including six that were larger than 350,000 (Atlanta, Detroit, Miami, San Antonio, San Francisco, and Seattle).

Cities that grew in population did better in relative income increases than those that did not grow. Most striking, however, was the poor relative income performance of cities that declined in occupied housing—zero increases in the 1970s, eight

Table 4.5
**Change in Income of Central Cities Relative to Metropolitan Median
Family Income 1970 to 2000 by Change in Occupied Housing Units**

| 542 Cities | Changes Relative to Metropolitan Median Family Income | | | | | |
| | Declined by 2.5% or More | | Stable: Less than 2.5% Change | | Increased by 2.5% or More | |
	Number	Percent	Number	Percent	Number	Percent
1970 to 1980[1]						
Occupied Housing						
Increased	300		133		48	
Decreased	56		2		0	
All Cities:	356	66.0	135	25.0	48	8.9
1980 to 1990						
Occupied Housing						
Increased	200		168		70	
Decreased	79		18		8	
All Cities:	279	51.5	185	34.1	78	14.4
1990 to 2000						
Occupied Housing						
Increased	208		154		71	
Decreased	80		18		11	
All Cities:	288	53.1	172	31.7	82	15.1

[1]In 1970, there were valid data for 539 cities.

Source: U.S. Department of Housing and Urban Development, *HUD User: State of the Cities Data System* (2003), http://socds.huduser.org.

increases in the 1980s, and 11 increases in the 1990s (Table 4.5). The importance of occupied housing change to relative income changes is another clue that housing characteristics deserve closer study.

WHITE FLIGHT?

In our sample of 40 central cities in 35 large metropolitan areas, the simple unweighted average for cities' per capita income relative to the metropolitan per capita income was .885 (or 88.5 percent) in 2000. The cities' relative median family income score was .786 (or 78.6 percent) of metropolitan median family income, reflecting less attraction of many large cities for families. The difference between per capita and family income measures is consistent with the general image of relative attraction of cities and suburbs for families and nonfamilies.

The simple unweighted average for per capita income of whites in cities actually was slightly higher (100.8 percent) than metropolitan per capita income. It had risen slightly from 1990, when white city residents had 99.5 percent of metropolitan per capita income of whites. Thus, incomes of whites were slightly higher in cities than

Table 4.6
Average City Income Ratio Relative to Metropolitan Incomes
for 40 Cities by Income Type for Whites, Blacks, and Hispanics

	Per Capita Income		Median Family Income	Median Nonfamily Income	Median Household Income
	1990	2000	2000	2000	2000
All Races	0.883	0.885	0.786	0.919	0.790
White[1]	0.995	1.008	0.907	0.983	0.845
Black[2]	0.929	0.915	0.874	0.885	0.872
Hispanic	0.918	0.929	0.858	0.891	0.853
White[1] Non-Hispanic		1.048	0.947	1.005	0.863

[1]In 2000, these figures are for those giving the "White Alone" census response to race.

[2]In 2000, these figures are for those giving the "Black Alone" census response to race.

Sources: U.S. Census Bureau, *Census 2000,* Summary File 4, PCT Matrices 89, 113, 126, 130, and *Census 1990,* Summary File 3, Matrix P114A, generated by William H. Lucy, using American FactFinder, http://factfinder.census.gov, August 2004.

in suburbs—the opposite of the general image of flight of middle- and upper-income whites to suburbs.

Blacks' incomes were going in the other direction. In 1990, blacks' per capita income in cities was 93.9 percent of metropolitan blacks' income. By 2000, city blacks' per capita income was 91.6 percent of metropolitan blacks, opening a 9 percentage point gap between whites and blacks.

Hispanics' intrametropolitan income balance was about the same in 1990 and 2000, with city per capita income at 91.8 percent of metropolitan Hispanic income in 1990 and 92.2 percent in 2000. Averages for 40 cities for relative per capita income for 1990 and 2000, and for relative incomes for families, nonfamilies, and all households in 2000 are presented in Table 4.6. Individual city values are presented in Appendix Tables 4.A1 and 4A.2 (located at the end of this chapter).

By this per capita income measure, it would seem that middle-class flight from cities became more of a black than a white phenomenon during the 1990s. Cities fared worse on these overall scores that used incomes for all races than when incomes for whites and blacks were analyzed separately. Black populations reduced the scores of cities, because blacks had much lower incomes than whites, and blacks constituted higher percentages of city than suburban populations.

Wide variations occurred among cities in income conditions and trends that were influenced by changes in shares of population by race, as well as movement between cities and suburbs within races. In some cities, white shares of total city populations increased, as in Atlanta, as well as incomes of whites in cities increasing relative to metropolitan whites' incomes. In such instances, cities' overall income ratios rose.

The general image that the only persons remaining in cities are those who have no choice is patently false. In addition, the image that the only whites in cities are poor clearly is mistaken. Evidence about high per capita incomes among city whites is cause for some hope that cities can revive. More progress by cities in retaining or attracting middle-income white families would contribute to greater prospects for revival of incomes in cities, as would narrowing of the income gap between whites and blacks.

Research by Alan Berube and Thacher Tiffany has confirmed that diverse income patterns existed in the 100 largest U.S. cities in 2000. Dividing income distributions in cities by quintiles, Berube and Tiffany found that some cities had more households in the lowest quintile and declining proportions of residents in each higher quintile, but others had more high-income quintile residents than households in the lowest quintile. Other cities had bulges in the middle ranges, while others approximated the national income distribution with equal percentages of households within each quintile.[4]

Diversity in income distribution results suggests that diversity in causes has occurred. By extension, one can reason that diversity in prospects also are likely. Public policies to bring more cities in line with national income distributions among their households should reflect these diverse conditions and causes. Housing policies, we will argue, should play an important role in seeking more representative income distribution patterns in cities.

HOME OWNERSHIP

As home ownership increased nationally from 44 percent in 1940 to 62 percent in 1960,[5] cities and suburbs diverged in owner occupancy rates. In 1960, 47 percent of city households owned their residences, while 73 percent of suburban households were owner occupants. City and suburb home ownership proportions diverged partially because of different opportunities for ownership. Cities and suburbs both depended on having single-unit structures to accommodate this rising demand and opportunity for owner occupancy. The opportunity to buy homes was increased by greater affluence and easier loans—lower down payments in particular. The desire for owner occupancy was paramount, and more influential, we suspect, than other motivations for suburbanization of the middle class. Consequently, cities that had high percentages of single-unit structures in their housing stock, and cities with land where single-unit structures could be built, were in a much better position to accommodate the rise in home ownership by middle-class households.

Relative income nearly always declined where owner-occupied housing units and single-unit structures did not increase. Moreover, in neighborhoods where demand eroded due to social problems, some single-unit structures converted from owner occupancy to rental uses. These circumstances were much more likely in large cities than in smaller cities. Hence, large cities were more vulnerable to decline because opportunities for home ownership increased more in suburbs than in cities, and social problems in cities increased in the wake of middle-income households departing for suburbia.[6]

In the six metropolitan areas (Atlanta, Chicago, Los Angeles, Philadelphia, Richmond, and Washington, D.C.) that we analyze below and in Chapters 7 and 8, the home ownership and residential structure disadvantages of their central cities were apparent in 1960. In owner occupancy, only Philadelphia was close to the national home ownership average of 62 percent in 1960 (Table 4.7). The other five central cit-

Table 4.7
Percent Owner-Occupied and Single-Unit Structures
in Central Cities and Outside Central Cities in 1960

	Central City		Outside Central City		Difference Central City–Outside Central City		
	Percent Owner Occupied	Percent Single Unit*	Percent Owner Occupied	Percent Single Unit*	Percent Owner Occupied	Percent Single Unit*	Combined Indicator
Atlanta	45.6	59.0	72.6	87.9	-27.0	-28.9	-55.9
Chicago	34.3	24.8	76.2	79.8	-41.9	-55.0	-96.9
Los Angeles	46.2	60.8	62.7	78.8	-16.5	-18.0	-34.5
Philadelphia	61.9	74.7	77.5	87.4	-15.6	-12.7	-28.3
Richmond	47.7	68.1	80.9	94.2	-33.2	-26.1	-59.3
Washington, D.C.	30.0	42.2	63.1	73.6	-33.1	-31.4	-64.5
Unweighted Average:	44.3	54.9	72.2	83.6	-27.9	-28.7	-56.6

*Percent of Occupied Housing in Single-Unit Structures.

Source: U.S. Census Bureau, *Census of Population and Housing* (Washington, DC: U.S. Government Printing Office, 1960).

ies ranged from owner occupancy of 30 percent in Washington, D.C., to 48 percent in Richmond.

These six central cities also had a lesser share of occupied dwellings in single-unit structures (55 percent) than the national average (75 percent) in 1960. Other than Philadelphia, these cities ranged from 24.8 percent of occupied housing units in single-unit structures in Chicago to 68 percent in Richmond. Differences between these five central cities and their suburbs in occupied housing proportions in single-unit structures also were substantial, ranging from 18 percent in the Los Angeles area to 55 percent in the Chicago area (Table 4.7). These central cities' single-unit structure proportions of occupied housing put them at a disadvantage versus their suburbs as desires and capacities for home ownership increased. We suspect that the shares of single-unit and multiunit structures in cities in 1960 contributed to a downward spiral in these cities, which was reflected in wider relative median family income gaps between cities and suburbs from 1970 through 2000.

Where the middle class went, relative income rose. In places where the middle class left, relative income fell. As suburbs grew, spread, and diversified, however, some of their appeal faded, reduced by congestion, time lost in traffic, inconvenience in running errands, dependence of children on parents to drive, loss of green space, and uncertainties about neighborhood change, school change, and housing investment. As noted in Chapter 1, 57 percent of persons surveyed in 2000 thought sprawl had become a very important or somewhat important problem. When they were asked to specify the biggest problem associated with sprawl, 30 percent said loss of green space, forests, and farm land; 21 percent said more traffic and longer commute times; 6 percent said poor air quality, 6 percent said high suburban infrastructure costs; and 5 percent said deterioration of cities and inner suburbs.[7]

As these frustrations with suburbs increased, we suspect that more people aspired to walk to some destination other than neighborhood friends, to have public transportation alternatives for some purposes, to recapture some of the variety and ambiance of walkable neighborhoods, to be closer to more types of restaurants and entertainment, and to be able to share more driving and provide alternatives for some transportation destinations for teenagers. Questions about teenagers' safety while driving substantial distances for routine activities in suburbs also produced anxiety for some parents.

Dowell Myers and Elizabeth Gearin cite the American LIVES survey to conclude: "Resale buyers, . . . who favored the open space, gardens, and easy walking access to shared recreation space and stores represent an increasing number of homebuyers."[8] Myers and Gearin suggest that differences between consumers of new and resale housing "are instructive because some have speculated that the consumer base for TND [Traditional Neighborhood Development] is satisfying its desires through existing housing built in the decades before World War II."[9] We think some of these attitudes grew in the 1980s and then increased and became a noticeable force in metropolitan housing markets in the 1990s.

If we are correct in these hypotheses, diverse results would occur. Cities would continue to have housing that was less compatible with home ownership than suburban housing because of inertia embedded in multiunit structures. On the other hand, some parts of cities might have advantages of convenience and ambiance. Consequently, any neighborhood in a city that had single-unit housing for ownership and convenience with ambiance might have more potential for revival in relative income than other neighborhoods.

The minimum trend that would support, or at least not disprove, this hypothesis would occur if more city neighborhoods rose in relative median family income in the 1990s than in the 1980s. To test this hypothesis, we conducted a census tract scale analysis.

RELATIVE INCOME IN SIX CENTRAL CITIES

Census tracts typically have 3,000 to 5,000 residents. They approximate neighborhoods, although they may not correspond to local impressions of neighborhood boundaries. Here we consider whether relative average family income had increased or decreased by 2.5 percent or more during the 1980s and 1990s in central cities and outside central cities in the metropolitan areas of Atlanta; Chicago; Los Angeles; Philadelphia; Washington, D.C.; and Richmond. Median family income data were not available. Census tract data in the Neighborhood Change Database compiled by the Urban Institute in collaboration with GeoLytics, Inc., were used in this analysis.[10] We chose these six metropolitan areas because of their large size, coast-to-coast geographic range, diverse economies, and, in the case of Richmond, accessibility for a case study (see Chapter 12).

During the 1980s, a modest number and percentage of census tracts were increasing in relative average family income in these six central cities. Washington, D.C. (37 percent) and Atlanta (34 percent) did best; Philadelphia (15 percent) and Chicago (20 percent) did worst.

During the 1990s, average family income increases of 2.5 percent or more occurred in 39 percent of census tracts in these six central cities, up from 24 percent in the 1980s. Atlanta (52 percent) and Chicago (45 percent) did best; Philadelphia (23 percent) again was worst. More census tracts decreased in relative average family income than increased, as would be consistent with a citywide decline in relative income. However, in Atlanta, far more tracts increased than decreased by 2.5 percent or more (52 to 34 percent) in the 1990s. Overall, Atlanta went up citywide in relative median family income by 4 percent and in relative per capita income by 14 percent. Washington, D.C., was the only city in which fewer census tracts increased in the 1990s than in the 1980s.

As with citywide indicators for population and relative income, central city neighborhoods tended to do better in the 1990s than they had in the 1980s. In this modest sense, these relative income data are consistent with our hypothesis that evolving consumer preferences for neighborhood characteristics made more city neighborhoods attractive to more families than in the 1980s.

In addition, analysis of repeat house sales in Chicago from 1983 to 1998 revealed higher values toward the center, with an average housing value decline of 8 percent with each mile farther from downtown Chicago. This discovery by Daniel P. McMillen reversed a trend that had been observed in the 1980s for house values to be relatively flat with distance from the center.[11] Relatively flat housing values in relation to distance from the center was a change from the traditional strength of the center in the monocentric metropolitan area that preceded the dominance of suburbia. McMillen concluded that repeat house sales in the 1990s demonstrated a "dramatic return of centralization to the Chicago housing market."[12] These housing value changes in the 1990s point in the same direction of central city revival as the increase in average family income of 2.5 percent or more in 45 percent of Chicago census tracts in the 1990s compared with such increases in 20 percent in the 1980s, as noted above.

POVERTY IN CITIES

Poverty has continued to be much more of a city than a suburban problem, despite signs of income revival in more city neighborhoods in the 1990s than in the 1980s. In 1970, 310 of 539 cities (58 percent) had poverty rates for individuals that exceeded their metropolitan poverty rate. By 2000, 432 of 542 cities (80 percent) had higher poverty rates. Large cities were more likely than small cities to have poverty rates higher than metropolitan rates. Ninety percent or more of cities with 350,000 or more residents had higher poverty rates than their metropolitan rates from 1970 through 2000.

In 1970, less than 50 percent of cities under 50,000 had poverty rates exceeding metropolitan rates but, by 2000, poverty rates were higher than metropolitan rates in more than 70 percent of small cities. Overall, poverty rates were higher in cities than metropolitan rates in 76 percent of cities in 1990 and 80 percent of cities in 2000. This rate of increase in the 1990s was less, however, than the increase in the 1970s and 1980s. Given the increasing concentration of poverty in cities relative to suburbs in the 1990s, the reduction in highly concentrated poverty in city census tracts, as described next, is surprising.

CONCENTRATED NEIGHBORHOOD POVERTY

Neighborhoods with concentrated poverty seem least amenable to turning around. Poverty, when concentrated, often breeds more poverty.[13] Successful role models for neighborhood youths are rare. Employment networking is anemic. Pathologies abound. Health care is in short supply. Housing is deteriorated, often abandoned. Why would such neighborhoods rebound? Demolition and rebuilding sometimes occur. A massive influx of investment, such as a new subway stop followed by entrepreneurs' private investments, is another possibility. In general, however, such neighborhoods seem more likely to be stable or escalating in their poverty concentrations rather than subject to widespread diminished poverty when the number of poverty households nationally is stable.

As one would expect, poverty concentrations increased in the 1970s and 1980s. Using 40 percent of residents below the poverty level as the benchmark for extreme poverty concentrations, Paul Jargowsky found that the number of people in extreme poverty neighborhoods doubled between 1970 and 1990.[14] ". . . the physical size of the blighted sections of many central cities increased even more dramatically," Jargowsky wrote. "By contrast, poverty—measured at the family level—did not increase during this period. Thus, there was not a change in poverty per se, but a fundamental change in the spatial organization of poverty. The poor became even more physically isolated from the social and economic mainstream of society."[15]

In the 1990s, however, the number of people in extreme poverty concentrations dropped significantly—24 percent, about 2.5 million people.[16] Extreme poverty concentrations diminished in central cities and rural areas but did not change much in suburbs. Jargowsky observed that this trend in the 1990s countered the assumption "that high-poverty neighborhoods were an unavoidable aspect of urban life and would continue to grow inexorably in size and population."[17]

G. Thomas Kingsley and Kathryn L.S. Pettit discovered, in addition, that the number of metropolitan poor who lived in high-poverty neighborhoods, defined as having 30 percent or more of residents below the poverty line, also diminished from 31 percent in 1990 to 26 percent in 2000. This decline in poverty concentrations above the 30 percent poverty rate depended, however, on reductions in extreme poverty tracts above 40 percent poverty rates. By 2000, only 12 percent of the metropolitan poor lived in extreme poverty districts (40 percent or more poverty rate), down from 17 percent in 1990, and down, as well, from 13 percent in 1980.[18]

These high-poverty census tracts (30 percent or more poverty) accounted for 6.7 million poor persons compared with 3.1 million in the extreme poverty census tracts (40 percent or more poverty). There was some compensating increase, however, in census tracts with 20 to 30 percent poverty rates, with 21 percent of the metropolitan poor living there, up from 18 percent in 1990. In addition, the number of persons living in tracts with poverty rates between 10 and 30 percent increased from 10.4 million to 12.7 million in the 1990s.

Poverty concentrations declined in the 1990s for blacks as well as whites, reversing a 20-year increase in black poverty concentrations from 1970 to 1990. In 1990, 30 percent of poor blacks lived in high-poverty neighborhoods (40 percent or more below the poverty level). By 2000, only 19 percent of poor blacks resided in high-poverty neighborhoods. Concentrations of poor blacks decreased in 227 metropolitan areas, increased in 55, and remained the same in 49.[19] Moreover, the share of high-poverty census tracts in which blacks comprised more than 60 percent of the residents decreased from 48 percent in 1980 to 39 percent in 2000. The share of high-poverty tracts with no predominant race, on the other hand, increased from 21 percent in 1980 to 26 percent in 2000.[20]

These findings about reductions in high- and extreme poverty concentrations in the largest 100 metropolitan areas are consistent with our census tract findings about rising average family income in more census tracts in Atlanta, Chicago, Los Angeles, Philadelphia, and Richmond during the 1990s. Why would extreme poverty concentrations be increasing in the 1970s and 1980s and diminishing in the 1990s? Why should more census tracts experience rising relative income in the 1990s compared with the 1980s in several large cities? Jargowsky does not attempt an answer, despite vague mention that the economic boom of the 1990s may have contributed.

Kingsley and Pettit add to the mystery by providing additional information about frequent changes in which tracts had high poverty: "The way concentrated poverty changes is generally not well understood. Contrary to what the name might imply, levels of concentrated poverty are not much influenced by population growth or decline in tracts that were in the high- or extreme poverty categories at the beginning of the decade. Rather, the outcome is determined more by the number of tracts moving in and out of those categories. And it is important to know that when tracts reach high-poverty status, further deterioration is not at all inevitable."[21] By 2000, for example, high-poverty tracts with 22 percent of the high-poverty tract population in 1990 had less poverty and were no longer classified as high-poverty tracts.[22]

These surprising trends in high-poverty census tracts in the 1990s were foreshadowed by trends in the 1980s, which perhaps were even more surprising. In a conference paper, Roberto Quercia, George Galster, and Alvaro Cortes report that high-poverty tracts (40 percent or more of residents below the poverty rate in 1980) were more likely to have stable or declining poverty rates than rising poverty rates in the 1980s.[23] ". . . unlike the contentions of the traditional filtering and neighborhood life cycle models," they wrote, "the fortunes of poor neighborhoods are not necessarily predetermined."[24] Continuing, they wrote, "Nationally, neighborhoods with 1980 poverty rates that were 40 percent or greater were nearly as likely to experience succession (greater incidences of poverty over time) (36%), as stability (33%), or displacement (lower incidences of poverty over time) (31%) . . . This confounds an oft-repeated nostrum based on neighborhood life cycle theory: extreme poverty neighborhoods only get progressively poor."[25]

In a commentary on the Jargowsky and Kingsley/Pettit findings for the 1990s, George Galster offered "A Cautionary Tale" in two respects.[26] First, Galster notes that previous empirical literature suggests that "increasing numbers of poor neighbors apparently has [sic] indecipherable effects on the individual until they exceed roughly 5 to 20 percent of the census tract population (depending on the indicator), whereupon the marginal impact rises dramatically."[27] Examples of negative effects of neighborhood poverty from the literature cited by Galster were lower incomes, longer poverty durations, and more property crimes.

Describing the reduction in concentrated high-poverty tracts from 1990 to 2000 as "astonishing," Kingsley and Pettit ask: "Why did it happen? More research will be needed to answer that in a fully satisfying way. However, it is hard to believe that the booming economy of the late 1990s did not have a great deal to do with it."[28] Perhaps, but the number of persons below the poverty level increased from 31.7 million in 1990 to 33.9 million in 2000, despite the booming economy. Therefore, why should highly concentrated poverty decline, while the general poverty totals increased slightly, and while poverty in central cities increased? Neither Jargowsky nor Kingsley and Pettit addressed these questions. Evidently, in the 1990s, more than in the 1980s, the trickle-down process of neighborhood change did not proceed inexorably, contrary to standard forecasts.

SINGLE-UNIT STRUCTURES AND HOME OWNERSHIP

The presence of single-unit residential structures in cities, cities' home ownership rates, and the decade in which housing was constructed provide some clues about strengths and weaknesses of cities from 1950 to 2000. Owner occupancy of single-unit structures accounted for nearly all home ownership in the United States before 1970. After 1970, ownership of units in condominiums and cooperatives became increasingly common, primarily in large cities and some inner suburbs. However, in large cities, even in 2000, 94 to 99 percent of owner occupancy usually was in single-unit structures or duplexes, with 92 percent or more in single-unit structures.

In the 1950s and 1960s, single-unit structures were particularly important as the home ownership rate increased from 44 percent in 1940 to 55 percent in 1950, 62 percent in 1960, and 63 percent in 1970.[29] Cities that fell short of 60 or 70 percent of their housing in single-unit structures had more difficulty, other things being equal, in competing with their suburbs for middle- and upper-income residents. When cities had significantly lower home ownership rates than their suburbs, their demographic characteristics were less hospitable to families with children, who wanted neighbors similarly situated and playmates for their children.

On the other hand, if large numbers of single-unit structures and other housing were constructed in cities in the 1945 to 1970 period, another problem occurred. The median size, single-unit house built in 1950 had 1,100 square feet. By 1970, the median size still was only 1,375 square feet. Typical size houses increased steadily thereafter, with 2,000 square feet becoming the median size by the year 2000.[30] As houses age, and become outmoded in size, style, and internal attributes, extensive remodeling and expansion is required to make them competitive to attract middle-income households. This remodeling occasionally occurred, but it was not the norm. Consequently, cities with modest or low amounts of single-unit structures in 1950 and 1960, and cities that added substantially to their housing stock in the 1950s and 1960s, were positioned weakly to compete with their suburbs for middle-income households from 1970 to the present.

Elements of new houses changed greatly between 1970 and 2000. For the five years from 1968 to 1972, 72 percent of new owner-occupied, single-unit houses were single story, 47 percent had two or more baths, and 36 percent had central air conditioning.[31] In 2000, 47 percent of new owner-occupied, single-unit houses were single story, 93 percent had two or more baths, and 85 percent had central air conditioning.[32] The market had changed. In 2000, 26.4 percent of all housing had been constructed between 1950 and 1970. Cities and suburbs with more than that share of 1950s and 1960s housing often would be at a competitive disadvantage.

Cities could compete to some extent if they had very strong employment centers in their cores or elsewhere, and if their public policies and private development sector accommodated condominiums and cooperatives, effectively permitting extensive ownership other than in single-unit structures. Cities also could compete more effectively with suburbs if they retained some capacity to construct single-unit structures in the 1980s and 1990s.

SINGLE-UNIT STRUCTURES AND RELATIVE INCOME

Of the 40 central cities in the 35 large metropolitan areas in our sample, 14 had more than 60 percent, and 24 had more than 50 percent, of their dwellings in single-unit structures in 2000. These 14 central cities had average relative per capita incomes that were 91 percent of metropolitan per capita incomes, above the 40 cities' percentage (88 percent) and above the average for the remaining 26 central cities' percentage (87 percent). These 14 cities with high percentages of single-unit structures also did well in the 1990s in preserving their relative income positions, with essentially no loss of standing relative to their suburbs between 1990 and 2000 (Table 4.8).

Four of these 14 cities had noticeably lower relative income proportions in 2000 than the other 10 cities. These cities—Baltimore, Detroit, Philadelphia, and Sacramento—were distinguishable by the large percentage differences between their high percentage of structures in single units (65 percent in Baltimore to 70 percent in Detroit) and their considerably lower percentages of owner-occupied units (50 percent Sacramento to 59 percent Philadelphia). The relative per capita income ratios of these cities ranged from .60 for Detroit to .84 for Sacramento. The mean per capita income ratio for the remaining 10 cities with high single-unit structure and home ownership percentages was 1.01, with cities slightly higher than their metropolitan per capita income. Conversely, these four cities had an average per capita income ratio of .71, with an average median family income ratio of .65.

Why didn't high single-unit structure rates lead to fairly strong standing in relative income in these four cities? One possibility is that the housing units and lots are quite small. High percentages of housing in three of these cities (Baltimore, Detroit, and Philadelphia) were built before 1940 and in the 1940s and 1950s, when housing sizes tended to be small. Baltimore and Philadelphia have a substantial proportion of two-story row houses that would be difficult to expand. Detroit's housing was more heavily concentrated in the 1945 to 1960 construction period, when small, detached, single-family houses were standard, and in Detroit they were built mainly to the budgets of industrial workers. These houses also may be difficult to expand. Sacramento is a more mysterious case.

SMALL HOUSES, OWNERSHIP, AND RELATIVE INCOME

By the 1990s, housing units built in the 1940s and 1950s would be middle aged and in need of major reinvestment, upgrading, and expansion. If substantial percentages of housing in some cities were built either before 1940 or in the 1940s and 1950s, these cities might have little capacity to accommodate newer, larger, more upscale housing built to contemporary preferences in the 1980s and 1990s. These cities might be particularly vulnerable to downward pressure on relative income.

Table 4.8
Single Units Exceeding 60 Percent of Occupied Units,
Owner Occupancy and Relative Income in Central Cities

14 Cities	Census 2000 Percentages		Relative Per Capita Income		Relative Median Family Income	
	Single Units	Owner Occupied	2000	Changes 1990-2000	2000	Changes 1990-2000
Baltimore	65.1	50.3	.70	.96	.60	.89
Charlotte	61.5	57.5	1.15	1.00	1.05	.99
Detroit	69.9	54.9	.60	1.00	.57	1.04
Indianapolis	65.6	58.6	.93	.98	.88	.95
Kansas City	66.3	57.7	.89	.97	.83	.94
Las Vegas	62.6	59.1	1.04	1.07	1.04	1.04
Philadelphia	68.2	59.3	.69	.94	.63	.88
Phoenix	62.8	60.7	.91	.96	.91	.96
Portland	63.0	55.8	.97	1.01	.90	1.02
Sacramento	65.4	50.1	.84	.92	.78	.91
San Antonio	67.8	58.1	.94	1.03	.92	1.03
St. Petersburg	61.0	63.5	.97	.99	.95	.98
Tampa	60.8	55.0	1.01	1.09	.89	1.01
Virginia Beach	74.5	65.6	1.10	.97	1.08	.96
Mean			.91	.99	.86	.97
Mean[1]			.96	1.00	.92	.98
Mean[2]			.99	1.01	.95	.99

[1] Omits Baltimore, Detroit, and Sacramento, with a gap of 14.8 to 15.3 between single-unit and owner-occupied percentages.

[2] Omits Baltimore, Detroit, Philadelphia, and Sacramento, with a gap of 8.9 to 15.3 between single-unit and owner-occupied percentages.

Source: U.S. Department of Housing and Urban Development, *HUD User: State of the Cities Data System* (2003), http://socds.huduser.org.

In 2000, 16 of the 40 central cities in this sample had 67 percent (two-thirds) or more of their housing constructed before 1960, and they also had less than 10 percent of their housing constructed after 1980 (Table 4.9). For these 16 cities, their average relative per capita income ratio in 2000 was .79 and their average relative median family income ratio was .68. These ratios were well below the 40-city average ratios of .88 and .79, and much below the average ratios for the other 24 central cities in this sample—a .95 ratio for relative per capita income and .86 for relative median family income.

Boston, Chicago, and New York are interesting examples of cities that would seem to be especially disadvantaged on three of these indicators of housing supply. They had high percentages of housing constructed before 1960 (Boston, 73 percent; Chicago, 69 percent; and New York, 67 percent). They had low percentages of housing constructed in the 1980s and 1990s (Boston, 9; Chicago, 9; and New York, 9). They also had the lowest shares of single-unit structures in the 40-city sample. However, they also were unusual in having home ownership rates that were much higher than their percentages of single-unit structures—16.6 percent single-unit structures in Boston, 16 percent in New York, and 28 percent in Chicago. Percentages of owner occu-

Table 4.9
Cities With More than 67 Percent of 2000 Housing Built Pre-1960

City	Percent of 2000 Housing Units Built		Relative Per Capita Income		Relative Median Family Income	
	Pre-1960	Post-1980	2000	Changes 1990-2000	2000	Changes 1990-2000
Baltimore	73.7	7.2	.70	.96	.60	.89
Boston	72.7	9.2	.80	.99	.65	.93
Buffalo	86.0	4.4	.74	.97	.62	.91
Chicago	69.4	8.5	.81	1.03	.70	.95
Cincinnati	68.7	6.8	.87	1.01	.68	.95
Cleveland	81.4	4.3	.64	1.02	.58	.97
Detroit	81.4	3.8	.60	1.00	.57	1.04
Milwaukee	69.5	6.7	.70	.93	.67	.92
Minneapolis	72.5	8.7	.87	.98	.74	.97
New York	67.2	9.0	.84	.98	.70	.93
Philadelphia	75.4	4.4	.69	.94	.63	.88
Pittsburgh	78.3	6.0	.90	1.00	.82	.98
San Francisco	74.6	9.0	1.09	1.12	.89	1.06
St. Louis	79.1	5.9	.71	.98	.60	.95
St. Paul	69.4	8.7	.77	.95	.75	.96
Washington, DC	68.4	7.7	.94	1.07	.64	.96
Mean	74.2	6.9	.79	1.00	.68	.95

Source: U.S. Department of Housing and Urban Development, *HUD User: State of the Cities Data System* (2003), http://socds.huduser.org.

pancy increased in Boston (25 percent in 1950 to 32 percent in 2000) and New York (19 percent in 1950 to 30 percent in 2000), but not in Chicago (44 percent in 1950 to 44 percent in 2000). We speculate that greater opportunities to own condominiums and cooperatives in Boston and New York contributed to meeting the desires for many middle- and upper-income households to own their residences, and thereby prevented even greater declines in their incomes relative to metropolitan norms.

The problem with old housing may not be the old housing itself but the elimination of sites where significant amounts of new housing can be constructed. In the sample of 40 cities, only two cities—Portland and Seattle—had more than 30 percent of their housing constructed before 1940 and had at least 15 percent of their housing constructed in the 1980s and 1990s. Portland and Seattle scored much higher in their relative per capita income ratios (.97 and1.09) and median family income ratios (.90 and .98) than the 40-city averages. Portland and Seattle also increased in relative median owner-occupied housing value. Portland increased from a .81 ratio of city to metropolitan values in 1990 to .89 in 2000, while Seattle increased from 1.01 in 1990 to 1.14 in 2000. These cities and their metropolitan regions have reputations for effective planning, development, and public transportation policies. Perhaps these policies also have had positive effects on the central cities.

Cities that have a substantial amount of new housing should have more housing built to contemporary preferences in size and quality than cities with little new housing. Therefore, cities with new housing also should be more successful than older cities in attracting and retaining middle- and upper-income households. Sixteen cities in our sample of 40 cities had 20 percent or more of their year 2000 housing constructed in the 1980s and 1990s (Table 4.10). In these cities, the average per capita income ratios in 2000 were .97 compared with an average of .88 in all 40 cities and .83 in the 24 other cities. For relative median family income, the average for these 16 cities was .88 compared with .78 for 40 cities and .72 for the remaining 24 cities. Employment opportunities, social problems, lifestyle amenities, housing density, condominium construction, and local government policies are among the conditions that may influence how much new housing has been constructed in central cities.

CONDOMINIUMS

An alternative to constructing new housing is to convert existing housing from rental to owner status, satisfying the desire of more middle-income households to own their residences. A substantial amount of the new housing that is built in cities is in multiunit structures, the type of structures in which units usually are rented. Condominiums and cooperatives make ownership possible in multiunit structures. Therefore, an indicator about how much of the owner-occupied housing in a city is in multiunit structures may reveal successful efforts to appeal to middle-class preferences for ownership of residences.

In our sample of 40 central cities in 35 large metropolitan areas, seven central cities had 10 percent or more of their owner-occupied housing in structures other than single-unit buildings, mobile homes, and two- to four-unit buildings (often duplexes). These cities had relative per capita income ratios (.92) slightly above the 40-city average (.88) in 2000. More significant, however, was that they improved in their relative income standing in the 1990s in per capita income and stayed nearly even in their relative median family income standing compared with 1990 (Table 4.11).

Table 4.10
Cities Where 20 Percent or More Year 2000
Housing Was Built from 1980 to 2000

	Percent of Housing Built 1980 to 2000	Relative Per Capita Income		Relative Median Family Income	
		2000	Changes 1990- 2000	2000	Changes 1990- 2000
Atlanta	20.4	1.03	1.14	.63	1.04
Charlotte	47.5	1.15	1.00	1.05	.99
Columbus	33.1	.89	.98	.86	.96
Dallas	32.6	.91	.92	.73	.91
Houston	28.9	.92	.98	.79	.96
Indianapolis	27.5	.93	.98	.88	.95
Kansas City	20.1	.89	.97	.83	.94
Las Vegas	67.9	1.04	1.07	1.04	1.04
Newport News	36.3	.88	.93	.86	.96
Orlando	45.5	1.00	1.07	.85	1.00
Phoenix	42.9	.91	.96	.91	.96
Sacramento	27.4	,84	.92	.78	.91
San Antonio	38.4	.94	1.03	.92	1.03
San Diego	31.9	1.03	1.02	.99	1.01
Tampa	28.3	1.01	1.09	.89	1.01
Virginia Beach	49.8	1.10	.97	1.08	.96
Mean	36.2	.97	1.00	.88 .90*	.98

*Omitting Atlanta

Source: U.S. Department of Housing and Urban Development, *HUD User: State of the Cities Data System* (2003), http://socds.huduser.org.

Table 4.11
Seven Cities with 10 Percent or More Owner Occupants
in Other than 1-Unit, 2- to 4-Unit, and Mobile Structures

| | Other Than 1-Unit, 2- to 4-Unit, and Mobile Structures | Relative Per Capita Income | | Relative Median Family Income | |
		2000	Changes 1990-2000	2000	Changes 1990-2000
New York	29.1	.84	.98	.70	.93
Boston	19.4	.80	.99	.65	.93
Washington, D.C.	18.0	.94	1.07	.64	.96
Chicago	17.5	.81	1.03	.70	.95
Denver	11.2	.92	.98	.79	.99
San Francisco	11.0	1.09	1.12	.89	1.06
Atlanta	9.9	1.03	1.14	.63	1.04
Mean	16.6	.92	1.04	.71	.98

Source: U.S. Department of Housing and Urban Development, *HUD User: State of the Cities Data System* (2003), http://socds.huduser.org.

HOUSING PAST AND FUTURE

Cities did better in the 1990s than in preceding decades in maintaining their standing relative to their suburbs in relative income and poverty. Cities differed considerably in how well they coped with attracting and retaining middle- and upper-income households. Housing supply differences were related to these relative income differences. Cities with significant amounts of housing constructed in the 1980s and 1990s tended to do better than other cities, as did cities whose home ownership rates exceeded the percentage of housing in single-unit structures. Cities with more than two-thirds of their housing constructed before 1940 and in the 1950s tended to fare worse in relative income trends in the 1990s. Next we will examine conditions and trends in suburbs. The role of housing supply characteristics will be considered as a cause of suburban decline.

POST-2000 TRENDS IN CITIES

Data about relative income trends since 2000 are sketchy. The available data confirm our optimistic hypothesis about central cities' potential for rebounding. During the 1990s, many more census tracts in cities rebounded in relative income compared with the 1980s. Based on that trend, as well as based on detailed data about relative income trends in relation to when housing was constructed (see Chapter 8), and our theory about changed beliefs and preferences altering housing markets, we anticipated that cities will do better during the early 21st century than during the late 20th century. The early returns are in. They indicate larger gains for cities than we anticipated.

The *American Community Survey* reports data periodically for samples of central cities and metropolitan areas.[33] For our sample of 40 cities in 35 large metropolitan areas, relative income calculations are feasible now for 20 cities for 2000 to 2003.

For the first time, central cities on average increased their relative per capita income and relative median family income compared with outside central city areas. For relative per capita income, cities increased from an average ratio of .85 in 2000 to .88 in 2003. In 1990, their per capita income ratio was .86. For relative median family income, cities increased from .75 in 2000 to .76 in 2003, after declining from .78 in 1990 (Table 4.12).

Between 1990 and 2000, only six of these cities increased in relative per capita income ratios (Atlanta, Chicago, Cleveland, San Antonio, San Diego, and Tampa). Between 2000 and 2003, 15 of these 20 cities increased in relative per capita income ratios (Atlanta, Boston, Buffalo, Chicago, Denver, Houston, Indianapolis, Philadelphia, Pittsburgh, Sacramento, San Antonio, San Diego, St. Louis, St. Petersburg, and Tampa). This list of improving cities included old northern industrial cities (Buffalo, Chicago, Philadelphia, Pittsburgh, and St. Louis), as well as northern financial and high-tech centers (Boston), diverse northern cities with wide boundaries (Indianapolis), and several southern and western cities.

Data for relative median family income changes reveal still more impressive gains for cities. Suburbs' strong appeal to families has been reflected in lower scores for cities in median family income ratios than per capita income ratios since 1960. Between 1990 and 2000, only three of these 20 cities registered gains in relative median family income ratios (Atlanta, Detroit, and San Antonio). From 2000 to 2003, 11 of these central cities increased in relative median family income ratios (Atlanta, Boston, Buffalo, Denver, Indianapolis, Kansas City, Philadelphia, Pittsburgh, San Antonio, St. Louis, and St. Petersburg). The diversity of regions and economic types of improving cities is striking, especially that seven of the 11 cities are in the Northeast or Midwest.

Caution is warranted. Only three years are tracked, and the sample sizes in the *American Community Survey* are small. However, the 2000 to 2003 trend is consistent with our discoveries about neighborhood changes from 1990 to 2000 that we discuss in Chapter 8. Moreover, the greater diversity and complexity of suburbs, including an increase in low-income suburbs during the 1990s, adds credibility to this post-2000 trend. Conditions in suburbs are analyzed next in Chapters 5, 6, and 7.

Table 4.12
Central City to Metropolitan Income in 1990, 2000, and 2003

City	Relative Per Capita Income Ratios				Relative Median Family Income Ratios			
	1990	2000	2003	Percent Change 2000 to 2003	1990	2000	2003	Percent Change 2000 to 2003
Atlanta	0.90	1.03	1.05	1.9	0.61	0.63	0.66	4.8
Boston	0.81	0.80	0.92	15.0	0.70	0.65	0.71	9.2
Buffalo	0.77	0.74	0.83	12.2	0.68	0.62	0.66	6.5
Chicago	0.78	0.81	0.82	1.2	0.74	0.70	0.70	0.0
Cleveland	0.63	0.64	0.63	-1.6	0.60	0.58	0.53	-8.6
Dallas	0.99	0.91	0.90	-1.1	0.81	0.73	0.71	-2.7
Denver	0.94	0.92	0.98	6.5	0.80	0.79	0.82	3.8
Detroit	0.60	0.60	0.57	-5.0	0.55	0.57	0.50	-12.3
Houston	0.95	0.92	0.93	1.1	0.82	0.79	0.77	-2.5
Indianapolis	0.96	0.94	0.95	1.1	0.93	0.89	0.92	3.4
Kansas City	0.92	0.89	0.80	-10.1	0.87	0.83	0.84	1.2
Milwaukee	0.75	0.70	0.70	0.0	0.73	0.67	0.67	0.0
Philadelphia	0.74	0.69	0.71	2.9	0.72	0.63	0.67	6.3
Pittsburgh	0.90	0.90	1.01	12.2	0.83	0.82	0.89	8.5
Sacramento	0.91	0.84	0.90	7.1	0.86	0.78	0.76	-2.6
San Antonio	0.92	0.94	0.95	1.1	0.90	0.92	0.94	2.2
San Diego	1.01	1.03	1.05	1.9	0.99	0.99	0.98	-1.0
St. Louis	0.72	0.71	0.73	2.8	0.64	0.60	0.63	5.0
St. Petersburg	0.98	0.97	1.04	7.2	0.98	0.95	0.96	1.1
Tampa	0.92	1.01	1.05	4.0	0.89	0.89	0.85	-4.5
				0.0				0.0
Average of Cities	0.86	0.85	0.88	3.0	0.78	0.75	0.76	0.9
Percent Change of Averages				3.1				0.9

Source: U.S. Census Bureau, *American Community Survey*, Detailed Tables generated by William H. Lucy using American FactFinder, http://factfinder.census.gov, May 2005.

Table Appendix 4.A1
Central City 2000 Income Relative to Metropolitan Income
for Each Racial or Hispanic Group—Per Capita Income

	Relative Per Capita Income Within Group				
City	All	White Alone	Black Alone	Hispanic	White Alone Non-Hispanic
Atlanta, GA	1.030	1.699	0.769	1.062	1.731
Baltimore, MD	0.696	0.891	0.816	0.844	0.893
Boston, MA	0.799	0.976	0.897	0.866	1.015
Buffalo, NY	0.744	0.825	0.948	0.879	0.834
Charlotte, NC	1.145	1.311	1.042	1.033	1.335
Chicago, IL	0.807	0.976	0.900	0.936	1.084
Cincinnati, OH	0.870	1.064	0.887	1.017	1.064
Cleveland, OH	0.640	0.738	0.813	0.818	0.752
Columbus, OH	0.888	0.931	0.965	0.986	0.933
Dallas, TX	0.911	1.079	0.874	0.885	1.270
Denver, CO	0.920	1.019	0.913	0.876	1.099
Detroit, MI	0.604	0.633	0.897	0.694	0.663
Houston, TX	0.922	1.026	0.924	0.929	1.179
Indianapolis, IN	0.939	0.993	0.988	0.909	0.998
Kansas City, MO	0.890	0.994	0.938	0.928	1.003
Las Vegas, NV	1.040	1.067	0.970	0.949	1.094
Los Angeles, CA	0.999	1.061	0.967	0.907	1.097
Miami, FL	0.818	0.841	0.795	0.822	1.136
Milwaukee, WI	0.699	0.803	0.959	0.862	0.827
Minneapolis, MN	0.865	1.016	0.874	0.814	1.031
New York, NY	0.842	0.991	0.933	0.903	1.066
Newport News, VA	0.878	0.910	0.939	0.846	0.913
Norfolk, VA	0.855	0.956	0.850	0.911	0.957
Oakland, CA	0.777	1.003	0.897	0.763	1.123
Orlando, FL	0.999	1.121	0.907	0.998	1.156
Philadelphia, PA	0.692	0.779	0.885	0.766	0.791
Phoenix, AZ	0.905	0.940	0.909	0.894	0.996
Pittsburgh, PA	0.899	1.005	0.938	1.026	1.006
Portland, OR	0.971	1.010	0.910	1.031	1.008
Sacramento, CA	0.839	0.959	0.896	0.892	0.997
San Antonio, TX	0.944	0.948	0.982	0.988	1.018
San Diego, CA	1.030	1.082	0.995	0.974	1.098
San Francisco, CA	0.943	1.034	0.927	1.084	1.025
Seattle, WA	1.092	1.177	0.974	1.110	1.179
St. Louis, MO	0.710	0.875	0.833	0.836	0.877
St. Paul, MN	0.771	0.886	0.890	0.859	0.900
St. Petersburg, FL	0.969	1.035	0.958	1.161	1.015
Tampa, FL	1.008	1.157	0.935	1.007	1.238
Virginia Beach, VA	1.100	1.051	1.084	1.049	1.055
Washington, D.C.	0.944	1.437	0.832	1.051	1.472
Unweighted Average:	0.885	1.008	0.915	0.929	1.048

Source: U.S. Census Bureau, *Census 2000*, Summary File 4, PCT Matrix 130, generated by
William H. Lucy, using American FactFinder, http://factfinder.census,gov, August 2004.

Table Appendix 4.A2
Central City 2000 Income Relative to Metropolitan Income
for Each Racial or Hispanic Group—Median Family Income

City	All	White Alone	Black Alone	Hispanic	White Alone Non-Hispanic
		Relative Median Family Income Within Group			
Atlanta, GA	0.628	1.511	0.611	0.816	1.554
Baltimore, MD	0.597	0.736	0.793	0.705	0.738
Boston, MA	0.646	0.808	0.884	0.815	0.840
Buffalo, NY	0.623	0.731	0.947	0.768	0.741
Charlotte, NC	1.049	1.208	1.014	1.013	1.217
Chicago, IL	0.698	0.793	0.859	0.889	0.863
Cincinnati, OH	0.680	0.893	0.802	0.853	0.893
Cleveland, OH	0.582	0.679	0.785	0.791	0.688
Columbus, OH	0.861	0.905	0.948	0.911	0.907
Dallas, TX	0.733	0.857	0.817	0.882	1.034
Denver, CO	0.788	0.858	0.905	0.869	0.923
Detroit, MI	0.572	0.571	0.909	0.713	0.571
Houston, TX	0.790	0.871	0.866	0.897	1.017
Indianapolis, IN	0.887	0.928	0.982	0.929	0.931
Kansas City, MO	0.825	0.908	0.922	0.903	0.917
Las Vegas, NV	1.042	1.065	0.918	0.990	1.083
Los Angeles, CA	0.860	0.925	0.874	0.844	1.018
Miami, FL	0.676	0.698	0.663	0.725	0.976
Milwaukee, WI	0.667	0.772	0.969	0.873	0.785
Minneapolis, MN	0.743	0.872	0.871	0.799	0.881
New York, NY	0.695	0.780	0.894	0.846	0.839
Newport News, VA	0.864	0.910	0.885	0.826	0.911
Norfolk, VA	0.750	0.841	0.760	0.673	0.844
Oakland, CA	0.644	0.899	0.819	0.754	1.028
Orlando, FL	0.851	0.946	0.794	0.887	0.972
Philadelphia, PA	0.634	0.713	0.871	0.737	0.727
Phoenix, AZ	0.909	0.945	0.898	0.911	0.991
Pittsburgh, PA	0.816	0.925	0.899	0.713	0.927
Portland, OR	0.903	0.922	0.873	0.959	0.920
Sacramento, CA	0.782	0.845	0.860	0.895	0.866
San Antonio, TX	0.924	0.932	0.888	0.969	0.996
San Diego, CA	0.993	1.034	0.969	0.904	1.059
San Francisco, CA	0.845	0.936	0.858	0.924	0.960
Seattle, WA	0.975	1.050	0.983	0.945	1.054
St. Louis, MO	0.602	0.752	0.794	0.694	0.755
St. Paul, MN	0.748	0.829	0.873	0.872	0.837
St. Petersburg, FL	0.952	1.016	0.958	1.108	1.005
Tampa, FL	0.893	1.043	0.858	0.870	1.126
Virginia Beach, VA	1.082	1.030	1.196	1.091	1.033
Washington, D.C.	0.641	1.351	0.679	0.762	1.435
Unweighted Average:	0.786	0.907	0.874	0.858	0.947

Source: U.S. Census Bureau, *Census 2000*, Summary File 4, PCT Matrix 113, generated by
William H. Lucy, using American FactFinder, http://factfinder.census,gov, August 2004.

NOTES

1. William H. Frey and Alan Berube, "City Families and Suburban Singles: An Emerging Household Story," in Bruce Katz and Robert E. Lang, eds., *Redefining Urban & Suburban America* (Washington, DC: The Brookings Institution, 2003), p. 261.
2. William H. Frey, "The New Geography of Population Shifts: Trends Toward Balkanization," in Reynolds Farley, ed., *State of the Union: America in the 1990s, Vol. 2* (New York: Russell Sage Foundation, 1995), p. 319.
3. Alan Altshuler, William Morrill, Harold Wolman, and Faith Mitchell, eds., *Governance and Opportunity in Metropolitan America* (Washington, DC: National Academy Press, 1999), p. 42.
4. Alan Berube with Thacher Tiffany, *The Shape of the Curve: Household Income Distribution in U.S. Cities, 1979-1999* (Washington, DC: The Brookings Institution, 2004).
5. U.S. Census Bureau, *1990 Housing Highlights: United States* (Washington, DC: U.S. Department of Commerce, 1991).
6. Kenneth T. Jackson, *Crabgrass Frontier* (New York: Oxford University Press, 1985).
7. Penn, Schoen, and Berland Associates, *Why Voters Care about the Quality of Life* (Storrs, CT: The Roper Center for Public Opinion Research, University of Connecticut, 2000).
8. Dowell Myers and Elizabeth Gearin, "Current Preferences and Future Demand for Denser Residential Environments," *Housing Policy Debate* 12, no. 4 (2001), p. 640.
9. Ibid.
10. Urban Institute (Washington, DC: Urban Institute, 2002) and Neighborhood Change Database (East Brunswick, NJ: GeoLytics, Inc., 2003).
11. Daniel P. McMillen, "The Return of Centralization to Chicago: Using Repeat Sales to Identify Changes in House Price Distance Gradients," *Regional Science and Urban Economics* 33 (2003), pp. 287-304.
12. Ibid., p. 287.
13. William Julius Wilson, *The Truly Disadvantaged: The Inner-City, the Underclass and Public Policy* (Chicago: University of Chicago Press, 1987).
14. Paul A. Jargowsky, *Poverty and Place* (New York: Russell Sage Foundation, 1997).
15. Paul A. Jargowsky, *Stunning Progress, Hidden Problems: The Dramatic Decline of Concentrated Poverty in the 1990s* (Washington, DC: The Brookings Institution, 2003), p. 2.
16. Ibid., p. 1.
17. Ibid., p. 2.
18. G. Thomas Kingsley and Kathryn L.S. Pettit, *Concentrated Poverty: A Change in Course* (Washington, DC: Urban Institute, 2003), pp. 1-2.
19. Paul A. Jargowsky, *Stunning Progress, Hidden Problems: The Dramatic Decline of Concentrated Poverty in the 1990s* (Washington, DC: The Brookings Institution, 2003), p. 10.
20. G. Thomas Kingsley and Kathryn L.S. Pettit, *Concentrated Poverty: A Change in Course* (Washington, DC: Urban Institute, 2003), p. 3.
21. Ibid., pp. 4-5.
22. Ibid., p. 5.
23. Roberto G. Quercia, George C. Galster, and Alvaro Cortes, "The Fortunes of Poor Neighborhoods." Annual meeting of the Association of Collegiate Schools of Planning (2000).
24. Ibid., p. 1.
25. Ibid., p. 9.
26. George C. Galster, "Consequences from the Redistribution of Urban Poverty During the 1990's: A Cautionary Tale," National Poverty Center Working Paper Series (Ann Arbor: Gerald R. Ford School of Public Policy, University of Michigan, 2003).
27. Ibid., pp. 1-2.

28. G. Thomas Kingsley and Kathryn L.S. Pettit, *Concentrated Poverty: A Change in Course* (Washington, DC: Urban Institute, 2003), p. 10.
29. U.S. Census Bureau, *1990 Housing Highlights: United States* (Washington, DC: U.S. Department of Commerce, 1991).
30. National Association of Home Builders, *Housing Facts, Figures, and Trends* (Washington, DC: National Association of Home Builders, 2003).
31. U.S. Census Bureau, *Statistical Abstract of the United States 1972* (Washington, DC: U.S. Government Printing Office, 1973).
32. U.S. Census Bureau, *Statistical Abstract of the United States 2002* (Washington, DC: U.S. Government Printing Office, 2003).
33. U.S. Census Bureau, American FactFinder, Data Sets, *American Community Survey,* Detailed Tables.

5

Scoping Suburban Decline

The first 50 years of metropolitan America in the 20th century belonged to the cities. The second 50 years, 1950 to 2000, were the era of suburban dominance. In the 1960s, the suburbs' population surpassed the population of central cities, as the 1970 census confirmed. By 1980, William H. Frey observed, "the suburbs achieved the undisputed dominance as the locus of population and jobs . . ."[1] In 2000, the suburbs had 62 percent of metropolitan population, and metropolitan areas comprised 80 percent of total United States' population. However, even as the suburbs became ascendant in the 1970s, elements of suburban decline also emerged.

In this chapter, we will present the bare outlines of suburban ascendancy and dominance, but our main focus is on chinks in the suburban armor. We will emphasize diversity in suburbs as we looked for diversity rather than uniformity in cities. Diversity, it turns out, was much easier to find than anticipated. Many suburbs have declined in population. Some have fewer housing units. Many have more minorities and immigrants. The elderly population is up and the proportion of families with children is down.

Having found so many signs of decline—in population, occupied housing, and, in the next chapter, income—reasons for suburban diversity become another interesting puzzle. It is interesting as a social science problem. More importantly here, it is a public policy problem and a problem for citizens attempting to make reasonable decisions for their households about where to live, where to move, and where to invest. We will describe conditions and trends in this chapter and the next, addressing income and, to a lesser extent, poverty in Chapter 6. Then we turn to explanations in Chapters 7 and 8, focusing on aspects of housing supply and neighborhood characteristics.

Many of the data in this chapter are drawn from an analysis of 2,586 suburbs in the 34 most populous metropolitan areas in 2000, plus the Buffalo metropolitan area, which in prior decades had been much higher in population rank. This analysis was conducted for The Brookings Institution.[2] The data set applies to the period from 1980 to 2000 and includes all the suburban places that had at least 2,500 residents in 1980, the minimum population for which the census reported economic and housing data consistently (see the section entitled "Methods" at the end of this chapter). We also report data for 40 central cities in these 35 metropolitan areas for contrast.

SUMMARY OF RESULTS

• Twenty-seven percent of the 2,586 suburbs in this study declined in population between 1990 and 2000. Of these 700 suburbs that lost population, 124 declined in population faster than their central cities. Suburbs declined in sectors 10 to 30 miles from central cities as well as adjacent to central cities.

• Outer suburbia, on the other hand, grew unabated, consuming land at an accelerating rate. In fact, slow-growing metropolitan areas sprawled more by consuming more land per person than fast-growing areas.

• Immigrants increased more rapidly in suburbs than in central cities, contributing to greater suburban diversity.

• Blacks in suburbs increased rapidly, and many owned homes in suburbs. Black home ownership increased at intermittent rates that did not coincide with the usual interpretations about the ebb and flow of housing discrimination against blacks from 1940 to 2000.

• Suburban population loss is not a new phenomenon, actually having peaked in the 1970s—the same decade when city population loss occurred most rapidly. Major reductions in average household size (AHS) in the 1970s seem mainly responsible for rapid population decline in that decade.

• In the 1990s, more elderly lived in suburbs, either aging in place or moving to suburbs with specialized facilities for the elderly.

• Of the 2,586 suburbs, 437 declined in occupied housing units during the 1990s. This 17 percent of suburbs that lost housing was close to the percentage of cities, 20 percent, that did so (109 out of 542).

These findings reveal suburbs more diverse, and with fewer differences from cities, than commonly believed.

SUBURBAN DOMINANCE

The typical image of central cities and suburbs is simple: Central cities have been losing population, while suburbs have continually gained population, often at cities' expense. Reality has changed. Suburban population declines have become common, as have some central city population increases. Between 1990 and 2000, for example, 700 of 2,586 suburbs declined in population in the United States' 35 most populous metropolitan areas. The average rate of decline was 6.1 percent per suburb.

Major population growth occurred outside central cities in most of the 35 metropolitan areas in this study, even though these 700 declining suburbs lost 638,543 residents between 1990 and 2000—a substantial number. The other suburbs in our sample accounted for growth of 7,417,836 (a 14.1 percent increase) out of the total outside central city growth of 12,461,292 (a 16.4 percent increase). In suburbs too small to include in this study and outside any census-designated place, population growth was 5,043,456, a rate of 21.7 percent. Growth was faster in the outside central city area that was not in our suburban sample in 25 of the 35 metropolitan areas—another indication that sprawl development was the norm.

Ironically, suburban population decreases in the Northeast and Midwest contributed to substantial sprawl in development patterns, even though metropolitan growth was slow or, in the Pittsburgh and Buffalo areas, negative. According to a study by William Fulton and his colleagues of 281 metropolitan areas, "..., the amount of urbanized land in the United States increased by 47 percent, from approximately 51 million acres in 1982 to approximately 76 million acres in 1997. During this same period, the nation's population grew by only 17 percent."[3] Sprawl, measured by acreage settled relative to population, increased most in slow-growing metropolitan areas.

Sprawl occurs for many reasons. Many developers like sprawl because greenfield sites are usually easier to develop than infill, refill, densification, or adaptive use sites. Many outer-suburban government officials like it because it churns the local economy and, if major investments in schools or other infrastructure have occurred, it spreads the burden of paying for the investments—until a new round of investments is needed. Many consumers also like it, some because it provides sites for large, exclusive homes, and some because it provides larger, more affordable dwellings closer to central cities. Some low-income people also like it because they can trade long driving times for cheaper sites and affordable dwellings. Amy Helling has found that "the most affordable housing in metropolitan areas is concentrated in the lowest and very highest density areas ... Thus, the sprawl occasioned by increasingly convenient, inexpensive transportation would accommodate some low income households, particularly on the more distant and less attractive fringes of metropolitan areas, and in pockets of high density (like trailer parks) in otherwise exurban areas."[4]

The lure in remote sprawl is a dream house, sometimes in a location with a dream view, which is traded for long commuting times. A new commuter from Charlestown, West Virginia, to a work location adjacent to Washington, D.C., drove 75 minutes each way, and got on the road by 5 AM each morning. "It's not that bad," the home owner and driver said. "We wanted to have a nice place that we could afford—so here we are."[5]

Regional sprawl tendencies vary with some surprises. Although metropolitan areas in the Northeast and Midwest continued to be denser than those in the West, they were consuming land at a faster rate per additional person than in the West. As Fulton et al. observed: "Metropolitan areas in the Northeast and Midwest are consuming land at a much greater rate than they are adding population, ... At the same time, the auto-oriented metropolitan areas of the West ... are currently growing at much higher densities than their counterparts anywhere else in the nation."[6] Carrying capacity played a role in the West, as water shortages prevented random well-digging and required public water and public approval of development plans.

Notable exceptions occurred to the norm that growth outside our study suburbs surpassed growth within them. Portland's suburbs in this study increased by 54 percent compared with only a 4.5 percent increase in Portland's other suburban territory. The Chicago and Seattle areas also had much faster growth in suburbs in this study than in their other suburbs—18 percent to 6.2 percent in the Chicago area, and 32 percent to 13 percent in the Seattle area. In several other metropolitan areas, residents in suburbs in this study grew by a much larger total increase than in other suburbs, especially Phoenix, Dallas, San Francisco–Oakland, Minneapolis–St. Paul, Los Angeles, Kansas City, and Norfolk.

Atlanta stood out as the metropolitan area where the largest numerical increase occurred in suburbs not included in this study, 863,014, compared with the increase in this study's suburbs, 266,777. Thus, sprawl patterns, as well as suburban governments' size, central cities' share of metropolitan population,[7] and the ratio of new dwellings to population growth[8] affect how many suburbs are in each metropolitan area and how many suburbs are growing, stable, and declining.

CITY DECLINE AND METROPOLITAN GROWTH

Although low-density sprawl is alive and accelerating, population decline in many suburbs also has been occurring. In our sample, 11 of 40 central cities (28 percent) lost population at an average rate of 8.3 percent per city, and 431 suburbs lost population in these 11 metropolitan areas where the central cities declined, at an average rate of 6.4 percent per suburb (Table 5.1). Perhaps more surprising, 124 suburbs declined in population faster than the central cities in these 11 metropolitan areas.

The highest frequency of suburbs declining faster than their declining central city occurred in the Philadelphia area—51 of 129 suburbs, 40 percent declining faster (Table 5.1). Pittsburgh was second with 18 percent; Detroit with 13 percent was third. The forces leading to central city population loss seemed to affect many suburbs also, sometimes with greater impacts than in cities.

The frequency of suburban population loss was higher where central cities lost population than in the other 24 metropolitan areas. Where cities declined, 49.7 percent of suburbs lost population compared with 15.6 percent where central cities grew. Since some central cities gained population, the population loss in their suburbs was greater, by definition, than in their cities. More than half of the declining suburbs in metropolitan areas with growing central cities occurred in New York (104), Chicago (28), Los Angeles (21), and Boston (20) (Table 5.2).

Suburban population decline also was related to metropolitan growth rates. We separated metropolitan areas into three groups: metropolitan areas that grew by more than 25 percent, between 10 and 25 percent, and by less than 10 percent. Suburban population decline was more frequent in the slow-growing metropolitan areas, where 37.6 percent declined. Suburban population decline was least common in fast-growing Metropolitan Statistical Areas (MSAs), where only 8.0 percent of the suburbs declined (Table 5.3). These fast-growing metropolitan areas were located in the South, Southwest, and West.

Table 5.1
Declining Cities and Their Declining Suburbs

City	City			Suburbs					
				All Suburbs in Study				Declining Faster than City	
	Population 1990	Population 2000	Percent Change 1990-2000	Number	Declining	Percent Declining	Average Percent Decline	Number	Average Percent Decline
Baltimore	736,014	651,154	-11.5	67	12	17.9	-3.1	0	0.0
Buffalo	328,123	292,648	-10.8	28	20	71.4	-5.1	0	0.0
Cincinnati	364,040	331,285	-9.0	67	27	40.3	-6.9	6	-12.3
Cleveland	505,616	478,403	-5.4	76	41	54.0	-3.8	8	-8.3
Detroit	1,027,974	951,270	-7.5	89	51	57.3	-5.6	12	-10.0
Milwaukee	628,088	596,974	-5.0	39	13	33.3	-3.0	3	-5.6
Norfolk	261,229	234,403	-10.3	10	1	10.0	-3.2	0	0.0
Philadelphia	1,585,577	1,517,550	-4.3	129	86	66.7	-6.4	51	-9.4
Pittsburgh	369,879	334,563	-9.5	128	108	84.4	-6.7	23	-13.3
St. Louis	396,685	348,189	-12.2	106	49	46.2	-10.1	12	-27.3
Washington, D.C.	606,900	572,059	-5.7	130	23	17.7	-8.7	9	-18.1
Totals for Declining Cities	6,810,125	6,308,498	-7.4	869	431	49.6	-6.4	124	-12.5
Average of Individual City's Percent Change			-8.3						

Sources: U.S. Census Bureau, *Census 2000, Profiles of General Demographic Characteristics 2000,* issued May 2001, for each separate state, www2.census.gov/census_2000/datasets/100_and_sample_profile; CensusCD 1990 (East Brunswick, NJ: GeoLytics, Inc., 2000).

Table 5.2
Suburban Decline Outside Growing Cities

City	City			All Suburbs in Study			
	Population 1990	Population 2000	Percent Change 1990-2000	Number	Declining	Percent Declining	Average Percent Decline
Atlanta	394,017	416,474	5.7	66	5	7.6	-27.6
Boston	574,283	589,141	2.6	78	20	25.6	-2.0
Charlotte	396,003	540,828	36.6	24	4	16.7	-4.7
Chicago	2,783,726	2,896,016	4.0	213	28	13.2	-3.8
Columbus	632,958	711,470	12.4	28	9	32.1	-7.2
Dallas	1,006,831	1,188,580	18.1	45	0	0.0	0.0
Denver	467,610	554,636	18.6	28	1	3.6	-35.7
Houston	1,630,672	1,953,631	19.8	43	4	9.3	-5.4
Indianapolis	731,321	781,870	6.9	26	1	3.9	-1.6
Kansas City	435,141	441,545	1.5	40	13	32.5	-4.4
Las Vegas	258,295	478,434	85.2	8	0	0.0	0.0
Los Angeles	3,485,398	3,694,820	6.0	138	21	15.2	-5.1
Miami	358,548	362,470	1.1	52	10	19.2	-11.4
Minneapolis and St. Paul	640,618	669,769	4.6	96	16	16.7	-2.7
New York	7,322,564	8,008,278	9.4	515	104	20.2	-3.2
Orlando	164,693	185,951	12.9	37	5	13.5	-13.3
Phoenix	983,403	1,321,045	34.3	28	3	10.7	-2.8
Portland	437,398	529,121	21.0	32	3	9.4	-8.7
Sacramento	369,365	407,018	10.2	29	2	6.9	-13.7
San Antonio	935,927	1,144,646	22.3	15	4	26.7	-4.2
San Diego	1,110,549	1,223,400	10.2	24	6	25.0	-29.8
San Francisco and Oakland	1,096,201	1,176,217	7.3	73	2	2.7	-3.1
Seattle	516,259	563,374	9.1	38	4	10.5	-22.7
Tampa	518,644	551,679	6.4	41	4	9.8	-9.4
Total for Growing Cities	27,250,424	30,390,413	11.5	1717	269	15.7	-5.6
Average of Individual City's Percent Change			15.3				

Sources: U.S. Census Bureau, *Census 2000, Profiles of General Demographic Characteristics 2000*, issued May 2001, for each separate state, www2.census.gov/census_2000/datasets/100_and_sample_profile; CensusCD 1990 (East Brunswick, NJ: GeoLytics, Inc., 2000).

Table 5.3
Declining Suburbs by Rate of Metropolitan Growth

GROWTH RATE GROUP Metropolitan Area	Metropolitan Area			Suburbs			
	Population 1990	Population 2000	Percent Change 1990-2000	Suburbs in Study	Number Declining	Percent Declining	Average Percent Decline
1) LESS THAN 10%							
Baltimore, MD PMSA	2,552,994	2,382,172	7.2	67	12	17.9	-3.1
Boston, MA–NH PMSA	3,406,829	3,227,707	5.5	78	20	25.6	-2.0
Buffalo–Niagara Falls, NY MSA	1,170,111	1,189,288	-1.6	28	20	71.4	-5.1
Cincinnati–Hamilton, OH–KY–IN CMSA	1,979,202	1,817,571	8.9	67	27	40.3	-6.9
Cleveland–Lorain–Elyria, OH PMSA	2,250,871	2,202,069	2.2	76	41	54.0	-3.8
Detroit, MI PMSA	4,441,551	4,266,654	4.1	89	51	57.3	-5.6
Los Angeles and Orange County, CA PMSAs	12,366,637	11,270,720	9.6	138	21	15.2	-5.1
Milwaukee–Waukesha, WI PMSA	1,500,741	1,432,149	4.8	39	13	33.3	-3.0
New York–NY-NJ-CT-PA CMSA	21,199,865	19,549,649	8.4	515	104	20.2	-3.2
Norfolk–Va. Beach–Newport News, VA-NC MSA	1,569,541	1,443,244	8.8	10	1	10.0	-3.2
Philadelphia, PA–NJ PMSA	5,100,931	4,922,175	3.6	129	86	66.7	-6.4
Pittsburgh, PA MSA	2,358,695	2,394,811	-1.5	128	108	84.4	-6.7
St. Louis, MO–IL MSA	2,603,607	2,492,525	4.5	106	49	46.2	-10.1
Group Totals:	62,501,575	58,590,734	6.7	1,471	553	37.6	

Table 5.3 (cont.)
Declining Suburbs by Rate of Metropolitan Growth

GROWTH RATE GROUP Metropolitan Area	Metropolitan Area Population 1990	Population 2000	Percent Change 1990-2000	Suburbs Suburbs in Study	Number Declining	Percent Declining	Average Percent Decline
2) 10% TO 25%							
Chicago, IL PMSA	8,272,768	7,410,858	11.6	213	28	13.2	-3.8
Columbus, OH MSA	1,540,157	1,345,450	14.5	28	9	32.1	-7.2
Indianapolis, IN MSA	1,607,486	1,380,491	16.4	26	1	3.9	-1.6
Kansas City, MO–KS MSA	1,776,062	1,582,875	12.2	40	13	32.5	-4.4
Miami, FL PMSA	2,253,362	1,937,094	16.3	52	10	19.2	-11.4
Minneapolis–St. Paul, MN–WI MSA	2,968,806	2,538,834	16.9	96	16	16.7	-2.7
Sacramento–Yolo, CA CMSA	1,796,857	1,481,102	21.3	29	2	6.9	-13.7
San Antonio, TX MSA	1,592,383	1,324,749	20.2	15	4	26.7	-4.2
San Diego, CA MSA	2,813,833	2,498,016	12.6	24	6	25.0	-29.8
San Francisco and Oakland, CA PMSAs	4,123,740	3,686,592	11.9	73	2	2.7	-3.1
Seattle–Bellevue–Everett, WA PMSA	2,414,616	2,033,156	18.8	38	4	10.5	-22.7
Tampa–St. Petersburg–Clearwater, FL MSA	2,395,997	2,067,959	15.9	41	4	9.8	-9.4
Washington, DC–MD–VA–WV PMSA	4,923,153	4,223,485	16.6	130	23	17.7	-8.7
Group Totals:	38,479,220	33,510,661	14.8	806	122	15.1	

Table 5.3 (cont.)
Declining Suburbs by Rate of Metropolitan Growth

GROWTH RATE GROUP Metropolitan Area	Metropolitan Area Population 1990	Population 2000	Percent Change 1990-2000	Suburbs in Study	Suburbs Number Declining	Suburbs Percent Declining	Suburbs Average Percent Decline
3) 25% OR MORE							
Atlanta, GA MSA	4,112,198	2,959,950	38.9	66	5	7.6	-27.6
Charlotte–Gastonia–Rock Hill, NC–SC MSA	1,499,293	1,162,093	29.0	24	4	16.7	-4.7
Dallas, TX PMSA	3,519,176	2,676,248	31.5	45	0	0.0	0.0
Denver, CO PMSA	2,109,282	1,622,980	30.0	28	1	3.6	-35.7
Houston, TX PMSA	4,177,646	3,322,025	25.8	43	4	9.3	-5.4
Las Vegas, NV–AZ MSA	1,563,282	852,737	83.3	8	0	0.0	0.0
Orlando, FL MSA	1,644,561	1,224,852	34.3	37	5	13.5	-13.3
Phoenix–Mesa, AZ MSA	3,251,876	2,238,480	45.3	28	3	10.7	-2.8
Portland–Vancouver, OR–WA PMSA	1,918,009	1,515,452	26.6	32	3	9.4	-8.7
Group Totals:	23,795,323	17,574,817	35.4	312	25	8.0	
Study Totals:	124,776,118	109,676,212	13.8	2,586	700	27.1	

CMSA = Consolidated Metropolitan Statistical Area; MSA = Metropolitan Statistical Area; PMSA = Primary Metropolitan Statistical Area

Sources: U.S. Census Bureau, *Census 2000, Profiles of General Demographic Characteristics 2000*, issued May 2001, for each separate state, www2.census.gov/census_2000/datasets/100_and_sample_profile; CensusCD 1990 (East Brunswick, NJ: GeoLytics, Inc., 2000).

RING, SECTOR, AND SCATTERED POPULATION DECLINE

Suburban decline often is referred to as an inner-suburb phenomenon. Sometimes it is, but some inner suburbs grew between 1990 and 2000, while other suburbs separated from the central city declined. Alexandria and Arlington, Virginia, adjacent to Washington, D.C., for example, grew by 15 and 11 percent, respectively, between 1990 and 2000. Suburban decline around Washington, D.C., was common, but it occurred primarily in a sector pattern, concentrated in Prince Georges County, Maryland, not in inner suburbs in Montgomery County, Maryland, or in suburbs in Virginia.

To analyze ring, sector, and scattered patterns of decline, we created maps to locate suburban decline geographically. Population decline was more common in inner than in intermediate or outer locations, but a diverse array of patterns was found.

Decline patterns in the Cleveland and Chicago metropolitan areas illustrate these differences. In the Cleveland Primary Metropolitan Statistical Areas (PMSA), most inner suburbs declined in population, as did many intermediate suburbs. However, a number of outer suburbs declined, including Elyria and Lorain far to the west, which are classified as central cities in the census, and several suburbs far to the east (Map 5.1).

Many large metropolitan areas, including those discussed below, have grown to encompass formerly independent cities, like Elyria and Lorain, and other small municipalities. They are not the same as developments that have emerged entirely since World War II as bedroom suburbs. Suburbs included in this study are shaded on each map. Suburbs lacking 2,500 residents in 1980 and new post-1980 suburbs are shown on each metropolitan map with an outline and no shading. By displaying them, sprawl development patterns can be observed.

In the Chicago PMSA, some inner suburbs declined but most grew in population. Suburban decline was scattered, with more in a south-side sector than elsewhere. However, some suburbs declined that were separated from the central city by six or seven other suburbs, most of which increased in population (Map 5.2).

In the Philadelphia, St. Louis, and Detroit metropolitan areas, a variety of spatial population trends occurred (Maps 5.3, 5.4, and 5.5). These metropolitan examples reveal diverse patterns of suburban population decline. They demonstrate that suburban population decline is not limited to inner suburbs and that many inner suburbs grew. They also demonstrate that suburban population decline cannot be explained as merely the contagion of central city population decline spreading to their suburbs, especially because 71 percent of the central cities increased in population.

Map 5.1
Cleveland–Lorain–Elyria, OH Primary Metropolitan Statistical Area
Population Change in Suburban Places 1990 to 2000

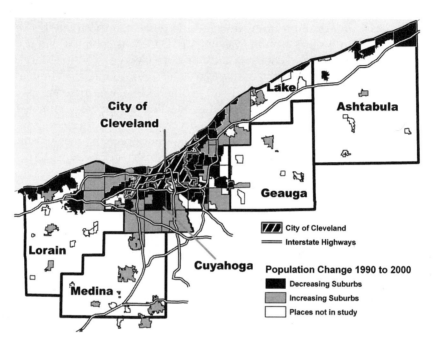

Sources: U.S. Census Bureau, *Census 2000, Profiles of General Demographic Characteristics 2000*, issued May 2001, for each separate state, www2.census.gov/census_2000/datasets/100_and_sample_profile; CensusCD 1990 (East Brunswick, NJ: GeoLytics, Inc., 2000).

Map 5.2
Chicago, IL Primary Metropolitan Statistical Area
Population Change in Suburban Places 1990 to 2000

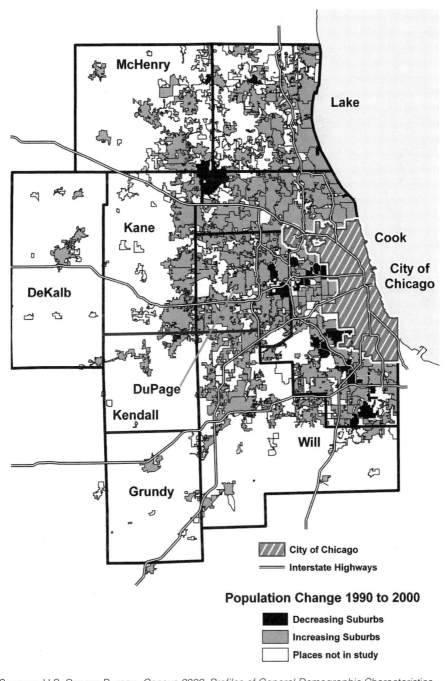

Population Change 1990 to 2000

■ Decreasing Suburbs
▨ Increasing Suburbs
□ Places not in study

Sources: U.S. Census Bureau, *Census 2000, Profiles of General Demographic Characteristics 2000*, issued May 2001, for each separate state, www2.census.gov/census_2000/datasets/100_and_sample_profile; CensusCD 1990 (East Brunswick, NJ: GeoLytics, Inc., 2000).

Map 5.3
Philadelphia, PA Primary Metropolitan Statistical Area
Population Change in Suburban Places 1990 to 2000

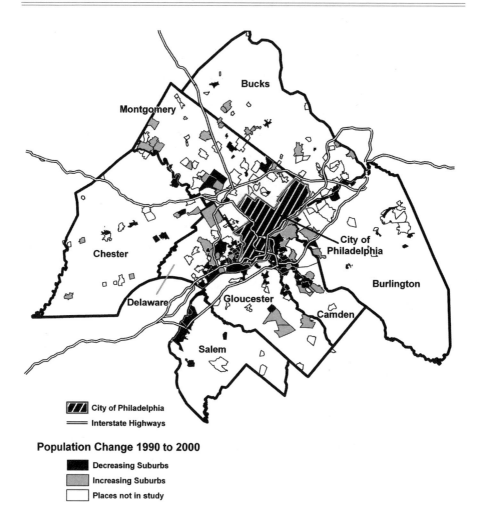

Sources: U.S. Census Bureau, *Census 2000, Profiles of General Demographic Characteristics 2000*, issued May 2001, for each separate state, www2.census.gov/census_2000/datasets/100_and_sample_profile; CensusCD 1990 (East Brunswick, NJ: GeoLytics, Inc., 2000).

Map 5.4
St. Louis, MO Metropolitan Statistical Area
Population Change in Suburban Places 1990 to 2000

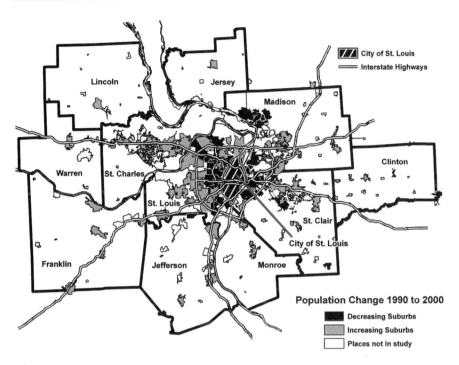

Sources: U.S. Census Bureau, *Census 2000, Profiles of General Demographic Characteristics 2000*, issued May 2001, for each separate state, www2.census.gov/census_2000/datasets/ 100_and_sample_profile; CensusCD 1990 (East Brunswick, NJ: GeoLytics, Inc., 2000).

Map 5.5
Detroit, MI Primary Metropolitan Statistical Area
Population Change in Suburban Places 1990 to 2000

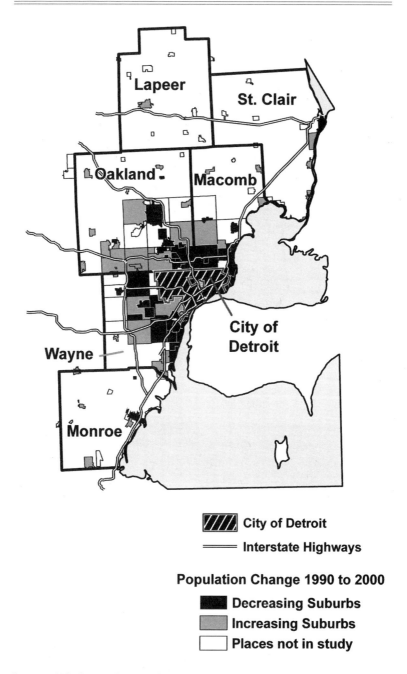

Sources: U.S. Census Bureau, *Census 2000, Profiles of General Demographic Characteristics 2000*, issued May 2001, for each separate state, www2.census.gov/census_2000/datasets/100_and_sample_profile; CensusCD 1990 (East Brunswick, NJ: GeoLytics, Inc., 2000).

POPULATION SIZE IN SUBURBS

Some observers argue that small suburban jurisdictions are better because public service and tax preferences of constituents may be more homogeneous than in large jurisdictions, enabling local governments to be more responsive.[9] On the other hand, small size and homogeneity make greater distinctions in resources more likely among jurisdictions, as well as distinctions in race and income.[10] Small jurisdictions increase the number of governments that must be consulted, and whose approval may be needed, for regional projects and policies. Metropolitan areas with numerous local governments have had more sprawl at low densities than less governmentally fragmented regions.[11] Employers also are more likely to locate far from central city downtowns in metropolitan areas with greater government fragmentation.[12] Small jurisdictions are subject to rapid change from residential mobility, which averages 50 percent of metropolitan residents moving every five years. Substantial change also can occur from suburban residents aging in place, with fewer families with children being present as the years pass. Because of these governance implications of small size, we considered jurisdiction population size in analyzing suburban decline.

We separated suburbs into five population size categories (Table 5.4). In the metropolitan areas where more than 40 percent of suburbs declined, the small suburbs were as likely to decline as larger ones. Small suburbs were not protected from

Table 5.4
Decreasing and Increasing Population by Size of Suburbs

Population of Suburbs	Decreasing Suburbs			Increasing Suburbs			Total Suburbs in Study	
	Number of Suburbs	Percent Suburbs in Size Class	Average Percent Decrease	Number of Suburbs	Percent Suburbs in Size Class	Average Percent Increase	Number of Suburbs	Average Percent Change
Less than 5,000	207	39.1	-6.8	321	60.9	22.7	529	11.2
5,000 to 10,000	195	28.1	-5.6	499	71.9	28.1	694	18.6
10,000 to 25,000	190	24.4	-5.8	587	75.6	20.7	777	14.2
25,000 to 50,000	60	16.6	-7.0	302	83.4	18.2	362	14.0
More than 50,000	48	21.4	-5.7	176	78.6	17.6	224	12.6
Total Suburbs	700	27.0	-6.1	1886	72.9	22.3	2586	14.6

Sources: U.S. Census Bureau, *Census 2000, Profiles of General Demographic Characteristics 2000*, issued May 2001, for each separate state, www2.census.gov/census_2000/datasets/100_and_sample_profile; CensusCD 1990 (East Brunswick, NJ: GeoLytics, Inc., 2000).

decline, despite their alleged greater responsiveness to constituents' preferences. Small suburbs were less numerous in regions where decline was less common—the South, Southwest, and West—but in these regions, suburbs with populations less than 10,000 were more likely than larger suburbs to decline.

SEVERE SUBURBAN POPULATION LOSS

Suburban population loss was heaviest in the Northeast, where 39 percent of metropolitan suburbs lost population, and the Midwest, where population declines occurred in 32 percent of suburbs. In the Southwest, in contrast, 8 percent of suburbs declined, as did 10 percent in the West, and 13 percent in the south (Table 5.5).

The Pittsburgh metropolitan area experienced the most frequent population loss. One hundred and eight of its 128 suburbs (84 percent) declined in population, at an average rate of 6.7 percent per suburb. In four other metropolitan areas, most suburbs declined in population—Buffalo, 71 percent; Philadelphia, 67 percent; Detroit, 57 percent; and Cleveland, 54 percent.

Twenty percent or more of suburbs declined in population in nine other metropolitan areas—St. Louis, 46 percent; Cincinnati, 40 percent; Milwaukee, 33 percent; Kansas City, 33 percent; Columbus, 32 percent; San Antonio, 27 percent; Boston, 26 percent; San Diego, 25 percent; and New York, 20 percent (Table 5.5). In addition, 19 percent declined in the Miami area and 18 percent declined in the Baltimore and Washington, D.C., areas.

PROSPECTS FOR INCREASING DENSITY

Many suburbs, especially small ones, probably have little chance to annex territory. Often their development pattern has been built out. Population increase then depends on adding housing units in denser configurations or increasing household size. Neither trend has been common. Politics and public policy in small suburbs will not usually favor increased density, because Americans generally prefer low density, open space, and ample landscaping.[13] The strongest preferences for suburban living have been held by two-parent families with children and by mothers not employed outside the home.[14] They have tended to resist denser development, but the proportion of such householders has been declining,[15] potentially reducing opposition to denser living patterns.

In central cities where there has been a history of declining population, political support for increasing population often develops. Transportation networks often can support, and profit from, greater density in certain locations, especially downtown. Many downtowns grew in population in the 1990s, including in cities that overall declined in population.

Suburbs are less likely than central cities to have a recognized history of population decline. They probably are less likely to have political support for increasing density. Their transportation systems are less likely to support increased density and they are less likely to have downtown assets that will attract more residents. These conditions probably will persist, contributing to forces that may lead to more suburban population decline in the future.

Table 5.5
Metropolitan Areas and Declining Suburbs

REGION / Metropolitan Area	Metropolitan Area			Suburbs			
	Population 1990	Population 2000	Percent Change 1990–2000	Suburbs in Study	Number Declining	Percent Declining	Average Percent Decline
NORTHEAST							
Boston, MA–NH PMSA	3,406,829	3,227,707	5.5	78	20	25.6	-2.0
Buffalo–Niagara Falls, NY MSA	1,170,111	1,189,288	-1.6	28	20	71.4	-5.1
New York–NY–NJ–CT–PA CMSA	21,199,865	19,549,649	8.4	515	104	20.2	-3.2
Philadelphia, PA–NJ PMSA	5,100,931	4,922,175	3.6	129	86	66.7	-6.4
Pittsburgh, PA MSA	2,358,695	2,394,811	-1.5	128	108	84.4	-6.7
Regional Total	33,236,431	31,283,630	6.2	878	338	38.5	
MID-ATLANTIC							
Baltimore, MD PMSA	2,552,994	2,382,172	7.2	67	12	17.9	-3.1
Washington, DC–MD–VA–WV PMSA	4,923,153	4,223,485	16.6	130	23	17.7	-8.7
Regional Total	7,476,147	6,605,657	13.2	197	35	17.8	
SOUTH							
Atlanta, GA MSA	4,112,198	2,959,950	38.9	66	5	7.6	-27.6
Charlotte–Gastonia–Rock Hill, NC–SC MSA	1,499,293	1,162,093	29.0	24	4	16.7	-4.7
Miami, FL PMSA	2,253,362	1,937,094	16.3	52	10	19.2	-11.4
Norfolk–Va Beach–Newport News, VA–NC MSA	1,569,541	1,443,244	8.8	10	1	10.0	-3.2
Orlando, FL MSA	1,644,561	1,224,852	34.3	37	5	13.5	-13.3
Tampa–St. Petersburg–Clearwater, FL MSA	2,395,997	2,067,959	15.9	41	4	9.8	-9.4
Regional Total	13,474,952	10,795,192	24.8	230	29	12.6	

Table 5.5 (cont.)
Metropolitan Areas and Declining Suburbs

REGION Metropolitan Area	Metropolitan Area			Suburbs			
	Population 1990	Population 2000	Percent Change 1990–2000	Suburbs in Study	Number Declining	Percent Declining	Average Percent Decline
MIDWEST							
Chicago, IL PMSA	8,272,768	7,410,858	11.6	213	28	13.2	-3.8
Cincinnati–Hamilton, OH–KY–IN CMSA	1,979,202	1,817,571	8.9	67	27	40.3	-6.9
Cleveland–Lorain–Elyria, OH PMSA	2,250,871	2,202,069	2.2	76	41	54.0	-3.8
Columbus, OH MSA	1,540,157	1,345,450	14.5	28	9	32.1	-7.2
Detroit, MI PMSA	4,441,551	4,266,654	4.1	89	51	57.3	-5.6
Indianapolis, IN MSA	1,607,486	1,380,491	16.4	26	1	3.9	-1.6
Kansas City, MO–KS MSA	1,776,062	1,582,875	12.2	40	13	32.5	-4.4
Milwaukee–Waukesha, WI PMSA	1,500,741	1,432,149	4.8	39	13	33.3	-3.0
Minneapolis–St. Paul, MN–WI MSA	2,968,806	2,538,834	16.9	96	16	16.7	-2.7
St. Louis, MO–IL MSA	2,603,607	2,492,525	4.5	106	49	46.2	-10.1
Regional Total	28,941,251	26,469,476	9.3	780	248	31.8	
SOUTHWEST							
Dallas, TX PMSA	3,519,176	2,676,248	31.5	45	0	0.0	0.0
Houston, TX PMSA	4,177,646	3,322,025	25.8	43	4	9.3	-5.4
San Antonio, TX MSA	1,592,383	1,324,749	20.2	15	4	26.7	-4.2
Regional Total	9,289,205	7,323,022	26.8	103	8	7.8	

Table 5.5 (cont.)
Metropolitan Areas and Declining Suburbs

REGION Metropolitan Area	Metropolitan Area			Suburbs			
	Population 1990	Population 2000	Percent Change 1990–2000	Suburbs in Study	Number Declining	Percent Declining	Average Percent Decline
WEST							
Denver, CO PMSA	2,109,282	1,622,980	30.0	28	1	3.6	-35.7
Las Vegas, NV–AZ MSA	1,563,282	852,737	83.3	8	0	0.0	0.0
Los Angeles and Orange County, CA PMSAs	12,366,637	11,270,720	9.6	138	21	15.2	-5.1
Phoenix-Mesa, AZ MSA	3,251,876	2,238,480	45.3	28	3	10.7	-2.8
Portland-Vancouver, OR–WA PMSA	1,918,009	1,515,452	26.6	32	3	9.4	-8.7
Sacramento-Yolo, CA CMSA	1,796,857	1,481,102	21.3	29	2	6.9	-3.7
San Diego, CA MSA	2,813,833	2,498,016	12.6	24	6	25.0	-29.8
San Francisco and Oakland, CA PMSAs	4,123,740	3,686,592	11.9	73	2	2.7	-3.1
Seattle–Bellevue-Everett, WA PMSA	2,414,616	2,033,156	18.8	38	4	10.5	-22.7
Regional Total	32,358,132	27,199,235	19.0	401	42	10.5	
Study Totals:	124,776,118	109,676,212	13.8	2,586	700	27.1	

CMSA = Consolidated Metropolitan Statistical Area; MSA = Metropolitan Statistical Area; PMSA = Primary Metropolitan Statistical Area

Sources: U.S. Census Bureau, *Census 2000, Profiles of General Demographic Characteristics 2000*, issued May 2001, for each separate state, www2.census.gov/census_2000/datasets/100_and_sample_profile; CensusCD 1990 (East Brunswick, NJ: GeoLytics, Inc., 2000).

SUBURBAN DIVERSITY

More blacks in suburbs is an important dimension of their diversity. During the 1950s, blacks actually decreased in suburbs of northern metropolitan areas. Mass-produced suburbs were part of the reason. Levittown on Long Island in New York had 82,000 residents by 1960, but not a single black resident. Developer William Levitt observed: "We can solve a housing problem, or we can try to solve a racial problem. But we cannot combine the two."[16] While the proportion of blacks in suburbs rose in the 1960s, the pace was slow. Meager black suburbanization spawned concerns like the Advisory Commission on Civil Disorders' fear that the U.S. was heading toward "two separate societies," one black in cities and one white in suburbs,[17] and to Anthony Downs' appeal in *Opening Up the Suburbs*.[18]

Blacks in suburbs were much more likely to be home owners in 1960 (51.6 percent) and 1970 (54.1 percent) than were blacks in central cities, but there were only 334,000 black home owners in suburbs in 1960 compared with 11,836,000 white home owners. By 1970, there were 490,000 black home owners in suburbs compared with 15,300,000 white home owners.[19]

Most home ownership by blacks occurred in central cities and in nonmetropolitan areas. Total black home ownership was much larger than suburban black home ownership. A huge change occurred after 1940, when nationwide only 23.6 percent of black households were owner occupants. By 1950, 34.9 percent of black households were home owners, as were 38.2 percent in 1960.[20]

This home ownership increase of 11.3 percent for blacks in the 1940s equaled the increase for whites, whose home ownership increased from 45.7 percent in 1940 to 57.0 percent in 1950. These data, which describe home ownership rate increases for both blacks and whites of 11.3 percent, do not match well with conventional explanations of discrimination against blacks in housing. In addition, another analysis discovered an even larger black home ownership increase from 20.3 percent in 1940 to 39.1 percent in 1960.[21] The conventional critique of the 1940s is that "white people were strongly encouraged to buy homes in the suburbs on long-term, federally insured mortgages ... African-Americans and other racial minorities were not included in this housing boom."[22]

These home ownership data by race lead to two puzzles. First, if blacks were explicitly discriminated against in Federal Housing Administration and Department of Veterans Affairs mortgage guarantee programs after World War II, how did the black ownership rate increase as much as the white rate in the 1940s? Were blacks discriminated against in suburbs but not in central cities or not in some city neighborhoods? Second, after lending practices allegedly became more neutral in the 1960s and 1970s, why did the black home ownership rate decline in the suburbs (54.1 percent in 1970 to 50.6 percent in 1980)[23] while it increased in central cities (34.8 percent in 1970 and 36.8 percent in 1980)? Were blacks still discriminated against in suburbs but not, or less, in central cities? Why did black home ownership increase by more than the white increase in both central cities and suburbs in the 1960s, when discrimination against blacks allegedly, according to the Commission on Civil Disorders, was greater than in the 1970s? The changes in owner occupancy rates were: blacks in central cities, 35.7 percent in 1960 and 38.5 percent in 1970; whites in central cities, 62.1 percent in 1960 and 62.3 percent in 1970; blacks outside central cities, 51.6

percent in 1960 and 54.1 percent in 1970; whites outside central cities, 73.4 percent in 1960 and 71.1 percent in 1970. The home ownership rate for blacks increased in sub-urbs in the 1960s, when the conventional critique says they were victims of discrimi-nation, and it decreased for whites who, by the conventional wisdom, were the favored group. This puzzle deserves a separate investigation, but it is beyond our scope here.

In the 1970s, the pace of black suburbanization, but not black home ownership, quickened. As summarized by William H. Frey and Alden Speare: "The magnitude of the 1970-1980 black suburbanization shift outdistanced that shown in any previ-ous postwar decade, and participation in this movement was not limited to only the most well-off segments of the black population."[24] By the 1980s, diversity of suburbs received much more attention. Differences in population trends between older and newer residential areas were recognized, as were quasi-city characteristics in subur-ban employment and retail centers.[25]

Frey anticipated noticeable advances in suburban racial integration in the 1980s due to greater population diversity from increases in Hispanic and Asian residents and from increases in incomes of some blacks.[26] While Frey found that neither black suburbanization nor neighborhood segregation had changed appreciably in the aggregate, "in some regions of the country significant changes have occurred, hap-pily, they are the regions that grew in population."[27] In sum, Frey discovered: "Nationally, minorities comprised 41 percent of the central city population and less than 18 percent of the suburban population [in 1990]. The minority share of both populations grew by about 5 percent over the 1980s, so the city-suburb minority dis-parity remained about the same."[28] While discovering wide variation in minority res-idential disparities among metropolitan areas, Frey concluded: "These patterns [in the North] indicate that the door for black suburbanization is not open very wide, and that future gains are most likely to be made in metro areas that house and con-tinue to attract a growing black middle-class population."[29]

By 2000, Frey found that minorities comprised 27 percent of suburban populations in the 102 largest metropolitan areas, up from 19 percent in 1990. Forty-seven percent of minorities lived in suburbs in 2000, up from 40 percent in 1990. In 65 of these 102 metropolitan areas, minorities were responsible for more than half of suburban pop-ulation increases in the 1990s.[30]

Surprisingly, suburbs of 24 metropolitan areas experienced losses of whites, raising curiosity about the meaning of "white flight," a term used in the past to refer to whites moving from central cities to suburbs. By 2000, 55 percent of Asians and 50 percent of Hispanics lived in suburbs, as did 39 percent of black metropolitan residents.

IMMIGRANTS

Immigration also has increased suburban diversity. In the 1990s, the biggest increase in immigrants was by Hispanics. In numerous suburbs, mainly in the South and West, Hispanics are the largest minority group. They also are a major presence in public schools, complicating language issues in numerous ways and adding to bur-dens on teachers.

Cities are accustomed to helping immigrants adjust to life in the United States. Tra-ditionally, cities have been the point of entry. Metropolitan areas still are the point of entry, except for farm workers, but frequently suburbs have become the first place of residence for immigrants.

In 1970, more immigrants lived in cities than suburbs. By 1980, about 100,000 more immigrants were in suburbs than in cities. The gap grew to one million by 1990, and in 2000, the suburbs had three million more immigrants than cities. While immigrant settlers contributed considerably to city growth in the 1990s, the rate of increase in suburbs was greater—66 percent to 43 percent.[31]

Immigrants and blacks constituted two major aspects of growing suburban diversity in the 1990s. Other aspects of diversity were an increase in the elderly and an increase in the low-income and poverty population.

SUBURBAN DECLINE IN THE 1960s AND 1970s

Substantial suburban decline has been a fairly recent subject for analysis. Most studies of suburban decline have been journalistic examinations of individual metropolitan areas or studies of moderate-size suburban samples in numerous metropolitan areas. Some suburban decline in the 1980s has been found in these studies.

We examined population changes between 1980 and 1990 as well as between 1990 and 2000. We found that suburban population decline was also prevalent in the 1980s; in fact, it was more common in the 1980s than in the 1990s. Within this 2,586-suburbs sample, 42 percent declined between 1980 and 1990 compared with 27 percent from 1990 to 2000. When a stable category (plus or minus 2.5 percent population change) was added, 33 percent declined between 1980 and 1990 compared with 18 percent that declined between 1990 and 2000.

We also studied suburban population decline for a smaller sample—554 suburbs in the 24 most populous urbanized areas in 1960. They constituted an older set than the 2,586 suburbs in 35 large metropolitan areas that had reached 2,500 or more residents by 1980. For this older group of suburbs, suburban population decline peaked in the 1970s. In the 1960s, only 115 suburbs (21 percent) declined in population, followed by 351 suburbs (63 percent) in the 1970s, 313 suburbs (57 percent) in the 1980s,[32] and 219 suburbs (40 percent) in the 1990s.[33] In a study of trends in 39 metropolitan areas, Frey and Speare found that central cities declined much more in population in the 1970s than in the 1950s and 1960s.[34]

The dominant influence on suburbs, as well as cities, that lost population probably was household size reductions. The national AHS fell from 3.33 in 1960 to 3.11 in 1970, to 2.75 in 1980, to 2.63 in 1990, and to 2.59 in 2000. These AHS reductions were 6.6 percent in the 1960s, 11.6 percent in the 1970s, and 4.4 percent in the 1980s. While the reduction in the 1990s was only 1.5 percent, that was a national average, the mean of a large range. The large number of suburbs that lost population in the 1970s coincides with the largest AHS decline.

AVERAGE HOUSEHOLD SIZE, FAMILIES
WITH CHILDREN, AND THE ELDERLY

Of the 700 suburbs that declined in population between 1990 and 2000, 615 decreased in AHS (Table 5.6). AHSs rise and fall for many reasons. Changes over time in the number of children per household, the rate of divorce, marriage later in life, frequency of older children and grandparents living in extended families, and age dis-

Table 5.6
Occupied Housing and Household Size Changes in Suburbs with Declining Population 1990 to 2000

	Number of Suburbs	Population Change 1990 to 2000		Change in Occupied Housing Units 1990 to 2000		Average Household Size (Persons Per Occupied Unit)			Average Demographic Composition Ratio*		
		Average Change	Average Percent Change	Average Change	Average Percent Change	1990	2000	Average Percent Change	1990	2000	Percent Change
Household Size Change in Population-Declining Suburbs											
Households Size Decreased	615	-835	-5.8	-55	-1.0	2.61	2.49	-4.8	2.71	2.13	-10.7
Household Size Increased	85	-1,468	-8.8	-671	-9.1	2.56	2.62	2.6	2.31	2.60	23.4
Total Suburbs	700										
Occupied Housing Unit Change in Population-Declining Suburbs											
Occupied Housing	366	-1,322	-8.9	-395	-6.6	2.55	2.48	-2.6	2.48	2.17	0.8
Occupied Housing	334	-463	-3.1	161	3.1	2.68	2.53	-5.4	2.86	2.20	-14.6
Total Suburbs	700										
Both Occupied Housing Unit and Household Size Changes											
Occupied Housing Units Decreased											
Household Size Decreased	288	-1,257	-9.0	-302	-5.5	2.55	2.44	-4.0	2.53	2.06	-5.6
Household Size Increased	78	-1,563	-8.6	-737	-10.4	2.55	2.62	2.7	2.27	2.59	24.2
Occupied Housing Units Increased											
Household Size Decreased	327	-464	-2.9	163	3.0	2.68	2.53	-5.5	2.86	2.19	-15.2
Household Size Increased	7	-413	-10.4	73	5.6	2.61	2.66	1.9	2.65	2.69	14.3
Summary for Population	700	-912	-6.1	-130	-1.9	2.61	2.5	-3.9	2.66	2.18	-6.5

*Demographic Composition Ratio: Ratio of Percent of Households with Families with Children Divided by Percent of Population 65 Years and Older.

Sources: U.S. Census Bureau, *Census 2000, Profiles of General Demographic Characteristics 2000*, issued May 2001, for each separate state, www2.census.gov/ census_2000/datasets/100_and_sample_profile; CensusCD 1990 (East Brunswick, NJ: GeoLytics, Inc., 2000).

tribution of the population can influence household size. Here we will emphasize two types of information that are available in the 2000 census reports: percentage of households composed of families with children under 18 and percentage of the population composed of persons 65 and over. Although these data are not identical in composition—one is a percentage of households and the other is a percentage of population—the ratio between these two items of information is revealing.

Household size would be expected to diminish as the elderly population increases. If the percentage of households composed of families with children goes up, AHS usually should increase. The ratio between these percentages of families with children and the elderly, therefore, may be related to whether population in suburbs increased or decreased. In 2000, the national average was that 32.8 percent of households was composed of families with children under 18. Persons age 65 and over constituted 12.4 percent of the total population. The ratio of one category to the other was 32.8 to 12.4, which was 2.65 families with children to one elderly person.

This ratio of families with children to elderly also dramatized differences between metropolitan areas dominated by growing and declining suburbs. In Atlanta, a rapidly growing metropolitan area, the ratio was very high in 1990 in suburbs that grew in the 1990s—3.89 to 1. It increased by 2000 to 4.09 to 1, indicating these suburbs were overwhelmingly dominated by families with children relative to the elderly population. In Atlanta's five suburbs that lost population, on the other hand, the families with children to elderly ratio fell from 4.16 in 1990 to 2.88 in 2000, an average change of 23.6 percent in a single decade.

In the slow-growing Cleveland region, a majority of suburbs—41 of 76—lost population. The average ratios of families with children to elderly fell from 2.36 in 1990 to 1.88 in 2000, a 20 percent drop in the declining suburbs. In the 35 growing suburbs, the average ratios of families with children also declined, from 2.52 to 2.07. Its influence on reducing population was outweighed by an average 18.7 percent increase in occupied housing units.

In their study of the 102 metropolitan areas with more than 500,000 residents in 2000, William H. Frey and Alan Berube found that "nonfamilies now represent a larger share of total suburban households than do traditional 'married with children' households."[35] Moreover, "the majority of household growth in suburbs of the North's metros came in the form of single-parent families and smaller nonfamilies," according to Frey and Berube.[36] Both the family and nonfamily characteristics of the suburbs changed in the 1990s, and reductions in suburbs' population often resulted.

HIGH ELDERLY POPULATIONS

The declining proportions of families with children to persons 65 and over in many suburbs indicate that suburbia is no longer preeminently a child-oriented arena. Elderly persons are becoming more prominent, either by staying in place as they age or by moving into places that specialize in appealing to the elderly. To explore this trend, we used a category for suburbs that "specialized in the elderly." Persons 65 and over constituted 12.4 percent of the United States' population in 2000. Suburbs that "specialized in the elderly" exceeded the national elderly proportion by 50 percent. The threshold for membership in the "specialized in the elderly" category is 18.6 percent.

In 2000, 13.8 percent of the suburbs (357 of 2,586) specialized in the elderly. A majority of those suburbs (183, which is 51 percent) declined in population in the

1990s. In 183 declining suburbs specializing in the elderly, the average proportion of elderly was 22.6 percent in 2000, nearly as high as the 25.2 percent that families with children constituted of households in these suburbs (a ratio of 1.17 to 1).

In 118 instances, the elderly proportion of the population exceeded the families-with-children proportion of households. We call these elderly-dominant suburbs. Some of these were retirement suburbs. Seventy of the 118 elderly-dominant suburbs were growing. The largest numbers of growing elderly-dominant suburbs were in Tampa–St. Petersburg, 21; Orlando, 6; Miami, 5; Phoenix, 5; and New York, 10.

AVERAGE HOUSEHOLD SIZE AND OCCUPIED HOUSING UNITS

The potential influence of changes in occupied housing units can be examined directly. We found that 437 suburbs had fewer occupied housing units in 2000 than in 1990—17 percent of 2,586 suburbs. Of the 700 declining suburbs, 366 (52 percent) had fewer occupied housing units. In these 366 suburbs, the average population loss from 1990 to 2000 was 8.9 percent, considerably higher than the 6.1 percent average loss in all 700 declining suburbs. The average decline in occupied housing units in these 366 suburbs was 6.6 percent. On average, these 366 suburbs also experienced a 2.6 percent reduction in AHS from 2.55 in 1990 to 2.48 in 2000.

In most of these 366 suburbs, demand for housing was less than supply, vacancy rates rose, and perhaps some abandonment and demolition occurred. Small declines in the number of occupied units could have been caused by demolition for public works, private development of commercial or industrial buildings, or census errors. However, a 6.6 percent reduction in occupied units in a decade is rather large. Low demand for housing seems the likely explanation of population decline in most of these 366 suburbs.

In all 2,586 suburbs, 437 suburbs (17 percent) declined in occupied housing units in the 1990s. In the 542 cities in 326 metropolitan areas that we analyzed in Chapter 3, 109 cities (20 percent) declined in occupied housing. Considering the general image that cities are declining and suburbs are growing, the similarity in these occupied-housing loss percentages is surprising.

SUBURBAN TRENDS

Suburban diversity has been increasing. Many pre-World War II suburbs had industrial or rural support economies and town centers, in addition to serving some commuters who worked in central cities. Post-World War II suburbs more often were bedroom settings, serving commuters and providing public schools. Edge cities have added major employment centers in some suburbs. The aging of middle-aged, post-World War II suburbs has added another dimension to suburban diversity.

By the 1990s, many suburbs had passed beyond their origins, which were based on families with children. Many suburbs now are dominated by uncertainties. They are mediating between long-time residents aging in place and newcomers, as well as potential buyers and renters who are considering whether these formerly child-oriented suburbs still are satisfactory places to raise families.

In a surprising number of instances, fewer households have chosen to replace suburban households who have moved or died. This outcome was reflected in fewer occupied dwellings, as occurred in 366 suburbs in the 35 metropolitan areas we analyzed. In addition, diminished household size occurred in 615 suburbs. When smaller household size intersected with less occupied housing, suburbs experienced substantial population losses.

Public policy tensions follow these demographic changes. Where demand for housing slackens, property tax bases usually will grow less than inflation—or even decline. Where AHS declines, a smaller proportion of households will have children in schools. Some public schools will close for lack of students.

If housing construction lags behind population growth, housing prices rise. Then old and middle-aged places, with less inflated housing prices, look more appealing and attract more replacement in-movers. Where metropolitan growth was slow or absent, fewer replacement households were available. Population decline then increased in suburbs as in central cities, becoming the norm in some metropolitan areas.[37]

Suburban population decline rivals, and often exceeds, population decline in central cities. Suburban decline bears some relationship to central city decline and to rates of metropolitan growth. The size of suburbs makes little difference, with decline in small suburbs about as likely as in large ones. The geographic location of population decline in suburbs does not conform to uniform patterns within, nor is it consistent among, metropolitan areas.

Why have some places declined while others have grown? Have some places lost residents who have moved or died and who have not been replaced by an equal number of new residents because of real or perceived deficiencies in their place? May these perceived deficiencies involve the age of structures, especially housing, and characteristics associated with age? May they involve social characteristics, such as race, schools, crime, public services, and employment? Do the development histories and locations of suburbs matter, such as whether they developed as balanced, independent jurisdictions or grew during the era when suburbs served mainly as bedroom settings for employment centers nearby?

The "what difference does it make" question also is difficult. Many observers are not convinced that growth conveys social benefits. Clearly, growth involves environmental stresses, yet population decline seems at first glance to be undesirable. If growth is not necessarily good, is decline necessarily bad? Growth and decline in themselves, for example, do not identify whether a suburb or central city is getting richer or poorer, either in terms of residents' income and other resources or in terms of the tax base that can be accessed by public agencies. The significance of variation and changes in income in suburbs will be examined in Chapter 6.

METHODS

In this study, we examined the 34 most populous metropolitan areas in the United States in 2000, plus the Buffalo metropolitan area, which in previous decades had ranked higher than many of these 34 metropolitan areas. Individual suburbs were chosen based on a population in 1980 of 2,500 or more. The 35 metropolitan areas in this study had 2,586 suburban governments and Census Designated Places (CDPs) in 1980. Military CDPs were eliminated when we could identify them. Population size of 2,500 or more residents in 1980 and consistent presence in U.S. censuses since 1980 were the only criteria for including suburbs in this study. Population density and government powers were not considered. Distance came into play only through the requirement that a place be within each metropolitan boundary.

The 35 metropolitan areas had 40 main central cities. Minneapolis–St. Paul, San Francisco–Oakland, and Tampa–St. Petersburg were treated equally as central cities in this chapter. Virginia Beach and Newport News in the Norfolk metropolitan area, and another 10 secondary central cities, were included in the sample of 2,586 suburbs.

Large suburbs, sometimes referred to as boomburbs, have complicated the distinction between central cities and suburbs. The largest of these suburbs, Mesa, outside Phoenix, has more than 400,000 residents—larger than the populations of old central cities like St. Louis, Pittsburgh, and Buffalo.

The Northeast and Midwest had more suburbs per metropolitan area (91 in the Northeast, excluding New York's 515, and 78 in the Midwest) than the South (38), Southwest (34), and West (45). The Mid-Atlantic region was an anomaly (99 suburbs per metropolitan area) in that the census included many CDPs as separate suburbs that lacked governmental responsibilities in the Baltimore and Washington, D.C., metropolitan areas.

Census designations for MSAs, PMSAs, and Consolidated Metropolitan Statistical Areas were chosen, depending on which category included most of the suburbs of a given central city without, if possible, including other major central cities with their own metropolitan areas. The spread of metropolitan areas into each other's territory makes some metropolitan boundary distinctions awkward and arguable. The choices we made among metropolitan designations did not alter significantly the percentages of suburban decline. In the metropolitan areas experiencing frequent suburban decline, most suburbs had substantial governance responsibilities. Of the 108 declining suburbs in the Pittsburgh area, for example, 92 had governance responsibilities.

NOTES

1. William H. Frey, "The New Geography of Population Shifts: Trends Toward Balkanization," in Reynolds Farley, ed., *State of the Union: America in the 1990s, Vol. 2* (New York: Russell Sage Foundation, 1995).

2. William H. Lucy and David L. Phillips, "Suburbs: Patterns of Growth and Decline," in Bruce Katz and Robert E. Lang, eds., *Redefining Urban & Suburban America* (Washington, DC: The Brookings Institution, 2003).

3. William Fulton, Rolf Pendall, Mai Nguyen, and Alicia Harrison, *Who Sprawls Most? How Growth Patterns Differ Across the U.S.* (Washington, DC: The Brookings Institution Survey Series, 2001), p. 1.

4. Amy Helling, "Transportation, Land Use, and the Impacts of Sprawl on Poor Children and Families," in Gregory Squires, ed., *Urban Sprawl* (Washington, DC: Urban Institute Press, 2002), p. 125.

5. Peter Whoriskey, "Washington's Road to Outward Growth," *The Washington Post*, August 9, 2004.

6. William Fulton, Rolf Pendall, Mai Nguyen, and Alicia Harrison, *Who Sprawls Most? How Growth Patterns Differ Across the U.S.* (Washington, DC: The Brookings Institution Survey Series, 2001), p. 2.

7. David Rusk, *Cities Without Suburbs* (Baltimore: Johns Hopkins University Press, 1993).

8. Thomas Bier and Charlie Post, *Vacating the City: An Analysis of New Homes vs. Household Growth* (Washington, DC: The Brookings Institution, 2003).

9. Robert Bish, *The Public Economy of Metropolitan Areas* (Chicago: Markham, 1971); Charles M. Tiebout, "A Pure Theory of Local Expenditures," *Journal of Political Economy* 64 (1956), pp. 416-424.

10. Alan Altshuler, William Morrill, Harold Wolman, and Faith Mitchell, eds., *Governance and Opportunity in Metropolitan America* (Washington, DC: National Academy Press, 1999).

11. William Fulton, Rolf Pendall, Mai Nguyen, and Alicia Harrison, *Who Sprawls Most? How Growth Patterns Differ Across the U.S.* (Washington, DC: The Brookings Institution Survey Series, 2001), p. 1.

12. Edward L. Glaeser, Matthew Kahn, and Chenghuan Chu, *Job Sprawl: Employment Location in U.S. Metropolitan Areas* (Washington, DC: The Brookings Institution Survey Series, 2001), p. 1.

13. Ivonne Audirac, "Stated Preferences for Pedestrian Activity: An Assessment of New Urbanist Sense of Community," *Journal of Planning Education and Research* 19 (1999), pp. 53-66.

14. Daphne Spain, "An Examination of Residential Preferences in the Suburban Era," *Sociological Focus* 21, no. 1 (1988), pp. 1-8.

15. Richard K. Green and Stephen Malpezzi, *A Primer on U.S. Housing Markets and Housing Policy* (Washington, DC: Urban Institute Press, 2003).

16. Kenneth T. Jackson, *Crabgrass Frontier* (New York: Oxford University Press, 1985).

17. Advisory Commission on Civil Disorders, *A Report* (Washington, DC: U.S. Government Printing Office, 1968).

18. Anthony Downs, *Opening Up the Suburbs* (New Haven, CT: Yale University Press, 1973).

19. U.S. Census Bureau, *Statistical Abstract of the U.S. 1982* (Washington, DC: U.S. Government Printing Office, 1983), p. 752.

20. U.S. Census Bureau, *Statistical Abstract of the U.S. 1972* (Washington, DC: U.S. Government Printing Office, 1973), p. 759.

21. William J. Collins and Robert A. Margo, "Race and Home Ownership: A Century-Long View." Working Paper No. 00-W12 (Nashville: Department of Economics, Vanderbilt University, May 2000).

22. John Powell, "Sprawl, Fragmentation, and the Persistence of Racial Inequality," in Gregory Squires, ed., *Urban Sprawl* (Washington, DC: Urban Institute Press, 2002), p. 78.

23. U.S. Census Bureau, *Statistical Abstract of the U.S. 1982* (Washington, DC: U.S. Government Printing Office, 1983), p. 758.

24. William H. Frey and Alden Speare, Jr., *Regional and Metropolitan Growth and Decline in the United States* (New York: Russell Sage Foundation, 1988), pp. 316-317.

25. William H. Frey, "The New Geography of Population Shifts: Trends Toward Balkanization," in Reynolds Farley, ed., *State of the Union: America in the 1990s, Vol. 2* (New York: Russell Sage Foundation, 1995), p. 315; Joel Garreau, *Edge City: Life on the New Frontier* (New York: Doubleday, 1991).

26. William H. Frey, "The New Geography of Population Shifts: Trends Toward Balkanization," in Reynolds Farley, ed., *State of the Union: America in the 1990s, Vol. 2* (New York: Russell Sage Foundation, 1995), p. 320.

27. Ibid.

28. Ibid., p. 321.

29. Ibid., p. 324.

30. William H. Frey, "Melting Pot Suburbs: A Study of Suburban Diversity," in Bruce Katz and Robert E. Lang, eds., *Redefining Urban & Suburban America* (Washington, DC: The Brookings Institution, 2003).

31. Audrey Singer, *The Rise of New Immigrant Gateways* (Washington, DC: The Brookings Institution, 2004), p. 10.

32. David L. Phillips and William H. Lucy, *Suburban Decline Described and Interpreted, 1960 to 1990: 554 Suburbs in 24 Largest Urbanized Areas* (Charlottesville: School of Architecture, University of Virginia, 1996).
33. William H. Lucy and David L. Phillips, "Suburban Population and Income Change: 554 Suburbs in 24 Metropolitan Areas, 1960 to 2000." Report to the The Brookings Institution, June 19, 2001.
34. William H. Frey and Alden Speare, Jr., *Regional and Metropolitan Growth and Decline in the United States* (New York: Russell Sage Foundation, 1988), pp. 512-513.
35. William H. Frey and Alan Berube, "City Families and Suburban Singles: An Emerging Household Story," in Bruce Katz and Robert E. Lang, eds., *Redefining Urban & Suburban America* (Washington, DC: The Brookings Institution, 2003), p. 272.
36. Ibid., p. 277.
37. Thomas Bier and Charlie Post, *Vacating the City: An Analysis of New Homes vs. Household Growth* (Washington, DC: The Brookings Institution, 2003).

CHAPTER

6

Discovering Poor Suburbs

Traditional images of suburbia as middle and upper income, growing, white, family oriented, and conservative are out of date. Instead, suburbs have become diverse in income, some have lost population, minorities are common, single-person households including elderly persons are frequent, and politics is in flux. Some opportunities may exist for finding order among these diverse elements, however, such as connections between population and income changes.

Because income embodies capacities of individuals to pay for goods and services, relative income changes in cities and suburbs are a more direct measure of economic and social strength than are population changes. Intrametropolitan inequalities include differences among suburbs, but "virtually all of the research examines only central city and suburban differences . . ., because of the way data are presented . . ."[1] William H. Frey, in his analysis of 1980 to 1990 metropolitan conditions, took care to note that "the broad territory surrounding major central cities has become a patchwork that includes inner suburbs, large suburban cities, office parks, retail centers, a few manufacturing communities dating from World War I, and even low-density, rural territory—in addition to the stereotypic bedroom communities."[2] However, Frey's analysis emphasized central city versus the remainder of the metropolitan area comparisons. Here, we do the opposite—differences among suburbs are given more attention than differences between central cities and suburbs collectively.

A notable exception to the analytic norm is the work of Myron Orfield, first in *Metropolitics*[3] and then in *American Metropolitics*.[4] In *American Metropolitics*, Orfield analyzes central city and suburban fiscal and social conditions in the 25 largest U.S. metropolitan areas. Four types of areas are classified: central cities with 28 percent of metropolitan population, at-risk suburbs (40 percent), bedroom-developing suburbs (26 percent), and affluent job centers (7 percent). Only the affluent job centers have adequate public sector resources, according to Orfield, and they have few social needs on which to spend them.[5] The U.S. Department of Housing and Urban Development in its *State of the Cities* report also warned that conditions commonly associated with troubled cities had been discovered in nearly 400 suburbs in 24 states, including poverty rates of more than 20 percent.[6]

In this chapter, we emphasize income changes in 2,586 suburbs in 35 large metropolitan areas. We focus on relationships between income and population changes. Most suburbs increased in population between 1990 and 2000, but 700 of 2,586 suburbs, 27 percent, declined in population. In the United States, growth usually is believed to be associated with prosperity and rising incomes. Population losses seem to imply stagnation and diminished opportunities, but did the 700 population-losing suburbs usually go down in income? We will examine those relationships.

SUMMARY OF FINDINGS

Suburbs were discovered to be diverse in relative income conditions and trends. However, they differed from common beliefs that growing suburbs also are prosperous, and that inner suburbs are the ones that are stressed, to the extent that any suburbs are. Neither belief held up well to close examination.

- Approximately half of the suburbs had relative incomes below their metropolitan areas' incomes in 1990 and 2000.
- Half of the suburbs declined in relative income between 1990 and 2000, including half of the suburbs that increased in population.
- Suburbs declined in relative income in sectors stretching as much as 40 miles from city centers, as well as suburbs adjacent to cities often declining.
- Many suburbs declined faster, or increased slower, than their central cities between 1990 and 2000, 33 percent of them in relative median family income and 52 percent of them in relative per capita income.
- In 2000, 155 suburbs had per capita income less than 60 percent of metropolitan incomes, with 88 suburbs below that level in median family income.
- Concentrated poverty in suburban neighborhoods nearly doubled between 1980 and 2000. The number of low- and moderate-income suburbs (below 80 percent relative median family income) increased by four times between 1960 and 1990.
- In four metropolitan areas (Atlanta, Chicago, Los Angeles, and Philadelphia) examined with detailed maps, suburbs declining in relative income were widely distributed geographically, and some suburbs adjacent to cities improved.

METHODOLOGY

Income changes are measured in relative income, as we explained in Chapter 4. That is, incomes of residents in each suburb and central city are measured relative to income for their metropolitan area in 2000, 1990, and 1980, and are expressed as a ratio. A ratio of more than 1.0 means that suburbs or cities' income is higher than their metropolitan area's income. A ratio of less than 1.0 means that their incomes are lower than their metropolitan area's income. The income status of each suburb and central city at each decade can be compared relative to metropolitan income, as can income changes between decades. For example, if a suburb's income ratio is 1.08 in 1990 and .95 in 2000, it has shifted from having income higher than its metropolitan area in 1990 to lower than its metropolitan area in 2000. We say the suburb in this example declined in relative income. The ratio of .95/1.08 = .88, which is a 12 percent relative income decline. The difference between 1.08 and .95, which is .13, when divided by 1.08, the 1990 base year, equals .12—a 12 percent relative income decline. Income data were reported by census respondents in 2000, 1990, and 1980 for the prior year. Population data are for 2000, 1990, and 1980. To avoid unnecessary repetition in reporting income details, we refer to the year in which the income was reported—2000, 1990, and 1980—to simplify the narrative.

Income of residents captures the cumulative decisions of residents to remain in, move from, and move to different parts of these metropolitan areas. Because location decisions are primarily a matter of residents making choices among many opportunities in housing markets within commuting distance of work, relative income captures changes in the perceived attractiveness of different parts of metropolitan areas over time. Income is valuable as an indicator of economic and social conditions. It determines much of the capacity of individuals, households, and families to purchase goods and services and to pay taxes and fees for public services.

RELATIVE INCOME CONDITIONS AND TRENDS

Metropolitan median family income and per capita income are the baselines from which differences among suburbs and central cities are measured for each decade, as well as changes from decade to decade. In 2000, for example, 44.6 percent of 2,586 suburbs in the 35 metropolitan areas had lower median family incomes than their metropolitan area, and 55.2 percent of their per capita income ratios were lower. These suburban income conditions in 2000 were similar to 1990, but more suburbs were below metropolitan income levels in 2000 than in 1980 (Figure 6.1).[7]

The metropolitan norms are medians or averages of the entire metropolitan area. Some central cities were 20 to 40 percent below metropolitan income levels, creating a mathematical necessity that many suburbs would be above the metropolitan norms. With large populations, these relatively low-income cities pull the metropolitan medians and averages toward their values relative to their proportion of their metropolitan areas. In addition, many suburbs had to be above the metropolitan median and mean income because large percentages of the population in these metropolitan areas were outside central cities. Large percentages of suburbs below metropolitan norms were somewhat surprising because most central cities were below the metropolitan norms—37 of 40 central cities in terms of median family income ratios in 2000, and 32 in terms of per capita income ratios, leaving room for more suburbs above metropolitan norms.

Twenty-five of 40 central cities declined in relative median family income, eight were stable, and seven increased from 1990 to 2000; 12 of 40 declined in relative per capita income, 18 were stable, and 10 increased. A slight majority of sample suburbs declined in relative income (50.1 percent in median family income and 53.1 percent in per capita income) (Figure 6.2). After accounting for a stable category, 39.3 percent of the suburbs declined in relative median family income as did 42.3 percent in relative per capita income (Table 6.1).

Figure 6.1
Percent of Suburbs Below Metropolitan Income Levels by Region

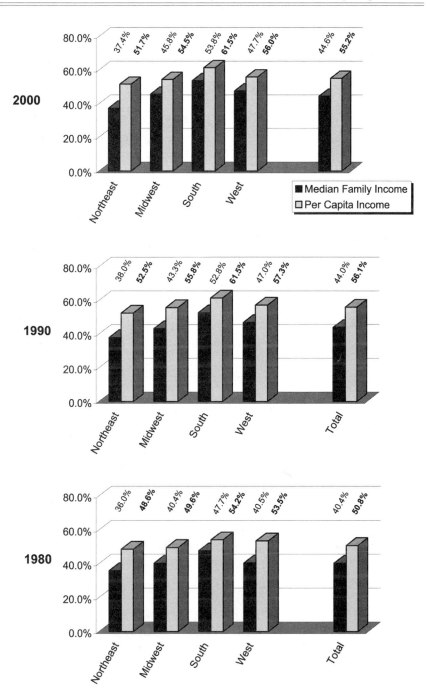

Sources: U.S. Census Bureau, *Census 2000,* Demographic Profiles: 100-percent and Sample Data, issued May 2002, for each separate state, www2.census.gov/census_2000/datasets/100_and_sample_profile; CensusCD 1980 (East Brunswick, NJ: GeoLytics, Inc., 1999) and CensusCD 1990 (East Brunswick, NJ: GeoLytics, Inc., 2000).

Figure 6.2
Percent of Suburbs Decreasing in
Income Relative to Metropolitan Income

Relative Median Family Income

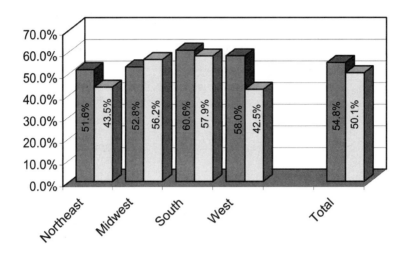

Relative Per Capita Income

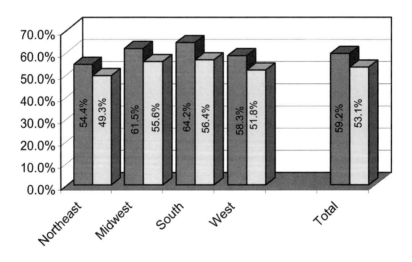

◼ 1980 to 1990   ◻ 1990 to 2000

Sources: U.S. Census Bureau, *Census 2000,* Demographic Profiles: 100-percent and Sample Data, issued May 2002, for each separate state, www2.census.gov/ census_2000/datasets/100_and_sample_profile; CensusCD 1980 (East Brunswick, NJ: GeoLytics, Inc., 1999) and CensusCD 1990 (East Brunswick, NJ: GeoLytics, Inc., 2000).

Table 6.1
Relative Suburban Income Decline by Region

Region	Suburbs in Study	Suburbs Deceasing in Income Relative to Metropolitan Income by At Least 2.5 Percent							
		1980 to 1990				1990 to 2000			
		Median Family		Per Capita		Median Family		Per Capita	
		Number	Percent	Number	Percent	Number	Percent	Number	Percent
Northeast	878	343	39.1	409	46.6	298	33.9	323	36.8
Midwest	780	326	41.8	406	52.1	346	44.4	358	45.9
South	530	263	49.6	295	55.7	247	46.6	245	46.2
West	398	184	46.2	200	50.3	125	31.4	168	44.2
Total	2586	1116	43.2	1310	50.7	1016	39.3	1094	42.3

Sources: U.S. Census Bureau, *Census 2000*, Demographic Profiles: 100-percent and Sample Data, issued May 2002, for each separate state, www2.census.gov/census_2000/datasets/100_and_sample_profile; CensusCD 1980 (East Brunswick, NJ: GeoLytics, Inc., 1999) and CensusCD 1990 (East Brunswick, NJ: GeoLytics, Inc., 2000).

REGIONS AND GROWTH MATTER LITTLE

Suburban population declines were concentrated in the Northeast and Midwest, where 38.5 percent and 31.8 percent of their suburbs lost population in the 1990s. In the South, only 13.6 percent of suburbs had fewer residents in 2000; in the West, only 10.5 percent lost population.

In contrast, the highest percentages of relative median family income decline were in the South (57.9 percent) followed by the Midwest (56.2 percent), and the lowest decline rates were in the West (42.5 percent) and Northeast (43.5 percent). Decline percentages were higher for relative per capita income in the West (51.8 percent) and Northeast (49.3 percent) than for relative median family income (Figure 6.2).

The highest relative income decline was in the South, not the expected trend, because 86.4 percent of southern suburbs increased in population. In the Northeast, where population losses in suburbs were most frequent, relative income decline was much less.

In most growing suburbs (except those that increased more than 50 percent in population), relative income was as likely to decrease as increase between 1990 and 2000. A majority of suburbs that decreased in population also decreased in relative median family income and per capita income.

Relative income declines were approximately as frequent in suburbs of fast-growing metropolitan areas (more than 25 percent growth) as in suburbs of slow-growing metropolitan areas (less than 10 percent growth). High frequencies of relative income increases during the 1990s occurred only in specific suburbs that grew by more than 50 percent, reflecting the influence of high percentages of new housing.

SPATIAL PATTERNS

Maps of relative income patterns in the Midwest and Northeast between 1990 and 2000 revealed that the Chicago and Cleveland metropolitan areas came closest to the expectation that inner suburbs would be the main locations of suburban income decline. Suburban relative income decline in these metropolitan areas, however, was not limited to the inner suburbs. In the Chicago area, in particular, considerable second-tier suburban income decline occurred to the south and northwest, with the northwest sector of decline extending to the third and fourth tiers of suburbs as much as 40 miles from the center of Chicago. References to inner-suburban decline have become common,[8] but limiting decline to inner suburbs understates the phenomenon.

In suburban territories in other Midwest and Northeast metropolitan areas (Buffalo, Cincinnati, Detroit, Philadelphia, Pittsburgh, and St. Louis), irregular geographic sequences were typical of declining and increasing relative income in suburbs adjacent to central cities.

In the Atlanta metropolitan area, the southeast sector was dominated by suburbs declining in relative median family income as far as 40 miles from the center of Atlanta. Los Angeles was distinctly different in its suburban decline pattern. Nearly all the suburbs that were adjacent to or surrounded by the City of Los Angeles were stable or increased in relative median family income. Other metropolitan areas in the South and West exhibited similar diversity, countering the belief that decline is concentrated in inner suburbs.

Neither concentric rings nor sectors radiating from the central cities were sufficient images of suburban income decline, although parts of most metropolitan areas exhibited these tendencies to varying degrees. Metropolitan maps of suburban income characteristics in the Atlanta, Chicago, Los Angeles, and Philadelphia areas are included later in this chapter.

GROWING SUBURBS AND METROPOLITAN AREAS

Of the suburbs that grew in population between 2.5 and 50 percent, more decreased (559) than increased (545) in relative median family income (341 were stable—stable is defined as less than plus or minus 2.5 percent change), and for relative per capita income, 668 decreased and 498 increased (279 were stable). Thus, most population growth was associated with relative income decreases instead of increases. For relative per capita income, income decline among growing suburbs even exceeded the income decline frequency among suburbs that lost population.

Only among suburbs growing by 50 percent or more from 1990 to 2000 were relative income increases much more common than decreases. These suburbs constituted only 7.4 percent (191) of the sample. Why would very rapidly growing suburbs frequently increase in relative income? Most new housing is priced so that only middle- and upper-income households can afford it. The size of new housing increased dramatically during the 1990s. Because large, new houses were affordable to a small income spectrum of the population, rapid growth tends to concentrate part of the population that is relatively well off financially. Rapid growth of this income segment would tend to lift relative incomes in such suburbs. Much of this growth occurred in outer areas that were transitioning from rural to urban status. Incomes in

Table 6.2
Metropolitan Population Growth Rates
and Relative Income Changes 1990 to 2000

	Metropolitan Population Increases 1990 to 2000					
	Less Than 10 Percent		10 to 25 Percent		More Than 25 Percent	
	Number of Suburbs	Percent	Number of Suburbs	Percent	Number of Suburbs	Percent
Change in Relative Median Family Income						
Decreased	528	35.9	359	44.6	129	41.5
Stable	327	22.2	183	22.7	55	17.7
Increased	615	41.8	263	32.7	127	40.8
Total	1470	100.0	805	100.0	311	100.0
Change in Relative Per Capita Income						
Decreased	590	40.1	384	47.7	120	38.6
Stable	325	22.1	138	17.1	63	20.3
Increased	555	37.8	283	35.2	128	41.2
Total	1470	100.0	805	100.0	311	100.0

Suburbs were Increasing or Decreasing during the decade if they changed by more than 2.5%; otherwise, they were classed as "Stable."

Sources: U.S. Census Bureau, *Census 2000,* Demographic Profiles: 100-percent and Sample Data, issued May 2002, for each separate state, www2.census.gov/census_2000/datasets/100_and_sample_profile; CensusCD 1990 (East Brunswick, NJ: GeoLytics, Inc., 2000).

rural areas typically are lower than in urban areas. Therefore, suburban sprawl into rural areas usually was accompanied by relative income increases there.

On the other hand, increases and decreases in relative income were about the same in fast-growing (25 percent or more) and slow-growing (less than 10 percent) metropolitan areas. Moderate-growing metropolitan areas (10 to 25 percent) were more likely to have suburbs with decreasing relative income (Table 6.2). Strong growth at metropolitan scale was not reflected in significant relative income growth in suburbs in the study sample.

POPULATION SIZE AND INCOME CHANGES

Population size of suburbs may influence income changes, but arguments for the relevance of population size diverge toward opposite hypotheses. Small size sometimes is argued to more readily reflect residents' preferences for public services and for neighbors with similar characteristics. Hence, small size might contribute to stability in retaining current residents and attracting similar replacement residents. With residential mobility rates averaging between 45 and 50 percent in five years, small jurisdictions are vulnerable to rapid changes in the make-up of their population. Just as

Table 6.3
Population Size of Suburbs and Relative Change in Median Family Income 1990 to 2000

2000 Population of Suburb	Relative Income Change in Median Family Income between 1990 and 2000							
	Decreased		Stable		Increased		Totals	
	Number of Suburbs	Percent	Number of Suburbs	Percent	Number of Suburbs	Percent	Number of Suburbs	Percent
Less than 5,000	189	41.4	77	16.8	191	41.8	457	100.0
5,000 to 9,999	234	37.3	112	17.8	282	44.9	628	100.0
10,000 to 24,999	285	34.8	198	24.2	336	41.0	819	100.0
25,000 to 49,999	166	41.4	116	28.9	119	29.7	401	100.0
More than 50,000	142	50.5	62	22.1	77	27.4	281	100.0
Total Suburbs	1016	39.3	565	21.8	1005	38.9	2586	100.0

Suburbs were Increasing or Decreasing during the decade if they changed by more than 2.5%; otherwise they were classed as "Stable."

Sources: U.S. Census Bureau, *Census 2000*, Demographic Profiles: 100-percent and Sample Data, issued May 2002, for each separate state, www2.census.gov/census_2000/datasets/100_and_sample_profile; CensusCD 1990 (East Brunswick, NJ: GeoLytics, Inc., 2000).

inelastic central cities are vulnerable to decline,[9] inelastic suburbs also are vulnerable, perhaps even more than central cities. Suburbs' small size may restrict them to a narrow range of housing ages that are difficult to renew and replace as housing units reach 30 or more years in age, an aging process accompanied by structural deterioration. Housing deterioration commonly is associated with income decline in the process known as the trickle-down process of neighborhood change.[10]

In the 2,586 suburbs in this study, the relationship of population size to relative income decline was inconsistent. Taking into account stable categories of suburbs (2.5 percent or less of relative income change), 39.3 percent of suburbs decreased in relative median family income. The lowest decline frequency was in the mid-size category (10,000 to 25,000) at 34.8 percent. The smallest (less than 5,000) and next largest (25,000 to 50,000) suburbs were equally likely to decrease in relative median family income with decline frequencies of 41.4 percent. The largest suburbs (more than 50,000) were most likely to decline in relative median family income (50.5 percent) (Table 6.3).

CITY AND SUBURB INCOMES

Many large central cities have reputations for serious social and fiscal problems, especially problems related to poverty concentrations. However, significant percentages of suburbs had relative incomes lower than their central cities in 2000, with 14.1 percent of suburbs being lower in relative median family income and 33.5 percent being lower in relative per capita income. More surprising was the change in these relationships between 1990 and 2000: relative median family income declined faster or improved at slower rates in 33 percent of suburbs compared with their central cities, and 52 percent of suburbs were behind their central cities in relative per capita income changes.

In part, more suburbs were lagging behind their central cities because more cities were doing better—seven of 40 central cities increased in relative median family income in the 1990s with eight stable compared with three that increased in the 1980s with 11 stable. Ten of 40 central cities increased in relative per capita income in the 1990s, with 18 stable compared with two that increased in the 1980s with 16 stable (Table 6.4).

THE LOWEST RELATIVE INCOME SUBURBS

Suburbs with low relative income are another useful group to examine. We chose income ratios of .60 or less (40 percent below equality with the metropolitan norms) for this category. Besides intuitively seeming rather extreme cases, this criterion also matches well with the lowest relative income central city, Detroit, which had a median family income ratio of .57 and a per capita income ratio of .60 in 2000.

Suburbs were below this ratio in 15 of 35 metropolitan areas for median family income ratios and 23 of 35 for per capita income ratios. In all, 88 suburbs had median family income ratios below .60, as did 155 suburbs for per capita income ratios. Metropolitan areas, where the highest percentages of suburbs are below .60, are in the South and West rather than in the Northeast or Midwest. For per capita income ratios, most suburbs below .60 were in Los Angeles, 22 percent; Phoenix, 18 percent; Miami, 17 percent; Houston, 16 percent; and Atlanta, 15 percent. Outside the South and West, St. Louis had the most low-income suburbs with 10 percent.

Some suburbs were much lower in relative income than .60. The five suburbs with the lowest per capita income ratios were Wellston (St. Louis), .36; East Compton (Los Angeles), .37; Guadalupe (Phoenix), .37; Washington Park (St. Louis), .37; and Prairie View (Houston), .38.

For median family income, most suburbs with relative income ratios lower than .60 were in the South—Atlanta, 14 percent, and Miami, 10 percent—followed by St. Louis, 9 percent in the Midwest. The five lowest median family income ratios were Rankin (Pittsburgh), .39; Lincoln Heights (Cincinnati), .41; Lithonia (Atlanta), .42; Wellston (St. Louis), .42; and Camden, New Jersey (Philadelphia), .42.

Wellston was the only suburb in the lowest five for both median family and per capita income. Interestingly, East St. Louis, which may have gotten the most news attention over the years as a depressed industrial suburb, did not appear among the 10 lowest income suburbs for either indicator of relative income. Metropolitan areas and the number and percentage of suburbs with income ratios below .60 are listed in Table 6.5. Individual suburbs below .60 for per capita income appear in Table Appendix 6.A, located at the end of this chapter.

Low relative income is associated with problems: poverty, crime, unemployment, poor health, and low school test scores. They constitute "push" factors that reduce willingness of middle- and upper-income households to live in low-income jurisdictions. Consequently, when low relative income occurs, cities and suburbs face mobility and location decision pressures that tend to further reduce the incomes of residents.

An important question is whether a "point of no return" exists in relative income below which cities and suburbs cannot revive or reverse direction. David Rusk in

Table 6.4
Central Cities and Their Declining Suburbs 1990 to 2000

REGION/City	Central City — Percent Population Change 1990 to 2000	Central City — Percent Change in Relative Income 1990-2000 Median Family	Central City — Percent Change in Relative Income 1990-2000 Per Capita	Suburbs — Number of Suburbs in Study	Suburbs — Number Decreasing in Relative Income 1990-2000 Median Family	Suburbs — Number Decreasing in Relative Income 1990-2000 Per Capita	Suburbs — Number Decreasing Faster or Growing Slower Than Central City Median Family	Suburbs — Number Decreasing Faster or Growing Slower Than Central City Per Capita
NORTHEAST								
Boston	2.6	-7.4	-1.1	78	35	45	8	38
Buffalo	-10.8	-8.6	-3.4	28	17	15	1	6
New York City	9.4	-7.3	-2.0	515	171	236	64	191
Philadelphia	-4.3	-11.7	-6.3	129	85	79	11	30
Pittsburgh	-9.5	-1.9	0.4	128	74	58	67	61
				878	382	433	151	326
MIDWEST								
Chicago	4.0	-5.1	2.9	213	143	140	93	160
Cincinnati	-9.0	-5.0	0.5	67	49	35	27	36
Cleveland	-5.4	-3.3	2.3	76	35	40	17	50
Columbus	12.4	-3.6	-1.9	28	17	17	11	14
Detroit	-7.5	3.8	0.4	89	44	50	59	52
Indianapolis	6.9	-4.9	-2.3	26	10	13	5	11
Kansas City, MO	1.5	-5.6	-2.9	40	22	23	9	19
Milwaukee	-5.0	-8.1	-7.0	39	19	18	3	5
Minneapolis	3.9	-2.7	-1.7	96	44	38	35	31
St. Paul (secondary)	5.5	-4.4	-5.4					
St. Louis	-12.2	-5.4	-2.0	106	55	60	42	52
				780	438	434	301	430

Table 6.4 (cont.)
Central Cities and Their Declining Suburbs 1990 to 2000

REGION/City	Percent Population Change 1990 to 2000	Percent Change in Relative Income 1990-2000 Median Family	Per Capita	Number of Suburbs in Study	Number Decreasing in Relative Income 1990-2000 Median Family	Per Capita	Number Decreasing Faster or Growing Slower Than Central City Median Family	Per Capita
SOUTH								
Atlanta	5.7	3.8	13.9	66	48	41	53	61
Baltimore	-11.5	-10.6	-3.7	67	48	51	8	37
Charlotte	36.6	-1.2	-0.3	24	15	17	15	15
Dallas	18.1	-9.3	-8.0	45	14	11	2	3
Houston	19.8	-3.7	-2.5	43	22	21	16	18
Miami	1.1	6.7	14.2	52	27	29	37	47
Norfolk	-10.3	-2.7	-0.9	10	5	5	4	4
Orlando	12.9	-0.3	7.2	37	17	15	16	24
San Antonio	22.3	2.9	2.9	15	10	10	13	11
St. Petersburg	4.0	-2.4	-1.4					
Tampa	8.4	0.9	9.1	41	28	18	31	37
Washington, D.C.	-5.7	-4.4	7.1	130	73	81	46	107
				530	307	299	241	364
WEST								
Denver	18.6	-1.1	-2.4	28	17	19	15	13
Las Vegas	85.2	3.8	6.6	8	4	4	5	5
Los Angeles	6.0	-3.7	-1.0	138	47	71	21	66
Phoenix	34.3	-4.0	-3.9	28	9	9	5	5
Portland	21.0	2.4	1.1	32	14	12	17	14
Sacramento	10.2	-8.6	-8.2	29	15	16	5	6
San Diego	10.2	0.5	1.8	24	10	11	10	13
Oakland (secondary)	7.3	-5.3	-5.0					
San Francisco	7.3	6.1	11.6	73	33	40	57	67
Seattle	9.1	6.5	6.9	38	20	24	27	30
				398	169	206	162	219
Total				2,586	1,296	1,372	855	1,339

Sources: U.S. Census Bureau, *Census 2000,* Demographic Profiles: 100-percent and Sample Data, issued May 2002, for each separate state, www2.census.gov/census_2000/datasets/100_and_sample_profile; CensusCD 1990 (East Brunswick, NJ: GeoLytics, Inc., 2000).

Table 6.5
Number of Suburbs with Income 40 Percent or More Below Metropolitan Income

	Number in Study	Number and Percent of Suburbs with Relative Income Ratio of 0.600 or Below (Income 40 or More Below Metropolitan Income)							
		Median Family Income				Per Capita Income			
		1990		2000		1990		2000	
		Number	Percent	Number	Percent	Number	Percent	Number	Percent
NORTHEAST									
Boston PMSA	78	1	1.3	2	2.6	1	1.3	3	3.8
Buffalo–Niagara Falls MSA	28	0	0.0	0	0.0	0	0.0	0	0.0
New York CMSA	515	6	1.2	13	2.5	16	3.1	18	3.5
Philadelphia PMSA	129	5	3.9	6	4.7	5	3.9	8	6.2
Pittsburgh MSA	128	2	1.6	7	5.5	7	5.5	2	1.6
Total for Northeast	878	14	1.6	28	3.2	29	3.3	31	3.5
MIDWEST									
Chicago PMSA	213	0	0.0	4	1.9	5	2.3	12	5.6
Cincinnati CMSA	67	1	1.5	3	4.5	1	1.5	2	3.0
Cleveland PMSA	76	1	1.3	1	1.3	0	0.0	1	1.3
Columbus, OH MSA	28	1	3.6	0	0.0	0	0.0	0	0.0
Detroit PMSA	89	4	4.5	4	4.5	2	2.2	4	4.5
Indianapolis, IN MSA	26	0	0.0	0	0.0	0	0.0	0	0.0
Kansas City MSA	40	0	0.0	0	0.0	0	0.0	1	2.5
Milwaukee PMSA	39	0	0.0	0	0.0	0	0.0	0	0.0
Minneapolis–St.Paul MSA	96	0	0.0	0	0.0	0	0.0	0	0.0
St. Louis, MO—IL MSA	106	7	6.6	10	9.4	8	7.5	11	10.4
Total for Midwest	780	14	1.8	22	2.8	16	2.1	31	4.0
SOUTH									
Atlanta MSA	66	5	7.6	9	13.6	5	7.6	10	15.2
Baltimore, MD PMSA	67	0	0.0	0	0.0	1	1.5	0	0.0
Charlotte, NC MSA	24	0	0.0	1	4.2	0	0.0	2	8.3
Dallas PMSA	45	1	2.2	0	0.0	5	11.1	4	8.9
Houston PMSA	43	2	4.7	2	4.7	5	11.6	7	16.3
Miami PMSA	52	4	7.7	5	9.6	9	17.3	9	17.3

Table 6.5 (cont.)
Number of Suburbs with Income 40 Percent or More Below Metropolitan Income

Number and Percent of Suburbs with Relative Income Ratio of 0.60 or Below (Income 40 or More Below Metropolitan Income)

	Number in Study	Median Family Income				Per Capita Income			
		1990		2000		1990		2000	
		Number	Percent	Number	Percent	Number	Percent	Number	Percent
SOUTH (cont.)									
Norfolk–Va. Beach MSA	10	0	0.0	0	0.0	0	0.0	0	0.0
Orlando, FL MSA	37	1	2.7	0	0.0	1	2.7	2	5.4
San Antonio, TX MSA	15	0	0.0	0	0.0	0	0.0	0	0.0
Tampa–St. Petersburg MSA	41	1	2.4	1	2.4	1	2.4	2	4.9
Washington, D.C. PMSA	130	3	2.3	6	4.6	7	5.4	12	9.2
Total for South	530	17	3.2	24	4.5	34	6.4	48	9.1
WEST									
Denver PMSA	28	0	0.0	0	0.0	2	7.1	2	7.1
Las Vegas MSA	8	0	0.0	0	0.0	1	12.5	0	0.0
Los Angeles & Orange Co. PMSAs	138	10	7.2	11	8.0	27	19.6	31	22.5
Phoenix–Mesa MSA	28	4	14.3	1	3.6	7	25.0	5	17.9
Portland PMSA	32	1	3.1	0	0.0	1	3.1	0	0.0
Sacramento–Yolo, CA CMSA	29	0	0.0	0	0.0	0	0.0	0	0.0
San Diego, CA MSA	24	0	0.0	1	4.2	1	4.2	1	4.2
San Francisco–Oakland PMSAs	73	1	1.4	1	1.4	3	4.1	6	8.2
Seattle PMSA	38	0	0.0	0	0.0	0	0.0	0	0.0
Total for West	398	16	4.0	14	3.5	42	10.6	45	11.3
TOTALS	2586	61	2.4	88	3.4	121	4.7	155	6.0

CMSA = Consolidated Metropolitan Statistical Area; MSA = Metropolitan Statistical Area; PMSA = Primary Metropolitan Statistical Area

Sources: U.S. Census Bureau, *Census 2000,* Demographic Profiles: 100-percent and Sample Data, issued May 2002, for each separate state, www2.census.gov/census_2000/datasets/100_and_sample_profile; CensusCD 1990 (East Brunswick, NJ: GeoLytics, Inc., 2000).

Cities Without Suburbs hypothesized that cities have passed the "point of no return" when city incomes are 70 percent or less of suburban incomes, because "city-suburb economic disparities become so severe that the city, in a broad sense, no longer is a place to invest or create jobs . . ."[11]

In our study, we chose a more extreme indicator of cities and suburbs' disadvantages—below 60 percent of metropolitan incomes—to examine whether such places continued to decline or whether they stabilized or rebounded. In 1990, 61 suburbs and one city (Detroit) were at or below .60 in median family income ratio, and in 2000 there were 88 suburbs and three cities (Cleveland, Detroit, and Baltimore) at or below .60. No cities were below .60 in 2000 for relative per capita income, but 121 suburbs were below it in 1990 with 155 below it in 2000.

These were surprising numbers, given the general impression that cities are worse off than suburbs. It was surprising also that so many of the suburbs were far below .60 income ratios, with many below .50 ratios. More surprising was the large number of these very low income suburbs that improved in income between 1990 and 2000, even as more suburbs were falling below these strikingly low income levels.

Of the 61 suburbs below .60 for their median family income ratios in 1990, 39 increased by 2000, with 29 increasing by more than 2.5 percent. Of the 121 instances of suburbs below .60 in per capita income ratios in 1990, 68 increased by 2000, with 54 increasing by more than 2.5 percent. With low-income suburbs embodying many problems that constitute "push" factors to drive away households with enough income to have many housing and neighborhood choices, why would so many of these low-income suburbs stabilize or improve?

Region seemed to matter, but the regional data also contained more mysteries. Most low-income suburbs in the Northeast, for example, decreased in relative income between 1990 and 2000 but, in other regions, a substantial majority of them were stable or increased in income in the 1990s. The highest rate of increase was in the Midwest, where nine of 14 suburbs below .60 in median family income ratios increased in the 1990s, and nine of 16 increased in per capita income ratios. Many low-income suburbs in the South and West also improved in the 1990s (Table 6.6).

Why were there so many low-income suburbs in the South and West, more than in the Northeast and Midwest, even though the Northeast and Midwest had far more suburbs? Why did so many of these low-income suburbs in the South increase in population as well as in income ratios? Why did so many of the low-income suburbs in other regions decline in population, even as they were improving in their income ratios? From these disparate trends, it would seem to follow that many forces have been at work that require more detailed analysis, and perhaps numerous individual case studies, to unearth the reasons for their income conditions and trajectories.

POVERTY IN SUBURBS

Few suburbs had individual or family poverty rates higher than their central cities in either 1990 or 2000. Very little change, in this respect, occurred in our sample of 2,586 suburbs. In 1990, 6.6 percent of suburbs had family poverty rates higher than their central cities, as did 6.4 percent of suburbs in 2000. Individual poverty rates rarely were higher in suburbs—in 6.3 percent of cases in 1990 and in 6.1 percent of cases in 2000. Even such small numbers of poverty-impacted suburbs may seem inconsistent with traditional impressions, since central cities have had reputations

Table 6.6
Relative Income Change among Suburbs with 1990 Income
40 Percent or More Below Metropolitan Income

Relative Median Family Income

Region	Number of Suburbs	Relative Income Change between 1990 and 2000			Change in Population 1990 to 2000		
		Decreased	Stable	Increased	Decreased	Stable	Increased
Northeast	14	10	2	2	8	2	4
Midwest	14	4	1	9	12	1	1
South	17	4	5	8	5	4	8
West	16	2	4	10	11	3	2
Total	61	20	12	29	36	10	15

Relative Per Capita Income

Region	Number of Suburbs	Relative Income Change between 1990 and 2000			Change in Population 1990 to 2000		
		Decreased	Stable	Increased	Decreased	Stable	Increased
Northeast	29	15	5	9	15	2	12
Midwest	16	5	2	9	13	1	2
South	34	7	9	18	13	4	17
West	42	12	12	18	33	7	2
Total	121	39	28	54	74	14	33

Suburbs were Increasing or Decreasing during the decade if they changed by more than 2.5%; otherwise they were classed as "Stable."

Sources: U.S. Census Bureau, *Census 2000,* Demographic Profiles: 100-percent and Sample Data, issued May 2002, for each separate state, www2.census.gov/census_2000/datasets/ 100_and_sample_profile; CensusCD 1990 (East Brunswick, NJ: GeoLytics, Inc., 2000).

for decades as the locations of concentrated poverty neighborhoods. Some metropolitan areas had considerably higher percentages of suburbs with family poverty rates above central city levels, including: Charlotte,14 of 24 (58 percent); Phoenix, 8 of 28 (29 percent); Houston, 9 of 43 (21 percent); San Diego, 4 of 24 (17 percent); Los Angeles, 22 of 138 (16 percent); Pittsburgh, 20 of 128 (16 percent); Miami, 8 of 52 (15 percent); Orlando, 5 of 37 (14 percent); San Francisco, 9 of 73 (12 percent); and Portland, 4 of 32 (12 percent).

Of these 10 metropolitan areas, only Pittsburgh was in the Northeast or Midwest. Although each region had some high-poverty suburbs, the largest shares of high family poverty suburbs were in the West (15.1 percent) and South (8.5 percent) (Table 6.7). Although income decline was common in the Northeast and Midwest, poverty concentrations remained mainly a central city phenomenon in those regions. However, when St. Louis (in the Midwest) had a 20.8 percent family poverty rate (compared with a national average of 9.2 percent, a metropolitan average of 8.7 percent, and a central city average of 13.6 percent), and nine of its suburbs had higher family poverty rates than the City of St. Louis, that indicates some suburbs have severe poverty concentrations.

Miami in the South with a 23.5 percent family poverty rate and eight suburbs with higher poverty is another striking example of concentrated suburban poverty, as was Los Angeles in the West—18.2 percent family poverty rate in the city and 22 suburbs with higher poverty rates. Given the large number of suburbs with median family income ratios (14.1 percent) and per capita income ratios (33.5 percent) below central cities in our 2,586 sample of suburbs, one might have expected more than 6.4 percent of suburbs to surpass central cities in family poverty rates. The downward relative income trend in many suburbs may foreshadow higher poverty levels in more suburbs in the 2010 census.

POVERTY IN SUBURBAN NEIGHBORHOODS

Other researchers have examined high-poverty concentrations in suburban census tracts and found significant changes. In the 100 largest metropolitan areas, G. Thomas Kingsley and Kathryn L.S. Pettit found that suburbs "have experienced the most rapid growth in concentrated poverty" compared with central cities and rural areas. In 1980, only 408 of the 23,974 census tracts in these 100 metropolitan areas had more than 30 percent of their residents below the poverty level compared to 772 tracts in 2000. Although still a modest number, suburbs' share of metropolitan high-poverty neighborhoods increased from 11 percent in 1980, to 13 percent in 1990, and 15 percent in 2000.[12]

Researching 330 metropolitan areas, Paul Jargowsky found that high poverty (40 percent or more below the poverty level) declined by 4 percent in suburbs compared with a 24 percent reduction in central cities, from 1990 to 2000.[13] ". . . poverty rates actually increased along the outer edges of central cities and in the inner-ring suburbs of many metropolitan areas, including those that saw a dramatic decline in poverty concentration," Jargowsky wrote, including Chicago, Cleveland, Dallas, and Detroit.[14] "The fact that inner-ring suburbs declined during this period is really quite astonishing," he said, because the census coincided "with the peak of a long economic boom." Therefore, Jargowsky worried that these inner-ring suburbs "may well have a bleak future . . ."[15]

Table 6.7
Suburban Poverty Compared with Central Cities

REGION/ Central City	Central Cities Income as Reported in 2000 Census		Income Relative to Metropolitan Area		Central Cities Poverty Rates (Percent)		Total Suburbs in Study	Suburbs with Poverty Rates Higher than Central City Family Poverty Rate		Person Poverty Rate	
	Median Family	Per Capita	Median Family	Per Capita	Family	Persons		Number	Percent	Number	Percent
NORTHEAST											
Boston	$44,151	$23,353	0.65	0.80	15.3	19.5	78	1	1.3	1	1.3
Buffalo	$30,614	$14,991	0.62	0.74	23.0	26.6	28	0	0.0	0	0.0
New York City	$41,887	$22,402	0.70	0.84	18.5	21.2	515	8	1.6	10	1.9
Philadelphia	$37,036	$16,509	0.63	0.69	18.4	22.9	129	6	4.7	5	3.9
Pittsburgh	$38,795	$18,816	0.82	0.90	15.0	20.4	128	20	15.6	18	14.1
							878	35	4.0	34	3.9
MIDWEST											
Chicago	$42,724	$20,175	0.70	0.81	16.6	19.6	213	5	2.3	5	2.3
Cincinnati	$37,543	$19,962	0.68	0.87	18.2	21.9	67	3	4.5	2	3.0
Cleveland	$30,286	$14,291	0.58	0.64	22.9	26.3	76	1	1.3	1	1.3
Columbus	$47,391	$20,450	0.86	0.89	10.8	14.8	28	3	10.7	2	7.1
Detroit	$33,853	$14,717	0.57	0.60	21.7	26.1	89	2	2.2	2	2.2
Indianapolis	$48,755	$21,640	0.88	0.93	9.1	11.9	26	2	7.7	3	-1.5
Kansas City, MO	$46,012	$20,753	0.82	0.89	11.1	14.3	40	2	5.0	2	5.0
Milwaukee	$37,879	$16,181	0.67	0.70	17.4	21.3	39	0	0.0	0	0.0
Minneapolis	$48,602	$22,685	0.74	0.87	11.9	16.9	96	0	0.0	0	0.0
St. Paul (secondary)	$48,925	$20,216	0.75	0.77	11.7	15.6					
St. Louis	$32,585	$16,108	0.60	0.71	20.8	24.6	106	9	8.5	9	8.5
							780	27	3.5	26	3.3

Table 6.7 (cont.)
Suburban Poverty Compared with Central Cities

REGION/Central City	Central Cities Income as Reported in 2000 Census		Income Relative to Metropolitan Area		Central Cities Poverty Rates (Percent)		Total Suburbs in Study	Suburbs with Poverty Rates Higher than Central City			
								Family Poverty Rate		Person Poverty Rate	
	Median Family	Per Capita	Median Family	Per Capita	Family	Persons		Number	Percent	Number	Percent
SOUTH											
Atlanta	$37,231	$25,772	0.63	1.03	21.3	24.4	66	2	3.0	2	3.0
Baltimore	$35,438	$16,978	0.60	0.70	18.8	22.9	67	0	0.0	0	0.0
Charlotte	$56,517	$26,823	1.05	1.15	7.8	10.6	24	14	58.3	14	58.3
Dallas	$40,921	$22,183	0.73	0.91	14.9	17.8	45	2	4.4	4	8.9
Houston	$40,443	$20,101	0.79	0.92	16.0	19.2	43	9	20.9	10	23.3
Miami	$27,225	$15,128	0.68	0.82	23.5	28.5	52	8	15.4	8	15.4
Norfolk	$36,891	$17,372	0.75	0.85	15.5	19.4	10	0	0.0	0	0.0
Orlando	$40,648	$21,216	0.85	1.00	13.3	15.9	37	5	13.5	8	21.6
San Antonio	$41,331	$17,487	0.92	0.94	14.0	17.3	15	2	13.3	2	13.3
Tampa	$40,517	$21,953	0.89	1.01	14.0	18.1	41	3	7.3	2	4.9
St. Petersburg	$43,198	$21,107	0.95	0.97	9.2	13.3					
Washington, D.C.	$46,283	$28,659	0.64	0.94	16.7	20.2	130	0	0.0	0	0.0
							530	45	8.5	50	9.4

Table 6.7 (cont.)
Suburban Poverty Compared with Central Cities

REGION/ Central City	Central Cities						Total Suburbs in Study	Suburbs with Poverty Rates Higher than Central City			
	Income as Reported in 2000 Census		Income Relative to Metropolitan Area		Poverty Rates (Percent)			Family Poverty Rate		Person Poverty Rate	
	Median Family	Per Capita	Median Family	Per Capita	Family	Persons		Number	Percent	Number	Percent
WEST											
Denver	$48,195	$24,101	0.79	0.92	10.6	14.3	28	1	3.6	1	3.6
Los Angeles	$39,942	$20,671	0.78	0.95	18.3	22.1	138	22	15.9	18	13.0
Las Vegas	$50,465	$22,060	1.04	1.04	8.6	11.9	8	3	37.5	3	37.5
Phoenix	$46,467	$19,833	0.91	0.91	11.5	15.8	28	8	28.6	7	25.0
Portland	$50,271	$22,643	0.90	0.97	8.5	13.1	32	4	12.5	2	6.3
Sacramento	$42,051	$18,721	0.78	0.84	15.3	20.0	29	3	10.3	4	13.8
San Diego	$53,060	$23,609	0.99	1.03	10.6	14.6	24	4	16.7	4	16.7
San Francisco	$63,545	$34,556	0.89	1.09	7.8	11.3	73	8	11.0	9	12.3
Oakland (secondary)	$44,384	$21,936	0.62	0.69	16.2	19.4					
Seattle	$62,195	$30,306	0.98	1.09	6.9	11.8	38	7	18.4	3	7.9
Totals							398	60	15.1	51	12.8
							2586	167	6.5	161	6.2

Source: U.S. Census Bureau, *Census 2000,* Demographic Profiles: 100-percent and Sample Data, issued May 2002, for each separate state, www2.census.gov/census_2000/datasets/100_and_sample_profile.

In 2002, the national poverty rate rose to 12.1 percent from 11.7 percent in 2001. According to the U.S. Census Bureau, the poverty level increased in suburbs from 8.2 to 8.9 percent, adding 1.2 million suburban residents in poverty. The poverty rate did not change in inner cities.[16]

INCOME CHANGES IN THE 1980S AND 1990S

Relative income decline in the 1980s was not consistently followed by income decline in the same suburbs in the 1990s, nor were relative income increases in the 1990s preceded consistently by income increases in the same suburbs in the 1980s. Decade-to-decade sequences were highly varied. Of 1,417 suburbs that decreased in relative median family income in the 1980s, only 772 (54 percent) continued to decrease between 1990 and 2000. Conversely, of 1,168 suburbs that increased in relative median family income in the 1980s, only 644 (55 percent) continued to increase from 1990 to 2000.

Similar trends occurred with per capita income. Of 1,530 suburbs that declined in relative per capita income in the 1980s, 878 (57 percent) declined in the 1990s. Of 1,058 suburbs that increased in relative per capita income in the 1980s, 562 (53 percent) increased in the 1990s.

Persistent income trends would illuminate expectations for policy makers and citizens. If income increases were followed by more increases, and income decreases were followed by more decreases, then opportunities and challenges would be clearer. Suburban income change tendencies have been fragile and flexible. Variation indicates that many economic and social forces for change are at work. Moreover, public policies and the quality of governance also may make a difference through impacts on residential location decisions. We found that inconsistency was nearly as common as consistency, identifying another puzzle about whether market forces, public policies, or other conditions affected income trends.

DECLINE IN OLD AND MIDDLE-AGED SUBURBS

Several years before analyzing these 2,586 suburbs in 35 metropolitan areas, we studied 554 suburbs that had 2,500 or more residents in 1960. We traced their evolution from 1960 through 1990. We classified these suburbs in terms of their median family income ratios by deciles: below .7, .7 to .8, .8 to .9, .9 to 1.0, 1.0 to 1.1, 1.1 to 1.2, and 1.2 and above.

A larger number of suburbs had income ratios exceeding 1.1 in 1960 compared with subsequent decades. In 1960, 267 of 554 suburbs (48.1 percent) had income ratios of 1.1 or more compared with 199 of 521 (38.2 percent) in 1970, 197 of 554 (35.6 percent) in 1980, and 190 of 554 (34.3 percent) in 1990.

The number of relatively low-income suburbs also increased greatly. In 1960, only six suburbs (1.1 percent) had median family income ratios below .7; by 1990, there were 38 (6.9 percent). Only 16 suburbs (2.9 percent) were between .7 and .8 in median family income ratios in 1960; by 1990, there were 52 (9.4 percent). Between 1960 and 1990, the number of suburbs below a .8 median family income ratio grew from 22 (4.0 percent) to 90 (16.2 percent), a four-fold increase.

In contrast, the category of the wealthiest suburbs was replenished after it declined, regaining a similar share by 1990 (25.6 percent) of the total that was in this category in 1960 (26.7 percent). Thus, the old and middle-aged suburbs were becoming more polarized between low- and high-income suburbs.

VOLATILITY IN SUBURBS

If a suburb or central city declined by 20 percent or more, we classified it as a rapid decliner. Suburbs and central cities that declined between 10 and 19.9 percent were classified as substantial decliners. Rapid and substantial increasers changed at these same rates. Two central cities (Philadelphia and Baltimore) declined by as much as 10 percent in relative median family income between 1990 and 2000, while no cities declined by 10 percent in relative per capita income.

Among the 2,586 suburbs in 35 metropolitan areas, 43 were rapid decliners in relative median family income (20 percent or more) in 14 metropolitan areas, and 265 were substantial decliners (10 to 19.9 percent) in 32 metropolitan areas. For relative per capita income, 50 suburbs declined rapidly and 315 declined substantially. Conversely, there were 97 rapid increasers and 309 substantial increasers in relative median family income, with 97 rapid increasers and 283 substantial increasers in relative per capita income.

Suburbs are volatile. High residential mobility rates, typically in the 45 to 50 percent range in five years, contribute to income volatility. Twenty-eight percent of suburbs increased or decreased by 10 percent or more in relative median family income from 1990 to 2000. Twenty-nine percent of suburbs changed by 10 percent or more in relative per capita income. The greatest volatility was in the South, where 34 percent of suburbs changed by 10 percent or more in both relative income indicators.

Small suburbs potentially are most susceptible to major changes in relative income due to high rates of residential mobility. Small suburbs were the major size category among the rapid decliners. Among the 43 suburbs that declined by 20 percent or more in relative median family income, 35 (81 percent) were small suburbs of 10,000 or fewer residents. Among the 50 suburbs that declined by 20 percent or more in relative per capita income, 36 (72 percent) were suburbs of 10,000 residents or less.

The rapid decliners also tended to be rich or poor suburbs. For example, among the 50 rapid decliners in relative per capita income, 16 had income ratios of 1.20 or higher (20 percent or more above the metropolitan norm), and 30 had income ratios below .80, of which 15 were below .60 in 2000. Only four rapidly declining suburbs were in the middle-income range between .80 and 1.20 in relative income in 2000. Among 43 rapid decliners in relative median family income, 30 were below .80, six were above 1.20, and seven were between .80 and 1.20 in income ratios. Thus, out of 93 rapid decliners by the two relative income indicators, only 11 (12 percent) were in the middle-income range between .80 and 1.20 ratios. Sixty-five percent (60 of 93) had relative income ratios below .80, indicating that more vulnerability to rapid decline occurred among low- and moderate-income suburbs.

The Atlanta metropolitan area had the highest percentage of rapid and substantial declining suburbs from 1990 to 2000, with 32 percent for relative median family and 23 percent for relative per capita income. This metropolitan area also had the highest percentage of suburbs that declined at rapid or substantial rates in both the 1980s and 1990s. The percentage of rapidly declining Atlanta suburbs diminished in the 1990s compared with the 1980s. The biggest increase in the percentage of substantially declining suburbs occurred in the Chicago metropolitan area, where only 10 suburbs declined substantially in relative median family income from 1980 to 1990 and 41 (20 percent) did so from 1990 to 2000.

SUBURBAN INCOME CHANGE VARIATIONS

In Figures 6.3 and 6.4, a great deal of information is packed into a small space. The range of relative income change ratios are shown for each metropolitan area. The values above and below the rectangular box plot are the minimum and maximum income change ratios. The rectangular box designates the middle 50 percent of the suburbs in the metropolitan area. The "whiskers" at the bottom and top of the rectangular box plots represent the first and fourth quartiles of the distribution. Consequently, the lines below and above the rectangular box represent one-quarter of each metropolitan area's suburbs.

In these figures, one can see that six metropolitan areas (San Antonio; Miami; Washington, D.C.; Chicago; Atlanta; and San Francisco) had one-fourth or more of their suburbs declining by 10 percent or more from 1990 to 2000 in relative per capita income (Figure 6.3). Eight metropolitan areas (Atlanta, San Antonio, Miami, St. Louis, Chicago, Cincinnati, Charlotte, and Pittsburgh) had one-fourth or more of their suburbs declining by 10 percent or more in relative median family income (Figure 6.4). Conversely, in four metropolitan areas (Dallas, Las Vegas, Phoenix, and Orlando), one-fourth or more of the suburbs increased by 10 percent or more in per capita income (Figure 6.3), with nearly one-fourth of the Dallas suburbs increasing by 20 percent or more. For median family income, more than one-fourth of the suburbs increased by 10 percent or more in three metropolitan areas (Dallas, Phoenix, and Orlando) (Figure 6.4).

Very wide ranges of rates of change also can be discerned. For per capita income, the most extreme differences between the largest decline and increase rates were in the metropolitan areas for Phoenix (.76 to 1.80), New York (.74 to 1.76), and Minneapolis–St. Paul (.67 to 1.48) (Figure 6.3). For median family income ratios, the biggest change rate ranges were in St. Louis (.64 to 1.38), New York (.77 to 1.50), and Atlanta (.69 to 1.32) (Figure 6.4).

Figures 6.3 and 6.4 also reveal whether the middle 50 percent, between the first and fourth quartiles, were huddled around the midpoint with little change, as in Norfolk, Baltimore, and Buffalo for per capita income ratios (Figure 6.3) and Norfolk, San Francisco, and Columbus for median family income (Figure 6.4). In general, these figures reveal great diversity among metropolitan areas in their pattern and rates of suburban income change, with considerable diversity also occurring within regions.

Figure 6.3

Distribution of Suburbs in Each Metropolitan Area by Relative Change in Per Capita Income 1990 to 2000

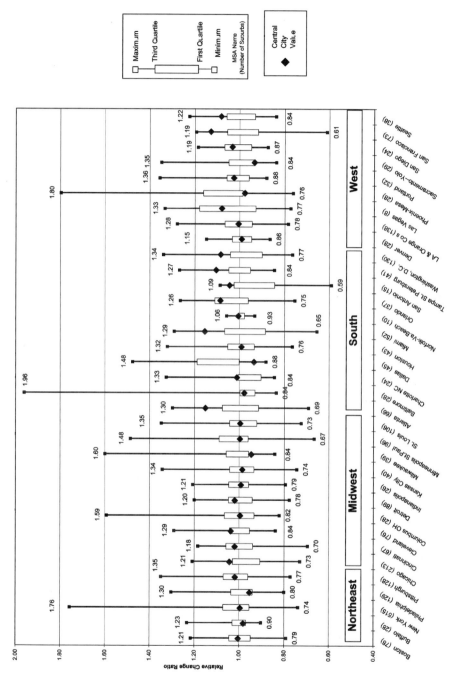

Sources: U.S. Census Bureau, *Census 2000*, Demographic Profiles: 100-percent and Sample Data, issued May 2002, for each separate state, www2.census.gov/census_2000/datasets/100_and_sample_profile; CensusCD 1990 (East Brunswick, NJ: GeoLytics, Inc., 2000).

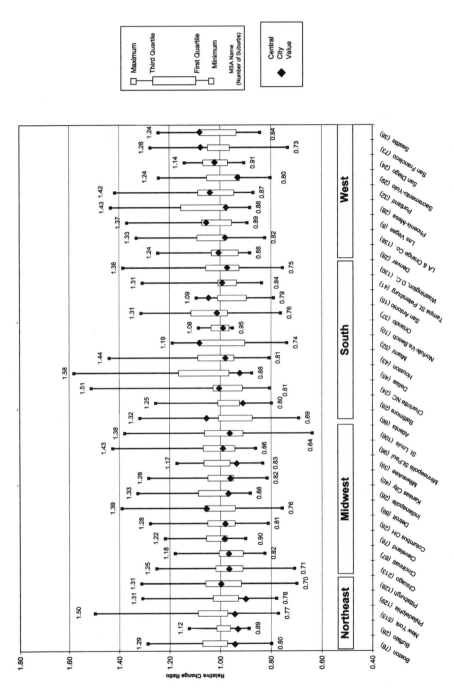

Figure 6.4
Distribution of Suburbs in Each Metropolitan Area
by Relative Change in Median Family Income 1990 to 2000

Sources: U.S. Census Bureau, *Census 2000*, Demographic Profiles: 100-percent and Sample Data, issued May 2002, for each separate state, www2.census.gov/census_2000/datasets/100_and_sample_profile; CensusCD 1990 (East Brunswick, NJ: GeoLytics, Inc., 2000).

METROPOLITAN PROFILES OF INCOME CHANGES

In this section, we will present the geographic array of declining and increasing suburbs in relative income for four metropolitan areas for Atlanta, Chicago, Los Angeles, and Philadelphia (Maps 6.1 through 6.8).

Atlanta, Georgia

The City of Atlanta is unique in the vast difference in its income status depending on whether it is measured with a median family income ratio (.63) in 2000 or with a per capita income ratio (1.03). This large spread was rivaled only by Washington, D.C., where the difference was between .64 for its median family income ratio and .94 for its per capita income ratio in 2000. Between 1990 and 2000, the City of Atlanta increased its income ratios relative to its metropolitan area by 3.8 percent for median family income and 13.9 percent for per capita income.

Atlanta's higher per capita income ratio depended on whites. Atlanta blacks had only one-fourth the per capita income of Atlanta whites. The white population of Atlanta had an extraordinary 1.70 per capita relative income ratio to whites in the metropolitan area in 2000, up from 1.60 in 1990. Conversely, the per capita relative income ratio for Atlanta blacks was .77 in 2000, down from .80 in 1990. The city was gaining more middle- and upper-income whites in nonfamily households, and the suburbs were gaining more moderate- and middle-income blacks.

Given Atlanta's high per capita income ratio, it is not surprising that many suburbs were below it. Yet it was not expected that 50 of Atlanta's 66 suburbs in this study would be below the central city per capita income ratio, or that 62 of 66 suburbs lagged behind the central city increase in this ratio between 1990 and 2000.

Moreover, given Atlanta's low median family income ratio (.63), it was surprising that 15 suburbs (22.7 percent) scored below the central city for this ratio in 2000—an increase from only four in 1990. Using a .60 relative income ratio again as a benchmark, nine Atlanta suburbs were lower in relative median family income. Ten (15 percent) of Atlanta's suburbs were below a .60 per capita income ratio (Table Appendix 6.A, located at the end of this chapter).

The geographic distribution of income declines encompassed the areas adjacent to Atlanta, including the high-income suburbs to the north (Map 6.1). However, income declines also projected a considerable distance from the central city, especially southeast, where suburbs were declining 30 and 40 miles from the center. A majority of suburbs close to the city were declining, but rapid increases in median family income occurred in adjacent suburbs to the east, and other adjacent suburbs to the east and west were stable. Many of the middle and outer suburbs were stable or increasing in relative median family income.

Despite the stability and increases in some middle and outer suburbs, the spatial distribution of suburban incomes relative to the Atlanta metropolitan area's income is particularly striking (Map 6.2). Most suburbs near the boundary of the central city were below the metropolitan area's median family income ratio in 2000, except for a small area to the north and northeast. However, in every direction, suburbs with income ratios below the metropolitan level were found in circumferential rings 20 to 40 miles from the center of the city. Thus, Atlanta's spatial income pattern contrasts with the traditional image that lower-income residents live near the center with mid-

**Map 6.1
Atlanta, GA Metropolitan Statistical Area
Change in Relative Median Family Income 1990 to 2000 in Suburban Places**

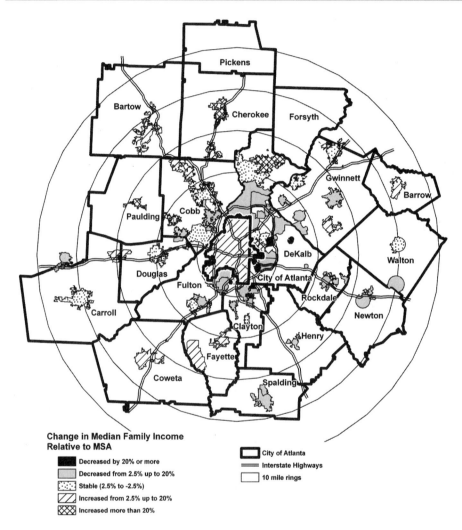

Change in Median Family Income
Relative to MSA

- Decreased by 20% or more
- Decreased from 2.5% up to 20%
- Stable (2.5% to -2.5%)
- Increased from 2.5% up to 20%
- Increased more than 20%

- City of Atlanta
- Interstate Highways
- 10 mile rings

Sources: U.S. Census Bureau, *Census 2000,* Demographic Profiles: 100-percent and Sample Data, issued May 2002, for each separate state, www2.census.gov/census_2000/datasets/ 100_and_sample_profile; CensusCD 1990 (East Brunswick, NJ: GeoLytics, Inc., 2000).

Map 6.2
Atlanta, GA Metropolitan Statistical Area
2000 Relative Median Family Income in Suburban Places

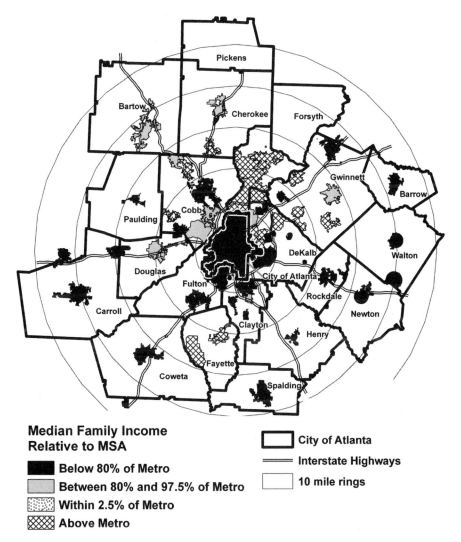

Median Family Income
Relative to MSA

■ Below 80% of Metro
▨ Between 80% and 97.5% of Metro
▦ Within 2.5% of Metro
▨ Above Metro

▢ City of Atlanta
═ Interstate Highways
▢ 10 mile rings

Source: U.S. Census Bureau, *Census 2000,* Demographic Profiles: 100-percent and Sample Data, issued May 2002, for each separate state, www2.census.gov/census_2000/datasets/ 100_and_sample_profile.

dle-income residents in the next rings, and higher-income residents on the metropolitan periphery.

Chicago, Illinois

Of the four metropolitan areas for which maps are presented, Chicago exhibits the most consistent pattern of relative income decline in suburbs that are adjacent to the central city. The only exceptions are Evanston (stable) to the north and Oak Park (increasing slightly) on the west. Even more striking, however, are the large sectors of relative income decline that extend south and northwest to the edge of the area of contiguous suburbs (40 miles northwest) from the central city. This pattern of decline is strongest for relative median family income (Map 6.3).

The median family income status map (Map 6.4) is quite different, however, as the declining northwest area is a high-income sector. Perhaps this sector is described well as not keeping up with high-income suburbs in the outer suburban areas due west of Chicago and north along Lake Michigan. South of Chicago is a low-income sector that stretches along most of the city's western border. Lower-income suburbs also are scattered around the fringe of the metropolitan area. Myron Orfield found a similar geographic distribution of local government revenue capacity, observing that "most of the lower-capacity suburbs are in the south and east, with higher capacities in the west and north."[17]

Of the Chicago area's 213 suburbs in this study, 140 decreased and 73 increased in relative median family income from 1990 to 2000—the same numbers of decrease and increase as for relative per capita income changes. The central city declined by 5 percent in relative median family income, but it increased by 3 percent in relative per capita income. Between 1990 and 2000, 91 suburbs declined faster than the City of Chicago in relative median family income, and 160 either declined or increased slower than the city in relative per capita income. These were increases from the numbers of suburbs that declined faster than the central city in the 1980s.

Due to a series of relative income declines in previous decades, the City of Chicago by 2000 had a median family income that was 30 percent below the metropolitan median, while its per capita income was 19 percent below the metropolitan level. Despite Chicago's low-income level, 10 suburbs were below the city's median family income level and 49 suburbs below its per capita income level in 2000, doubling the 1990 numbers of five and 25 suburbs that were below the city's income levels.

Only five suburbs (Dixmoor, Harvey, Phoenix, Riverdale, and Robbins) had family and person poverty levels below Chicago's. Using another benchmark, four of Chicago's suburbs had fallen below a .60 median family income ratio. Twelve suburbs had fallen below a .60 per capita income ratio (Table Appendix 6.A).

Relative income decline was the most prominent characteristic of Chicago's suburbs in this study, especially for per capita income. Moreover, more suburbs were falling below the income level of the central city. The large difference between median family income and per capita income findings indicates that Chicago was competing more effectively in attracting and holding single persons and households without children than families with children. Still, the presence of many minorities in suburban schools indicates that the distribution of family characteristics also has shifted. As Myron Orfield observed: "In Chicago, many south- and west-side suburban [school] districts actually have a higher percentage of blacks and Latinos than

Map 6.3
Chicago, IL Primary Metropolitan Statistical Area
Change in Relative Median Family Income 1990 to 2000 in Suburban Places

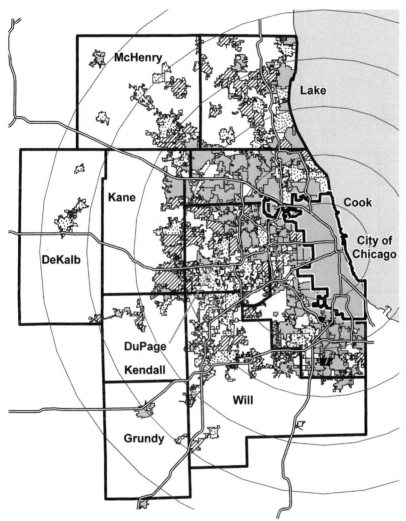

Change in Median Family Income Relative to PMSA

- ■ Decreased by 20% or more
- ▓ Decreased from 2.5% up to 20%
- ▒ Stable (2.5% to -2.5%)
- ▨ Increased from 2.5% up to 20%
- ▩ Increased more than 20%

- ▭ City of Chicago
- ═ Interstate Highways
- ▭ Ten Mile Rings

Sources: U.S. Census Bureau, *Census 2000,* Demographic Profiles: 100-percent and Sample Data, issued May 2002, for each separate state, www2.census.gov/census_2000/datasets/ 100_and_sample_profile; CensusCD 1990 (East Brunswick, NJ: GeoLytics, Inc., 2000).

Map 6.4
Chicago, IL Primary Metropolitan Statistical Area
2000 Relative Median Family Income in Suburban Places

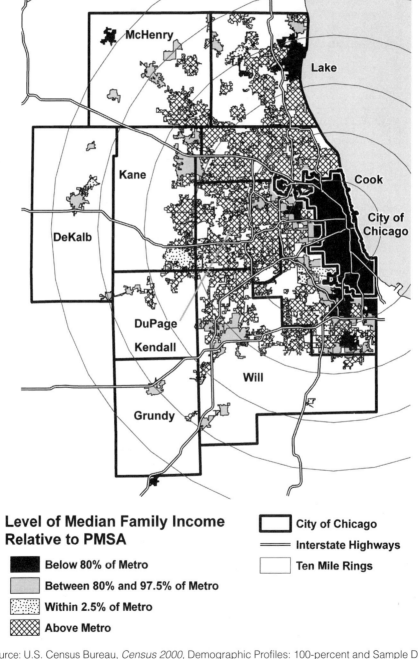

Level of Median Family Income Relative to PMSA

■ Below 80% of Metro

▨ Between 80% and 97.5% of Metro

▦ Within 2.5% of Metro

▧ Above Metro

☐ City of Chicago

═ Interstate Highways

☐ Ten Mile Rings

Source: U.S. Census Bureau, *Census 2000*, Demographic Profiles: 100-percent and Sample Data, issued May 2002, for each separate state, www2.census.gov/census_2000/datasets/ 100_and_sample_profile.

did the city itself . . . all of suburban Cook County is experiencing rapid racial change at the elementary school level, . . ."[18]

The Chicago metropolitan area does not fit the image of a central city whose middle- and upper-income whites have abandoned the city for the suburbs. The per capita relative income ratio of city whites to metropolitan whites in 2000 was .98, higher than in 1990 (.92), and considerably higher than the overall city to metropolitan ratio of .81 in 2000. The ratio of city black per capita relative income was .90 in 2000, slightly less than .92 in 1990. These ratios indicate slight trends for middle- and upper-income blacks to move to the suburbs, with some middle- and upper-income whites moving to the city.

Los Angeles, California

The suburbs of Los Angeles in this study are more like Chicago's than Philadelphia or Atlanta's suburbs in that they grew moderately (9.8 percent) in the 1990s and included 91.8 percent of the outside central city population. The average population of Los Angeles' 138 suburbs was 57,656—much larger than average suburb sizes in the other three metropolitan areas.

Twenty-one of these suburbs declined in population in the 1990s, and five of these also declined in relative median family income, with six declining in relative per capita income. Of the 117 that increased in population, however, only 75 increased in relative median family income, while 52 increased in relative per capita income.

The relationship between incomes in the suburbs to the central city's income was the most striking finding. There were 25 suburbs with a lower median family income ratio than the central city, and 69 suburbs (50 percent) were below Los Angeles in per capita income. The City of Los Angeles' median family income ratio was .78 and its per capita income ratio was .95. Like Atlanta, Los Angeles' whites had high per capita income—a 1.09 ratio in 2000 to metropolitan whites. Blacks in the city were almost as high as metropolitan blacks with a .98 ratio in 2000. The ratio for whites fell a little from 1.13 in 1990, while it rose for blacks from .94. Movement between city and suburbs seemed rather moderate in effects on income ratios for whites and blacks during the 1990s.

This relationship between suburbs and central cities was illuminated further by a comparison with a .60 income ratio. Eleven suburbs were below .60 in their median family income ratios and 31 suburbs (22 percent) were below a .60 per capita income ratio (Table Appendix 6.A)

The City of Los Angeles maintained its relative standing fairly well during the 1990s, declining by 3.7 percent in relative median family income and only 1.0 percent in relative per capita income. Many suburbs slipped more, with 21 suburbs declining more than the central city in relative median family income and 66 declining more in relative per capita income.

Overall, 47 of Los Angeles' 138 suburbs declined in relative median family income during the 1990s, with 71 declining in relative per capita income. The rate of suburban decline was moderate, as only six suburbs declined by 10 percent or more in relative median family income and 13 declined by 10 percent or more in relative per capita income.

Geographically, the pattern of income change was distinctive, contradicting the typical expectation that inner, especially adjacent, suburbs would be most likely to decline. Nearly all the suburbs adjacent to and surrounded by the City of Los Angeles were stable or increased in relative per capita income, with the exception of three decliners to the south. Several pockets or ribbons of income decline stretched as much as 30 miles to the east, and another bunch of declining suburbs was perched 35 to 50 miles to the north beyond a mountain range (Map 6.5).

As for the income status of Los Angeles' suburbs in 2000, per capita income ratios in the adjacent suburbs to the south and northeast, as well as those embedded in the city's fabric, generally were higher in income than the metropolitan average (Map 6.6). The eastern and southeastern suburbs were substantially below the metropolitan average, and this low-income sector extended 30 miles from the eastern part of the central city. A remote area 35 to 50 miles to the north was also a low-income collection of suburbs. Thus, neither the image of declining inner suburbs nor the image of a low-income center surrounded by progressively higher-income areas moving outward from the center was an accurate portrayal of the income geography of the Los Angeles metropolitan area.

Philadelphia, Pennsylvania

The City of Philadelphia declined more rapidly from 1990 to 2000 than any other central city in the sum of its median family income ratio (11.7 percent) and per capita income ratio (6.3 percent), for a total of 18.0 percent and a 9.0 percent average.

The suburbs in this study constituted only 30.6 percent of Philadelphia's outside central city population, and they had an average population size of 8,503. Much of the Philadelphia area's suburban population is in townships, which are not counted as places in census reports. Townships also contain places, so using townships would require eliminating places, creating difficult data problems. The geographic array of suburbs declining and increasing in income is spotty. Most suburbs adjacent to the city declined in relative median family income, but less than half of the boundary of the city was covered by the study sample. In relative per capita income in adjacent suburbs, a more diverse pattern of decreases and increases occurred (Map 6.7). Farther out, there were scattered declining suburbs in each direction (Map 6.7).

In per capita income status, nearly all the suburbs adjacent to Philadelphia were lower income in 2000 (Map 6.8). Middle- and upper-income suburbs were scattered in the mid-range suburban areas, with most of the outer suburbs in the lower-income categories. Many of these outer suburbs increased in relative per capita income, and some were stable, between 1990 and 2000. The Philadelphia area comes closer to the typical image of a poor central city, from which progressively higher-income areas emanate outward. However, fingers of low-income suburbs project into this mid-range area, and many of the outer suburbs also were low income.

Most suburbs in this study decreased in relative median family income—85 of 129. For relative per capita income, 79 suburbs decreased and 50 increased. Of the 86 suburbs that decreased in population, 60 also decreased in relative median family income while 53 decreased in relative per capita income. Of the 43 suburbs that increased in population, 25 decreased in relative median family income and 26 decreased in relative per capita income.

Map 6.5
Los Angeles and Orange County, CA Metropolitan Statistical Areas
Change in Relative Median Family Income 1990 to 2000 in Suburban Places

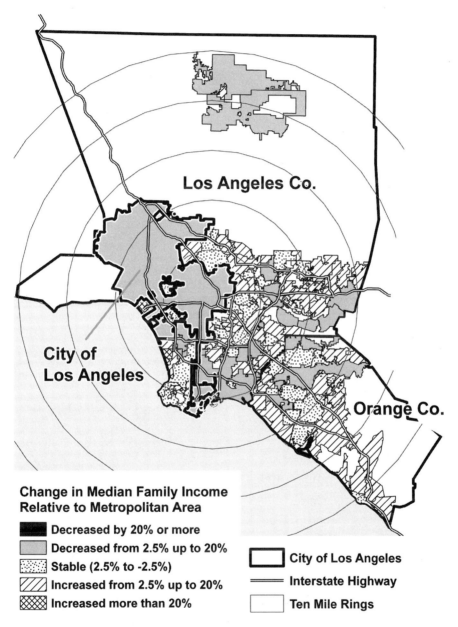

Change in Median Family Income
Relative to Metropolitan Area

■ Decreased by 20% or more
▨ Decreased from 2.5% up to 20%
▨ Stable (2.5% to -2.5%)
▨ Increased from 2.5% up to 20%
▨ Increased more than 20%

□ City of Los Angeles
══ Interstate Highway
□ Ten Mile Rings

Sources: U.S. Census Bureau, *Census 2000,* Demographic Profiles: 100-percent and Sample
Data, issued May 2002, for each separate state, www2.census.gov/census_2000/datasets/
100_and_sample_profile; CensusCD 1990 (East Brunswick, NJ: GeoLytics, Inc., 2000).

Map 6.6
Los Angeles and Orange County, CA Metropolitan Statistical Areas
2000 Relative Median Family Income in Suburban Places

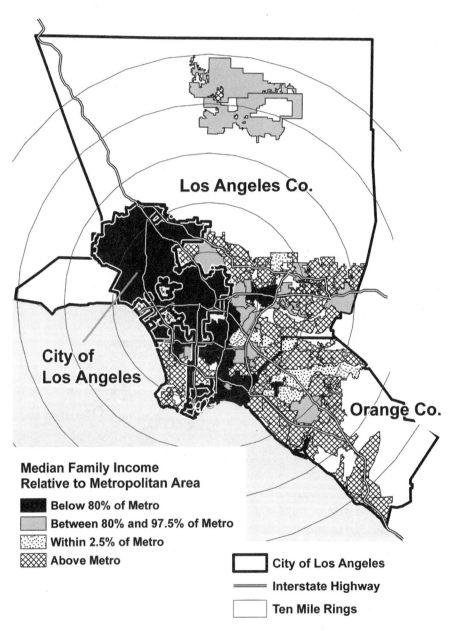

Source: U.S. Census Bureau, *Census 2000*, Demographic Profiles: 100-percent and Sample Data, issued May 2002, for each separate state, www2.census.gov/census_2000/datasets/100_and_sample_profile.

Map 6.7
Philadelphia, PA Primary Metropolitan Statistical Area
1990 to 2000 Change in Relative Median Family Income

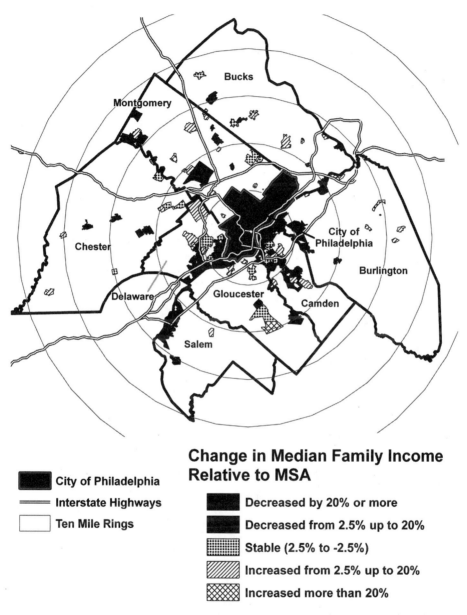

Change in Median Family Income Relative to MSA

City of Philadelphia

Interstate Highways

Ten Mile Rings

- Decreased by 20% or more
- Decreased from 2.5% up to 20%
- Stable (2.5% to -2.5%)
- Increased from 2.5% up to 20%
- Increased more than 20%

Sources: U.S. Census Bureau, *Census 2000,* Demographic Profiles: 100-percent and Sample Data, issued May 2002, for each separate state, www2.census.gov/census_2000/datasets/100_and_sample_profile; CensusCD 1990 (East Brunswick, NJ: GeoLytics, Inc., 2000).

Map 6.8
Philadelphia, PA Primary Metropolitan Statistical Area
2000 Relative Median Family Income in Suburban Places

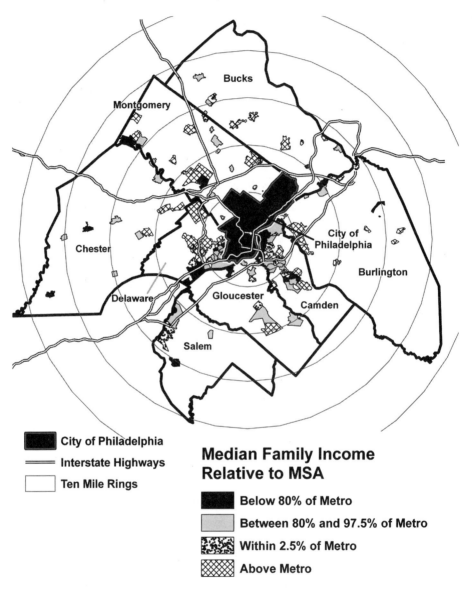

City of Philadelphia
Interstate Highways
Ten Mile Rings

Median Family Income Relative to MSA

Below 80% of Metro

Between 80% and 97.5% of Metro

Within 2.5% of Metro

Above Metro

Source: U.S. Census Bureau, *Census 2000,* Demographic Profiles: 100-percent and Sample Data, issued May 2002, for each separate state, www2.census.gov/census_2000/datasets/100_and_sample_profile.

Philadelphia fit the image of a central city struggling to retain affluent whites, in contrast with Atlanta, Chicago, and Los Angeles. Whites in the city had a per capita relative income ratio of only .78 in 2000, down from .82 in 1990. The ratio for black income also declined slightly from .92 to .89.

Although Philadelphia declined fastest among central cities in relative median family income from 1990 to 2000, 11 of its suburbs declined faster, and 30 suburbs declined faster than the city's 6.3 percent decline in relative per capita income. There also were 16 suburbs that declined by 10 percent or more in relative median family income, and 14 declined 10 percent or more in relative per capita income. Five suburbs exceeded a 10 percent decline rate in both the 1980s and 1990s in relative median family income, as did three in relative per capita income.

The City of Philadelphia had fallen to a low level in its median family income ratio (.63) and its per capita income ratio (.69). Nevertheless, 10 of the city's suburbs were lower in median family income ratios in 2000, and 13 suburbs were lower in per capita income ratios than the central city. Using .60 as an additional benchmark for low-income status, six Philadelphia suburbs were lower for relative median family income, and eight were lower for relative per capita income (Table Appendix 6.A, located at the end of this chapter).

SUMMARY AND INTERPRETATION

Awareness has been growing about diversity in suburbs,[19] including recognition that some suburbs are having social and fiscal problems.[20] The extent of suburban decline, however, continues to surprise. Based on analyses of income trends during the 1980s,[21] we anticipated finding considerable suburban relative income decline in the 1990s. Our current sample of 2,586 suburbs is based on suburbs that had 2,500 residents in 1980. It includes many new suburbs, and newness is thought to be a buffer against decline. Consequently, we were surprised to find that 50.1 percent of these 2,586 suburbs declined in relative median family income and 53.1 percent declined in relative per capita income.

From previous research, we knew that relative income decline was not limited to suburbs of large cities in the Northeast and Midwest where population decline was concentrated.[22] However, we did not expect that the most prevalent suburban relative income decline in the 1990s would be in the South—57.9 percent of suburbs in the South declined in relative median family income as did 56.4 percent in relative per capita income. We also expected that some relative income decline occurred in fast-growing metropolitan areas, but we did not expect that the frequency of relative income decline would be as great in fast-growing metropolitan areas (25 percent or more growth) as in slow-growing metropolitan areas (less than 10 percent growth) in the 1990s.

We had expected, based on previous research, that suburban relative income decline would not be limited to older, inner suburbs. We knew that some suburbs adjacent to central cities have been stable or increased in income in the 1980s, but we did not expect that relative income decline would be common 30 to 50 miles from the center of the central city, as occurred in the Atlanta, Chicago, Los Angeles, and Philadelphia metropolitan areas during the 1990s.

In addition, we knew of clues that some central cities had stabilized in the 1990s after several decades of persistent income decline, partly due to some downtown revitalization and population increases. However, we did not expect that 28 of the 40 central cities increased or were stable in relative per capita income in the 1990s, or that 15 cities increased or were stable in relative median family income, nor did we expect that a majority of suburbs—52 percent—would lag behind their central cities in relative per capita income changes, declining faster or increasing more slowly.

We hypothesized that small suburbs would be more subject to rapid relative income decline than larger ones, due to the vulnerability of small units to changes from residential mobility rates that average between 45 and 50 percent in five years. For rapidly declining suburbs, small size turned out to be a common characteristic, but in aggregate, small suburbs were not more likely than large ones to experience relative income decline in the 1990s.

We shared the belief that very low relative income levels constituted a major disadvantage so that these jurisdictions, whether cities or suburbs, were unlikely to be stable and rarely would increase in relative income. Yet numerous low-income cities were stable or revived, and many of the lowest income suburbs increased in relative income at sizable rates.

How might these trends be explained? With so many departures from expectations, these findings call for careful research into numerous possible explanations, but a few useful interpretations are possible now.

We acknowledge that some increases and decreases are mathematical as well as reality-based phenomena. When suburbs become very wealthy or very poor, as measured by departure from a ratio of 1.0 between the suburb's income and metropolitan income, a modest change in conditions can lead to a substantial percentage change.

A housing market attraction may be one explanation. If neighborhood conditions constitute strong forces "pushing" people to move elsewhere, then much of the housing stock may be sound but inexpensive relative to its internal quality. Some buyers may see the housing as an important opportunity for them to move up in housing quality, even though the neighborhood's social quality may be low. If enough people make this judgment, then relative incomes will rise even in very poor cities and suburbs.

Population increases may involve either more occupied housing units or larger households in the same number of housing units. Lower-income households are larger, on average, than households with higher incomes. Minority households and immigrant households tend to be larger than local norms, and they also tend to have lower incomes. If these groups constitute substantial portions of population growth, then population increases would lead to lower relative incomes in those suburbs.

On the other hand, if negative neighborhood factors have reduced the attraction of some suburbs, they may have less occupied housing, as housing stays vacant longer or is abandoned. Population decline may occur in such instances, accompanied by lower relative income as replacement in-moving households have lower incomes than out-moving households. If the in-moving households have larger families—as may occur if they are minorities, immigrants, or low-income households—then population might go up, even as the number of occupied housing units diminished.

Rapid population increases may indicate that metropolitan areas are attractive and that more middle- and upper-income persons are moving to them in strong job markets. Perhaps, but job growth does not equal higher earnings. In some states—Florida, for example—population and job growth were associated with lower earnings per job in the 1980s. Moreover, rapid metropolitan growth occurs mainly in a sprawl pattern with much of it outside suburbs that existed in 1980. In such instances, modest numbers of newcomers may move into established suburbs. Rapid construction of new residences within commuting distances may entice many middle- and upper-income residents to move to better quarters, leaving their previous residences to be occupied by lower-income persons. Rapid population growth leads to volatile housing markets and neighborhoods, leaving many possible paths of evolution for particular suburbs. Some suburbs may decline as other suburbs, especially newer ones, increase in relative income.

Overall, we found that suburbs where relative income increased in the 1980s were nearly as likely to experience income decreases as increases in the 1990s. The reverse applied to suburbs that decreased in relative income in the 1980s. They were nearly as likely to increase as decrease in relative income in the 1990s. This limited persistence in income trends suggests that multiple forces are operating with diverse effects. Some of these forces changed during the 1980s and 1990s.

The size of new housing increased rapidly during the 1980s and 1990s, constituting an inducement for households desiring more space to move.[23] Because of sprawl development patterns, moves to new housing often were to residences farther out from the center of metropolitan areas. Many downtowns of large cities revived during the 1990s and downtown populations increased.[24] Suburbanization of minorities increased rapidly in the 1990s,[25] and there is some evidence that avoidance of minorities by whites has diminished since the 1950s and 1960s. New employment and commercial concentrations in edge cities sprang up at a rapid rate, often superseding such centers that had been built in the 1960s and 1970s.[26] Highways became congested, reducing the attractiveness of some suburbs and perhaps negatively impacting entire sectors of suburbs. In some instances, fixed-rail mass transit was constructed, giving suburbs in its path major new advantages. Perhaps the quality of local governance has fluctuated, having its own effect on competitive advantages.

These forces would be expected to impact suburbs collectively in many different ways. Any, or many, of these forces might influence trends in a given suburb, altering its competitive attractiveness several times, perhaps, between 1980 and 2000. Overlaying these disparate forces would be persistent changes in housing composition—aging and deterioration of physical structures, varying reinvestment rates, and diverse frequencies of constructing new housing in specific suburbs.

There is another plausible explanation of these relative income trends. The comeback, or stability, of many central cities in the 1990s is consistent with the theory that some positive and negative influences on residential location decisions have turned to the advantage of central cities. Suburban commuting distances have lengthened, and the stress of commuting has increased, including increased uncertainty about how accidents or bad weather may further complicate a stressful experience. More social problems have come to some suburbs, reducing the difference between social problems in cities and many suburbs. Perhaps some public policy changes in cities involving community development corporations, community policing, reinvestment lending required of community banks, and welfare reform have had positive effects.[27] If proximity to culture and entertainment is important, if alternative modes of transportation are significant, and if walking to activities other than workplaces is a goal, then central cities are more likely to offer these options today, as in decades past, than suburbs. A combination of "pushes" from suburbs related to commuting, and "pulls" to cities related to accessibility and cultural variety, may explain some of central cities' revival. This interpretation also is consistent with central cities being stronger on per capita than median family income measures.

How might one explain the relative income increases in some of the poorest suburbs? Perhaps similar forces are at work there. They may be older suburbs close to central cities. They may have some advantages of central cities, including a housing stock that is more interesting aesthetically, and housing that also may be larger than the housing stock of many newer suburbs that were built mainly after World War II. In this theory, a combination of accessibility, cultural diversity, and an interesting housing stock worth fixing up may have induced more young and middle-income households to locate in these low-income suburbs. This is a theory worth exploring.

Table Appendix 6.A
Suburban Places with 60 Percent or Less of Metropolitan Per Capita Income in 2000
(ordered by Region, Metropolitan Area, and Relative Per Capita Income in 2000)

REGION Metropolitan Area Suburban Place	Relative Per Capita Income Ratio			Population and Change			
	1990	2000	Change Ratio	1990	2000	Change	Percent Change
NORTHEAST							
Boston, MA–NH PMSA							
Chelsea city, MA	0.599	0.500	0.835	28,710	35,080	6,370	22.2
Lynn city, MA	0.675	0.598	0.886	81,245	89,050	7,805	9.6
North Plymouth CDP, MA	0.758	0.599	0.791	3,450	3,593	143	4.1
New York–Northern New Jersey–Long Island, NY–NJ–CT–PA CMSA							
Lakewood CDP, NJ	0.523	0.444	0.849	26,095	36,065	9,970	38.2
Passaic city, NJ	0.583	0.484	0.829	58,041	67,861	9,820	16.9
Newark city, NJ	0.497	0.489	0.983	275,221	273,546	-1,675	-0.6
Wyandanch CDP, NJ	0.534	0.494	0.925	8,950	10,546	1,596	17.8
Paterson city, NJ	0.555	0.498	0.898	140,891	149,222	8,331	5.9
Newburgh city, NJ	0.527	0.502	0.953	26,454	28,259	1,805	6.8
Asbury Park city, NJ	0.594	0.508	0.855	16,799	16,930	131	0.8
Union City city, NJ	0.585	0.526	0.899	58,012	67,088	9,076	15.6
Monsey CDP, NJ	0.548	0.526	0.960	13,986	14,504	518	3.7
New Brunswick city, NJ	0.594	0.538	0.906	41,711	48,573	6,862	16.5
Trenton city, NJ	0.581	0.550	0.945	88,675	85,403	-3,272	-3.7
Spring Valley village, NJ	0.724	0.559	0.772	21,802	25,464	3,662	16.8
Perth Amboy city, NJ	0.599	0.563	0.941	41,967	47,303	5,336	12.7
Elizabeth city, NJ	0.639	0.568	0.889	110,002	120,568	10,566	9.6
Haverstraw village, NJ	0.581	0.580	0.999	9,438	10,117	679	7.2
New Cassel CDP, NJ	0.682	0.589	0.864	10,257	13,298	3,041	29.6
Hempstead village, NJ	0.701	0.591	0.843	49,453	56,554	7,101	14.4
Brentwood CDP, NJ	0.705	0.595	0.844	45,218	53,917	8,699	19.2
Philadelphia, PA–NJ PMSA							
Camden city, NJ	0.444	0.411	0.926	87,492	79,904	-7,588	-8.7
Chester city, PA	0.556	0.547	0.983	41,856	36,854	-5,002	-12.0
Penns Grove borough, NJ	0.567	0.558	0.985	5,228	4,886	-342	-6.5
Salem city, NJ	0.599	0.568	0.949	6,883	5,857	-1,026	-14.9
Marcus Hook borough, PA	0.612	0.575	0.940	2,545	2,314	-231	-9.1
Colwyn borough, PA	0.688	0.582	0.846	2,613	2,453	-160	-6.1
Darby borough, PA	0.629	0.586	0.932	11,140	10,299	-841	-7.5
Coatesville city, PA	0.645	0.590	0.914	11,038	10,838	-200	-1.8
Pittsburgh, PA MSA							
Rankin borough, PA	0.484	0.475	0.981	2,503	2,315	-188	-7.5
Duquesne city, PA	0.598	0.576	0.964	8,525	7,332	-1,193	-14.0

Table Appendix 6.A (cont.)
Suburban Places with 60 Percent or Less of Metropolitan Per Capita Income in 2000
(ordered by Region, Metropolitan Area, and Relative Per Capita Income in 2000)

REGION Metropolitan Area Suburban Place	Relative Per Capita Income Ratio			Population and Change			
	1990	2000	Change Ratio	1990	2000	Change	Percent Change
MIDWEST							
Chicago, IL PMSA							
Robbins village, IL	0.494	0.393	0.797	7,498	6,635	-863	-11.5
Dixmoor village, IL	0.582	0.468	0.804	3,681	3,934	253	6.9
Harvey city, IL	0.528	0.493	0.933	29,767	30,000	233	0.8
Cicero town, IL	0.650	0.499	0.768	67,436	85,616	18,180	27.0
Stone Park village, IL	0.706	0.515	0.730	4,383	5,127	744	17.0
Phoenix village, IL	0.498	0.573	1.150	2,221	2,157	-64	-2.9
Riverdale village, IL	0.761	0.578	0.759	13,637	15,055	1,418	10.4
North Chicago city, IL	0.557	0.582	1.045	34,978	35,918	940	2.7
Summit village, IL	0.618	0.584	0.945	9,971	10,637	666	6.7
Markham city, IL	0.602	0.595	0.987	13,136	12,620	-516	-3.9
Maywood village, IL	0.650	0.596	0.917	27,139	26,987	-152	-0.6
Chicago Heights city, IL	0.672	0.598	0.891	33,072	32,776	-296	-0.9
Cincinnati--Hamilton, OH–KY–IN CMSA							
Lincoln Heights village, OH	0.459	0.528	1.151	4,805	4,113	-692	-14.4
Elmwood Place village, OH	0.607	0.587	0.966	2,936	2,681	-255	-8.7
Cleveland–Lorain–Elyria, OH PMSA							
East Cleveland city, OH	0.610	0.565	0.926	33,096	27,217	-5,879	-17.8
Detroit, MI PMSA							
Highland Park city, MI	0.461	0.498	1.079	20,121	16,746	-3,375	-16.8
Hamtramck city, MI	0.609	0.521	0.855	18,372	22,976	4,604	25.1
River Rouge city, MI	0.565	0.564	0.997	11,314	9,917	-1,397	-12.3
Ecorse city, MI	0.623	0.594	0.953	12,180	11,229	-951	-7.8
Kansas City, MO–KS MSA							
Cameron city, MO	0.713	0.531	0.744	4,845	8,312	3,467	71.6
St. Louis, MO–IL MSA							
Wellston city, MO	0.324	0.364	1.124	3,612	2,460	-1,152	-31.9
Washington Park village, IL	0.403	0.374	0.929	7,437	5,345	-2,092	-28.1
Kinloch city, MO	0.373	0.388	1.038	2,702	449	-2,253	-83.4
Pagedale city, MO	0.560	0.485	0.866	3,771	3,616	-155	-4.1
Centreville city, IL	0.482	0.491	1.019	7,489	5,951	-1,538	-20.5
East St. Louis city, IL	0.430	0.492	1.143	40,944	31,542	-9,402	-23.0
Venice city, IL	0.456	0.506	1.108	3,571	2,528	-1,043	-29.2
Pine Lawn city, MO	0.497	0.525	1.056	5,092	4,204	-888	-17.4
Moline Acres city, MO	0.750	0.561	0.749	2,676	2,662	-14	-0.5
Bel-Ridge village, MO	0.794	0.576	0.725	3,202	3,082	-120	-3.7
Madison city, IL	0.619	0.577	0.931	4,623	4,545	-78	-1.7

Table Appendix 6.A (cont.)
Suburban Places with 60 Percent or Less of Metropolitan Per Capita Income in 2000
(ordered by Region, Metropolitan Area, and Relative Per Capita Income in 2000)

REGION Metropolitan Area Suburban Place	Relative Per Capita Income Ratio			Population and Change			
	1990	2000	Change Ratio	1990	2000	Change	Percent Change
SOUTH							
Atlanta, GA MSA							
Lithonia city, GA	0.464	0.424	0.912	2,186	2,187	1	0.0
Experiment CDP, GA	0.444	0.450	1.013	3,649	3,233	-416	-11.4
Conley CDP, GA	0.610	0.465	0.762	5,528	6,188	660	11.9
Fair Oaks CDP, GA	0.662	0.529	0.799	6,996	8,443	1,447	20.7
Clarkston city, GA	0.826	0.571	0.692	5,385	7,231	1,846	34.3
Villa Rica city, GA	0.539	0.572	1.060	6,542	4,134	-2,408	-36.8
College Park city, GA	0.614	0.574	0.935	20,236	20,382	146	0.7
Gresham Park CDP, GA	0.613	0.584	0.953	9,000	9,215	215	2.4
Monroe city, GA	0.531	0.592	1.116	9,759	11,407	1,648	16.9
Forest Park city, GA	0.707	0.596	0.844	16,925	21,447	4,522	26.7
Charlotte–Gastonia–Rock Hill, NC–SC MSA							
Dallas town, NC	0.684	0.590	0.863	3,012	3,402	390	12.9
Wingate town, NC	0.616	0.593	0.962	2,845	2,406	-439	-15.4
Dallas, TX PMSA							
Cockrell Hill city, TX	0.470	0.414	0.882	3,746	4,443	697	18.6
Hutchins city, TX	0.571	0.592	1.037	2,733	2,805	72	2.6
Commerce city, TX	0.587	0.593	1.011	6,825	7,669	844	12.4
Balch Springs city, TX	0.590	0.595	1.008	17,406	19,375	1,969	11.3
Houston, TX PMSA							
Prairie View city, TX	0.316	0.377	1.192	3,972	4,410	438	11.0
Jacinto City city, TX	0.535	0.518	0.968	9,343	10,302	959	10.3
Hempstead city, TX	0.693	0.530	0.765	3,581	4,691	1,110	31.0
Aldine CDP, TX	0.618	0.537	0.869	11,133	13,979	2,846	25.6
Galena Park city, TX	0.604	0.560	0.927	10,033	10,592	559	5.6
South Houston city, TX	0.561	0.564	1.007	14,207	15,833	1,626	11.4
Barrett CDP, TX	0.571	0.566	0.991	2,991	2,872	-119	-4.0
Miami, FL PMSA							
Gladeview CDP, FL	0.390	0.429	1.101	15,637	14,468	-1,169	-7.5
FL City city, FL	0.502	0.447	0.891	5,808	7,843	2,035	35.0
Goulds CDP, FL	0.460	0.468	1.016	7,284	7,453	169	2.3
Opa-locka city, FL	0.494	0.516	1.043	15,283	14,951	-332	-2.2
Brownsville CDP, FL	0.461	0.526	1.139	15,607	14,393	-1,214	-7.8
Leisure City CDP, FL	0.684	0.539	0.787	19,379	22,152	2,773	14.3
Pinewood CDP, FL	0.574	0.550	0.958	15,518	16,523	1,005	6.5
Opa-locka North CDP, FL	0.572	0.583	1.019	6,568	6,224	-344	-5.2
Sweetwater city, FL	0.591	0.600	1.016	13,909	14,226	317	2.3

Table Appendix 6.A (cont.)
Suburban Places with 60 Percent or Less of Metropolitan Per Capita Income in 2000
(ordered by Region, Metropolitan Area, and Relative Per Capita Income in 2000)

REGION Metropolitan Area Suburban Place	Relative Per Capita Income Ratio			Population and Change			
	1990	2000	Change Ratio	1990	2000	Change	Percent Change
SOUTH (cont.)							
Orlando, FL MSA							
South Apopka CDP, FL	0.454	0.512	1.127	6,360	5,800	-560	-8.8
Oak Ridge CDP, FL	0.771	0.582	0.754	15,388	22,349	6,961	45.2
Tampa–St. Petersburg–Clearwater, FL MSA							
Dade City North CDP, FL	0.367	0.465	1.267	3,058	3,319	261	8.5
Ruskin CDP, FL	0.703	0.594	0.845	6,046	8,321	2,275	37.6
Washington, DC–MD–VA–WV PMSA							
Langley Park CDP, MD	0.482	0.420	0.870	17,474	16,214	-1,260	-7.2
Brentwood town, MD	0.598	0.517	0.866	2,989	2,844	-145	-4.9
East Riverdale CDP, MD	0.634	0.519	0.820	14,187	14,961	774	5.5
College Park city, MD	0.627	0.528	0.843	21,927	24,657	2,730	12.5
Culpeper town, VA	0.629	0.555	0.883	8,581	9,664	1,083	12.6
Bladensburg town, MD	0.655	0.562	0.858	8,064	7,661	-403	-5.0
Mount Rainier city, MD	0.692	0.579	0.836	7,954	8,498	544	6.8
Dumfries town, VA	0.619	0.582	0.939	4,285	4,937	652	15.2
Seat Pleasant city, MD	0.597	0.587	0.983	5,359	4,885	-474	-8.8
Coral Hills CDP, MD	0.563	0.589	1.047	11,032	10,720	-312	-2.8
Front Royal town, VA	0.563	0.590	1.047	11,880	13,589	1,709	14.4
Chillum CDP, MD	0.712	0.590	0.829	31,309	34,252	2,943	9.4
WEST							
Denver, CO PMSA							
Commerce City city, CO	0.523	0.513	0.981	16,466	20,991	4,525	27.5
Derby CDP, CO	0.544	0.528	0.971	6,043	6,423	380	6.3
Los Angeles & Orange County PMSAs							
Florence-Graham CDP, CA	0.319	0.370	1.160	57,147	60,197	3,050	5.3
East Compton CDP, CA	0.394	0.371	0.940	7,967	9,286	1,319	16.6
Bell Gardens city, CA	0.361	0.385	1.065	42,355	44,054	1,699	4.0
Lennox CDP, CA	0.380	0.389	1.022	22,757	22,950	193	0.8
Cudahy city, CA	0.350	0.397	1.135	22,817	24,208	1,391	6.1
Maywood city, CA	0.409	0.408	0.999	27,850	28,083	233	0.8
Huntington Park city, CA	0.427	0.427	1.000	56,065	61,348	5,283	9.4
Lynwood city, CA	0.428	0.436	1.019	61,945	69,845	7,900	12.8
East Los Angeles CDP, CA	0.392	0.436	1.115	126,379	124,283	-2,096	-1.7
Westmont CDP, CA	0.508	0.447	0.880	31,044	31,623	579	1.9
Willowbrook CDP, CA	0.424	0.451	1.065	32,772	34,138	1,366	4.2
Bell city, CA	0.419	0.453	1.081	34,365	36,664	2,299	6.7
South El Monte city, CA	0.475	0.463	0.976	20,850	21,144	294	1.4
Walnut Park CDP, CA	0.466	0.470	1.009	14,722	16,180	1,458	9.9
El Monte city, CA	0.475	0.472	0.993	106,209	115,965	9,756	9.2

Table Appendix 6.A (cont.)
Suburban Places with 60 Percent or Less of Metropolitan Per Capita Income in 2000
(ordered by Region, Metropolitan Area, and Relative Per Capita Income in 2000)

	Relative Per Capita Income Ratio			Population and Change			
REGION							
Metropolitan Area							
Suburban Place	**1990**	**2000**	**Change Ratio**	**1990**	**2000**	**Change**	**Percent Change**
WEST (cont.)							
Los Angeles & Orange County PMSAs (cont.)							
Compton city, CA	0.463	0.475	1.027	90,454	93,493	3,039	3.4
South Gate city, CA	0.494	0.485	0.982	86,284	96,375	10,091	11.7
Hawaiian Gardens city, CA	0.492	0.491	0.997	13,639	14,779	1,140	8.4
Commerce city, CA	0.532	0.508	0.955	12,141	12,568	427	3.5
South San Jose Hills CDP, CA	0.516	0.518	1.003	17,814	20,218	2,404	13.5
La Puente city, CA	0.535	0.518	0.970	36,955	41,063	4,108	11.1
San Fernando city, CA	0.524	0.525	1.003	22,580	23,564	984	4.4
Paramount city, CA	0.556	0.525	0.944	47,669	55,266	7,597	15.9
Baldwin Park city, CA	0.523	0.529	1.012	69,330	75,837	6,507	9.4
Rosemead city, CA	0.578	0.555	0.961	51,638	53,505	1,867	3.6
Santa Ana city, CA	0.591	0.556	0.940	293,742	337,977	44,235	15.1
West Compton CDP, CA	0.694	0.560	0.807	5,451	5,435	-16	-0.3
West Puente Valley CDP, CA	0.556	0.586	1.053	20,254	22,589	2,335	11.5
West Athens CDP, CA	0.626	0.590	0.942	8,859	9,101	242	2.7
Valinda CDP, CA	0.674	0.592	0.878	18,735	21,776	3,041	16.2
Pico Rivera city, CA	0.617	0.595	0.965	59,177	63,428	4,251	7.2
Phoenix–Mesa, AZ MSA							
Guadalupe town, AZ	0.330	0.372	1.127	5,458	5,228	-230	-4.2
Eloy city, AZ	0.390	0.420	1.077	7,201	10,375	3,174	44.1
El Mirage city, AZ	0.397	0.472	1.188	5,001	7,609	2,608	52.1
Florence town, AZ	0.675	0.515	0.763	7,510	17,054	9,544	127.1
Superior town, AZ	0.483	0.570	1.180	3,376	3,254	-122	-3.6
San Diego, CA MSA							
National City city, CA	0.534	0.505	0.946	54,249	54,260	11	0.0
San Francisco and Oakland,CA PMSAs							
East Palo Alto city, CA	0.493	0.434	0.879	23,451	29,506	6,055	25.8
San Pablo city, CA	0.520	0.450	0.866	25,158	30,215	5,057	20.1
Cherryland CDP, CA	0.654	0.533	0.815	11,088	13,837	2,749	24.8
Ashland CDP, CA	0.665	0.571	0.858	16,590	20,793	4,203	25.3
Pittsburg city, CA	0.677	0.574	0.848	47,564	56,769	9,205	19.4
North Fair Oaks CDP, CA	0.555	0.577	1.039	13,912	15,440	1,528	11.0

Sources: U.S. Census Bureau, *Census 2000,* Demographic Profiles: 100-percent and Sample Data, issued May 2002, for each separate state, www2.census.gov/census_2000/datasets/100_and_sample_profile; CensusCD 1990 (East Brunswick, NJ: GeoLytics, Inc., 2000).

NOTES

1. Alan Altshuler, William Morrill, Harold Wolman, and Faith Mitchell, eds., *Governance and Opportunity in Metropolitan America* (Washington, DC: National Academy Press, 1999), p. 41.
2. William H. Frey, "The New Geography of Population Shifts: Trends Toward Balkanization," in Reynolds Farley, ed., *State of the Union: America in the 1990s, Vol. 2* (New York: Russell Sage Foundation, 1995), p. 311.
3. Myron Orfield, *Metropolitics* (Washington, DC: The Brookings Institution, 1997).
4. Myron Orfield, *American Metropolitics* (Washington, DC: The Brookings Institution, 2002).
5. Ibid., pp. 2-3.
6. U.S. Department of Housing and Urban Development, *The State of the Cities* (Washington, DC: U.S. Government Printing Office, 1999), p. xiii.
7. Each of the 2,586 suburbs is listed with pertinent data on the author's Web site, www.arch.virginia.edu/~dlp/incomemaps.
8. Peter Dreier, John Mollenkopf, and Todd Swanstrom, *Place Matters* (Lawrence: University Press of Kansas, 2001).
9. David Rusk, *Cities Without Suburbs* (Baltimore: Johns Hopkins University Press, 1993).
10. Anthony Downs, *Neighborhoods and Urban Development* (Washington, DC: The Brookings Institution, 1981).
11. David Rusk, *Cities Without Suburbs* (Baltimore: Johns Hopkins University Press, 1993), pp. 75-77.
12. G. Thomas Kingsley and Kathryn L.S. Pettit, *Concentrated Poverty: A Change in Course* (Washington, DC: Urban Institute, 2003), p. 4.
13. Paul A. Jargowsky, *Stunning Progress, Hidden Problems: The Dramatic Decline of Concentrated Poverty in the 1990s* (Washington, DC: The Brookings Institution, 2003), p. 12.
14. Ibid.
15. Ibid., p. 13.
16. Jonathan Weisman, "U.S. Income Fell, Poverty Rose in 2002," *The Washington Post*, September 27, 2003, p. 1.
17. Myron Orfield, *American Metropolitics* (Washington, DC: The Brookings Institution, 2002), p. 20.
18. Ibid., p. 14.
19. William H. Frey, *Melting Pot Suburbs: A Census 2000 Study of Suburban Diversity* (Washington, DC: The Brookings Institution, 2001).
20. William H. Lucy and David L. Phillips, *Confronting Suburban Decline: Strategic Planning for Metropolitan Renewal* (Washington, DC: Island Press, 2000); Myron Orfield, *Metropolitics* (Washington, DC: The Brookings Institution, 1997); Myron Orfield, *American Metropolitics* (Washington, DC: The Brookings Institution, 2002).
21. David L. Phillips and William H. Lucy, "Suburban Decline Described and Interpreted, 1960 to 1990, 554 Suburbs in 24 Largest Urbanized Areas." Report to the Center for Urban Development (Richmond: Virginia Commonwealth University, 1996).
22. William H. Lucy and David L. Phillips, *Suburbs and the Census: Patterns of Growth and Decline* (Washington, DC: The Brookings Institution, 2001).
23. William H. Lucy and David L. Phillips, *Confronting Suburban Decline: Strategic Planning for Metropolitan Renewal* (Washington, DC: Island Press, 2000).
24. Rebecca R. Sohmer and Robert E. Lang, *Downtown Rebound* (Washington, DC: Fannie Mae Foundation and The Brookings Institution, 2001).
25. William H. Frey, *Melting Pot Suburbs: A Census 2000 Study of Suburban Diversity* (Washington, DC: The Brookings Institution, 2001).
26. Edward L. Glaeser and Matthew Kahn, *Job Sprawl: Employment Location in U.S. Metropolitan Areas* (Washington, DC: The Brookings Institution, 2001).
27. Paul Grogan and Tony Proscio, *Comeback Cities* (Boulder, CO: Westview Press, 2000).

7

Do Middle-Aged Suburbs Need to Reinvent Themselves?

Population growth is not always good for local governments in fiscal capacity, environmental effects, and quality of life. Still, a vague, popular expectation persists that population growth is synonymous with economic health. Population growth, economic health, and stable or rising incomes are expected by many people to occur together.

In the previous chapter, we examined changes in suburbs' income relative to metropolitan income during the 1990s. We discovered that relative income decline often occurred when population increased. In this chapter, we will concentrate on exploring possible explanations of suburban income decline.

SUMMARY OF FINDINGS

To examine the role of age of housing, we classify suburbs by when their housing was constructed. Housing data for suburban places in the 2000 census were broken into six periods of construction: the 1990s, 1980s, 1970s, 1960s, 1940 through 1959, and pre-1940. We classified suburbs in terms of their concentration of housing built during each of these periods compared with when housing was built in their metropolitan area overall. We classified them as specializing in housing of a given time period by 1.5 times more than the metropolitan norm, or 2.0 times more, or 2.5 times or greater.

Three major findings emerged. First, suburbs specializing 1.5 times or more in pre-1940 housing were more likely to increase in relative income than suburbs specialized in any time period except the 1990s. Second, suburbs specializing in 1.5 times or more in 1960s housing were least likely to increase in relative income. Third, suburbs specializing in 1940 through 1959 housing were next least likely to increase in relative income. We hypothesize that when 1950s housing specialization can be isolated—as for census tracts, which we will do in Chapter 8—1950s areas will be approximately as unlikely to increase in relative income as 1960s areas.

We also conducted a factor analysis to include a wider array of housing and demographic variables and to relate them to relative income changes. We found that:

- Large owner-occupied dwellings were most likely to be associated with high relative income in suburbs, and to some extent to be associated with increases in relative income during the 1990s.
- Suburbs characterized by having middle-aged housing that was built in the 1960s and 1970s were associated with declines in relative income in the 1990s.

THREE THEORIES: POPULATION, CONTAGION, AND AGE OF HOUSING

Many suburbs declined in relative income during the 1990s despite population growth. Where population increased, relative per capita income was slightly more likely to decrease than increase between 1990 and 2000. There was a modest association between relative median family income increase and population increase. After eliminating a stable category of suburbs that increased or decreased by 2.5 percent or less, however, suburbs that increased by more than 2.5 percent in population were more likely to decrease than increase in relative median family and per capita income. An exception was that relative income increased in suburbs in which population grew by more than 50 percent. Hence, it is mistaken, as the population growth theory does implicitly, to equate population increase with suburban economic health. In addition, population loss was not associated with ill health in suburbs, at least as far as relative income is concerned.

The contagion theory of suburban decline also is suspect. In the contagion theory, social problems are believed to ooze over the boundary of declining central cities and infect nearby suburbs, leading to the decline of inner suburbs. Two trends between 1990 and 2000 confounded this idea. Many central cities increased in relative income in the 1990s. Hence, they might be in remission, with the jury out as to whether malignant citywide, rather than neighborhood focused, contagious conditions would re-emerge in these cities.

Suburban relative income decline also was widely dispersed geographically in rings 10 to 40 miles from central cities in numerous metropolitan areas, negating the image of cancerous inner suburbs infecting only adjacent suburbs. Myron Orfield also has found widely dispersed patterns of low and moderate income and fiscally stressed suburbs in his study of more than 4,000 suburbs in the 25 largest metropolitan areas.[1] Furthermore, many inner suburbs increased or were stable in relative income, indicating resistance to this nearby contagion that needs to be explained. On the other hand, diversity in suburban income decline may be related to neighborhood decline in sectors of cities as suburbs adjacent to declining city neighborhoods may have negative "push" influences develop on their border.

The third theory is that neighborhoods decline as housing ages and, by extension, that cities and suburbs decline as housing ages. In this study, we turn age of housing in a different direction. Rather than treating housing age from new to old as an explanation of decline in a roughly linear direction, we hypothesize that the decade in which housing was constructed, rather than old housing, seems on preliminary analysis to be useful in explaining some relative income trends. That is, decades of housing construction are not equal or linear in their effects on decline. Suburbs with substantial post-World War II housing appear to have been more vulnerable to relative income decline in the 1990s than suburbs with more older or newer housing. Prior to 1980, suburbs with more pre-1940 housing were more vulnerable to relative income decline. We describe preliminary findings for decade of construction below.

METHODOLOGY

As in the preceding chapter, this study sample includes 2,586 suburbs in 35 metropolitan areas. The 2,586 sample included all the suburbs that had 2,500 or more residents in 1980, and for which data remained available in 1990 and 2000 censuses.

In this study, we use relative median family income and relative per capita income data. Income changes are measured in relative income. That is, incomes of residents in each suburb and central city are measured relative to income for their metropolitan area in 2000 and 1990 and are expressed as a ratio. A ratio of more than 1.0 means that suburbs or cities' income is higher than their metropolitan area's income. A ratio of less than 1.0 means those suburbs' incomes are lower than their metropolitan area's income. The income status of every suburb and central city at each decade can be compared relative to metropolitan income, as can income changes between decades.

In some metropolitan areas, extreme divergence occurred between relative per capita income and relative median family income. In Atlanta, the central city's per capita income ratio was 1.03—3 percent higher than metropolitan per capita income in 2000, but Atlanta's median family income ratio was .63—37 percent below the metropolitan median. Similar income differences are possible in suburbs. However, central cities with their traditional allure for younger, single people and childless couples may have larger gaps than suburbs between per capita and family income measures.

We also define stable suburbs as those with 2.5 percent or less population change in a decade—a 5 percent stable spread. With population changes, we adopted this stable category to avoid exaggerating the number of declines and increases. With income data that are based on a 17 percent sample of households, small differences may be as much a sampling variation issue as a real difference. The 5 percentage point spread for a stable category acknowledges that variation without resorting to computing specific variations for different size suburbs.

DESCRIBING AND EXPLAINING INCOME TRANSITIONS

Previous findings about influences on residential mobility within metropolitan areas have emphasized housing and neighborhood conditions. Housing characteristics have been found in survey research to most often be associated by respondents with reasons for moving from their residential locations. Consequently, indicators of housing conditions should be included in any attempt to describe, explain, or predict which conditions may influence relative income changes through residential mobility. Relevant housing conditions involve tenure, size, cost, and quality. The timing of moves often is triggered by life-cycle changes, such as marriage, births, children leaving home, divorce, and death of one spouse. Many researchers have contributed to this perspective, including Adams; Clark and Burt; Farley; Frey; Galster; Goodman; Guest; Logan; Michelson; Rossi and Shlay; Spain; Speare, Goldstein, and Frey; and Varady and Raffel.[2]

Neighborhood conditions that may influence moving decisions include safety; schools; race and ethnicity; access and convenience; exterior housing conditions;

street noise; sanitation; and traffic, transportation alternatives, and architectural ambiance. These conditions are complex. Residents' interpretations of conditions will vary with personal preferences. Conditions change, and residents process clues about changes that may, or may not, indicate future changes. More research has been conducted about reasons for moving from a residence than about reasons for choosing the next residence. One exception is the research of Thomas Bier, in which he discovered strong tendencies for sellers of residences in metropolitan areas to buy larger, more expensive residences farther from central cities.[3] In its survey of home buyers' reasons for choosing a residence, the National Association of Home Builders has found that safety is the most important neighborhood influence.[4]

Neighborhood conditions with potential to influence income trends can be summarized in two concepts. One concept focuses on individuals' decisions and states that people will weigh "pushes and pulls," which incline them to avoid perceived problems ("pushes") and to seek better conditions ("pulls"). Because individuals are the units of decision, one should expect a variety of influences within a group of individuals that may vary by region of the nation, from one metropolitan area to another, and among categories of individuals differentiated by age, race, income, gender, family status, and other characteristics. The spatial effect of these influences has tended to be that older areas are preferred less often than newer settlements by people who can afford more expensive housing choices. Relative income decreases in older areas and relative income increases in newer ones have been common outcomes of mobility decisions.

The second concept—the trickle-down process of neighborhood change—emphasizes housing and, by extension, neighborhood physical characteristics. Most new housing is built at costs affordable by middle- to upper-income households and is too expensive for low- and moderate-income households to purchase. Housing filtering subsequently occurs. The filtering concept has been used to describe life-cycle changes of households and dwellings.[5] As a household moves up (filters up) in housing quality and cost, a vacancy chain is created, permitting another household to move into vacated housing. Households throughout the income spectrum can improve their housing quality, provided housing supply overall keeps up with or exceeds demand. If demand exceeds supply, prices will rise. If supply exceeds demand, prices will fall.

As housing ages, it needs more maintenance to sustain its quality. If affluence in society has increased, and housing technology has changed, or preferences have changed, then the housing of any era will tend to deteriorate physically as middle- and upper-income households choose housing better suited to current tastes and that embodies less physical deterioration. These physically driven transitions are from higher to lower incomes in housing and, by extension, in neighborhoods. Typically, these physical changes are accompanied by social changes, which lead to deterioration of neighborhood social conditions that may speed up physical deterioration through inadequate reinvestment. This neighborhood change process often is referred to as the trickle-down neighborhood change process.[6] The life cycle of households influences their housing preferences. The life cycle of neighborhoods transitions from better to worse quality as dwellings age, unless substantial reinvestment interrupts or lengthens neighborhood viability. Age of housing is a key indicator of the process of neighborhood decline in this theory.

These "push-pull" and neighborhood change theories identify decisions of individual households as the active agents of changes. Spatial data embody aggregate information about individuals, families, and households for places rather than providing direct information about households' reasons for moving. Interpretations of aggregate outcomes, therefore, depend upon inferences about reasons for decisions by individuals, families, and households. At some stage, closing this gap with direct information about moving and relocating decisions also would be useful.

SCALE AND TIME

These theories have a common-sense plausibility to them. Measuring these conditions, however, is not a simple matter. Indicators must be chosen. The specification of indicators of a given housing condition may affect findings, and findings about income or population changes in relation to housing characteristics have not been consistent.

Scale of analysis may be one of the distinctions that matters. Our own previous work, for example, has dealt with three scales. In an analysis of median family income change between central cities and outside central cities in 147 metropolitan areas from 1960 to 1980, we found that old housing mattered. A wider gap in the percentage of pre-1940 housing between central cities and outside central cities was associated with a growing gap in relative median family income—to the disadvantage of the central cities with more old housing. However, in an analysis of income change in 554 suburbs in 24 metropolitan areas from 1960 to 1990, we found that neither the percentage of pre-1940 housing nor the percentage of pre-1960 housing was associated with relative median family income decline in suburbs. Just as many suburbs went up as down in relative median family income based on their percentages of old housing relative to the metropolitan percentages.[7]

In another study, we analyzed income changes at census tract scale—usually 3,000 to 5,000 residents—between 1980 and 1990 in 770 census tracts in three metropolitan areas in Virginia. There we found the opposite of the predicted direction of change. Census tracts with substantial amounts of pre-1940 housing tended to go up in income, sometimes at rapid rates, even if they were in central cities that were experiencing substantial citywide relative median family income decline. Conversely, it was in suburbs where post-World War II housing (1950 to 1969) was prominent that relative median family income decline was most common and substantial. Thus, scale of analysis (central city versus outside central city, suburbs versus other suburbs, or census tracts versus other census tracts) may matter.[8]

Time also may matter. Conditions in the 1980s and 1990s may have been considerably different than in the 1960s or 1970s. Indeed, if something about post-World War II housing and neighborhoods where such housing is prominent had acquired characteristics amounting to "push" factors, the passage of time would lead to more deterioration in later decades, following the trickle-down process of neighborhood change. In addition, perhaps some problems with suburban sprawl (traffic, commuting time, stress, and public school costs) led to some old central city neighborhoods having more appeal to a growing segment of persons in the housing market, leading in the 1980s and 1990s to more of those old neighborhoods rising in relative income. Perhaps images of good community patterns also have shifted toward more people seeking mixed land-use settings with more functions and activities within walking distance and within reach of public transportation.

DECADE OF HOUSING CONSTRUCTION
AND RELATIVE INCOME CHANGES

We hypothesized that suburbs with a large proportion of housing built in the 1950s and 1960s would tend to be declining in relative income in the 1990s. We based this prediction on our previous findings at the scale of census tract analysis for changes in metropolitan areas in Virginia in the 1980s. We also based it on our judgment that these declines occurred for two reasons: one involving housing and the other involving neighborhoods. For housing, size and quality are likely to influence location decisions. In 1950, the median size, new, single-unit house was 1,100 square feet. By 1970, it still was only 1,375 feet. By 2000, the median size was 2,000 square feet, and the average size was considerably larger. Moreover, the typical 1950 house lacked air conditioning, had one bathroom, its kitchen was outmoded by current standards, and it had other deficiencies. These limitations in size and quality seem certain to influence location decisions of contemporary buyers who, when they buy new houses, are purchasing structures nearly twice the size of the 1950 house.[9]

Neighborhood effects are less clear, partly because many involve social problems rather than physical ones. Still, physical characteristics have some effects, and they are also associated with social problems. The typical 1950s and 1960s neighborhoods were designed as single-use, residential-only districts, where walking to other functions and activities was difficult. They often were inconvenient to public transportation, although not as inconvenient as neighborhoods constructed in subsequent decades. Unless they have attracted substantial reinvestment, the physical structures have deteriorated. Aesthetic charm is likely to be limited. These characteristics may have been attractive previously, partly because they were associated with middle-class occupants of the housing. As the housing aged and the neighborhood became less competitive with newer neighborhoods, the middle-income character of the occupants has eroded, and the "push" qualities of some neighborhoods increased. Consequently, some neighborhoods will be less competitive than previously due to housing and neighborhood conditions.

If these deficiencies of 1950s and 1960s neighborhoods have increased, then some older, pre-1940 neighborhoods may have become more attractive in comparison. Older neighborhoods sometimes have larger houses with more character. They are in neighborhoods that are more walkable and accessible by public transportation. Unless social problems counteract these assets, some of these neighborhoods are likely to make comebacks. These comebacks will occur in suburbs, just as they occur in some central city neighborhoods. Because suburbs are smaller, if they have enough of the positive aspects of these pre-1940 neighborhood characteristics, suburbs' potential for seeing overall increases in relative income may be better than the prospects of cities.

Our preliminary findings are consistent with these interpretations. In this narrative, we will emphasize relative income changes in suburbs with substantially more than the typical amount of a given period's housing proportion. The full arrays of income changes by decade of construction proportionate to metropolitan norms are displayed in Tables 7.1 through 7.3.

The clearest distinctions can be seen in comparing findings for pre-1940s, 1960s, and 1990s housing proportions. For suburbs with 2.5 or more times the typical metropolitan share of pre-1940s housing, for example, 65.6 percent increased in relative median family income between 1990 and 2000. If the suburbs had 2.0 to 2.5 times the typical proportion, then 55.7 percent of them increased in relative median family income. This contrasted with suburbs with less than 0.5 (one-half) the typical proportion, among which 45.2 percent increased.

The opposite tendency occurred where 1960s housing predominated, but to a considerably greater degree. In each of the categories of substantially higher proportions of 1960s housing than the metropolitan norms (1.5 to 2.0 times, 2.0 to 2.5 times, and 2.5 or more times), only 23.7 percent to 33.9 percent of those suburbs increased in relative median family income in the 1990s. This means that two-thirds to three-fourths of them declined in relative income (Table 7.1).

On the other hand, in suburbs where new housing construction was common in the 1990s, meeting contemporary preferences, relative median family income usually increased (78.9 percent of instances with 2.5 or more times the typical proportion of 1990s housing and 69.7 percent where the suburbs' housing stock exceeded the metropolitan norm by 2.0 to 2.5 times). Differences among these decades of construction and the relative income change trends can be seen in Figure 7.1.

The proportions of increase and decrease for the other decades fell between these extremes in the direction hypothesized. Because data are not available for the 1950s alone, inferences are limited at the scale of suburbs. The 1950 decade of construction data are combined with the 1940s in the 2000 census. Still, the tendency appears for suburbs with substantial proportions of such housing to decline in relative median family income (only 42.7, 41.2, and 42.5 percent of suburbs with 1.5 or more times the typical proportion of such housing rose in relative median family income in the 1990s). We hypothesize, however, that there would be differences between the 1940s and 1950s. We think the 1940s housing may be less distinctive in its income trend, and that the 1950s housing may be more like the 1960s housing in the downward income trend of its suburbs. We anticipate that the 1940s housing had more location advantages, there was less of it, and it was more diverse in construction characteristics, including size, than the 1950s housing. We expect that the 1950s housing was more uniform in style, with more small houses, and more often dominated the character of substantial proportions of some suburbs. To get at these hypotheses, we will separate the 1940s from the 1950s housing in a census tract analysis in Chapter 8.

Data for the relative income status of suburbs in 1990 and 2000 are consistent with traditional theories that, as housing ages, it tends to be occupied by persons of lower incomes. Suburbs with the most pre-1940 housing were most likely to be below the metropolitan median family income level in 1990. Suburbs with a great deal of housing built in the 1970s, 1980s, and 1990s were most likely to be above the metropolitan median family income level. The same tendency with respect to suburbs with new housing occurred in 2000. Suburbs with substantial amounts of pre-1940 housing were more likely to increase in relative median family income than any except suburbs where 1990s housing was prevalent (Table 7.1). Neighborhoods with at least 2.5 times the metropolitan proportion of pre-1940 housing had revived enough by 2000, so that in sum they ranked nearly as high in relative income as neighborhoods specializing in 1940s and 1950s housing (Figure 7.2).

Table 7.1
Suburbs Increasing in Relative Median Family Income 1990 to 2000 by Specialization of Period of Housing Unit Construction

| Period of Construction | Degree of Specialization | | | |
	1.0 to 1.5	1.5 to 2.0	2.0 to 2.5	More than 2.5
Pre-1940				
Suburbs	416	232	97	96
Increasing Suburbs	224	125	54	63
Percent Increasing	53.8%	53.9%	55.7%	65.6%
1940-1959				
Suburbs	703	344	148	82
Increasing Suburbs	332	147	61	35
Percent Increasing	47.2%	42.7%	41.2%	42.7%
1960s				
Suburbs	777	336	129	76
Increasing Suburbs	348	114	36	18
Percent Increasing	44.8%	33.9%	27.9%	23.7%
1970s				
Suburbs	712	309	118	55
Increasing Suburbs	329	131	54	32
Percent Increasing	46.2%	42.4%	45.8%	58.2%
1980s				
Suburbs	596	217	110	79
Increasing Suburbs	312	109	59	47
Percent Increasing	52.3%	50.2%	53.6%	59.5%
Since 1990				
Suburbs	408	241	119	147
Increasing Suburbs	220	165	83	116
Percent Increasing	53.9%	68.5%	69.7%	78.9%

Specialization in Decade of Occupied Housing Construction uses data reported in the *Census of Population and Housing 2000.* Degree of Specialization is calculated as the suburb percent of housing units built in a period divided by the metropolitan percent of housing units built in the same period.

A specialization of 2.5 indicates a suburb has two and one-half times the metropolitan percentage of housing built in that period.

Sources: U.S. Census Bureau, *Census 2000,* Demographic Profiles: 100-percent and Sample Data, issued May 2002, for each separate state, www2.census.gov/census_2000/datasets/100_and_sample_profile; CensusCD 1990 (East Brunswick, NJ: GeoLytics, Inc., 2000).

Figure 7.1
Percent of Suburbs Increasing in Relative Median Family Income 1990 to 2000

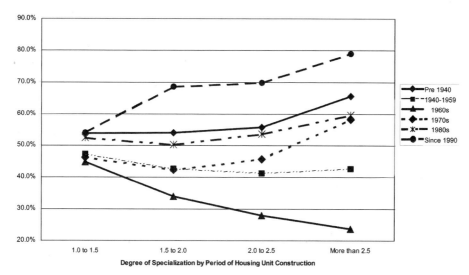

Degree of Specialization is calculated as the suburb percent of housing units built in a period divided by the metropolitan percent of housing units built in the same period. Data shown are for suburbs with more than their share of housing built in the period.

Sources: U.S. Census Bureau, *Census 2000,* Demographic Profiles: 100-percent and Sample Data, issued May 2002, for each separate state, www2.census.gov/census_2000/datasets/ 100_and_sample_profile; CensusCD 1990 (East Brunswick, NJ: GeoLytics, Inc., 2000).

Figure 7.2
Percent of Suburbs Above Metropolitan Median Family Income 2000

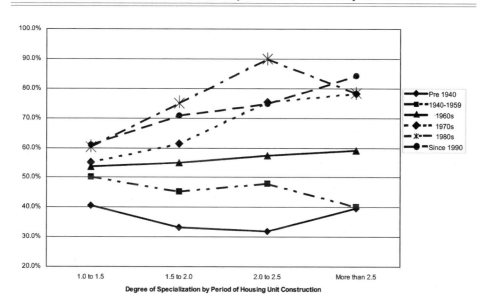

Degree of Specialization is calculated as the suburb percent of housing units built in a period divided by the metropolitan percent of housing units built in the same period. Data shown are for suburbs with more than their share of housing built in the period.

Source: U.S. Census Bureau, *Census 2000,* Demographic Profiles: 100-percent and Sample Data, issued May 2002, for each separate state, www2.census.gov/census_2000/datasets/ 100_and_sample_profile.

The support evidenced for traditional theories that age of housing is associated with declining incomes in a roughly linear manner adds to the interest in the converse finding for relative median family income changes in the 1990s. These income change and status patterns are similar for relative per capita income, but with stronger gains for pre-1940s suburbs (Table 7.2 and Figure 7.3). Suburbs with 1.5 times or more of the metropolitan proportion of pre-1940s housing were more likely to increase in relative per capita income in the 1990s than all but the suburbs with large proportions of 1990s housing. By 2000, suburbs with more than 2.5 times the metropolitan proportion of pre-1940s housing had passed suburbs with 2.5 times the metropolitan proportion of 1940s and 1950s housing in relative per capita income (Table 7.3 and Figure 7.4).

FACTORS IN DIFFERENTIATING NEIGHBORHOODS

Decade of housing construction is meaningful for its associations. As discussed previously, we associate pre-1940 housing with mixed-use, walkable, public transit-accessible neighborhoods. The quality and size of the pre-1940 housing will be diverse, including more multifamily units than housing built after World War II. We expect housing built from 1945 to 1970 to be relatively small, modestly equipped, somewhat out of fashion, and located with intermediate levels of walkability and accessibility compared with more recent housing, but with markedly less mixed use and accessibility than pre-1940 housing and neighborhoods. Post-1970 housing and, in particular, post-1980 housing, will be larger and more contemporary in structural elements and design, but it will be considerably less accessible than earlier housing—more consistently single use and considerably farther from land uses and activities other than housing. On the other hand, pre-1940 neighborhoods are more likely to have social issues, racial and ethnic diversity, and uncertain ambiance.

As awareness of suburban diversity has spread, attempts to classify suburbs to clarify diversity have increased. These efforts have been summarized usefully by Brian A. Mikelbank, who also conducted clustering and discriminating procedures to develop a new classification array.[10] Mikelbank included several housing variables, and found that a type of aging suburb tended to be successful, which he defined as including "higher incomes and higher rates of bachelor's degrees."[11] He observed that "the defining characteristic of Aging suburbs is that their population and housing are older and more densely settled."[12] To identify aging suburbs, Mikelbank relied on one indicator: median age of housing.[13]

We conducted a factor analysis to focus on housing and transport accessibility characteristics. The variables used are listed in Table 7.4. For age of housing, we used decade of construction, and pre-1940 construction, rather than median age of housing. We collapsed 21 variables into six factors that described 76 percent of the variation in the original 21 indicators (Table 7.5). These independent factors were then correlated with our measures of poverty, population change, and income. Suburbia often is characterized as the location of large, single-family, detached, owner-occupied dwellings. Factor #1, "Owner-Occupied Housing & Multiple Vehicles," distinguishes these suburbs from their opposite—suburbs with high proportions of apartments and renters. Factor #2, "New Housing," distinguishes suburbs by when their housing was built, which often was dominated by housing built during two or three most recent decades. The highest positive factor loadings (.85 and .79) are asso-

Table 7.2
Suburbs Increasing in Relative Per Capita Income 1990 to
2000 by Specialization of Period of Housing Unit Construction

	Degree of Specialization			
	1.0 to 1.5	1.5 to 2.0	2.0 to 2.5	More than 2.5
Period of Construction				
Pre-1940				
Suburbs	416	232	97	96
Increasing Suburbs	203	129	54	54
Percent Increasing	48.8%	55.6%	55.7%	56.3%
1940-1959				
Suburbs	703	344	148	82
Increasing Suburbs	317	128	48	32
Percent Increasing	45.1%	37.2%	32.4%	39.0%
1960s				
Suburbs	777	336	129	76
Increasing Suburbs	324	120	37	26
Percent Increasing	41.7%	35.7%	28.7%	34.2%
1970s				
Suburbs	712	309	118	55
Increasing Suburbs	328	126	58	31
Percent Increasing	46.1%	40.8%	49.2%	56.4%
1980s				
Suburbs	596	217	110	79
Increasing Suburbs	299	104	56	36
Percent Increasing	50.2%	47.9%	50.9%	45.6%
Since 1990				
Suburbs	408	241	119	147
Increasing Suburbs	210	151	84	103
Percent Increasing	51.5%	62.7%	70.6%	70.1%

Specialization in Decade of Occupied Housing Construction uses data reported in the *Census of Population and Housing 2000*. Degree of Specialization is calculated as the suburb percent of housing units built in a period divided by the metropolitan percent of housing units built in the same period.

A specialization of 2.5 indicates a suburb has two and one-half times the metropolitan percentage of housing built in that period.

Sources: U.S. Census Bureau, *Census 2000,* Demographic Profiles: 100-percent and Sample Data, issued May 2002, for each separate state, www2.census.gov/census_2000/datasets/100_and_sample_profile; CensusCD 1990 (East Brunswick, NJ: GeoLytics, Inc., 2000).

Figure 7.3
Percent of Suburbs Increasing in Relative Per Capita Income 1990 to 2000

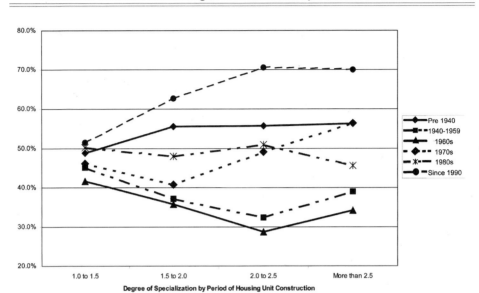

Degree of Specialization is calculated as the suburb percent of housing units built in a period divided by the metropolitan percent of housing units built in the same period. Data shown are for suburbs with more than their share of housing built in the period.

Sources: U.S. Census Bureau, *Census 2000,* Demographic Profiles: 100-percent and Sample Data, issued May 2002, for each separate state, www2.census.gov/census_2000/datasets/ 100_and_sample_profile; CensusCD 1990 (East Brunswick, NJ: GeoLytics, Inc., 2000).

Table 7.3
Suburbs above Metropolitan Per Capita Income in 2000
by Specialization of Period of Housing Unit Construction

	Degree of Specialization			
	1.0 to 1.5	**1.5 to 2.0**	**2.0 to 2.5**	**More than 2.5**
Period of Construction				
Pre-1940				
Suburbs	416	232	97	96
Suburbs above Metro Median	143	66	31	39
Percent Above	34.4%	28.4%	32.0%	40.6%
1940-1959				
Suburbs	703	344	148	82
Suburbs above Metro Median	299	123	60	27
Percent Above	42.5%	35.8%	40.5%	32.9%
1960s				
Suburbs	777	336	129	76
Suburbs above Metro Median	335	160	59	34
Percent Above	43.1%	47.6%	45.7%	44.7%
1970s				
Suburbs	712	309	118	55
Suburbs above Metro Median	316	163	70	28
Percent Above	44.4%	52.8%	59.3%	50.9%
1980s				
Suburbs	596	217	110	79
Suburbs above Metro Median	280	137	82	56
Percent Above	47.0%	63.1%	74.5%	70.9%
Since 1990				
Suburbs	408	241	119	147
Suburbs above Metro Median	196	134	65	98
Percent Above	48.0%	55.6%	54.6%	66.7%

Specialization in Decade of Occupied Housing Construction uses data reported in the *Census of Population and Housing 2000.* Degree of Specialization is calculated as the suburb percent of housing units built in a period divided by the metropolitan percent of housing units built in the same period.

A specialization of 2.5 indicates a suburb has two and one-half times the metropolitan percentage of housing built in that period.

Sources: U.S. Census Bureau, *Census 2000,* Demographic Profiles: 100-percent and Sample Data, issued May 2002, for each separate state, www2.census.gov/census_2000/datasets/100_and_sample_profile.

Figure 7.4
Percent of Suburbs Above Metropolitan Per Capita Income 2000

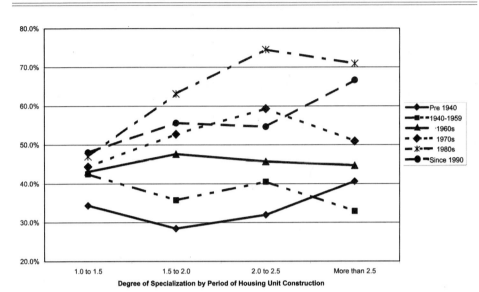

Degree of Specialization is calculated as the suburb percent of housing units built in a period divided by the metropolitan percent of housing units built in the same period. Data shown are for suburbs with more than their share of housing built in the period.

Source: U.S. Census Bureau, *Census 2000,* Demographic Profiles: 100-percent and Sample Data, issued May 2002, for each separate state, www2.census.gov/census_2000/datasets/100_and_sample_profile.

**Table 7.4
Variables Used in Factor Analysis of Suburbs**

Variables Used for Housing Stock Analysis

1. Percent Occupied Housing Units
2. Percent Vacant Housing Units
3. Percent Owner-Occupied Housing Units
4. Percent Renter-Occupied Housing Units
5. Percent of Workers Driving Alone
6. Percent of Workers Taking Public Transit
7. Mean Time to Work
8. Percent 1-Unit, Detached Housing Units
9. Percent 1-Unit, Attached Housing Units
10. Percent 20 Units or More Structures
11. Percent Mobile Homes
12. Percent of Units Built Since 1990
13. Percent of Units Built Between 1980 and 1990
14. Percent of Units Built Between 1970 and 1980
15. Percent of Units Built Between 1960 and 1970
16. Percent of Units Built Between 1940 and 1960
17. Percent of Units Built in 1939 or Earlier
18. Median Rooms in Unit
19. Percent of Occupied Units with No Vehicle
20. Percent of Occupied Units with 1 to 2 Vehicles
21. Percent of Occupied Units with 3 or More Vehicles

Variables Used for Correlation of Factors with

1. Median Owner-Occupied Unit Value 2000
2. Median Rent 2000
3. Median Household Income in 2000
4. Median Family Income in 2000
5. Per Capita Income in 2000
6. 2000 Family Poverty Rate
7. 2000 Personal Poverty Rate
8. Relative Median Household Income in 2000
9. Relative Median Family Income in 2000
10. Relative Per Capita Income in 2000
11. Change in Relative Median Family Income Between 1990 and 2000
12. Change in Relative Median Household Income Between 1990 and 2000
13. Change in Relative Per Capita Income Between 1990 and 2000
14. Change in Relative Median Family Income Between 1980 and 2000
15. Change in Relative Median Household Income Between 1980 and 2000
16. Change in Relative Per Capita Income Between 1980 and 2000

Sources: U.S. Census Bureau, *Census 2000,* Demographic Profiles: 100-percent and Sample Data, issued May 2002, for each separate state, www2.census.gov/census_2000/datasets/100_and_sample_profile; CensusCD 1980 (East Brunswick, NJ: GeoLytics, Inc., 1999) and CensusCD 1990 (East Brunswick, NJ: GeoLytics, Inc., 2000).

Table 7.5
Loadings of Variables on Housing Factors

| | Rotated Component Matrix | | | | | |
| | Factors | | | | | |
	#1 Owner-Occupied Housing & Multiple Vehicles	#2 New Housing	#3 Robust Housing Markets	#4 Transit-Oriented Suburbs	#5 Middle-Aged Housing	#6 Townhouse-Dominated Suburbs
1. Percent Occupied Housing Units	**	**	0.81	**	**	**
2. Percent Vacant Housing Units	-0.35	**	-0.77	**	-0.22	**
3. Percent Owner-Occupied Housing Units	0.92	**	**	**	**	**
4. Percent Renter-Occupied Housing Units	-0.92	**	**	**	**	**
5. Percent of Workers Driving Alone	0.43	**	**	-0.76	**	**
6. Percent of Workers Taking Public Transit	-0.21	-0.29	**	0.84	**	**
7. Mean Time to Work	0.26	**	**	0.77	**	**
8. Percent 1-Unit, Detached Housing Units	0.87	**	**	**	**	-0.30
9. Percent 1-Unit, Attached Housing Units	**	0.22	**	**	**	0.88
10. Percent 20 Units or More Structures	-0.68	**	-0.26	**	0.21	-0.50
11. Percent Mobile Homes	**	0.38	**	**	**	**
12. Percent of Units Built Since 1990	**	0.79	**	**	-0.22	**
13. Percent of Units Built Between 1980 and 1990	**	0.85	**	**	**	**
14. Percent of Units Built Between 1970 and 1980	**	0.58	**	**	0.61	**
15. Percent of Units Built Between 1960 and 1970	**	-0.31	**	**	0.84	**
16. Percent of Units Built Between 1940 and 1960	**	-0.84	**	**	**	**
17. Percent of Units Built in 1939 or Earlier	**	-0.49	**	**	-0.66	**
18. Median Rooms in Unit	0.86	**	**	**	**	**
19. Percent of Occupied Units with No Vehicle	-0.66	-0.32	-0.39	0.26	**	**
20. Percent of Occupied Units with 1 to 2 Vehicles	**	**	0.85	-0.25	**	**
21. Percent of Occupied Units with 3 or More Vehicle	0.75	**	**	**	0.32	**

Extraction Method: Principal Component Analysis.
Rotation Method: Varimax with Kaiser Normalization.
Rotation converged in 6 iterations.
**Factor loading less than .2.

Source: U.S. Census Bureau, *Census 2000*, Demographic Profiles: 100-percent and Sample Data, issued May 2002, for each separate state, www2.census.gov/census_2000/datasets/100_and_sample_profile.

ciated with suburbs with housing built in the 1980s and 1990s, while the high negative score (–.84) associated with suburbs with 1940s and 1950s housing indicates that few suburbs had substantial amounts of housing built during both periods. The score for suburbs with pre-1940 housing (–.49) indicates that more of these suburbs had housing built in the 1980s and 1990s than did suburbs built substantially in the 1940s and 1950s. We speculate that some infill development occurred, especially in the 1990s, blurring the housing age distinctiveness of pre-1940 suburbs.

Factor #5, "Middle-Aged Housing," separated suburbs with a high proportion of housing built in the 1960s and 1970s. Thus, two housing age factors (Factor #2 at 15 percent and Factor #5 at 9 percent) accounted for 24 percent of the housing variation among the suburbs. Factor #6, "Townhouse-Dominated Suburbs," also identified an aspect of physical structures. These suburbs were concentrated around major cities: Boston, Chicago, Los Angeles, Philadelphia, San Francisco, and Washington, D.C. The other factors—Factor #3, "Robust Housing Markets" and Factor #4, "Transit-Oriented Suburbs"—identified market demand and neighborhood access as characteristics that distinguished suburbs from each other.

The strongest correlations were between Factor #1 that reflected larger, owner-occupied, single-unit housing and relative income indicators. Size was measured by the median number of rooms in all housing in each suburb. The correlations in 2000 were .55 with higher median family income, .40 with higher per capita income and .49 with lower family poverty and this large, single-unit, owner-occupied housing factor. For change between 1980 and 2000, the correlation with increasing relative median family income was .34, and it was .21 between 1990 and 2000 (Table 7.6 for these and other correlations below). Owner occupancy and larger size were associated with higher relative incomes and less poverty, regardless of housing age.

Considering housing age independently, suburbs with concentrations of housing constructed between 1960 and 1979, with little housing built before 1940, were most strongly correlated (.26), significantly though weakly, with relative income decline between 1990 and 2000. Perhaps the correlation would have been stronger had we been able to isolate housing built from 1950 to 1969. The census place profiles aggregated housing built between 1940 and 1959, preventing our preferred 1950 to 1969 combination from being calculated.

It is worth noting that size and age emerged as separate factors in the analysis. Age provides only limited guidance about size of housing measured by median number of rooms in all housing. Age and size of single-unit housing are associated, as we have discussed previously, but both new and old housing include many multi-family units that have fewer rooms than single-unit housing. According to the 2000 census, the median number of rooms in all occupied housing was 5.4; however, in owner-occupied housing, the median number of rooms was 6.1, while it was 4.0 in renter-occupied housing. Considering only bedrooms rather than all rooms, 4.6 percent of renter-occupied housing had four or more bedrooms compared with 24.4 percent of owner-occupied housing. Thus, new housing is not all large, mainly because it includes considerable multiunit rental housing. Middle-aged housing, while small, includes both single-unit housing and multiunit housing. There probably has been less variation over time in the number of rooms and square footage in multiunit than in single-unit housing.

Table 7.6
Correlations of Housing Factors with Population Growth, Housing, Poverty, and Income Indicators

	Housing Factors					
	#1 Owner-Occupied Housing & Multiple Vehicles	#2 New Housing	#3 Robust Housing Markets	#4 Transit-Oriented Suburbs	#5 Middle-Aged Housing	#6 Townhouse-Dominated Suburbs
Population Indicators						
Change 1980-1990	**	0.43	**	**	**	**
Change 1990-2000	**	0.42	**	**	**	**
Change 1980-2000	**	0.46	**	**	**	**
Percent Change 1980-1990	**	0.60	**	**	**	**
Percent Change 1990-2000	**	0.49	**	**	**	**
Percent Change 1980-2000	**	0.60	**	**	**	**
Housing Indicators						
Median Value Owner-Occupied Housing 2000	0.29	**	**	0.36	**	**
Median Contract Rent 2000	0.37	**	0.27	0.39	**	**
Poverty Indicators						
Family Poverty Rate 2000	-0.49	**	-0.54	**	**	**
Person Poverty Rate 2000	-0.54	**	-0.53	**	**	**
Income Indicators						
Relative Median Household Income 2000	0.63	**	0.26	**	**	**
Relative Median Family Income 2000	0.55	**	0.27	**	**	**
Relative Per Capita Income 2000	0.40	**	0.20	**	**	**
Change in Income Indicators						
Relative Median Household Income 1990-2000	**	**	**	**	-0.30	**
Relative Median Family Income 1990-2000	0.21	**	**	**	-0.26	**
Relative Per Capita Income 1990-2000	**	**	**	**	-0.24	**
Relative Median Household Income 1980-2000	0.27	0.21	**	**	-0.32	**
Relative Median Family Income 1980-2000	0.34	0.22	**	**	-0.24	**
Relative Per Capita Income 1980-2000	0.38	0.21	**	**	**	**

Sources: U.S. Census Bureau, *Census 2000,* Demographic Profiles: 100-percent and Sample Data, issued May 2002, for each separate state, www2.census.gov/census_2000/datasets/100_and_sample_profile; CensusCD 1980 (East Brunswick, NJ: GeoLytics, Inc., 1999) and CensusCD 1990 (East Brunswick, NJ: GeoLytics, Inc., 2000).

INTERPRETATION

These findings about the relevance of decade of housing construction and size of housing variables begin to support our hypothesis that housing and neighborhood continue to influence location decisions but in a somewhat altered pattern. Middle-aged housing stands out as a distinct and problematic characteristic of some suburbs. Positive and negative effects of decade of housing construction on relative income, poverty, and relative housing value also may be influenced by numerous aspects of neighborhood context.

What will be discovered by separating construction decade data for the 1950s from the 1940s, and from extending the income change analysis backward to include the 1980s, supplementing changes observed in the 1990s? What happened at census tract scale where decade of construction differences were more pronounced than for suburbs, which usually are larger than census tracts? We address these questions in Chapter 8.

NOTES

1. Myron Orfield, *American Metropolitics* (Washington, DC: The Brookings Institution, 2002).
2. John S. Adams, *Housing America in the 1980s* (New York: Russell Sage Foundation, 1987); W.A.V. Clark and James Burt, *The Impact of Workplace on Residential Relocation.* Annals of the Association of American Geographers 70, no. 1 (March 1980), pp. 59-67; Reynolds Farley, "Suburban Persistence," *American Sociological Review* 29 (February 1964), pp. 38-47; William H. Frey, "Central City White Flight: Racial and Nonracial Causes," *American Sociological Review* 44 (June 1979), pp. 425-448; George C. Galster, *Homeowners and Neighborhood Reinvestment* (Durham, NC: Duke University Press, 1987); John L. Goodman, Jr., "Reasons for Moves out of and into Large Cities," *Journal of the American Planning Association* 45, no. 4 (Autumn 1979), pp. 407-416; Avery M. Guest, "Suburban Social Status: Persistence or Evolution," *American Sociological Review* 43 (1978), pp. 251-264; John R. Logan, "Industrialization and the Stratification of Cities in Suburban Regions," *American Journal of Sociology* 82, no. 2 (1976), pp. 333-348; William Michelson, *Environmental Choice, Human Behavior, and Residential Satisfaction* (New York: Oxford University Press, 1977); Peter H. Rossi and Anne B. Shlay, "Residential Mobility and Public Policy Issues: 'Why Families Move' Revisited," *Journal of Social Issues* 38, no. 3 (1982), pp. 21-34; Daphne Spain, "Why Higher Income Households Move to Central Cities," *Journal of Urban Affairs* 11, no. 3 (1989), pp. 283-299; Alden Speare, Jr., Sidney Goldstein, and William H. Frey, *Residential Mobility, Migration and Metropolitan Change* (Cambridge, MA: Ballinger, 1974); David P. Varady and Jeffrey A. Raffel, *Selling Cities: Attracting Homebuyers through Schools and Housing Programs* (Albany: State University of New York Press, 1995).
3. Thomas Bier, *Moving Up, Filtering Down: Metropolitan Housing Dynamics and Public Policy* (Washington, DC: The Brookings Institution, 2001).
4. Dowell Myers and Elizabeth Gearin, "Current Preferences and Future Demand for Denser Residential Environments," *Housing Policy Debate* 12, no. 4 (2001), pp. 633-659.
5. George Galster, "William Grigsby and the Analysis of Housing Sub-markets and Filtering," *Urban Studies* 33, no. 10 (1996), p. 1800.
6. Anthony Downs, *Neighborhoods and Urban Development* (Washington, DC: The Brookings Institution, 1981); John P. Blair, *Urban and Regional Economics* (Homewood, IL: Irwin, 1991); George Galster, "William Grigsby and the Analysis of Housing Sub-markets and Filtering," *Urban Studies* 33, no. 10 (1996), pp. 1797-1805; Truman Asa Hartshorn, *Interpreting the City: An Urban Geography* (New York: John Wiley & Sons, 1992); Alan M. Hay, "The Economic Basis of Spontaneous Home Improvement: a Graphical Analysis," *Urban Studies* 18 (1981),

pp. 359-364; Colin Jones, Chris Leishman, and Craig Watkins, "Intra-Urban Migration and Housing Submarkets: Theory and Evidence," *Housing Studies* 19, no. 2 (2004), pp. 269-283; John Knox, *Urbanization: An Introduction to Urban Geography* (Englewood Cliffs, NJ: Prentice-Hall, 1994); Harry L. Margulis, "Predicting the Growth and Filtering of At-risk Housing: Ageing, Poverty and Redlining," *Urban Studies*, 35, no. 8 (1998), pp. 1231-1258; Edwin S. Mills, *Urban Economics* (Glenview, IL: Scott, Foresman and Company, 1980); Harvey S. Perloff, "The Development of Urban Economics in the United States," *Urban Studies* 10 (1973), pp. 289-301.

7. David L. Phillips and William H. Lucy. "Suburban Decline Described and Interpreted, 1960 to 1990: 554 Suburbs in the 24 Largest Metropolitan Areas." Report to the Center for Urban Development (Richmond: Virginia Commonwealth University, 1996).

8. William H. Lucy and David L. Phillips, "The Post-Suburban Era in the Hampton Roads Region: City Decline, Suburban Transition, and Farmland Loss." Report to the Center for Urban Development (Richmond: Virginia Commonwealth University, 1996); William H. Lucy and David L. Phillips, "The Post-Suburban Era in the Richmond-Petersburg Region: City Decline, Suburban Transition, and Farmland Loss." Report to the Center for Urban Development (Richmond: Virginia Commonwealth University, 1996); William H. Lucy and David L. Phillips, "The Post-Suburban Era in the Northern Virginia Region: City Decline, Suburban Transition, and Farmland Loss." Report to the Center for Urban Development (Richmond: Virginia Commonwealth University, 1996).

9. William H. Lucy and David L. Phillips, *Confronting Suburban Decline: Strategic Planning for Metropolitan Renewal* (Washington, DC: Island Press, 2000).

10. Brian A. Mikelbank, "A Typology of U.S. Suburban Places," *Housing Policy Debate* 15, no. 4 (2004), pp. 935-964.

11. Ibid., p. 953.

12. Ibid., p. 956.

13. Ibid., p. 945.

8

Discovering Virtues
of Old Neighborhoods

The era when housing was constructed has influenced the attractiveness of suburbs to middle- and upper-income families and individuals. Suburbs with housing constructed in the 1950s and especially the 1960s often signaled declining relative incomes in the 1990s. If housing and neighborhood characteristics influenced the ability of suburbs to compete for residents in the 1990s, then similar influences should operate and be discernible at neighborhood scale in suburbs and perhaps in central cities. Neighborhood analyses, using census tract data, revealed that pre-1940 neighborhoods in both cities and suburbs revived in the 1990s.

The results included the following:

- Relative incomes increased in census tracts in central cities and outside central cities more frequently in the 1990s than in the 1980s.

- Census tracts specializing in pre-1940 housing increased more often in relative income.

- Decreases in relative income occurred most often in tracts specializing in 1950s and 1960s housing.

- In 1970, census tracts specializing in pre-1940 housing were most likely to be low in relative income. However, by 2000, tracts specializing in 1940s and 1950s housing, especially in suburbs, were likely to be below pre-1940 tracts in relative income.

- Neighborhoods specializing in pre-1940 housing were more likely to increase in relative income in the 1990s than tracts specializing in any decade's housing other than housing built in the 1990s.

- Relative income was more likely to decline than increase in census tracts specializing in housing built in the 1950s, 1960s, 1970s, and 1980s.

- Tracts specializing in housing 30 to 40 years old were most likely to decline in relative income during the 1990s.

• Central cities were noticeably different from each other in some of these tendencies. In Atlanta, a majority of census tracts increased in relative income in the 1990s. In Philadelphia, less than one-fourth of the census tracts increased in relative income.

These trends can be interpreted plausibly as signaling a new era of substantial revival in most central cities and many older suburbs.

UNITS OF ANALYSIS

Geographic areas, such as census tracts, are closer than suburban jurisdictions as a whole to neighborhood scale. Census tracts typically range from 3,000 to 5,000 residents in central cities and sometimes reach 7,000 residents in suburbs before they are divided into two tracts. Census tract boundaries sometimes are changed by the U.S. Census Bureau, mainly by subdividing growing census tracts, recognizing small changes in cultural characteristics, or tracting counties added to metropolitan areas. Census tract boundary changes present problems for trend analyses. To facilitate census tract studies, the Urban Institute in collaboration with GeoLytics, Inc., has standardized census tract data from 1970 to 2000 to 2000 boundaries. The Urban Institute's methodology for standardizing boundaries is described in Note 1.[1] Data on income and housing for 2000 come from the *Census of Population and Housing 2000*. We use the Urban Institute's demographic data for prior decades.[2]

For this analysis, we used the Urban Institute's data for standardized census tract boundaries for all census tracts in six metropolitan areas—Atlanta, Chicago, Los Angeles, Philadelphia, Richmond, and Washington, D.C. Most of this analysis focuses on changes between 1990 and 2000, sometimes comparing them with the 1980 to 1990 decade. We also identified the relative income status of these census tracts in 1970 and 1980. The tract boundaries throughout are ones the census used in 2000. By using all census tracts, comparisons also can be made between neighborhood trends in central cities and outside central cities. The six metropolitan areas contained 8,471 census tracts. Of these tracts, 2,415 were in central cities and 6,056 were outside central cities. Not all tracts had families with income. Consequently, some totals in subsequent tables are slightly lower than these totals.

We selected the Atlanta, Chicago, Los Angeles, Philadelphia, and Washington, D.C., metropolitan areas to achieve east-to-west and north-to-south geographic distribution, to have large populations and numerous census tracts, to have a variety of industrial and post-industrial economic characteristics, to have considerable racial diversity including growing numbers of Hispanic residents, and to identify an ample number of census tracts containing old housing. Richmond was included due to its convenient access for a case study (described in Chapter 12) and was added to this sample. The six metropolitan areas had a population of nearly 40 million in 2000, almost one-seventh of the U.S. population. In the narrative, we often will refer to census tracts as neighborhoods. This term is more likely to be appropriate in central cities than in suburbs.

RELATIVE INCOME AND DECADE OF CONSTRUCTION

We rely on two indicators of conditions and trends. Relative average family income is the indicator of income used in these census tract studies. Because of problems of adapting median family income to altered boundaries over time, the Neighborhood

Change Database by the Urban Institute used average family income. The mean gives more weight to high-income residents than does the median. Here we will report relative incomes as being above or below the metropolitan average in any one census year, or increasing or decreasing over a decade, if the difference or change is greater than 2.5 percent.

The second indicator is decade (or period) of construction. For post-1940 construction, data for each decade are available. Pre-1940 housing is lumped into a single category. For each decade of construction, each census tract was compared with its metropolitan area and an index of housing specialization was computed. For example, if 12 percent of Atlanta metropolitan housing was constructed during the 1950s, and 20 percent of a central city census tract's housing was constructed in the 1950s, that tract would be categorized as a tract with a specialization of 1.67 and we will report it as "more than 1.5 times" the share of metropolitan housing built during that period. Conversely, if a suburban tract had only 4 percent of its housing constructed during the 1950s, it would be categorized as having less than 0.5 of its housing built during the 1950s. The reference for the ratios in each instance is the census tract's share of housing built during a particular time period compared with the share of its metropolitan area's housing built during that time period. This indicator of housing age was constructed using the inventory of occupied housing in the 2000 census.

In most of the tables in this chapter, we have focused on those census tracts with a decade of construction specialization of 1.5 or greater. Occasionally we use decade of construction specialization of 2.5 or greater. Using these categories, most tracts are specialized in occupied housing constructed in more than one decade.

In this way, we can classify neighborhoods as being old (with substantial shares of pre-1940 housing), or middle aged (tracts with substantial shares of 1950s and 1960s housing), or new (tracts with housing built in the two decades before the study year, which is the 1980s and 1990s for 2000 data). The 1940s are in an ambiguous category between old and middle aged, but we think they usually share more middle-aged than old characteristics because most construction occurred between 1945 and 1950, after World War II. The 1970s also are a transitional era, neither quite middle aged nor new. In Figure 8.1, the distribution of year 2000 housing by decade of construction is described for each of these six metropolitan areas and for their sum.

NEIGHBORHOOD LIFE CYCLES

An extensive literature about dynamics of neighborhood change exists in sociology, economics, geography, policy analysis, and planning. Useful summaries of these findings can be found in a point and counterpoint format in articles by John T. Metzger, Anthony Downs, Kenneth Temkin, George C. Galster, and Robert Lang in *Housing Policy Debate* in 2000. We will examine some of these arguments briefly in Chapter 9 where we consider interactions between patterns and beliefs, and how changes in beliefs may influence changes in patterns, as well as how policies may change patterns. Here we note merely that research on dynamics of neighborhood change has not applied, as far as we know, the data on which we rely in this chapter—decade of housing construction and average family income. We believe these are the best available data to flesh out, test, and elaborate theories of neighborhood change dynamics.

Figure 8.1
Distribution of Occupied Housing by Decade of Construction in Year 2000

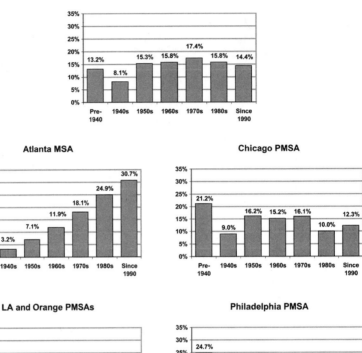

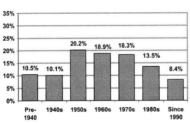

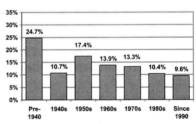

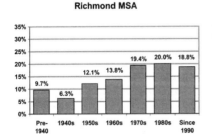

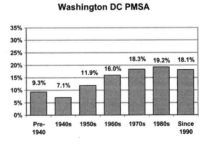

Source: Neighborhood Change Database (NCDB) Tract Data from 1970-2000 and CensusCD 2000 (East Brunswick, NJ: GeoLytics, Inc., 2003).

INCOME INCREASES IN
NEIGHBORHOODS IN THE 1980S AND 1990S

In central cities' neighborhoods in the 1980s, decreases in relative average family income were three times more likely than were increases. During the 1990s, this relationship changed dramatically. Thirty-nine percent of city neighborhoods increased in relative income compared with 51 percent that declined (Table 8.1). In Chicago and Richmond, virtual equality of rising and declining neighborhoods emerged in the 1990s, while increases were much more common than decreases in Atlanta. Philadelphia and Washington, D.C., were at the other extreme, with decreases two or three times more frequent than increases in relative income.

The suburban areas of these six metropolitan areas were little changed in the 1990s compared with the 1980s, except for improvements in the suburbs of Los Angeles. Central city neighborhoods were slightly more likely than suburban neighborhoods to increase in relative income during the 1990s. At this scale, little evidence of an increase in suburban decline appears, but improvement in central cities was vivid in the 1990s compared with the 1980s.

On the other hand, in repeating their income change trend of the 1980s in the 1990s, suburbs in these metropolitan areas continued a decline trend. The clearest demarcation was in the suburban tracts of Richmond, where two and one-half times more suburban tracts declined rather than increased in relative average family income in the 1990s. Suburban decline also was particularly strong in the Atlanta and Chicago areas.

If there has been a shift nationally in perceptions of difficulties of living in outer parts rather than inner parts of metropolitan areas, or if there has been a shift in positive attractions of one area, in general, versus the other, then these trends above are what one should find. At this very general level of analysis, the trend we expected emerged. Differences among metropolitan areas also are apparent. Interpretations of these differences will emerge gradually below.

EVIDENCE FOR TRICKLE-DOWN NEIGHBORHOOD CHANGE

In the filtering process of neighborhood change, most housing in the United States is built to high or fairly high standards and is occupied by persons of middle to higher income upon construction. As the housing ages, it deteriorates physically. Reinvestment nurtures some housing, and occasionally may upgrade it, but overall, physical deterioration predominates. Physical deterioration of structures is accompanied by social deterioration of neighborhoods. Social deterioration deters some reinvestment and creates obstacles to persons of similar or higher incomes from purchasing dwellings as occupants leave. With high mobility rates—50 percent of occupants moving within five years and 50 percent of owners moving within eight years—social and physical deterioration sometimes occurs rapidly.

Consequently, when neighborhoods are classified based on the decades in which their housing was constructed, the effects of trickle-down processes should be observable. Older neighborhoods should tend to have lower relative incomes than newer neighborhoods. In Table 8.2, effects of the trickle-down process can be discerned. In 1970, neighborhoods with 50 percent more pre-1940 housing (1.5 ratio) than their metropolitan area had the lowest proportion of tracts with relative average

Table 8.1

Changes in Relative Average Family Income in the 1980s and 1990s of Census Tracts in Six Metropolitan Areas

Metropolitan Area	Change from 1980 to 1990						Change from 1990 to 2000					
	Total		Central City		Outside City		Total		Central City		Outside City	
	Tracts	Percent	Tracts	Percent	Tracts	Percent	Tracts	Percent	Tracts	Percent	Tracts	Percent
Atlanta, GA												
Decreased In Relative Income	340	57.0	71	60.7	269	56.0	338	51.2	40	34.2	298	54.9
Stable (+ or - 2.5)	54	9.0	6	5.1	48	10.0	94	14.2	16	13.7	78	14.4
Increased In Relative Income	203	34.0	40	34.2	163	34.0	228	34.5	61	52.1	167	30.8
Number of Tracts	597		117		480		660		117		543	
Chicago, IL												
Decreased In Relative Income	1196	65.8	622	74.0	574	58.7	921	49.8	385	45.7	536	53.2
Stable (+ or - 2.5)	178	9.8	49	5.8	129	13.2	252	13.6	79	9.4	173	17.2
Increased In Relative Income	444	24.4	169	20.1	275	28.1	677	36.6	379	45.0	298	29.6
Number of Tracts	1818		840		978		1850		843		1007	
Los Angeles, CA												
Decreased In Relative Income	1828	55.0	501	60.2	1327	53.2	1538	46.3	411	49.4	1127	45.2
Stable (+ or - 2.5)	469	14.1	113	13.6	356	14.3	457	13.7	102	12.3	355	14.2
Increased In Relative Income	1029	30.9	218	26.2	811	32.5	1330	40.0	319	38.3	1011	40.6
Number of Tracts	3326		832		2494		3325		832		2493	
Philadelphia, PA												
Decreased In Relative Income	794	60.8	279	76.4	515	54.7	706	54.2	248	67.9	458	48.9
Stable (+ or - 2.5)	169	12.9	31	8.5	138	14.7	186	14.3	34	9.3	152	16.2
Increased In Relative Income	343	26.3	55	15.1	288	30.6	410	31.5	83	22.7	327	34.9
Number of Tracts	1306		365		941		1302		365		937	

Table 8.1 (cont.)

Changes in Relative Average Family Income in the 1980s and 1990s of Census Tracts in Six Metropolitan Areas

Metropolitan Area	Change from 1980 to 1990						Change from 1990 to 2000					
	Total		Central City		Outside City		Total		Central City		Outside City	
	Tracts	Percent	Tracts	Percent	Tracts	Percent	Tracts	Percent	Tracts	Percent	Tracts	Percent
Richmond, VA												
Decreased In Relative Income	162	64.5	42	64.6	120	64.5	145	57.5	29	44.6	116	62.0
Stable (+ or - 2.5)	21	8.4	5	7.7	16	8.6	32	12.7	8	12.3	24	12.8
Increased In Relative Income	68	27.1	18	27.7	50	26.9	75	29.8	28	43.1	47	25.1
Number of Tracts	251		65		186		252		65		187	
Washington, D.C.												
Decreased In Relative Income	479	49.8	94	54.7	385	48.8	530	51.5	102	59.6	428	49.9
Stable (+ or - 2.5)	149	15.5	15	8.7	134	17.0	138	13.4	11	6.4	127	14.8
Increased In Relative Income	333	34.7	63	36.6	270	34.2	361	35.1	58	33.9	303	35.3
Number of Tracts	961		172		789		1029		171		858	
Total In Study												
Decreased In Relative Income	4799	58.1	1609	67.3	3190	54.4	4178	49.6	1215	50.8	2963	49.2
Stable (+ or - 2.5)	1040	12.6	219	9.2	821	14.0	1159	13.8	250	10.4	909	15.1
Increased In Relative Income	2420	29.3	563	23.5	1857	31.6	3081	36.6	928	38.8	2153	35.7
Number of Tracts	8259		2391		5868		8418		2393		6025	

Source: Neighborhood Change Database (NCDB) Tract Data from 1970-2000 and CensusCD 2000 (East Brunswick, NJ: GeoLytics, Inc., 2003).

Table 8.2
Four Decades of Relative Average Family Income Above the Metropolitan Average
for Census Tracts Specialized in Housing Constructed in Different Decades

Decade of Housing Construction	Relative Family Income 1970			Relative Family Income 1980			Relative Family Income 1990			Relative Family Income 2000		
	All Tracts	Central City	Outside City	All Tracts	Central City	Outside City	All Tracts	Central City	Outside City	All Tracts	Central City	Outside City
Pre-1940												
Tracts	2280	1486	794	2328	1484	844	2392	1487	905	2398	1490	908
Above Metro	405	164	241	400	168	232	442	202	240	519	245	274
Percent Above	17.8%	11.0%	30.4%	17.2%	11.3%	27.5%	18.5%	13.6%	26.5%	21.6%	16.4%	30.2%
1940s												
Tracts	2205	1180	1025	2231	1181	1050	2261	1181	1080	2263	1182	1081
Above Metro	467	173	294	404	139	265	367	135	232	376	132	244
Percent Above	21.2%	14.7%	28.7%	18.1%	11.8%	25.2%	16.2%	11.4%	21.5%	16.6%	11.2%	22.6%
1950s												
Tracts	1819	551	1268	1844	553	1291	1857	551	1306	1858	551	1307
Above Metro	791	184	607	700	149	551	534	120	414	483	98	385
Percent Above	43.5%	33.4%	47.9%	38.0%	26.9%	42.7%	28.8%	21.8%	31.7%	26.0%	17.8%	29.5%
1960s												
Tracts	1574	322	1252	1590	321	1269	1598	321	1277	1602	322	1280
Above Metro	827	114	713	769	95	674	639	77	562	540	69	471
Percent Above	52.5%	35.4%	56.9%	48.4%	29.6%	53.1%	40.0%	24.0%	44.0%	33.7%	21.4%	36.8%

Table 8.2 (cont.)
Four Decades of Relative Average Family Income Above the Metropolitan Average for Census Tracts Specialized in Housing Constructed in Different Decades

Decade of Housing Construction	Relative Family Income 1970			Relative Family Income 1980			Relative Family Income 1990			Relative Family Income 2000		
	All Tracts	Central City	Outside City	All Tracts	Central City	Outside City	All Tracts	Central City	Outside City	All Tracts	Central City	Outside City
1970s												
Tracts				1629	152	1477	1641	150	1491	1646	151	1495
Above Metro				895	57	838	794	47	747	737	42	695
Percent Above				54.9%	37.5%	56.7%	48.4%	31.3%	50.1%	44.8%	27.8%	46.5%
1980s												
Tracts							1845	148	1697	1851	148	1703
Above Metro							942	53	889	927	56	871
Percent Above							51.1%	35.8%	52.4%	50.1%	37.8%	51.1%
Since 1990												
Tracts										1700	150	1550
Above Metro										851	45	806
Percent Above										50.1%	30.0%	52.0%

In this table, a tract is considered "specialized" if it has 1.5 times or more the metropolitan proportion of housing built in that decade. Specialization in Decade of Occupied Housing Construction uses data reported in the *Census of Population and Housing 2000.* The proportion of a census tract's occupied housing in a particular period of construction is compared with the proportion for its metropolitan area.

If a census tract's Average Family Income for the year preceding the census date exceeds the Metropolitan Average Family Income by 2.5% or more, it is reported here as "Above Metro."

Source: Neighborhood Change Database (NCDB) Tract Data from 1970-2000 and CensusCD 2000 (East Brunswick, NJ: GeoLytics, Inc., 2003).

family incomes above the metropolitan level. Each decade of more recent vintage had a higher share of neighborhoods with higher relative average family incomes than the metropolitan average. This same pattern was observable in 1980. However, examining the central cities and suburbs separately, the tracts specialized in pre-1940 and 1940s housing demonstrated similar proportions of tracts with income above the metropolitan level in 1980.

By 1990, a shift had occurred. Neighborhoods with 50 percent or more pre-1940 housing than the metropolitan norm were slightly more likely to have relative average family incomes above the metropolitan average than were tracts with that same percentage of housing built in the 1940s. In 2000, this trend had continued and was more apparent. In addition, the difference between incomes in the pre-1940 neighborhoods and the neighborhoods similarly specialized in 1950s housing had narrowed.

These trends were clear by 2000 when neighborhoods in central cities were examined separately from suburban neighborhoods. In suburbs' neighborhoods, relative average family incomes were as likely to be higher than metropolitan averages in neighborhoods specializing in pre-1940 housing compared with 1950s housing. In addition, central cities and suburbs' pre-1940 neighborhoods were more likely to be ahead of neighborhoods specializing in 1940s housing.

These patterns were even more evident in tracts with specialization greater than 2.5 times the metropolitan area. Relative income in old housing tracts was considerably higher than in 1950s neighborhoods in both cities and suburbs (Table 8.3). In central cities, 19.7 percent of census tracts specialized in pre-1940 housing were above the metropolitan average income compared with 12.5 percent of tracts specialized in housing built in the 1950s. Housing built in the 1940s also was more likely than the 1950s housing to be above the metropolitan average income. In suburbs, 40.1 percent of tracts specialized in pre-1940 housing, compared with 31.4 percent of 1950s housing, were above the metropolitan average. In central cities, nearly as high a percentage of pre-1940 specialized tracts (19.7 percent) were above the metropolitan average income as were tracts specialized in 1960s housing (21.0 percent) and 1970s housing (21.9 percent) (Table 8.3).

COUNTING CENSUS TRACTS

A clearer picture of the changing attractiveness of neighborhoods with housing of different vintages emerges by counting numbers of census tracts above the metropolitan average family income. In the six central cities, the number of census tracts above the metropolitan average declined each decade from 1970 to 2000 for tracts specializing in housing built in the 1940s, 1950s, and 1960s at both the 1.5 times and 2.5 times the metropolitan percentage of housing built in that decade. The pace of decline was slow in the 1940s neighborhoods, with little change from 1980 through 2000 (Table 8.2).

In contrast, neighborhoods specializing in housing built before 1940 were increasingly likely from 1970 through 2000 to have relative incomes above the metropolitan average. In 1970, 164 census tracts specializing 1.5 times in pre-1940 housing were above the metropolitan average. This number of census tracts increased to 168 in 1980, to 202 in 1990, and to 245 in 2000—an increase since 1980 of 46 percent.

Relative income decline in central city census tracts specializing 1.5 times in 1950s and 1960s housing was precipitous. In 1970, central cities had 184 census tracts spe-

Table 8.3
Four Decades of Relative Average Family Income Above the Metropolitan Average
for Census Tracts Highly Specialized in Housing Constructed in Different Decades

Decade of Housing Construction	Relative Family Income 1970			Relative Family Income 1980			Relative Family Income 1990			Relative Family Income 2000		
	All Tracts	Central City	Outside City	All Tracts	Central City	Outside City	All Tracts	Central City	Outside City	All Tracts	Central City	Outside City
Pre-1940												
Tracts	1051	776	275	1078	775	303	1102	777	325	1104	777	327
Above Metro	199	93	106	203	101	102	231	118	113	284	153	131
Percent Above	18.9%	12.0%	38.5%	18.8%	13.0%	33.7%	21.0%	15.2%	34.8%	25.7%	19.7%	40.1%
1940s												
Tracts	746	405	341	751	404	347	759	404	355	759	404	355
Above Metro	175	79	96	146	64	82	140	62	78	146	60	86
Percent Above	23.5%	19.5%	28.2%	19.4%	15.8%	23.6%	18.4%	15.3%	22.0%	19.2%	14.9%	24.2%
1950s												
Tracts	622	175	447	628	177	451	630	175	455	631	176	455
Above Metro	332	71	261	290	54	236	190	34	156	165	22	143
Percent Above	53.4%	40.6%	58.4%	46.2%	30.5%	52.3%	30.2%	19.4%	34.3%	26.1%	12.5%	31.4%
1960s												
Tracts	416	83	333	418	81	337	418	82	336	418	81	337
Above Metro	274	33	241	255	29	226	224	23	201	179	17	162
Percent Above	65.9%	39.8%	72.4%	61.0%	35.8%	67.1%	53.6%	28.0%	59.8%	42.8%	21.0%	48.1%

Table 8.3 (cont.)

Four Decades of Relative Average Family Income Above the Metropolitan Average for Census Tracts Highly Specialized in Housing Constructed in Different Decades

Decade of Housing Construction	Relative Family Income 1970			Relative Family Income 1980			Relative Family Income 1990			Relative Family Income 2000		
	All Tracts	Central City	Outside City	All Tracts	Central City	Outside City	All Tracts	Central City	Outside City	All Tracts	Central City	Outside City
1970s												
Tracts				436	32	404	435	31	404	438	32	406
Above Metro				288	13	275	260	8	252	238	7	231
Percent Above				66.1%	40.6%	68.1%	59.8%	25.8%	62.4%	54.3%	21.9%	56.9%
1980s												
Tracts							750	46	704	755	47	708
Above Metro							431	21	410	451	25	426
Percent Above							57.5%	45.7%	58.2%	59.7%	53.2%	60.2%
Since 1990												
Tracts										814	41	773
Above Metro										492	13	479
Percent Above										60.4%	31.7%	62.0%

In this table, a tract is considered "highly specialized" if it has 2.5 times or more the metropolitan proportion of housing built in that decade. Specialization in Decade of Occupied Housing Construction uses data reported in the *Census of Population and Housing 2000*. The proportion of a census tract's occupied housing in a particular period of construction is compared with the proportion for its metropolitan area.

If a census tract's Average Family Income for the year preceding the census date exceeds the Metropolitan Average Family Income by 2.5% or more, it is reported here as "Above Metro."

Source: Neighborhood Change Database (NCDB) Tract Data from 1970-2000 and CensusCD 2000 (East Brunswick, NJ: GeoLytics, Inc., 2003).

cializing 1.5 times in 1950s housing above the metropolitan average—a number that fell to 98 in 2000, a decline of 47 percent. For tracts specializing 1.5 times in 1960s housing, the number of tracts above the metropolitan average fell by 39 percent from 1970 to 2000. By 2000, more tracts specializing 1.5 times in pre-1940 housing (245 tracts) were above the metropolitan average income than the number combined of tracts specializing in 1960s, 1970s, 1980s, and 1990s housing (212) (Table 8.2). The number of census tracts specializing in pre-1940 housing was large—1,490 tracts in 2000. The fact that only 16.4 percent of these old housing tracts were above the metropolitan average by 2.5 percent or more indicates that the trickle-down process of neighborhood change had been occurring until 1980, and also indicates that if the pace of revival of old housing neighborhoods continues at the pace from 1980 to 2000, the potential for revival in central city neighborhoods also is quite large. Another 46 percent increase, repeating the pace of increase from 1980 to 2000, would add 113 tracts, bringing the number of pre-1940 specialized tracts above the metropolitan average to 357, which was 24 percent of the total.

For central city neighborhoods specializing 2.5 times in pre-1940 housing, the rate of census tracts moving above the metropolitan average family income was a little higher than for the neighborhoods specialized 1.5 times. These old neighborhoods specialized 2.5 times above the metropolitan income average increased by 51 percent from 1980 to 2000, with 30 percent of the increase occurring from 1990 to 2000 (Table 8.3).

Outside central cities in suburbs, pre-1940 specialized neighborhoods also were reviving. They differed from central cities in that revival of suburbs' old neighborhoods was concentrated in the 1990s, with little foreshadowing in the 1980s. Old neighborhoods specialized 1.5 times increased above the metropolitan average income by 34 (14 percent in the 1990s) and by 18 (16 percent) in old neighborhoods specialized 2.5 times. Conversely, the decline occurred in 1960s specialized neighborhoods in the 1990s, 16 percent for neighborhoods specialized 1.5 times, and 19 percent for neighborhoods specialized 2.5 times (Tables 8.2 and 8.3).

COMPARING THE 1990s AND 1980s

During the 1990s, housing preferences of some consumers may have been shifting from their previous distribution. Criticisms of traffic congestion and inconvenient access for family members to diverse locations for routine activities became more common. These criticisms were reflected in growing, though episodic, support for growth management. In addition, arguments about the virtues of walking to activities and organizing neighborhoods in traditional pre-auto densities with street grids and houses with front porches were stressed by advocates of new urbanism, which really was the old pre-auto urbanism. Perhaps the combination of extolling pre-auto virtues with growing stress from auto-dominated suburban land development patterns led to shifts in consumer preferences for housing and neighborhoods. We think that happened.

If we are correct, then relative income trends should reflect the accumulation of those consumer preference shifts. Old neighborhoods should have done better in relative income in the 1990s than in the 1980s. More old neighborhoods should have higher relative incomes in 2000 than in 1990, as we have seen in findings discussed above. More old neighborhoods should be rising in relative income compared to neighborhoods specializing in housing constructed in the 1950s and 1960s.

First, more neighborhoods specializing in pre-1940 housing increased in relative average family income in the 1990s than in the 1980s. In the 1980s, old neighborhoods were slightly less likely to increase in relative income than all neighborhoods—27.6 percent of old neighborhoods (Table 8.4) compared with 29.3 percent of all neighborhoods (Table 8.1). In the 1990s, pre-1940s specialized neighborhoods were more likely than all neighborhoods to increase in relative income (44.7 percent for old neighborhoods compared with 36.6 percent for all neighborhoods).

In addition, pre-1940 neighborhoods were more likely to increase in relative income in the 1990s than in the 1980s compared to neighborhoods specializing in each period of housing construction (Table 8.4). The largest gap concerning pre-1940s neighborhoods in the 1990s occurred versus neighborhoods specializing in 1960s housing. Whereas 44.7 percent of old neighborhoods increased in relative income in the 1990s, only 22.8 percent of 1960s neighborhoods increased.

Some advantages for pre-1940s neighborhoods had emerged in the 1980s. Although the margins were small, pre-1940s neighborhoods were slightly more likely to increase in relative income in the 1980s than neighborhoods specializing in housing built in the 1940s, 1950s, and 1960s. Thus, evidence had begun to emerge in the 1980s that old neighborhoods were increasing in comparative attractiveness.

This phenomenon became considerably stronger in the 1990s. Pre-1940s neighborhoods were more likely to increase in the 1990s in relative income in central cities and in suburbs, examined separately, than neighborhoods specializing in housing constructed in the 1940s, 1950s, 1960s, 1970s, and 1980s (Tables 8.4 and 8.5).

The number of census tracts that increased in relative income 2.5 percent or more also is worth noting. In central cities, 364 of pre-1940 census tracts specialized 1.5 times increased in relative income from 1980 to 1990, whereas 679 increased from 1990 to 2000—an increase of 87 percent. A very large jump occurred in central cities in the 1990s compared with the 1980s—an increase of 94 percent—for census tracts specializing 1.5 times in 1940s housing. Because pre-1940 and 1940s specialized neighborhoods constituted a substantial majority of central city census tracts (2,667 compared with 1,312 specializing in more recent housing), the revival of attractiveness of pre-1940 and 1940s neighborhoods bodes well for future prospects for these central cities (Table 8.4).

Large jumps in relative income also occurred in census tracts specializing 2.5 times in pre-1940 and 1940s housing, which is an additional reason to be optimistic about central cities' future (Table 8.5). For pre-1940 neighborhoods, 49.9 percent increased in average family income relative to metropolitan income from 1990 to 2000 compared with 28.6 percent of these neighborhoods from 1980 to 1990. This was the largest increase for neighborhoods of any vintage. The next largest increase was in 1940s neighborhoods, where the proportion of increasing tracts was 36.9 percent from 1990 to 2000, up from 21.0 percent from 1980 to 1990 (Table 8.5).

The substantial fall-off between the frequency of relative income increases in census tracts specializing in 1970s and 1980s housing compared with 1990s housing may be particularly important in anticipating future trajectories for suburbs. In the 1990s, for example, 50.9 percent of suburban census tracts specializing (at 1.5 or more times the metropolitan share) in housing built in the 1990s increased in relative income;

Table 8.4
Relative Average Family Income Increasing for Census Tracts
Specialized in Housing Constructed in Different Decades

Decade of Housing Construction	Change 1980 to 1990			Change 1990 to 2000		
	All Tracts	Central City	Outside City	All Tracts	Central City	Outside City
Pre-1940						
Tracts	2325	1482	843	2391	1486	905
Increased	642	364	278	1069	679	390
Percent Increased	27.6%	24.6%	33.0%	44.7%	45.7%	43.1%
1940s						
Tracts	2231	1181	1050	2261	1181	1080
Increased	445	215	230	803	418	385
Percent Increased	19.9%	18.2%	21.9%	35.5%	35.4%	35.6%
1950s						
Tracts	1842	551	1291	1855	549	1306
Increased	359	105	254	555	153	402
Percent Increased	19.5%	19.1%	19.7%	29.9%	27.9%	30.8%
1960s						
Tracts	1587	320	1267	1597	320	1277
Increased	355	67	288	364	90	274
Percent Increased	22.4%	20.9%	22.7%	22.8%	28.1%	21.5%
1970s						
Tracts	1625	151	1474	1640	150	1490
Increased	520	39	481	468	41	427
Percent Increased	32.0%	25.8%	32.6%	28.5%	27.3%	28.7%
1980s						
Tracts	1818	145	1673	1844	147	1697
Increased	758	47	711	697	57	640
Percent Increased	41.7%	32.4%	42.5%	37.8%	38.8%	37.7%
Since 1990						
Tracts				1674	146	1528
Increased				855	78	777
Percent Increased				51.1%	53.4%	50.9%

In this table, a tract is considered "specialized" if it has 1.5 times or more the metropolitan proportion of housing built in that decade. Specialization in Decade of Occupied Housing Construction uses data reported in the *Census of Population and Housing 2000*. The proportion of a census tract's occupied housing in a particular period of construction is compared with the proportion for its metropolitan area.

If a census tract's Average Family Income Relative to its Metropolitan Area's Average Family Income grew by more than 2.5%, it is reported here as having "Increased."

Source: Neighborhood Change Database (NCDB) Tract Data from 1970-2000 and CensusCD 2000 (East Brúnswick, NJ: GeoLytics, Inc., 2003).

Table 8.5
Relative Average Family Income Increasing for Tracts Highly
Specialized in Housing Constructed in Different Decades

Decade of Housing Construction	Change 1980 to 1990			Change 1990 to 2000		
	All Tracts	Central City	Outside City	All Tracts	Central City	Outside City
Pre-1940						
Tracts	1076	774	302	1101	776	325
Increased	349	221	128	547	387	160
Percent Increased	32.4%	28.6%	42.4%	49.7%	49.9%	49.2%
1940s						
Tracts	751	404	347	759	404	355
Increased	166	85	81	298	149	149
Percent Increased	22.1%	21.0%	23.3%	39.3%	36.9%	42.0%
1950s						
Tracts	626	175	451	629	174	455
Increased	93	30	63	177	43	134
Percent Increased	14.9%	17.1%	14.0%	28.1%	24.7%	29.5%
1960s						
Tracts	417	81	336	417	81	336
Increased	83	16	67	86	19	67
Percent Increased	19.9%	19.8%	19.9%	20.6%	23.5%	19.9%
1970s						
Tracts	434	32	402	435	32	403
Increased	165	8	157	120	10	110
Percent Increased	38.0%	25.0%	39.1%	27.6%	31.3%	27.3%
1980s						
Tracts	746	44	702	750	46	704
Increased	359	20	339	305	16	289
Percent Increased	48.1%	45.5%	48.3%	40.7%	34.8%	41.1%
Since 1990						
Tracts				790	38	752
Increased				449	23	426
Percent Increased				56.8%	60.5%	56.6%

In this table, a tract is considered "highly specialized" if it has 2.5 times or more the metropolitan proportion of housing built in that decade. Specialization in Decade of Occupied Housing Construction uses data reported in the *Census of Population and Housing 2000*. The proportion of a census tract's occupied housing in a particular period of construction is compared with the proportion for its metropolitan area.

If a census tract's Average Family Income Relative to its Metropolitan Area's Average Family Income grew by more than 2.5%, it is reported here as having "Increased."

Source: Neighborhood Change Database (NCDB) Tract Data from 1970-2000 and CensusCD 2000 (East Brunswick, NJ: GeoLytics, Inc., 2003).

only 37.7 percent of 1980s census tracts and 28.7 percent of 1970s census tracts did so (Table 8.4). A similar fall-off occurred in the 1980s. Whereas 42.5 percent of census tracts specializing in 1980s housing increased in relative income in the 1980s, only 32.6 percent of 1970s census tracts and 22.7 percent of 1960s census tracts did so. Again, the tracts specialized 2.5 times or more metropolitan proportions demonstrated these patterns more strongly (Table 8.5). Relative income in old housing tracts increased in more than twice the percentage of tracts specializing in 1960s housing in both cities and suburbs—49.9 percent in cities and 49.2 percent in suburbs for pre-1940 neighborhoods compared with 23.5 percent in cities and 19.9 percent in suburbs for 1960s neighborhoods (Table 8.5).

We interpret these differences to mean that consumers in housing markets were finding new houses appealing, but they were not finding similar appeal in settlement patterns. Therefore, as the housing aged slightly, by only 10 to 20 years, the ability of such areas to continue to appeal to more affluent buyers diminished substantially. Hence, increases in relative income in census tracts specializing in housing 10 to 30 years old were much less frequent than in census tracts with housing built in the most recent 10 years. Conversely, old neighborhoods, with housing built 60 or more years earlier, were more likely to be increasing in relative income in the 1990s than census tracts specializing in housing that was 10 to 30 years old. In these instances, the trickle-down process of neighborhood change was operating with considerable speed in relatively new and middle-aged suburban areas, but it had been interrupted and often reversed in old neighborhoods in central cities and suburbs.

WHICH OLD NEIGHBORHOODS INCREASED IN RELATIVE INCOME?

Pre-1940 neighborhoods may have revived for competing reasons. A few hypotheses:

• Housing prices fell so low that housing bargains attracted more affluent households than the average neighborhood resident. This hypothesis would be supported if low-income neighborhoods were significantly more likely to increase in relative income than other pre-1940 neighborhoods.

• The most likely neighborhoods to rise in relative income would be those with the highest incomes where the fewest adverse social and housing conditions occurred. This hypothesis, which is the opposite view from the first, would be supported if the highest income, pre-1940 neighborhoods were most likely to increase in relative income.

• Old housing was well located and often aesthetically attractive, lending itself to relative income increases throughout the income spectrum. This hypothesis would be supported if old neighborhoods increased in relative income as much or more than middle-aged and new neighborhoods in each segment or most segments of the income spectrum of neighborhoods.

Data pertinent to these hypotheses are displayed in Tables 8.6 and 8.7. Table 8.6 applies to census tracts specializing 1.5 times or more in pre-1940 housing. In Table 8.7, data are presented for census tracts specializing 2.5 times or more in pre-1940 housing. In these tables, census tracts specializing in pre-1940 housing are placed in categories based on their average family income ratios in 1990. The income categories are more than 30 percent below the metropolitan average, 10 to 30 percent

Table 8.6
Relative Average Family Income Increasing for Census Tracts
Specialized in Housing Constructed Before 1940 by Income Status in 1990

Relative Income Status in 1990	Tracts Specialized In Occupied Housing Built Before 1940			All Census Tracts		
	All Tracts	**Central City Tracts**	**Outside City Tracts**	**All Tracts**	**Central City Tracts**	**Outside City Tracts**
More than 30% Below Metro Income						
Total	1327	1001	326	2387	1323	1064
Increased	619	486	133	1018	598	420
Percent Increasing	46.6%	48.6%	40.8%	42.6%	45.2%	39.5%
10% to 30% Below Metro Income						
Total	476	232	244	1961	477	1484
Increased	158	70	88	582	123	459
Percent of Group	33.2%	30.2%	36.1%	29.7%	25.8%	30.9%
10% Below to 10% Above Metro Income						
Total	216	83	133	1460	213	1247
Increased	109	41	68	489	73	416
Percent of Group	50.5%	49.4%	51.1%	33.5%	34.3%	33.4%
10% to 100% Above Metro Income						
Total	259	110	149	1530	233	1297
Increased	137	58	79	598	86	512
Percent of Group	52.9%	52.7%	53.0%	39.1%	36.9%	39.5%

The column header spanning "All Census Tracts" columns: **Number of Census Tracts Increasing in Relative Average Family Income and Percentage of All Tracts in the Income Status Group**

Table 8.6 (cont.)
Relative Average Family Income Increasing for Census Tracts
Specialized in Housing Constructed Before 1940 by Income Status in 1990

Relative Income Status in 1990	Number of Census Tracts Increasing in Relative Average Family Income and Percentage of All Tracts in the Income Status Group					
	Tracts Specialized In Occupied Housing Built Before 1940			All Census Tracts		
	All Tracts	Central City Tracts	Outside City Tracts	All Tracts	Central City Tracts	Outside City Tracts
More than Double Metro Income						
Total	113	60	53	322	109	213
Increased	46	24	22	106	39	67
Percent of Group	40.7%	40.0%	41.5%	32.9%	35.8%	31.5%
For All Income Status Groups						
Increased	1069	679	390	2793	919	1874
Percent Increased	44.7%	45.7%	43.1%	36.5%	39.0%	35.3%
Stable	274	142	132	1047	247	800
Percent Stable	11.5%	9.6%	14.6%	13.7%	10.5%	15.1%
Decreased	1048	665	383	3820	1189	2631
Percent Decreased	43.8%	44.8%	42.3%	49.9%	50.5%	49.6%
Total	2391	1486	905	7660	2355	5305

In this table, a tract is considered "specialized" if it has 1.5 times or more the metropolitan proportion of housing built in that decade. Specialization in Decade of Occupied Housing Construction uses data reported in the *Census of Population and Housing 2000*. The proportion of a census tract's occupied housing in a particular period of construction is compared with the proportion for its metropolitan area.

If a census tract's Average Family Income Relative to its Metropolitan Area's Average Family Income changed by more than 2.5%, it is reported here as having "Increased" or "Decreased" accordingly.

Source: Neighborhood Change Database (NCDB) Tract Data from 1970-2000 and CensusCD 2000 (East Brunswick, NJ: GeoLytics, Inc., 2003).

Table 8.7
**Relative Average Family Income Increasing for Census Tracts Highly
Specialized in Housing Constructed Before 1940 by Income Status in 1990**

Relative Income Status in 1990	Number of Census Tracts Increasing in Relative Average Family Income and Percentage of All Tracts in the Income Status Group					
	Tracts Specialized In Occupied Housing Built Before 1940			All Census Tracts		
	All Tracts	Central City Tracts	Outside City Tracts	All Tracts	Central City Tracts	Outside City Tracts
More than 30% Below Metro Income						
Total	599	500	99	2387	1323	1064
Increased	303	257	46	1018	598	420
Percent Increasing	50.6%	51.4%	46.5%	42.6%	45.2%	39.5%
10% to 30% Below Metro Income						
Total	206	124	82	1961	477	1484
Increased	88	49	39	582	123	459
Percent of Group	42.7%	39.5%	47.6%	29.7%	25.8%	30.9%
10% Below to 10% Above Metro Income						
Total	95	51	44	1460	213	1247
Increased	57	31	26	489	73	416
Percent of Group	60.0%	60.8%	59.1%	33.5%	34.3%	33.4%
10% to 100% Above Metro Income						
Total	145	72	73	1530	233	1297
Increased	75	36	39	598	86	512
Percent of Group	51.7%	50.0%	53.4%	39.1%	36.9%	39.5%

Table 8.7 (cont.)
Relative Average Family Income Increasing for Census Tracts Highly
Specialized in Housing Constructed Before 1940 by Income Status in 1990

| Relative Income Status in 1990 | Number of Census Tracts Increasing in Relative Average Family Income and Percentage of All Tracts in the Income Status Group | | | | | |
| | Tracts Specialized In Occupied Housing Built Before 1940 | | | All Census Tracts | | |
	All Tracts	Central City Tracts	Outside City Tracts	All Tracts	Central City Tracts	Outside City Tracts
More than Double Metro Income						
Total	56	29	27	322	109	213
Increased	24	14	10	106	39	67
Percent of Group	42.9%	48.3%	37.0%	32.9%	35.8%	31.5%
For All Income Status Groups						
Increased	547	387	160	2793	919	1874
Percent Increased	49.7%	49.9%	49.2%	36.5%	39.0%	35.3%
Stable	124	79	45	1047	247	800
Percent Stable	11.3%	10.2%	13.8%	13.7%	10.5%	15.1%
Decreased	430	310	120	3820	1189	2631
Percent Decreased	39.1%	39.9%	36.9%	49.9%	50.5%	49.6%
Total	1101	776	325	7660	2355	5305

In this table, a tract is considered "highly specialized" if it has 2.5 times or more the metropolitan proportion of housing built in that decade. Specialization in Decade of Occupied Housing Construction uses data reported in the *Census of Population and Housing 2000*. The proportion of a census tract's occupied housing in a particular period of construction is compared with the proportion for its metropolitan area.

If a census tract's Average Family Income Relative to its Metropolitan Area's Average Family Income changed by more than 2.5%, it is reported here as having "Increased" or "Decreased" accordingly.

Source: Neighborhood Change Database (NCDB) Tract Data from 1970-2000 and CensusCD 2000 (East Brunswick, NJ: GeoLytics, Inc., 2003).

below, 10 percent above to 10 percent below, 10 to 100 percent above, and more than twice the metropolitan average.

The third hypothesis is most consistent with the findings in Tables 8.6 and 8.7. In each income category, pre-1940 neighborhoods were more likely to increase in relative income during the 1990s than middle-aged and new neighborhoods in the same income categories. In addition, each income category had substantial percentages of increasing census tracts, including the lowest and highest income pre-1940 neighborhoods. The most frequent increasing pre-1940 neighborhoods, however, were middle- or upper-middle-income ranges—10 to 100 percent of metropolitan income for tracts specializing 1.5 times or more in relative income (Table 8.6) and 10 percent above to 10 percent below metropolitan average income in tracts specializing 2.5 times or more in relative income (Table 8.7). Moreover, these tendencies occurred similarly in central cities and suburbs.

Pre-1940 census tracts with incomes 10 to 30 percent below metropolitan averages also were more likely than newer neighborhoods in this income category to increase in relative income. This tendency was especially marked in neighborhoods specializing 2.5 times or more in pre-1940 housing (Table 8.7). These neighborhoods were less likely than richer and poorer neighborhoods, however, to increase in relative income. Less success in this income category should be a concern in both cities and older suburbs, because many neighborhoods were in this category and this category is most likely to be in a condition of substantial decline but not overwhelming deterioration. Greater success in raising relative incomes in these neighborhoods would provide stronger confidence in future prospects of cities and old suburbs.

From these trends, we infer that both central cities and old suburbs have combinations of housing characteristics and accessibility to nonhousing resources (work, public transportation, entertainment, shopping, and culture) that appealed to more households during the 1990s than in previous decades. Given that social problems were greater generally in central cities and older suburbs than in newer suburbs, the rise in family incomes in these old neighborhoods would tend to reduce social problems, creating more auspicious conditions during the 2000 to 2010 period than during the 1990s. Pre-1940 neighborhoods, therefore, would be poised to achieve a stronger revival trend in coming years.

DIFFERENCES AMONG METROPOLITAN AREAS

Atlanta, Georgia

Much more than the other metropolitan areas, Atlanta features recent housing, with more than 55 percent of its housing constructed in the 1980s and 1990s (Figure 8.1). Does this make a difference in relative income trends in cities versus suburbs and by decade of construction? It seems to, because Atlanta stood out as the metropolitan area in which neighborhoods specializing in 1980s housing were least likely to increase in relative income.

The City of Atlanta made major strides in increasing relative average family income in the 1990s (Table 8.8). Neighborhoods with pre-1940 and 1940s housing were somewhat more likely than middle-aged neighborhoods to increase in relative income in the 1990s. The increases in Atlanta provide evidence for the attractiveness of old and middle-aged neighborhoods located closer to the center, because 52.1 per-

Table 8.8
Relative Average Family Income Increasing for Census Tracts Specialized in Housing Constructed in Different Decades—Atlanta Metropolitan Area

Decade of Housing Construction	Change 1980 to 1990			Change 1990 to 2000		
	All Tracts	Central City	Outside City	All Tracts	Central City	Outside City
Pre-1940						
Tracts	133	85	48	169	85	84
Increased	41	30	11	83	51	32
Percent Increased	30.8%	35.3%	22.9%	49.1%	60.0%	38.1%
1940s						
Tracts	161	97	64	186	97	89
Increased	45	34	11	81	49	32
Percent Increased	28.0%	35.1%	17.2%	43.5%	50.5%	36.0%
1950s						
Tracts	190	94	96	203	94	109
Increased	47	28	19	75	44	31
Percent Increased	24.7%	29.8%	19.8%	36.9%	46.8%	28.4%
1960s						
Tracts	187	63	124	195	63	132
Increased	26	10	16	48	27	21
Percent Increased	13.9%	15.9%	12.9%	24.6%	42.9%	15.9%
1970s						
Tracts	131	7	124	136	7	129
Increased	36	1	35	21	1	20
Percent Increased	27.5%	14.3%	28.2%	15.4%	14.3%	15.5%
1980s						
Tracts	113	1	112	115	1	114
Increased	47	1	46	20	1	19
Percent Increased	41.6%	100.0%	41.1%	17.4%	100.0%	16.7%
Since 1990						
Tracts				105	1	104
Increased				61	1	60
Percent Increased				58.1%	100.0%	57.7%

In this table, a tract is considered "specialized" if it has 1.5 times or more the metropolitan proportion of housing built in that decade. Specialization in Decade of Occupied Housing Construction uses data reported in the *Census of Population and Housing 2000.* The proportion of a census tract's occupied housing in a particular period of construction is compared with the proportion for its metropolitan area.

If a census tract's Average Family Income Relative to its Metropolitan Area's Average Family Income grew by more than 2.5%, it is reported here as having "Increased."

Source: Neighborhood Change Database (NCDB) Tract Data from 1970-2000 and CensusCD 2000 (East Brunswick, NJ: GeoLytics, Inc., 2003).

cent of Atlanta's city neighborhoods increased in relative income compared with relative income increases in 30.8 percent of Atlanta's suburban tracts (Table 8.1).

The number of old neighborhoods increasing in relative income by 2.5 percent or more increased dramatically in Atlanta in the 1990s compared with the 1980s. While 30 city census tracts specializing in pre-1940 housing increased in relative income in the 1980s, 51 increased in the 1990s. For census tracts specializing in 1940s housing, 34 increased in the 1980s and 49 increased in the 1990s (Table 8.8).

In suburban areas, the appeal of older neighborhoods was apparent in relative income change data by decade. Pre-1940 suburban neighborhoods were not as likely to increase in relative income in the 1990s as city neighborhoods of comparable age, but their attractiveness increased nearly threefold in the 1990s (32 increased) compared with old suburban neighborhoods in the 1980s (11 increased). Similar increases occurred in tracts specializing in 1940s housing. In the 1990s, neighborhoods specializing in pre-1940 and 1940s housing were about twice as likely to increase in relative income as neighborhoods specializing in 1960s, 1970s, and even 1980s housing.

This phenomenon of 1980s areas having so little appeal compared with the central city and older parts of the suburbs is unique. One wonders if the Atlanta metropolitan area's reputation for congested suburbs and explosive sprawl is justified, and perhaps it has had powerful effects on consumer preferences for housing locations. The fall-off from housing built in the 1990s, for which 57.7 percent of census tracts specializing in such housing increased, to a mere 16.7 percent of areas specializing in 1980s housing having increased is dramatically different from the other metropolitan areas. This small amount of relative income increases in 1980s neighborhoods may indicate that the neighborhoods had little place attraction as newness wore off the housing units. Frustration with driving times for commuting, errands, and entertainment in areas where 1980s housing was constructed also may have been intense in the sprawling Atlanta area.

Chicago, Illinois

Chicago is a much older metropolitan area than Atlanta. It has a much higher proportion (46 percent) of metropolitan census tracts in the central city. More pre-1940 housing existed than housing of any subsequent decade, and housing built in the 1950s, 1960s, and 1970s was more common than housing constructed in the 1980s and 1990s (Figure 8.1). Only 9.2 percent of old housing tracts in the city had relative incomes above the metropolitan average. Considerable old suburban neighborhoods (34.9 percent), in contrast, were above this average.

In the 1990s, however, old neighborhoods in both the city and suburbs were much more likely to increase in relative income than were middle-aged neighborhoods. In the city, 51 percent of neighborhoods specializing in pre-1940 housing went up in relative average family income in the 1990s compared with only 24.8 percent and 25.6 percent of neighborhoods specializing in 1950s and 1960s housing (Table 8.9). Thus, many city neighborhoods below middle income were rising in relative income in the 1990s. In the suburbs, 38.3 percent of neighborhoods specializing in pre-1940 housing increased compared with only 18.2 percent of 1940s areas, 18.9 percent of 1950s areas, 11.9 percent of 1960s areas, and only 21.7 percent of 1970s areas (Table 8.9). Old neighborhoods were more likely to increase in relative income in the 1980s than were

Table 8.9
Relative Average Family Income Increasing for
Census Tracts Specialized in Housing Constructed in
Different Decades—Chicago Primary Metropolitan Area

Decade of Housing Construction	Change 1980 to 1990			Change 1990 to 2000		
	All Tracts	Central City	Outside City	All Tracts	Central City	Outside City
Pre-1940						
Tracts	728	587	141	739	590	149
Increased	172	125	47	358	301	57
Percent Increased	23.6%	21.3%	33.3%	48.4%	51.0%	38.3%
1940s						
Tracts	617	448	169	618	448	170
Increased	69	48	21	189	158	31
Percent Increased	11.2%	10.7%	12.4%	30.6%	35.3%	18.2%
1950s						
Tracts	412	159	253	411	157	254
Increased	58	15	43	87	39	48
Percent Increased	14.1%	9.4%	17.0%	21.2%	24.8%	18.9%
1960s						
Tracts	337	86	251	339	86	253
Increased	57	15	42	52	22	30
Percent Increased	16.9%	17.4%	16.7%	15.3%	25.6%	11.9%
1970s						
Tracts	340	31	309	344	31	313
Increased	98	12	86	82	14	68
Percent Increased	28.8%	38.7%	27.8%	23.8%	45.2%	21.7%
1980s						
Tracts	330	40	290	338	42	296
Increased	152	19	133	135	26	109
Percent Increased	46.1%	47.5%	45.9%	39.9%	61.9%	36.8%
Since 1990						
Tracts				337	57	280
Increased				182	42	140

In this table, a tract is considered "specialized" if it has 1.5 times or more the metropolitan proportion of housing built in that decade. Specialization in Decade of Occupied Housing Construction uses data reported in the *Census of Population and Housing 2000*. The proportion of a census tract's occupied housing in a particular period of construction is compared with the proportion for its metropolitan area.

If a census tract's Average Family Income Relative to its Metropolitan Area's Average Family Income grew by more than 2.5%, it is reported here as having "Increased."

Source: Neighborhood Change Database (NCDB) Tract Data from 1970-2000 and CensusCD 2000 (East Brunswick, NJ: GeoLytics, Inc., 2003).

middle-aged neighborhoods, and the margins of advantages for old neighborhoods increased in the 1990s.

The appeal of old neighborhoods in the 1990s was greater than during the 1980s, when 125 census tracts specializing in pre-1940 housing increased in relative income. In the 1990s, 301 of the 590 tracts specializing in pre-1940 housing increased in relative income. The proportionate increase was even greater among tracts specializing in 1940s housing, as the number that increased in relative income went from 48 in the 1980s to 158 in the 1990s.

These results are consistent with the discovery of higher residential repeat sales prices nearer the center of Chicago during the 1990s than in the 1980s. Daniel P. McMillen found that estimates for repeat housing sales "suggest a dramatic return of centralization to the Chicago housing market. After a long period during which house prices were not affected by distance from the central business district, values now decline by more than 8 percent per mile."[3]

Los Angeles, California

Los Angeles was different in several respects. It was a middle-aged metropolitan area, with most of its housing having been constructed in the 1950s, 1960s, and 1970s (Figure 8.1). It had much less variation in the attractiveness of neighborhoods based on the age of housing. The Los Angeles area was unique in that pre-1940 neighborhoods did as well as 1990s neighborhoods in the proportion rising in relative income during the 1990s.

In the City of Los Angeles, neighborhoods that specialized in pre-1940 and in 1940s housing were more likely than neighborhoods specializing in 1990s housing to rise in relative average family income during the 1990s. This same relationship occurred in the suburbs, except that pre-1940, 1940, and 1990 areas had virtually the same success in rising during the 1990s (Table 8.10). As in most metropolitan areas, 1960s specialized neighborhoods were least likely to increase in relative income in the suburbs. In the central city, however, 1970s specialized neighborhoods fared worse in this respect. The variation from the most to least successful in rising in relative income varied much less than in other metropolitan areas. Limited variation by age of housing also occurred in the 1980s.

Oddly, 1960s neighborhoods in the central city were most likely to rise in relative income during the 1980s—the only instance in which 1960s neighborhoods were most popular. In the suburbs, new housing areas did best in the 1980s, with pre-1940 housing neighborhoods being more successful than middle-aged housing neighborhoods (Table 8.10).

In the City of Los Angeles, 38.3 percent of census tracts increased in relative income in the 1990s compared with 26.2 percent in the 1980s. Changes between decades were greatest in pre-1940 and 1940s census tracts. In the 1990s, 399 census tracts specializing in pre-1940 housing increased in relative income compared with only 202 in the 1980s. For tracts specializing in 1940s housing, the number of tracts increasing in relative income went from 180 in the 1980s to 393 in the 1990s (Table 8.10)

The average family income used for the Los Angeles metropolitan area is for the Los Angeles and Orange County Primary Metropolitan Statistical Areas combined,

Table 8.10
Relative Average Family Income Increasing for
Census Tracts Specialized in Housing Constructed
in Different Decades—Los Angeles Metropolitan Area

Decade of Housing Construction	Change 1980 to 1990			Change 1990 to 2000		
	All Tracts	Central City	Outside City	All Tracts	Central City	Outside City
Pre-1940						
Tracts	701	396	348	745	396	349
Increased	202	92	121	399	209	190
Percent Increased	28.8%	23.2%	34.8%	53.6%	52.8%	54.4%
1940s						
Tracts	710	300	446	747	300	447
Increased	180	75	109	393	152	241
Percent Increased	25.4%	25.0%	24.4%	52.6%	50.7%	53.9%
1950s						
Tracts	551	140	453	593	140	453
Increased	118	37	87	275	54	221
Percent Increased	21.4%	26.4%	19.2%	46.4%	38.6%	48.8%
1960s						
Tracts	417	73	443	516	73	443
Increased	132	28	135	199	24	175
Percent Increased	31.7%	38.4%	30.5%	38.6%	32.9%	39.5%
1970s						
Tracts	436	66	580	645	66	579
Increased	164	20	217	263	17	246
Percent Increased	37.6%	30.3%	37.4%	40.8%	25.8%	42.5%
1980s						
Tracts	447	83	783	870	83	787
Increased	194	20	335	386	25	361
Percent Increased	43.4%	24.1%	42.8%	44.4%	30.1%	45.9%
Since 1990						
Tracts				680	76	604
Increased				368	34	334
Percent Increased				54.1%	44.7%	55.3%

In this table, a tract is considered "specialized" if it has 1.5 times or more the metropolitan proportion of housing built in that decade. Specialization in Decade of Occupied Housing Construction uses data reported in the *Census of Population and Housing 2000*. The proportion of a census tract's occupied housing in a particular period of construction is compared with the proportion for its metropolitan area.

If a census tract's Average Family Income Relative to its Metropolitan Area's Average Family Income grew by more than 2.5%, it is reported here as having "Increased."

Source: Neighborhood Change Database (NCDB) Tract Data from 1970-2000 and CensusCD 2000 (East Brunswick, NJ: GeoLytics, Inc., 2003).

not the entire Consolidated Metropolitan Statistical Area. This territory was used to correspond to data in Chapters 5 and 6.

Philadelphia, Pennsylvania

Philadelphia is the oldest metropolitan area analyzed here, similar to Chicago in its housing age distribution, but with slightly more pre-1940 and 1950s housing (Figure 8.1). The City of Philadelphia also had the lowest proportion of its census tracts in which relative income increased in the 1980s and 1990s, as well as the biggest gap between the city tracts (22.7 percent) and suburban tracts (34.9 percent) increasing in relative income (Table 8.1). Few city tracts (10.8 percent) were above the metropolitan average family income in 2000. Many more tracts (47.2 percent) were above the metropolitan level in the suburbs in 2000.

Only 22.7 percent of the City of Philadelphia's neighborhoods increased in relative income during the 1990s—the lowest percentage in these six metropolitan areas. The city was almost wholly dependent on its old neighborhoods for attractive power. City neighborhoods that specialized in 1950s, 1960s, and 1970s housing had very low appeal in the 1990s, with only 5.3 percent, 15.7 percent, and 12.5 percent of their neighborhoods increasing in relative income. In comparison, the pre-1940 neighborhoods were fairly successful, with 26.8 percent of them increasing in relative income (Table 8.11). The number of pre-1940 tracts where relative income went up in the 1990s increased from 45 to 64—a significant increase but not as large as the increases in Atlanta, Chicago, and Los Angeles. Little appeal occurred in the 1980s in neighborhoods specializing in middle-aged housing, with only one tract increasing among the 57 specialized in 1950s housing. Old housing neighborhoods again did better than other neighborhoods in the 1980s (19.0 percent increasing), but not as well as in the 1990s.

In the suburbs, old neighborhoods had some appeal in the 1990s, but not as much as in Atlanta, Chicago, and Los Angeles. They were more likely to go up in relative income than 1940s, 1950s, and 1960s neighborhoods (33.9 percent to 21.2, 24.9, and 23.3 percent, respectively), but they trailed newer suburban neighborhoods, including those specializing in 1970s and 1980s housing, the only one of these six metropolitan areas where that occurred (Table 8.11). Philadelphia's pre-1940 suburban neighborhoods exhibited more housing market appeal than middle-aged neighborhoods in the city and suburbs, but relative to the other five metropolitan areas, the appeal of these old neighborhoods was less distinctive.

Richmond, Virginia

A much smaller metropolitan area than the other five, which rank in the largest eight in population, Richmond's housing age pattern is similar to that of Washington, D.C., with most of its housing constructed during the 1970s, 1980s, and 1990s (Figure 8.1). With 9.7 percent of its housing built before 1940, it had less than Philadelphia, Chicago, and Los Angeles, and slightly more than Washington, D.C.

The City of Richmond had about the same percentage of census tracts increasing in relative income as its suburbs in the 1980s, and many more increased in the city in the 1990s than in the suburbs (Table 8.1). The surprise in Richmond during the 1990s was, first, that 43.1 percent of its city neighborhoods increased in relative income—a

Table 8.11
Relative Average Family Income Increasing
for Census Tracts Specialized in Housing Constructed
in Different Decades—Philadelphia Metropolitan Area

Decade of Housing Construction	Change 1980 to 1990			Change 1990 to 2000		
	All Tracts	**Central City**	**Outside City**	**All Tracts**	**Central City**	**Outside City**
Pre-1940						
Tracts	411	237	174	413	239	174
Increased	84	45	39	123	64	59
Percent Increased	20.4%	19.0%	22.4%	29.8%	26.8%	33.9%
1940s						
Tracts	326	169	157	326	169	157
Increased	35	12	23	62	28	34
Percent Increased	10.7%	7.1%	14.6%	19.0%	16.6%	21.7%
1950s						
Tracts	262	57	205	262	57	205
Increased	35	1	34	54	3	51
Percent Increased	13.4%	1.8%	16.6%	20.6%	5.3%	24.9%
1960s						
Tracts	227	51	176	227	51	176
Increased	56	5	51	49	8	41
Percent Increased	24.7%	9.8%	29.0%	21.6%	15.7%	23.3%
1970s						
Tracts	282	32	250	282	32	250
Increased	97	4	93	92	4	88
Percent Increased	34.4%	12.5%	37.2%	32.6%	12.5%	35.2%
1980s						
Tracts	287	16	271	288	17	271
Increased	121	5	116	122	4	118
Percent Increased	42.2%	31.3%	42.8%	42.4%	23.5%	43.5%
Since 1990						
Tracts				278	9	269
Increased				150	5	145
Percent Increased				54.0%	55.6%	53.9%

In this table, a tract is considered "specialized" if it has 1.5 times or more the metropolitan proportion of housing built in that decade. Specialization in Decade of Occupied Housing Construction uses data reported in the *Census of Population and Housing 2000*. The proportion of a census tract's occupied housing in a particular period of construction is compared with the proportion for its metropolitan area.

If a census tract's Average Family Income Relative to its Metropolitan Area's Average Family Income grew by more than 2.5%, it is reported here as having "Increased."

Source: Neighborhood Change Database (NCDB) Tract Data from 1970-2000 and CensusCD 2000 (East Brunswick, NJ: GeoLytics, Inc., 2003).

larger percentage than any city except Atlanta. Second, there was virtually no difference among its neighborhoods by age of housing in their tendency to increase. Most of its neighborhoods specialized in pre-1940, 1940, or 1950s housing, however, and more than 40 percent of each of them increased in relative average family income. This was an improvement for all ages of neighborhoods in the 1990s compared with the 1980s (Table 8.12).

The striking aspect of the Richmond metropolitan area was how few suburban tracts (25.1 percent) increased compared with city tracts (43.1 percent) in the 1990s. In that respect, Richmond was similar to Atlanta and Chicago. Richmond was like Atlanta also in the immense fall-off in attractive power of suburban neighborhoods with housing 10 to 30 years old compared with the newest housing. Whereas 44.6 percent of suburban tracts specializing in 1990s housing increased in relative income, less than 10 percent of tracts specializing in 1970s and 1960s housing increased. Suburban neighborhoods with old housing (31.6 percent increased) did best after the 1990s areas.

Whereas Atlanta's precipitous decline in suburban attractiveness may be related to congestion, inconvenience, and frustration, there is little evidence in transportation data or common discussion that similar causes operate in the Richmond suburbs. One can speculate that either housing quality is lower in Richmond's suburbs, or housing is smaller, or neighborhoods are less attractive compared with the other metropolitan areas. Perhaps outward movement has been so rapid that households, which desire suburban lifestyles, have abandoned middle-aged and even recent suburban neighborhoods at a faster rate than in some other metropolitan areas and moved even farther out on the metropolitan fringe.

Washington, D.C.

The Washington, D.C., metropolitan area's housing was mostly built from 1970 through 2000 (Figure 8.1). In the city, only a handful of neighborhoods specialized in 1980s and 1990s housing. Old city neighborhoods were rather successful in the 1990s in attracting more affluent residents, with 41.9 percent increasing in relative average family income. That was more than twice the rate of increase in 1950s neighborhoods.

There were virtually the same numbers of old neighborhoods in the suburbs (130) as in the city (129). These old suburban neighborhoods performed even better at increasing in relative income, as 52.3 percent did in the 1990s. They performed with similar strength in the 1980s (51.3 percent increased), an unusual similarity between the appeal of old neighborhoods in the 1980s and 1990s. In fact, old suburbs were even more likely to increase in relative income in the 1980s than were suburban areas specializing in 1980s housing—51.3 percent to 37.6 percent (Table 8.13). Washington, D.C., was the only metropolitan area where old suburbs were more likely to increase in relative income than the areas with the newest housing in both the 1980s and 1990s.

Washington, D.C., also was the only city in which fewer census tracts increased in relative income in the 1990s (58) than in the 1980s (63). Nearly all of these specialized in pre-1940 housing—55 in the 1980s and 54 in the 1990s. High proportions of tracts that increased in relative income in the 1990s tended to specialize in pre-1940 housing in each of the central cities: 51 of 61 in Atlanta, 301 of 379 in Chicago, 209 of 396 in Los Angeles, 64 of 83 in Philadelphia, 21 of 28 in Richmond, and 54 of 58 in Washington, D.C. (Table 8.1).

Table 8.12
Relative Average Family Income Increasing for Census Tracts Specialized in Housing Constructed in Different Decades—Richmond Metropolitan Area

Decade of Housing Construction	Change 1980 to 1990			Change 1990 to 2000		
	All Tracts	Central City	Outside City	All Tracts	Central City	Outside City
Pre-1940						
Tracts	66	47	19	66	47	19
Increased	19	17	2	27	21	6
Percent Increased	28.8%	36.2%	10.5%	40.9%	44.7%	31.6%
1940s						
Tracts	75	45	30	75	45	30
Increased	15	13	2	27	20	7
Percent Increased	20.0%	28.9%	6.7%	36.0%	44.4%	23.3%
1950s						
Tracts	68	24	44	68	24	44
Increased	10	5	5	17	10	7
Percent Increased	14.7%	20.8%	11.4%	25.0%	41.7%	15.9%
1960s						
Tracts	61	18	43	61	18	43
Increased	6	2	4	9	6	3
Percent Increased	9.8%	11.1%	9.3%	14.8%	33.3%	7.0%
1970s						
Tracts	38	6	32	38	6	32
Increased	3	0	3	4	3	1
Percent Increased	7.9%	0.0%	9.4%	10.5%	50.0%	3.1%
1980s						
Tracts	45	1	44	45	1	44
Increased	16	0	16	10	1	9
Percent Increased	35.6%	0.0%	36.4%	22.2%	100.0%	20.5%
Since 1990						
Tracts				56	0	56
Increased				25	0	25
Percent Increased				44.6%	0.0%	44.6%

In this table, a tract is considered "specialized" if it has 1.5 times or more the metropolitan proportion of housing built in that decade. Specialization in Decade of Occupied Housing Construction uses data reported in the *Census of Population and Housing 2000*. The proportion of a census tract's occupied housing in a particular period of construction is compared with the proportion for its metropolitan area.

If a census tract's Average Family Income Relative to its Metropolitan Area's Average Family Income grew by more than 2.5%, it is reported here as having "Increased."

Source: Neighborhood Change Database (NCDB) Tract Data from 1970-2000 and CensusCD 2000 (East Brunswick, NJ: GeoLytics, Inc., 2003).

Table 8.13
Relative Average Family Income Increasing for
Census Tracts Specialized in Housing Constructed in Different
Decades—Washington, D.C., Primary Metropolitan Area

Decade of Housing Construction	Change 1980 to 1990			Change 1990 to 2000		
	All Tracts	Central City	Outside City	All Tracts	Central City	Outside City
Pre-1940						
Tracts	243	130	113	259	129	130
Increased	113	55	58	122	54	68
Percent Increased	46.5%	42.3%	51.3%	47.1%	41.9%	52.3%
1940s						
Tracts	306	122	184	309	122	187
Increased	97	33	64	104	35	69
Percent Increased	31.7%	27.0%	34.8%	33.7%	28.7%	36.9%
1950s						
Tracts	317	77	240	318	77	241
Increased	85	19	66	87	14	73
Percent Increased	26.8%	24.7%	27.5%	27.4%	18.2%	30.3%
1960s						
Tracts	259	29	230	259	29	230
Increased	47	7	40	47	5	42
Percent Increased	18.1%	24.1%	17.4%	18.1%	17.2%	18.3%
1970s						
Tracts	188	9	179	195	8	187
Increased	49	2	47	55	3	52
Percent Increased	26.1%	22.2%	26.3%	28.2%	37.5%	27.8%
1980s						
Tracts	177	4	173	188	3	185
Increased	67	2	65	73	2	71
Percent Increased	37.9%	50.0%	37.6%	38.8%	66.7%	38.4%
Since 1990						
Tracts				218	3	215
Increased				109	1	108
Percent Increased				50.0%	33.3%	50.2%

In this table, a tract is considered "specialized" if it has 1.5 times or more the metropolitan proportion of housing built in that decade. Specialization in Decade of Occupied Housing Construction uses data reported in the *Census of Population and Housing 2000*. The proportion of a census tract's occupied housing in a particular period of construction is compared with the proportion for its metropolitan area.

If a census tract's Average Family Income Relative to its Metropolitan Area's Average Family Income grew by more than 2.5%, it is reported here as having "Increased."

Source: Neighborhood Change Database (NCDB) Tract Data from 1970-2000 and CensusCD 2000 (East Brunswick, NJ: GeoLytics, Inc., 2003).

SUMMARY OF TRENDS

Central city neighborhoods were more likely to increase in relative income in the 1990s than in the 1980s. Old neighborhoods were much better prospects for income revival than were middle-aged neighborhoods. Because central cities had few neighborhoods with substantial amounts of new housing and generally were less well off, the revival of cities depends on stayers and buyers liking old housing and neighborhoods. With old neighborhoods frequently going up in relative average family income in the 1990s, the trajectory for cities may be better in the next decade as well.

In suburbs, there was a striking difference between the tendency for census tracts with the newest housing to rise in relative income combined with dramatically less likelihood of increases in census tracts with housing 10 to 30 years old. As in central cities, areas with considerable middle-aged housing from the 1950s and 1960s were least likely to increase in relative income. Old neighborhoods specializing in housing constructed before 1940 were most likely, next to the areas specializing in the most recent housing, to go up in relative income.

Evidence for trickle-down processes of neighborhood change was modest at best in the data about which census tracts by age of housing had incomes higher than metropolitan averages. More pre-1940 neighborhoods in cities and suburbs in 2000 had average family incomes higher than neighborhoods dominated by 1940s housing. In suburbs, a higher percentage of pre-1940 than 1940s neighborhoods increased faster than metropolitan income averages in 1970, 1980, and 1990, as well as in 2000, though by small margins. Moreover, pre-1940 suburban neighborhoods were as likely as 1950s neighborhoods in 2000 to have incomes above metropolitan averages. With the old neighborhoods having been most likely to increase in relative income in the 1990s, after the newest neighborhoods, they have prospects of passing the 1950s and 1960s neighborhoods in relative income in the near future.

For highly specialized tracts (2.5 times the metropolitan average), pre-1940 tracts in central cities and suburbs separately had higher relative incomes in 2000 than 1940s and 1950s tracts. Should these trends continue, there could be major changes in 10 or 20 years in the relative income status of central cities and many suburbs. In addition, substantially higher percentages of highly specialized, pre-1940 neighborhoods in suburbs had higher incomes relative to metropolitan incomes than 1940s neighborhoods. One can speculate that some of these prospering old suburbs were commuter rail suburbs before autos dominated commuting. However, there also were numerous industrial suburbs and farm service suburbs that subsequently were engulfed by sprawl in recent decades. These suburbs might be less likely to have incomes above metropolitan averages. By 2000, highly specialized, pre-1940s neighborhoods in cities also were more likely to have incomes exceeding metropolitan averages than were tracts highly specialized in 1940s and 1950s housing.

IMPENDING SUBURBAN TRIUMPH FROM A 1950 PERSPECTIVE

With hindsight, we know that the reordering of metropolitan settlements accelerated after World War II ended in 1945. By 1960, suburban population increase was apparent. The outward movement of middle- and upper-income residents was leading to alarm that central cities were heading toward economic and social disaster, but that was by 1960. What did the city and suburban relationship look like in 1950? We will explore that question by examining data for the six metropolitan areas we have emphasized in this chapter. We will consider population, value of owner-occupied housing, and median family income.

Population shifts were apparent in 1950. In 1940, these six central cities contained 63.6 percent of their metropolitan population. By 1950, the cities' share of metropolitan population had fallen to 57.0 percent. Each of the cities added population. Their average increase was 13.0 percent. The total city increase was 1,035,887 persons. In contrast, the outside central city area increased by 2,221,373 persons and by 49.5 percent. Still, four of these six central cities had a majority of metropolitan population within their borders in 1950. By 1960, however, only two of the six cities contained a majority of metropolitan population, and their average metropolitan population share had declined to 46.7 percent. Moreover, four of the six cities lost population between 1950 and 1960 (Table 8.14).

Values of owner-occupied housing scarcely changed between 1940 and 1950. On average, values were slightly higher in these six central cities than their outside cities, with city-to-metropolitan area averages of 101.8 percent in 1940 and 101.6 percent in 1950. By 1960, values in the six metropolitan areas had fallen to a city-to-metropolitan area average of 93.4 percent. The decline would have been greater except that city values held up relative to suburban values in Los Angeles (Table 8.15).

Median family income data were not available in 1940. In 1950, incomes were higher in each of the metropolitan suburbs than in the six central cities. However, the difference was moderate and, with trend data not available and housing values holding steady from 1940 to 1950, the moderate income deficiency in central cities may not have been alarming. By 1960, five of the six central cities had fallen significantly in relative median family income. The average decline was modest, however, because, in the City of Los Angeles, relative family incomes rose substantially (Table 8.16).

On balance, a policy analyst or public official searching census data for clues about the future of central cities and suburbs would have found a mixed picture in 1950. Population was up in cities, housing values were slightly higher in cities than suburbs, and relative median family income was moderately lower in central cities than suburbs. Only the population trend may have been alarming to cities grown accustomed to dominance within their metropolitan areas. These discoveries lead to a question: Were cities and old suburbs poised for recovery in 2000 similar to suburban territories that were poised for take-off in 1950?

Returning to the present, reflecting on the 2000 census from a vantage point in 2005, are clues available that might foreshadow a rearranging of thriving and declining parts of metropolitan areas? The broadest data trends seem more auspicious for suburbs collectively than for cities. Suburbs' population continued to rise dramatically in the 1990s, and relative income in suburbs was higher and continued to increase at a modest though diminishing rate.

However, when elements of changes are examined, other evidence surfaces. These are some of the trends that occurred between 1990 and 2000, in addition to the trends summarized above concerning relative income increases in old neighborhoods in cities and suburbs:

Table 8.14

Population in Six Central Cities and Metropolitan Areas: 1940, 1950, and 1960

	1940			1950			1960		
	Central Cities	Metro-politan Areas	Central City as Percent of Metro-politan Area	Central Cities	Metro-politan Areas	Central City as Percent of Metro-politan Area	Central Cities	Metro-politan Areas	Central City as Percent of Metro-politan Area
Atlanta	302,288	558,842	54.1	331,314	726,989	45.6	487,455	1,017,188	47.9
Chicago	3,396,808	4,569,643	74.3	3,620,962	5,177,868	69.9	3,550,404	6,220,913	57.1
Los Angeles	1,504,277	2,916,403	51.6	1,970,358	4,367,911	45.1	2,479,015	6,742,696	36.8
Philadelphia	1,931,334	3,199,637	60.4	2,071,605	3,671,048	56.4	2,002,512	4,342,897	46.1
Richmond	193,042	266,185	72.5	230,310	328,050	70.2	219,958	408,494	53.8
Washington, DC	663,091	967,985	68.5	802,178	1,464,089	54.8	763,956	2,001,897	38.2
Average	1,331,807	2,079,783	63.6	1,504,454	2,622,659	57.0	1,583,883	3,455,681	46.7

Source: U.S. Census Bureau, *Census of Population 1960, Vol. 1, Characteristics of the Population* (Washington, DC: U.S. Government Printing Office, 1963), Table 33.

Table 8.15
Median Value of Owner-Occupied Housing in Six Central Cities and Metropolitan Areas: 1940, 1950, and 1960

	1940*			1950			1960		
	Central Cities	Metropolitan Areas	Central City as Percent of Metropolitan Area	Central Cities	Metropolitan Areas	Central City as Percent of Metropolitan Area	Central Cities	Metropolitan Areas	Central City as Percent of Metropolitan Area
Atlanta	$3,492	$3,372	103.6	$8,204	$8,039	102.1	$12,000	$12,400	96.8
Chicago	4,975	5,215	95.4	12,232	11,977	102.1	18,000	18,600	96.8
Los Angeles	3,958	3,735	106.0	10,821	9,899	109.3	17,300	15,900	108.8
Philadelphia	3,265	3,548	92.0	7,009	7,818	89.7	8,700	10,900	79.8
Richmond	4,617	4,446	103.8	8,263	8,009	103.2	10,300	11,700	88.0
Washington, DC	7,926	7,221	109.8	14,498	14,022	103.4	15,400	17,100	90.1
Average	4,706	4,590	101.8	10,171	9,961	101.6	13,617	14,433	93.4

*In 1940 and 1950, values were limited to owner-occupied, one-unit dwellings.

Sources: U.S. Census Bureau, *Census of Housing 1940, Vol. III, Housing Characteristics by Monthly Value or Rent* (Washington, DC: U.S. Government Printing Office, 1943), Tables B-2, C-2; U.S. Census Bureau, *Census of Housing 1950, Vol. I, General Characteristics* (Washington, DC: U.S. Government Printing Office, 1953), Tables 26, 31; U.S. Census Bureau, *Census of Housing 1960, Vol. II, Metropolitan Housing* (Washington, DC: U.S. Government Printing Office, 1963), Tables A-1, B-1.

Table 8.16
Median Family Income in Six Central Cities
and Metropolitan Areas: 1950 and 1960

	1950			1960		
	Central Cities	Metro-politan Cities	Central City as Percent of Metro-politan Area	Central Cities	Metro-politan Cities	Central City as Percent of Metro-politan Area
Atlanta	$2,664	$2,936	90.7	$5,029	$5,758	87.3
Chicago	3,956	4,063	97.4	6,738	7,342	91.8
Los Angeles	3,575	3,650	97.9	6,896	6,177	111.6
Philadelphia	3,322	3,466	95.8	5,782	6,433	89.9
Richmond	3,283	3,383	97.0	5,156	6,071	84.9
Washington, D.C.	3,800	4,262	89.2	5,993	7,577	79.1
Average	3,433	3,627	94.7	5,932	6,560	90.8

Sources: U.S. Census Bureau, *Census of Population: 1950, Vol. II, Characteristics of the Population* (Washington, DC: U.S. Government Printing Office, 1953), Table 37; U.S. Census Bureau, *Census of Population: 1960, Vol. I, Characteristics of the Population* (Washington, DC: U.S. Government Printing Office, 1963),Tables 148 and 154.

- Many downtowns increased in population.
- Four of the 20 largest cities in 1930 hit their population peaks in 2000.
- Seventy-three percent of the central cities in 35 large metropolitan areas increased in population.
- The elderly population increased, and the size of the pre-elderly population presaged a much larger elderly population in the future.
- Condominium ownership increased significantly.
- The number of census tracts with extreme concentrated poverty diminished by 24 percent.
- Extreme concentrated poverty diminished among African-Americans.
- As will be seen in later chapters, some cities and old suburbs experienced large increases in owner-occupied housing sales prices and residential property assessments.

These changes were matched with the fact that:
- As many suburbs went down as up in relative income.
- More than one-fourth of suburbs lost population.
- Middle-aged housing bore the brunt of relative income declines.
- Numerous suburbs (155) had relative per capita income lower than Detroit.
- More suburbs had lower relative median family income than Detroit in 2000 than in 1990.

- Concentrated poverty increased in suburbs.
- Minority and immigrant populations increased in suburbs, reducing population composition differences between suburbs and cities.

In sum, the trickle-down process of neighborhood change seemed to be affecting transitions more in middle-aged neighborhoods that are the norm in suburbs, whereas old neighborhoods that are more common in cities and inner suburbs seemed to be overcoming previous effects of the trickle-down neighborhood change process.

Given these clues, is it plausible to foresee a rearrangement of where low-, moderate-, middle-, and upper-income households will be located by 2010 and 2020? May that rearrangement include the revival of many central cities and the decline of many middle-aged suburbs? It seems there are as many or more clues in 2005 that these changes are possible than there were clues in 1955 based on the 1950 census that the impending triumph of suburbia was at hand.

One major difference between conditions in 2005 and 1955, however, is that central cities and some older suburbs must recover from several decades of deterioration and a position of considerable disadvantage. Suburbs in 1950 were being created rather than being revived. The institutional framework in housing and local government fragmentation was present in 1950 for suburbs to grow rapidly, although the growth facilitation provided by interstate highways was not yet in place. The framework of institutions and the array of development, planning, and design ideas that was dominant in 1950 and thereafter also contained the seeds of a damaged, mutated crop of suburban nonplaces, which the following decades revealed. This damaged pattern of suburbia is part of the subjects examined in the second half of this book. Just as cities in 1950 contained elements of vulnerability—such as a housing stock that was not compatible with the goal of a major increase in home ownership—the suburbs of 2000 contain elements of inconvenience related to separated land uses and necessity for driving 10 or more trips per day per household, which may be incompatible with goals of reducing daily stress and increasing health and quality of life.

We have seen in Chapter 6 that many suburbs have fallen in relative income well below even the lowest relative income central cities. A key question now is whether cities will continue to improve relative to some suburbs because of the continued decline of suburbs if more people become frustrated with suburban conditions or change their preferences more in line with city conditions. In addition, other than having some potential attractiveness in old housing, do central cities have advantages and opportunities that may complement greater preferences for old neighborhoods? What role have myths (mixtures of accurate and inaccurate beliefs and miscalculations of future effects) had on suburbanization? May reshaping myths on which households have made location decisions alter some households' location preferences? We turn to those subjects in Chapters 9, 10, and 11.

NOTES

1. The Neighborhood Change Database produced by the Urban Institute in cooperation with GeoLytics, Inc., is used for population, housing units, and income levels for 1970, 1980, and 1990. This database remapped 1970, 1980, and 1990 census tracts to equivalent 2000 census tracts. Data for 2000 come from the *Census of Population and Housing 2000* as published by GeoLytics' CensusCD. Some income data for 1970, 1980, and on occasion 1990, are suppressed in the Neighborhood Change Database and data for those tracts are not included in the tables here.

2. Peter Tatian, *CensusCD Neighborhood Change Data Base: 1970-2000 Tract Data and Data Users Guide* (Washington, DC: The Urban Institute in cooperation with GeoLytics, Inc., 2002).

3. Daniel P. McMillen, "The Return of Centralization to Chicago: Using Repeat Sales to Identify Changes in House Price Distance Gradients," *Regional Science and Urban Economics* 33 (2003), p. 287.

Beliefs
and Places

9

Linking Patterns, Beliefs, and Policies

Residential spatial patterns—described by relative income in cities, suburbs, and census tracts, as analyzed in Chapters 3 through 8—evolve through location decisions. Beliefs and public policies shape decisions by private sector actors (home buyers and renters, lenders, developers, and mortgage purchasers) and public sector actors (local elected officials, planners, planning and zoning commissions, water and sewer authorities, state legislatures, courts, housing administrators, and transportation agencies). Institutional structures, including fragmented local governance, adopt and implement policies. They shape incentives for residents, investors, and government officials to act in specific ways. The tyranny of easy development decisions (see Chapter 1) is an example of a decision process with spatial effects that results from institutional structures and public policy incentives interacting with beliefs.

Policies may embody theories about how to achieve preferred results. Policies always reflect political access and usually some compromise. Policy implementation, especially in a federal system, is uneven. Each of these characteristics—theories, access, compromise, and implementation—may shift at any time. Policies, such as prohibitions against discrimination, may influence beliefs. Both policies and beliefs may influence behavior.

Beliefs have many sources—factual, ideological, mythical, rational, emotional, and subconscious. Beliefs include value preferences, perceptions of facts, and interpretations of events, trends, and prospects. Whether beliefs are accurate guides to probable behavior in markets has been disputed among economists and psychologists.[1] We expect beliefs and behavior to be related, but not uniformly or reliably. Beliefs are complex, intertwined, and inconsistent. Behavior often is habitual and driven by unrecognized sources in past experience. Sometimes beliefs are based on myths, by which we mean partially accurate but significantly distorted interpretations of reality. Consequently, market decisions will be driven by combinations of explicit beliefs, some of which are inaccurate in significant ways, by complex and inconsistent weighting of beliefs in specific contexts, and by habits and unconscious motivations.

These diverse components come into play unpredictably in mega-decisions. Mega-decisions have wide-ranging and long-term social and economic consequences. These are decisions like getting married, having children, choosing higher education settings, deciding on jobs and careers, and purchasing residences. These mega-decisions are more likely to involve bounded rationality, composed of mixtures of rational calculations, emotional reactions, and even irrational judgments.[2]

Results of residential location decisions, such as relative income spatial patterns, will vary from time to time and place to place based on interactions among beliefs, habits, institutional structures, and policies. In a rapidly changing society, changes in results may occur because each of these elements—beliefs, habits, institutions, and policies—are subject to change. For example, changes have occurred in beliefs about race, travel habits, government fragmentation in metropolitan areas, and public policies concerning highways and home ownership. Additional changes can occur in any of these subjects. Consequently, relative income patterns resulting from the trickle-down process of neighborhood change should not be expected to remain the same over time or the same in every metropolitan area. There are too many variables to expect spatial consistency. Too many changes in beliefs, habits, institutions, and policies can occur to expect each decade to be like other decades.

In previous chapters, we have tracked trends in spatial patterns. In this chapter, we discuss links among patterns, beliefs, and policies. We consider some arguments by policy analysts about these linkages. We note some changes in conditions, such as crime rates, that may have influenced beliefs about safety. We identify demographic changes in household composition that may have altered the clustering of beliefs. We consider some survey findings that may influence residential location choices. We also raise the possibility that some policy changes, or greater skill in implementing traditional policy concerns, may contribute to changing beliefs and therefore alter future spatial patterns. In subsequent chapters, we address mythical beliefs about safety on cul-de-sacs and safety anywhere in exurbia, and policy problems and opportunities concerning small houses and their settings.

A POLICY DEBATE ABOUT
TRICKLE-DOWN NEIGHBORHOOD CHANGE

Most theorists have presented the trickle-down process of neighborhood change as a function of two reinforcing conditions. The first condition is that housing as it ages becomes more expensive to maintain, as well as potentially being out of fashion with changing tastes. The second condition is that neighborhoods with aging housing, and aging public infrastructure, are likely to accumulate social problems that increasingly act as "push" factors, diminishing prospects that replacement in-movers will be as affluent as out-movers.[3] From this formulation, it follows that neighborhood stability or enhancement would depend upon especially attractive housing and locations to counteract these almost mechanical probabilities of decline.

A contrary view was offered in the aptly named journal, *Housing Policy Debate*, by John T. Metzger. Metzger turned the theory on its head. He blamed the authors and promoters of the theory, singling out Anthony Downs for special attention, for creating a self-fulfilling prophecy. Public policies, like urban renewal, Federal Housing Administration mortgage guarantees, and interstate highways, interacting with racially biased implementation of public and private lending practices, had promoted neighborhood decline. The most dramatic declines were caused by redlining by banks, in which banks refused to make mortgage loans and business loans in some neighborhoods, principally neighborhoods with "too many" blacks. The main beneficiaries of these lending practices and public policies have been middle- and upper-income suburban whites, and the developers and lenders who promoted suburbanization.[4] "The neighborhood life-cycle theory and triage planning," Metzger concluded, ". . . accelerated disinvestment in low-income and minority neighborhoods, exacerbating disparities in wealth, the wasteful consumption and desertion of urban land, and outward suburban sprawl."[5]

Anthony Downs claimed in the same issue of *Housing Policy Debate* that Metzger was confusing cause and effect. Downs wrote: "Local policies by city governments and lending institutions actually had little direct impact on the rates of abandonment occurring within city boundaries . . . In the nation as a whole, from 1950 to 1970, 32.5 million new housing units (including mobile homes) were built, but only 19.9 million households were added to the population. This excess suburban construction permitted so many households to move out of central cities that even the poorest of the remaining households had multiple choices of where to live; otherwise they would never have abandoned any units."[6]

While agreeing with Metzger that neighborhood life-cycle theory overstates the probability of decline, and acknowledging the importance of available capital, Kenneth Temkin added: "A neighborhood's trajectory is affected by many factors in addition to the availability of capital. Collective activity . . . may not be enough to stabilize a neighborhood if the residents do not believe it is a good place to live . . . Metzger's alternative model leaves . . . the impression that any neighborhood is viable: All that is needed is an increase in capital along with policies to ensure that residents remain there as their economic conditions improve."[7]

Metzger's argument reduced to a claim that public policies and private lending practices could determine spatial patterns. In this instance, Metzger added that a theory could determine public policies, and that one particular theorist could dominate an entire public policy domain. The counterarguments by Downs and Temkin claimed that social reality was more complex, including causal potential in the beliefs of household members making residential location decisions, as well as by those who own and build housing.

INFLUENCES ON PREFERENCES

In its benign form, the trickle-down neighborhood change process is attributed to aspects of neighborhood aging. Several "push" factors also have been specified that augment influences of neighborhood aging. Race is cited more often than other influences, reflecting volatile race relations, population redistribution, and territorial conflicts. In the 1950s and 1960s, the notion of a tipping point—a percentage of minorities, usually blacks, above which whites would rapidly move out—was common. The 1970s and 1980s were characterized by more complex trends and patterns. Barrett Lee and Peter Wood found that 46 percent of racially mixed tracts in 1970 were stable or had nonblack increases by 1980, rather than increasing their black proportion.[8] John Ottensmann discovered that about half of substantially African-American neighborhoods remained racially stable or declined in their black percentage from 1970 to 1990.[9] "Whites were moving into mixed neighborhoods in surprising numbers ... the tipping-point hypothesis ... no longer is adequate for understanding racial change," Ottensmann concluded.[10] These diverse trends would not occur if effects of a racial tipping point were inevitable.

Still, the notion that race trumps other neighborhood change forces persisted in the 1990s and beyond. David Rusk in *Inside Game Outside Game* argued that race and sprawl are intertwined, even though racial anxiety has lessened.[11] As evidence of less racial tension, Rusk cited a survey finding from 1939 that 41 percent of the 5,146 respondents believed "'there should be laws compelling Negroes to live in certain districts.'"[12] Then he cited a 1997 Gallup survey in which only 1 percent of whites said they would move if a black family moved next door. Despite this change in attitudes by whites, Rusk thought a television documentary was revealing and persuasive that discovered "uncomfortable feelings" occurred when blacks became too numerous at a shopping center, especially when whites thought they might become a minority, leading to desires by some whites to move away.[13] "Watching the show that evening," Rusk wrote, "I realized that I had probably never heard a more compelling man-on-the-street connection between the issues of race and sprawl."[14] Rusk apparently was referring to "uncomfortable feelings" so strong that racial anxieties still would motivate decisions by many whites to move out, even though responses to survey questions had changed dramatically.

Myron Orfield in *American Metropolitics* argued that the racial tipping point hypothesis, when allied with poverty, applied in public schools and, therefore, by extension, still was the leading indicator of impending neighborhood decline.[15] Orfield wrote "... when schools reach certain thresholds of poverty—and its attendant racial segregation—middle-class families of all races with children that have residential choices will leave the community ... once the minority share in a community's schools increases to a threshold level (10 to 20 percent), racial transition accelerates until minority percentages reach very high levels (greater than 80 percent). Change occurs fastest at levels of 20 to 50 percent and proceeds inexorably until schools are highly segregated."[16] Continuing, Orfield said that strong housing markets depend on interest by middle-class whites, because middle-class blacks and Latinos still are not numerous enough.[17]

Downs in *Housing Policy Debate* wrote about the 1950s and 1960s: "When most middle-income whites withdrew en masse from adjacent neighborhoods, that opened the way for rapid transition to all-black occupancy."[18] Concerning recent decades, Downs continued: "... repeated empirical surveys of white household's views on racial integration have confirmed their continuing predominance and their crucial role in affecting housing choices—and therefore neighborhood racial changes. Douglas Massey and Nancy Denton and Reynolds Farley et al. have summarized the latest factual evidence."[19]

Farley, in two articles published in 1993, found that whites had become more accepting of black neighbors. "The preferences of whites for neighborhood segregation have changed," Farley and his colleagues noted, "even in a metropolis as driven by race as Detroit. Whites increasingly report that they are comfortable with blacks as neighbors and that they will not move away when blacks arrive ... the tipping point in Detroit shifted from a 30 percent black neighborhood in 1976 to 40 percent in 1992."[20] The tipping point is the black percentage above which a smaller percentage of whites is willing to move in than wants to move out. Examining attitudes of whites and blacks to housing integration in national surveys conducted from 1942 to 1990, Farley concluded: "In the last half century, whites have changed their attitudes and have increasingly supported the principle of racial residential integration."[21] Patterns of white-black residential segregation had declined by 1990, but much less than attitudes had changed.

Survey data since Downs' "Comment" was published in 2000 reveal that beliefs about racial and ethnic harmony became more positive between 2001 and 2004. According to Gallup's annual *Minority Rights and Relations* survey, 72 percent of respondents considered white-black relations to be very good or somewhat good in 2004 compared with 63 percent in 2001. White-Hispanic relations were perceived to be very good or somewhat good by 74 percent in 2004, up from 66 percent in 2001. Moreover, blacks were nearly as likely as whites in 2004 to perceive white-black relations to be good—68 percent to 74 percent.[22]

To us, it seems unlikely that the role of race has been the same everywhere. It seems unlikely as well that the role of race has been the same in each decade since 1950. Racial attitudes have been more important in some places than others, as differences in racial isolation and indexes of racial dissimilarity attest. As Orfield has argued, social behavior associated with poverty amplifies anxieties about race. Blacks were less racially isolated in 1990 in metropolitan areas with small numbers of blacks than in metropolitan areas where they were more numerous.[23] We suspect that race was a less important influence on residential location decisions in many places in 2000 than it had been in 1950 and 1960, because of a growing black middle class. Findings described in Chapter 4 about reductions in the 1990s in extreme poverty concentrations in black neighborhoods and an increase in relative income among blacks in suburbs are consistent with this interpretation.

Downs argued that different conditions in the 1980s led to different actions by lenders than in the 1950s and 1960s. He cited "the explosive expansion of low-income African-American big-city populations" in the 1950s and 1960s as having income levels too low to repay mortgage loans without subsidies that were not then available. Whereas by the 1980s, African-American populations in many cities were declining and their incomes were higher, so that "possibilities for stability were much greater."[24]

If racial attitudes become more nuanced over time, then other influences on location patterns will become more important. If racial polarization has promoted suburbanization, as usually is claimed, then more neutrality concerning race, as well as more black suburbanization, may enhance prospects that central cities and some inner suburbs will become more attractive to middle- and upper-income whites. Indeed, per capita income of whites was higher in the central cities of Atlanta, Los Angeles, Richmond, and Washington, D.C., than in their suburbs in 2000, and it was nearly as high in Chicago as in its suburbs. Per capita income of central city whites was considerably lower than the income of suburban whites only in Philadelphia, of the six metropolitan areas we have emphasized.

By 2000, more racial mixing had occurred in the nation's 10 largest metropolitan areas. Racial mixing was influenced by the increase in Hispanics and Asian-Americans. Whites and blacks became less likely to live in neighborhoods where they predominated in 2000 than in 1990. Hispanics and Asian-Americans were more likely to be dominant in some neighborhoods than 10 years earlier. Mixed-race neighborhoods increased especially in suburbs, as racially homogeneous neighborhoods diminished.[25]

CONDITIONS AND IDEAS INFLUENCE BELIEFS AND ACTIONS

Other metropolitan conditions changed during the 1945 to 2000 period, leading to changes in beliefs and policies. Sprawl had continued throughout these 55 years, achieving the goal that most Americans preferred. However, success at low-density development led to opposition as well as support. "As a result of increasingly intrusive difficulties during the 1980s," Downs wrote, "a remarkable transformation occurred in the attitude of hundreds of local governments . . . many have come to regard growth as responsible for traffic congestion, air pollution, loss of open space, higher taxes to pay for additional infrastructure, and a lack of affordable housing. They have adopted policies designed to control growth in their communities."[26]

States adopted growth management programs in Oregon, Florida, Vermont, and New Jersey, among others.[27] Some metropolitan areas gave growth management serious attention, principally Minneapolis–St. Paul[28] and Portland, Oregon,[29] but only Portland achieved notable success. Mainly, growth management was conducted by individual counties, lacking power to command collaboration with other counties.[30] The consequence was leap-frog development beyond or next to the county or town (Ramapo and Petaluma) that attempted growth management on its own. This sprawl pattern, however, including edge cities[31] and then edgeless cities,[32] increased commuting-to-work times, increased traffic congestion on weekends, and probably increased the number of individuals who craved a different development pattern for themselves.

Critics of placeless metropolitan areas and advocates of creating places where people like to be, such as so-called third places for social interaction, reacted to these new conditions by advocating old ideas. These old ideas were:

• *Smart growth*, which mainly means compact development, infill, refill, densification, mixed use, neighborhood preservation, farmland preservation, and contiguous rather than leap-frog development.

• *New urbanism* (neotraditional neighborhood development), which means narrow, connected streets; small lots; front porches; occasional alleys; mixed uses; shopping nearby; and an absence or minimal use of cul-de-sacs.[33]

• *Downtown redevelopment*, especially adding housing, entertainment, and culture to existing downtowns, while retaining as much of traditional commercial and office uses, and some industrial uses, as late 20th century and early 21st century conditions permit.

• *Transit-oriented development*, which means dense development near subway stations, substantial development near above-ground mass transit and commuter rail suburban downtowns with housing, limited parking, mixed use, and linear mixed-use development along street car lines.[34]

More transportation alternatives would be provided by each of these development concepts. Compact and mixed-use development makes automobiles a choice rather than a necessity. As the car liberated households early in the 20th century, mixed-use densification in the 21st century can liberate households from excessive auto dependence in the contemporary metropolis. Excessive auto dependence is the condition to which each of these place-making ideas reacted. More people may have been ready to embrace or consider these physical development patterns in the late 20th century because of inconvenience and low accessibility that low-density development from 1945 to 2000 had brought about.[35]

CONSUMER PREFERENCES FOR NEIGHBORHOOD SETTINGS

The rise of interest in smart growth and neotraditional town and neighborhood design in the 1980s and 1990s prompted curiosity by researchers about consumer preferences and market prospects for more compact and mixed-use development versus low-density, single-use suburban development. Several studies have probed these questions.

Hazel Morrow-Jones, Elena Irwin, and Brian Roe attempted to identify the appeal of physical design characteristics in asking respondents in central Ohio to choose residential locations. The questions focused on neighborhood layout and density, parks, agricultural land, and commuting time, but they did not distinguish mixed land use, architectural style, or transit accessibility. One finding was that respondents preferred curvilinear cul-de-sac street networks with low housing density to grid street networks with higher density. Among the features tested, access to a park compensated best for the disfavor of grid street networks.[36]

Emily Talen, in a survey of residents of an affluent suburb 25 miles north of Dallas, found that respondents generally liked their suburban setting, and they disagreed with claims that suburban development harms the environment (77 percent) and excludes too many potential residents (72 percent). For the suburbanites most likely to accept arguments in favor of compact, mixed-use development, "time spent in the car was found to be the variable with the most significance," especially noncommuting travel time.[37] Consequently, Talen concluded, "increasing urbanization of suburban areas based on the same principles of separate land uses and automobile dependence are likely to increase resident discontent."[38]

Ivonne Audirac probed whether Floridians would trade large lot sizes for more walkable accessibility. Specifically, the question posed was this: "If you were to move into a new residence, how likely would you be to live on a smaller lot if you could live within walking distance of . . . (1) open space and parks, (2) shopping, . . . (3) jobs or employment, (4) entertainment, . . . (5) community centers such as post offices or churches?"[39] Audirac found that 30 percent of respondents would make that trade-off, favoring greater walkability. Single persons and apartment and condominium dwellers were most likely to favor the walking opportunity.[40]

Respondents in a survey of more than 2,000 California residents "were almost evenly split between those that would opt to live in residential-only neighborhoods, . . . and those that would choose mixed-use neighborhoods with schools, stores and services within walking distance. Residents were also evenly split between those that would opt for a small home with a small backyard and short commute and those that would opt for a large home with a large backyard and long commute."[41]

These survey results support two interpretations. First, a majority of respondents, but sometimes a slim majority, prefers traditional suburban development to compact, mixed-use settlements. Second, more respondents prefer compact, mixed-use developments than the percentage of new such developments being constructed. According to the National Governors Association, one-third of home seekers prefer mixed-use, compact, transit-accessible developments with community centers and open space, but less than 1 percent of total new housing is constructed in these settings.[42] Consequently, an additional source of demand for pre-1940 and 1940s neighborhoods in central cities and suburbs may be from home buyers and renters whose preferences have not been met in new developments. Close-in 1950s neighborhoods also have revival potential, if obstacles imposed by too many small houses can be overcome.

This interpretation also is consistent with the interesting, though ambiguous, findings from a survey conducted jointly by the National Association of Realtors (NAR) and Smart Growth America. In their news release about the survey, the Realtors and Smart Growth America said: "Asked to choose between two communities, six in ten prospective homebuyers chose a neighborhood that offered a shorter commute, sidewalks and amenities like shops, restaurants, libraries, schools and public transportation within walking distance over a sprawling community with larger lots, limited options for walking and a longer commute."[43] Ambiguity in how to interpret this finding came from the definition of the sprawling community, which was assigned a commuting time of 45 minutes or more. Respondents may have been rejecting the commuting time as much or more than the development pattern and the inconvenience of substantial distances for noncommuting purposes.

Perhaps as important as the survey findings was the joint sponsorship between the NAR and Smart Growth America. A reason for this alliance may be discerned from the comment of NAR President Walt McDonald: "Realtors don't just sell homes, we sell communities and neighborhoods. This survey shows that most Americans prefer to live in walkable communities with shorter commutes, sidewalks and amenities close by, a trend Realtors have seen first-hand."[44] Indeed, the findings reported here in Chapters 7 and 8 should have been observed in buyer preferences noticed by Realtors. Apparently they were.

CRIME RATES FELL IN THE 1990S

Neighborhood conditions constitute "pushes" and "pulls" that influence location choices. Crime is one such important neighborhood characteristic. Crime was considered a major national problem, as well as a neighborhood concern, from the late 1960s through 1977. In Gallup polls, a standard question has been: "What do you think is the most important problem facing this country today?" Variations on that wording have been used, but responses to basically that same question can be traced periodically from 1961 through 1984. In 1961, only 1 percent of respondents thought crime was the most important problem, even at the local level. In 1979, 1981, and 1984, only 2 or 3 percent thought crime was the most important problem. However, in 1969, 13 percent and, in 1977, 15 percent said crime was the most important problem. Moreover, in 1969, 8 percent thought riots were the most important problem and 1 percent said drugs. The combination of crime, riots, and drugs was cited as the most important problem by 22 percent of respondents in 1969. In 1977, 18 percent cited crime (15) and drugs (3), while riots were not cited at all.[45]

Crime rates fell sharply during the 1990s. Violent crime declined 31 percent and property crime declined 29 percent. Violent and property crime rates in 2000 were below the 1980 rates.[46] Interpretations of causes vary. They include a smaller proportion of males of prime crime-committing ages, a strong economy in the 1990s, and an ebbing of the crack cocaine epidemic that arose in the 1980s. Possible policy causes include increased rates of incarceration, more community policing, and more police on the streets. Informal social controls also may play a role, reflecting increases in middle-income residents in many central city neighborhoods. Changes in crime conditions reduced an obstacle to middle- and upper-income households living in cities. With less worry about crime, perhaps people gave more weight to convenience and accessibility.

Crime rates dropped dramatically from 1990 to 2000 in four of the five large central cities analyzed in Chapter 8 (Table 9.1).[47] Beliefs about crime also changed. According to Gallup polls archived at the Roper Center for Public Opinion Research at the University of Connecticut, the following changes occurred in percentages of respondents believing that cities were safe to live in or visit in 1990 and 2001 (Table 9.2).[48]

Each city was believed to be considerably safer in 2001 than in 1990. Atlanta, Chicago, and Philadelphia were much more likely to be perceived as safe than not safe in 2001. In each instance, crime may have been less of a "push" factor working against interest in residing in cities in 2001 than in 1990.

In 2004, this survey was repeated by Gallup with similar findings. Of 14 large cities, 11 were perceived to be safer in 2004 than in the preceding year. These 11 cities were Minneapolis, Seattle, Dallas, Boston, Houston, San Francisco, Atlanta, Chicago, New York, Miami, and Los Angeles. The exceptions were Detroit, Philadelphia, and Washington, D.C. All 14 cities were perceived as safer in 2004 than in 1990.[49]

Table 9.1
Percent Change in Crime Rates in Central Cities 1990 to 2000

	Violent Crime Index	Property Crime Index
Atlanta	-32	-30
Chicago	-43	-31
Los Angeles	-43	-48
Philadelphia	+11	-15
Washington, D.C.	-39	-31

Source: U.S. Census Bureau, *Statistical Abstract of the United States 2002* (Washington, DC: U.S. Government Printing Office, 2003).

Table 9.2
Perceptions of Crime in Central Cities 1990 and 2001

	1990			2001		
	Safe	Not Safe	Don't Know	Safe	Not Safe	Don't Know
Atlanta	45	39	16	62	33	5
Chicago	26	65	9	53	43	4
Los Angeles	26	64	10	39	57	4
Philadelphia	40	40	20	60	33	7
Washington, D.C.	22	71	7	36	58	6 *

*Washington, D.C., data are for 1990 and 2000.

Source: Gallup Organization, Gallup polls, *Perceptions of Crime Vulnerability* (Storrs, CT: The Roper Center for Public Opinion Research, University of Connecticut, 1990 and 2001).

BELIEFS ABOUT HEALTH AND MOTOR VEHICLE SAFETY

Everyday health considerations and occasional dangers from motor vehicle crashes also are possible influences on location decisions. Attempts to link being overweight to living in low-density suburban neighborhoods are a recent phenomenon. Dangers of using, or being struck by, motor vehicles rarely have deterred people from driving long distances to work, errands, and entertainment, but they may in the future.

During 2003 and 2004, health concerns about overweight and obese Americans became more prominent. Studies were published showing higher rates of diabetes and heart disease in people who were overweight. Overweight children also were a growing health concern, being associated with rising diabetes rates in children. Residential patterns were systematically analyzed for the first time for possible connections to people being overweight. Sprawl patterns were found to be associated slightly with more overweight residents and with walking less.[50] Rising sensitivity to development pattern effects on health is new, at least as far as mass media are concerned. Public opinion polls by mid-2004 had not registered rising concern about unhealthy residential living patterns, but awareness of health implications of being overweight was increasing due to national news coverage of medical studies.

Vehicle safety related to commuting, errands, and socializing is another possible influence on residential location decisions. Cul-de-sac street networks were created in response to motor vehicle dangers within neighborhoods (Chapter 10). Exurban development was partially a response to crime in cities and inner suburbs (Chapter 11). However, both cul-de-sac neighborhoods and exurban settlements exacerbate dangers of auto dependence for commuting, errands, and socializing.

Action on vehicle safety issues has focused on driver behavior and vehicle characteristics. Mothers Against Drunk Driving targets driving under the influence of alcohol and drugs, especially among teenagers. Seat belt laws have gradually toughened and seat belt use has increased. All new motor vehicles are required to have air bags, and the number of air bags has increased from one to as many as six per vehicle.

Consumer responses to vehicle danger also has included vehicle size and weight. Safety has been a selling point for sports utility vehicles (SUVs) and light trucks, whose greater size and weight is thought to make them less likely to be arenas of death and serious injuries in vehicle crashes.[51] In 2001 and 2002, more than 50 percent of the motor vehicles sold in the United States were SUVs, mini-vans, and light trucks.[52] Despite these presumed safety decisions, Americans were pessimistic about the future of motor vehicle safety. In a Harris poll in 1999, respondents were asked whether more or less people would die in the next 10 years from various diseases and accidents. Concerning automobile crashes, 68 percent expected that crashes will kill more people.[53]

The number of deaths from motor vehicle crashes has remained above 41,000 through the 1990s and into the 21st century, passing 43,000 in 2003. In part, this high death total may result from more vehicles being driven more miles, because the death rate per miles driven has decreased. One might say it takes more miles to drive to one's death because of changes in vehicles and drivers' behavior, and Americans kept traffic fatality rates high by living farther from their driving destinations.

As we introduce the idea that myths about safety on cul-de-sacs and in exurbia have influenced settlement patterns, it is worth noting here that another myth about motor vehicles has fueled sprawl for more than 50 years: the myth of automobile convenience. It has been the desire of most Americans to be able to live where they prefer and to get from home to everywhere else they want to go in a motor vehicle, alone, and to travel at fairly high speeds at any time of day or night.[54] Inexpensive gasoline is a complementary goal of drivers. Facilitating automobile convenience has been seen as one of the most important goals for elected and appointed public officials.[55] Awareness that automobile convenience is impossible if most people drive alone in large metropolitan areas has not made much headway. In her survey of suburban residents north of Dallas, Talen reported that residents preferred low-density housing and light traffic, and "a substantial majority (73 percent) of the respondents said that they had not heard many negative views expressed about low-density suburban development."[56]

Besides health and safety related to driving, the cost of driving also could become more relevant to location decisions. If households make financial calculations about the cost of motor vehicle ownership, locations where they can have one less vehicle also may influence their decisions. If a modest vehicle is purchased for $20,000 and financed at 6 percent interest for five years, the monthly vehicle payment of more than $400 would finance $70,000 in payments per month on a 30-year mortgage at a 6 percent interest rate. Additional savings would occur from avoiding auto insurance, repairs, and operating costs. Households can upgrade their housing quality and location advantages without increasing annual household costs if they can forego owning one motor vehicle. Such calculations may have influenced some households in choosing locations with old housing in the 1990s.

DEMOGRAPHY ALTERS THE
DISTRIBUTION OF LOCATION PREFERENCES

A standard finding has been that families with children of school age typically gravitate to suburbs, while singles and couples without children are relatively more inclined to prefer central cities. If this is so, and, hypothetically, if preferences are constant over time by household type, then changes in the distribution of household types would lead to changes in the clustering of preferences for residential locations. A plausible explanation of greater attractiveness of cities, some older suburbs, and older housing could be that demographic shifts have created a frequency distribution of preferences that is more favorable to these locations.

Numerous relevant population changes have occurred. The percentage of households in families declined from 81 percent in 1970 to 69 percent in 2000. The percentage of families with children under 18 declined from 52 percent in 1980 to 48 percent in 2000. The percentage of population foreign born increased from 4.8 percent in 1970 to 11.1 percent in 2000. The percentage of persons age 65 or above increased from 9.9 percent in 1970 to 12.4 percent in 2000. The median age increased from 28.1 in 1970, 30.0 in 1980, 32.8 in 1990, and 35.3 in 2000, and it was projected to increase to 37.4 by 2010. The percentage of women age 16 and over in the labor force increased from 51.5 percent in 1980 to 60.2 percent in 2000. The percentage of married women in the labor force increased from 49.8 percent in 1980 to 61.3 percent in 2000. The percentage of divorced persons 18 and over increased from 6.2 percent in 1980 to 9.8 percent in 2000. The percentage of married persons 18 and over went down from 65.5 in 1980 to 59.5 in 2000.[57]

Each of these changes in demographic characteristics could increase the proportion of households more inclined to central city and inner-suburban living. However, elderly prominence and sometimes dominance in some suburbs have increased. Households with foreign-born members were more likely to live in suburbs in 2000 than in central cities. Still, compared with 1970, and the period from 1945 to 1970, demographic conditions in 2000 were more favorable for people choosing central cities or older suburbs. If the distribution of beliefs and preferences has changed, demography may be one source of those changes.

Concerns about neighborhood conditions vary with age and family circumstances. Dowell Myers and Elizabeth Gearin have used National Association of Home Builders data for 1999 to demonstrate that the crime rate is the most important neighborhood concern for home buyers, with more than 80 percent of each age group considering it a very important factor. The school district, on the other hand, which was very important to more than 50 percent of households age 25 to 44, diminished to a very important factor to only 22 percent of households 55 and over. The location of shopping was very important to 32 percent of households age 55 and over, and public transportation was considered very important by 16 percent, more than by younger age groups.[58]

Myers and Gearin also found that households 55 and over were projected to constitute larger proportions of moving households during the 2000 to 2010 period. Moreover, households 55 and over were twice as likely as households age 44 and under to prefer town houses in cities close to public transportation rather than larger, single-family residences in suburbs—24 percent to 11 percent.[59] The combination of diminished crime rates in cities, rising perceptions that cities are safe, and a growing proportion of movers who are age 55 and above enhances prospects that cities and older suburbs with city qualities became more attractive in the 1990s than previously and may become still more attractive in the 21st century.

RESULTS MATTER

At subdivision, neighborhood, or village scales, developments may have provided less diversity than markets would have supported. Other analysts, such as Dowell Myers and Elizabeth Gearin[60] and Christopher Leinberger[61] have reached this conclusion. Evidence from surveys is consistent with such an interpretation.

On the other hand, we have interpreted another characteristic—the large size and configuration of single-family dwellings in the 1990s—as indicative of market demand. Just as subdivision scale development may not represent demand diversity, the size and configuration of new, single-family dwellings also may skew demand. Large houses, for example, may compensate for inconvenient, remote locations. They may be larger than buyers would require if the dwellings were accessible to more destinations. Perhaps large house sizes optimize sales prospects, partly because they signal similarity of neighbors and good prospects of enhanced resale values. If reliable resale values and satisfactory neighbors can be found in more diverse neighborhoods, and sometimes in smaller houses, perhaps such houses will be in sufficient demand to maintain or increase their value in market conditions of the early 21st century. Old neighborhoods might be most likely to meet those criteria. Accessibility to mixed land uses was combined with diversity in housing size and value in pre-1940 neighborhoods more often than in mass-produced, single-use developments since 1945.

Performance by governments may influence residential location choices. If governments contribute to creating and renewing places where people like to be, demand will be greater. If dwellings are launching pads for accessible social interactions, as well as structures in which to live, work opportunities, cultural experiences, and healthy activities, demand will increase. Downtowns and transit-oriented development are two settings where such place making and renewing are especially inviting. Downtown and transit stations are places where people with choices like to be and where they will pay high prices, given limited supply, to live there. Powerful sprawl forces do not inevitably prevent downtown revitalization and successful transit-oriented development.

Results may matter in terms of danger and safety. If danger from crime diminishes, and is perceived to have diminished, location preferences for home buyers may change. Given the finding that crime rates are a more important neighborhood factor to home buyers than any other neighborhood condition, actual changes in crime rates should affect beliefs and behavior. Furthermore, if crime is not as salient a problem, other aspects of physical danger may receive greater attention. Danger from motor vehicle crashes has received less attention than it merits, based on comparisons between risks from crime and vehicle crashes. Perhaps less salience for crime can be matched with greater awareness of vehicle crash implications and lead to further changes in location preferences based on more accurate and more widely known information.

In each of these instances—less dangerous residential settings, downtowns, and transit station areas—performance has a common characteristic whose benefits to individuals may become more salient. This common characteristic is that more transportation choices will be available to more people. Exclusive reliance on driving alone in a motor vehicle might diminish. If it does, muscle activity levels will increase—at least for getting about from home to other activities each day. If walking increases, at various times of day and night for various purposes, people may become healthier. Furthermore, personal well-being as measured by lower weight and greater health may occur, a relationship discussed briefly in Chapter 11. Performance in greater health could be another outcome—an ironic reversal of one of the motivations for creating low-density suburbs, which was the expectation that low-density suburban settings would promote health better than compact central cities.

MYTHS AND MEGA-DECISIONS

By linking patterns, beliefs, and policies, we are moving toward a richer interpretation of location decisions and spatial results in metropolitan areas. We suggest that location issues lead to mega-decisions with complex and enduring consequences. In making these decisions, people draw on their experiences, interpret current circumstances, and imagine short- and long-term implications for themselves and for other household members. It is unrealistic to reduce these decisions to outcomes decided by any one of such relevant matters as whether lenders make loans available, residents are stressed by racial issues, people fear crime, they ignore traffic dangers, parents emphasize schools, and empty nesters and the elderly are more concerned about shopping and public transportation.

Each of these subjects is relevant and each is subject to change—crime rates change, beliefs about which places are safe from crime change, and policies toward crime change. Beliefs about race change, racial stereotyping may diminish, and norms of interracial civility may increase. Policies change in the extent to which they emphasize race. Similarly, the houses and neighborhoods in which people live change, and the location of work and services in downtowns, transit station areas, edge cities, and peripheral locations change.

Spatial patterns, described here by relative median family income and relative per capita income, also change. Because those income patterns are pervasive, composing local government jurisdictions and every neighborhood, the implications of these spatial patterns and changes in them are momentous for property values, life savings, education opportunities, and access to employment. Equality of opportunity, the privileges of capital, and the outcome of democratic processes are in flux.

We have suggested in preceding chapters that age and size of housing may play leading roles in the sum of decisions that lead to these spatial patterns. However, from the beginning, in Chapter 1, we introduced concepts like the tyranny of easy development decisions, careerism, and consumerism to suggest that an operational culture of life styles and life goals also impact outcomes. In this chapter, we introduced the idea that partially accurate and partially distorted interpretations of conditions and prospects also influence spatial pattern outcomes. We call these interpretations myths. These include the myth of cul-de-sac safety (Chapter 10), the myth of exurban safety (Chapter 11), and the myth that driving alone for every purpose from every location at every time of day is feasible. In policy discussions in Chapter 13, we illustrate alternatives to the myth that driving alone for every daily purpose is desirable and feasible.

Another myth is that people who work hard—or inherit money honestly—should be able to advance to bigger and better houses through their lives. This is the so-called American Dream, as Fannie Mae and others remind us continually.[62] The strength of this American Dream myth, a particular aspect of consumerism and careerism, animates the compulsion to keep expanding house sizes, despite the costs in time and stress from inaccessible locations as well as high dollar costs. It is this myth of continual justified housing advance that makes the small house problem, discussed in more detail in Chapter 12, so pervasive and deleterious.

The sum of these influences also leads to considerable unhappiness—and no doubt some happiness. The unhappiness occurs because so many aspects of these operational culture myths are inaccurate and inconsistent that the net results for individuals, households, and society is far less desirable than anyone intends. This outcome leads to yet another self-defeating myth: someone else, some incompetent other, is responsible for our set of myths not leading to happiness, rather than accepting responsibility for our own unwise choices.

NOTES

1. Richard J. Hill, "Attitudes and Behavior," in M. Rosenberg and R.H. Turner, eds., *Social Psychology, Sociological Perspectives* (New York: Basic Books, 1981); Paul A. Samuelson, "Consumption Theory in Terms of Revealed Preferences," *Economica* 15 (1948), pp. 243-253; Herbert A. Simon, "Rationality in Psychology and Economics," in Robin M. Hogarth and Melvin W. Reder, eds., *Rational Choice: The Contrast between Economics and Psychology* (Chicago: University of Chicago Press, 1987).
2. Herbert A. Simon, *Models of My Life* (New York: Basic Books, 1991).

3. Anthony Downs, *Neighborhoods and Urban Development* (Washington, DC: The Brookings Institution, 1981); Ira Lowry, "Filtering and Housing Standards," *Land Economics* 36 (1960), pp. 362-370; Myron Orfield, *American Metropolitics* (Washington, DC: The Brookings Institution, 2002); Wallace Smith, *Filtering and Neighborhood Change* (Berkeley: University of California, Center for Real Estate and Urban Economics Research, 1964).

4. John T. Metzger, "Planned Abandonment: The Neighborhood Life-Cycle Theory and National Urban Policy," *Housing Policy Debate* 11, no. 1 (2000), pp. 7-40.

5. Ibid., p. 30.

6. Anthony Downs, "Comment," *Housing Policy Debate* 11, no. 1 (2000), pp. 48-49.

7. Kenneth Temkin, "Comment," *Housing Policy Debate* 11, no. 1 (2000), p. 59.

8. Barrett A. Lee and Peter B. Wood, "Is Neighborhood Racial Succession Place-Specific?," *Demography* 28, no. 1 (1991), pp. 21-40.

9. John R. Ottensmann, "Requiem for the Tipping-Point Hypothesis," *Journal of Planning Literature* 10, no. 2 (1995), pp. 131-141.

10. Ibid., p. 131.

11. David Rusk, *Inside Game Outside Game: Winning Strategies for Saving Urban America* (Washington, DC: The Brookings Institution, 1999), p. 319.

12. Ibid.

13. Ibid., p. 319.

14. Ibid., p. 320.

15. Myron Orfield, *American Metropolitics* (Washington, DC: The Brookings Institution, 2002).

16. Ibid., p. 10.

17. Ibid., pp. 13-14.

18. Anthony Downs, "Comment," *Housing Policy Debate* 11, no. 1 (2000), p. 45.

19. Ibid.

20. Reynolds Farley, Charlotte Steeh, Tara Jackson, Maria Krysan, and Keith Reeves, "Continued Racial Residential Segregation in Detroit: 'Chocolate City, Vanilla Suburbs' Revisited," *Journal of Housing Research* 4, no. 1 (1993), p. 32.

21. Reynolds Farley, "Neighborhood Preferences and Aspirations among Blacks and Whites," in G. Thomas Kingsley and Margery Austin Turner, eds., *Housing Markets and Residential Mobility* (Washington, DC: Urban Institute Press, 1993), p. 183.

22. Gallop Organization, Gallup poll, *Minority Rights and Relations Survey* (Storrs, CT: Roper Center for Public Opinion Research, University of Connecticut, April 8, 2004).

23. Reynolds Farley, "Neighborhood Preferences and Aspirations among Blacks and Whites," in G. Thomas Kingsley and Margery Austin Turner, eds., *Housing Markets and Residential Mobility* (Washington, DC: Urban Institute Press, 1993).

24. Anthony Downs, "Comment," *Housing Policy Debate* 11, no. 1 (2000), pp. 50-51.

25. David Fasenfest, Jason Booza, and Kurt Metzger, *Living Together: A New Look at Racial and Ethnic Integration in Metropolitan Neighborhoods, 1990-2000* (Washington, DC: The Brookings Institution, 2004).

26. Anthony Downs, *New Visions for Metropolitan America* (Washington, DC: The Brookings Institution, 1994), p. 3.

27. John M. DeGrove, *Land, Growth, and Politics* (Chicago: American Planning Association, 1984).

28. Myron Orfield, *Metropolitics* (Washington, DC: The Brookings Institution, 1997).

29. Gerrit J. Knaap and Arthur C. Nelson, *The Regulated Landscape: Lessons on State Land Use Planning from Oregon* (Cambridge, MA: Lincoln Institute of Land Policy, 1992).

30. Tom Daniels, *When City and Country Collide: Managing Growth in the Metropolitan Fringe* (Washington, DC: Island Press, 1999); Douglas R. Porter, *Managing Growth in America's Communities* (Washington, DC: Island Press, 1997).

31. Joel Garreau, *Edge City: Life on the New Frontier* (New York: Doubleday, 1991).

32. Robert Lang, *Edgeless Cities: Exploring the Elusive Metropolis* (Washington, DC: The Brookings Institution, 2003).
33. Andres Duany, Elizabeth Plater-Zyberk, and Jeff Speck, *Suburban Nation* (New York: North Point Press, 2000).
34. Peter Calthorpe and William Fulton, *The Regional City* (Washington, DC: Island Press, 2001).
35. Ivonne Audirac, "Stated Preference for Pedestrian Proximity: An Assessment of New Urbanist Sense of Community," *Journal of Planning Education and Research* 19 (1999), pp. 53-66; Emily Talen, "Traditional Urbanism Meets Residential Affluence: An Analysis of the Variability of Suburban Preference," *Journal of the American Planning Association* 67, no. 2 (2001), pp. 199-216.
36. Hazel A. Morrow-Jones, Elena G. Irwin, and Brian Roe, "Consumer Preference for Neotraditional Neighborhood Characteristics," *Housing Policy Debate* 15, no. 1 (2004), pp. 176, 186.
37. Emily Talen, "Traditional Urbanism Meets Residential Affluence: An Analysis of the Variability of Suburban Preference," *Journal of the American Planning Association* 67, no. 2 (2001), p. 213.
38. Ibid., p. 214.
39. Ivonne Audirac, "Stated Preference for Pedestrian Proximity: An Assessment of New Urbanist Sense of Community," *Journal of Planning Education and Research* 19 (1999), p. 57.
40. Ibid., p. 63.
41. Leonard Gilroy, *The American Dream Is Alive and Well in California* (Los Angeles: The Reason Foundation, 2002), www.reason.org.
42. Joel S. Hirschhorn and Paul Souza, *New Community Design to the Rescue* (Washington, DC: National Governors Association, 2001), www.nga.org/cda/files/072001NCDFULL.pdf.
43. National Association of Realtors and Smart Growth America, "Homebuyers Favor Shorter Commutes, Walkable Neighborhoods" (Chicago: National Association of Realtors, October 20, 2004), www.realtor.org.
44. Ibid.
45. Gallup Organization, Gallup poll, "What do you think is the most important problem facing this country today?" (Storrs, CT: Roper Center for Public Opinion Research, University of Connecticut, 1961, 1969, 1977, 1980, 1981, 1984).
46. U.S. Census Bureau, *Statistical Abstract of the United States 2002* (Washington, DC: U.S. Government Printing Office, 2003).
47. Ibid.
48. Gallup Organization, Gallup polls, *Perceptions of Crime Vulnerability* (Storrs, CT: Roper Center for Public Opinion Research, University of Connecticut, 1990 and 2001).
49. Miranda Hitti, "U.S. Cities: How Americans Rate Their Safety," *WebMD Medical News* (2004), http://my.webmd.com/content/Article/97/104006.htm?printing=true.
50. Reid Ewing, Tom Schmid, Richard Killingsworth, Amy Zlot, and Stephen Raudenbush, "Relationship between Urban Sprawl and Physical Activity, Obesity, and Morbidity," *American Journal of Health Promotion* (September/October 2003), pp. 47-57.
51. Jack Gillis, *The Truck, Van, and 4 x 4 Book 1999* (New York: HarperCollins Publishers, 1998).
52. Michigan Senate, "The U.S. and Michigan Motor Vehicle Statistical Report" (Lansing: Senate Fiscal Agency, September 2003), www.senate.michigan.gov/sfa/Economics/MVStatReport.pdf.
53. Harris Interactive Inc., Harris poll, *Future Death Rates* (Storrs, CT: Roper Center for Public Opinion Research, University of Connecticut, 1999).
54. E.M. Risse, *The Shape of the Future* (Fairfax, VA: Synergy Planning, 2000).
55. Anthony Downs, *Stuck in Traffic* (Washington, DC: The Brookings Institution, 1992).

56. Emily Talen, "Traditional Urbanism Meets Residential Affluence: An Analysis of the Variability of Suburban Preference," *Journal of the American Planning Association* 67, no. 2 (2001), p. 214.

57. U.S. Census Bureau, *Statistical Abstract of the United States 2002* (Washington, DC: U.S. Government Printing Office, 2003).

58. Dowell Myers and Elizabeth Gearin, "Current Preferences and Future Demand for Denser Residential Environments," *Housing Policy Debate* 12, no. 4 (2001), p. 642.

59. Ibid., p. 648.

60. Dowell Myers and Elizabeth Gearin, "Current Preferences and Future Demand for Denser Residential Environments," *Housing Policy Debate* 12, no. 4 (2001).

61. Christopher B. Leinberger, "The Beginning of the End of Sprawl," *Urban Land* (January 2000), pp. 74-78.

62. Robert J. Samuelson, "Pressure of the American Dream," *The Washington Post*, July 26, 2004, p. A11.

10

The Cul-de-Sac Safety Myth: Housing Markets and Settlement Patterns

In home buyer surveys, neighborhood meetings about development proposals, and critiques by architects as early as the 1920s, safety from neighborhood traffic has been a persistent source of anxiety. The cul-de-sac, literally the bottom of the bag, has been the prevalent design response in the United States.

The effect of cul-de-sacs has been like a corset. It changes appearance. The wearer, or resident, feels better superficially, but the underlying condition and danger remains. Perhaps the danger (traffic or excess weight) is worse because of a false feeling of being in control.

The dangers, after all, come from unavoidable basics—eating and leaving home. What should concern the wary is what they eat and how they move about from home to work, school, entertainment, friends' houses, shopping, cultural events, religious activities, and civic life. Corsets and cul-de-sacs do not help with these subjects. In this chapter, we will trace how this exaggerated belief in cul-de-sac safety came about. Perhaps, like the corset in its time, the cul-de-sac eventually will be a passing feature of the auto age.

THE ISSUE

Suburban development patterns are widely blamed for traffic congestion, waste of infrastructure resources, costly housing, and a mismatch between employment and residential locations.[1] These frequently criticized suburban patterns remained the norm at the turn of the 21st century.[2] Suburban development patterns evoke occasional praise from academic planners.[3] Usually praise for current practices includes the belief that they respond to consumer preferences. One motivation for consumer preferences and suburban development patterns is the search for a safe refuge from danger, especially danger to small children from automobile traffic. Street networks that terminate in cul-de-sacs are the principal means by which development patterns have provided refuge from dangerous traffic.

Patterns of suburban development reflect interactions between housing market dynamics and public policies. Developers build where they predict they can make sufficient profits. Profits depend on building and selling fast enough to limit carrying costs that occur before revenues accumulate. Sufficient buyers must be present. For buyers, the choice of purchasing a dwelling is a mega-decision—a decision with many long-lasting ramifications for household members.

The number of potential buyers is quite large. For example, assume a metropolitan area has a population of one million, an average household size of 2.6 (the national average in 2000), 385,000 households, and 258,000 home owners based on two-thirds of households being home owners (the national average in 2000). If an average of 50 percent of home owners move in eight years (the national average in 1990), then within 10 years more than 130,000 purchases would occur by home owners. The location of these purchases and sales probably will have greater social, economic, and political consequences than any explicit housing and development policies of local governments. From these numbers, it is evident that home owners' beliefs that influence locations of home buying can have enormous ramifications for settlement patterns and their consequences—suburban sprawl, income disparities, insufficient reinvestment in established neighborhoods, and poverty concentrations.

Here we examine the belief that cul-de-sac street networks are safer than connected streets that permit through traffic on more residential streets, and the history of several professional and government organizations promoting cul-de-sac street patterns because of their alleged safety. These professional perspectives can have large, cumulative impacts on development patterns, especially when several professions, which are crucial to development decisions, have compatible beliefs about how development should occur.[4]

Myths and Realities

The shapers of, and believers in, myths think they are true in some sense. Myths simplify reality and are believed to embody its essence. Here we use the term myth as suggested by Judith I. De Neufville and Stephen E. Barton. They argued that "behind widely accepted problem definitions are myths, stories which draw on tradition and taken for granted knowledge. These myths, which may or may not be true in a factual sense, are important to the definition of problems because they link public issues to widely accepted ways of understanding the world and to shared moral evaluations of conditions, events, and possible solutions to problems."[5] The belief about safety on cul-de-sacs is an example of a myth that has influenced the physical pattern of cities and suburbs since the 1930s.

Bedroom suburbs, in part, represent an escape from city problems and a search for security, control, and the pleasure of a garden in nature.[6] The post-World War II residential development pattern is dominated by curvilinear roads terminating in cul-de-sacs. The cul-de-sac is a variation of a dead-end street, providing a bulb at the end of the street wide enough for uninterrupted forward turning space for automobiles and sometimes enough for snow-removal trucks and fire trucks. The cul-de-sac embodies desires by residents to control their physical setting. By preventing through traffic, residents, invited guests, and delivery personnel or occasional repair personnel are the only drivers with a legitimate reason to drive on the street. Cul-de-sacs, therefore, minimize the presence of moving vehicles. They also limit the speed of the relatively few vehicles that use the street by eliminating through traffic.

This opinion about cul-de-sac street networks being relatively safe is widely shared. Not only has the cul-de-sac concept dominated development practices and been included in many guidelines and regulations, it also is believed to be safe even by critics of the development pattern that results from it. Professional planners and architects, for example, often are skeptical about the large-scale consequences of the incremental accumulation of curvilinear cul-de-sac street networks. However, these professionals are inhibited in arguing against cul-de-sac-based patterns, especially in public meetings, because they may believe that cul-de-sac networks are safer than the alternatives.

Confronted by such beliefs at public meetings, professionals who criticize cul-de-sacs may feel defensive and insecure about advocating alternative patterns with more connected streets they believe are more dangerous. If they share a belief in the cul-de-sac safety myth, they must argue that other land development goals outweigh the merit of arguments about safety. Developers and lenders, as well as buyers and residents, are likely to share this belief in the cul-de-sac safety myth. They also may predict that cul-de-sac developments will sell faster at higher prices, so they may resist plans for alternative patterns. As stated by Ted Danter, a real estate consultant in the Columbus, Ohio, area: "The reality is people still pay a premium to get a lot on a cul de sac."[7] While evidence for this view rarely is presented, it often is stated adamantly, as by Danter, as though it is indisputable.

The belief that cul-de-sac street networks are safer than the alternatives is a myth in the sense that it was advocated without a demonstration that such networks were safer. There was also no recognition by advocates of cul-de-sacs for safety reasons about how cul-de-sac networks would work in reality, after they emerged in the ad hoc, incremental land development processes that dominate land development practices. The absence of empirical and theoretical justification for cul-de-sac-based networks continues to the present. There are some conceptual reasons to believe that cul-de-sac networks actually may be more dangerous, or at least as dangerous, as grid networks and other modified grid street patterns, which emphasize connections among streets that facilitate vehicular and pedestrian access for residents in every direction.

The gridiron street pattern of rectangular or square blocks in which streets are aligned at right angles was claimed as far back as the 1920s to be the most dangerous street pattern. The antigrid argument had taken root by the 1930s among many experts. Then it was incorporated into federal housing guidelines and other sources of official influence. After World War II, the belief that cul-de-sac street networks were safer and settings for sounder housing investments became the conventional wisdom.

The conventional wisdom is buttressed by ethical concerns. Potential residential buyers may believe that personal ethics require them to consider buying on cul-de-sacs. If cul-de-sacs are safer, especially for children, then many parents feel a moral obligation to weigh that factor in making location decisions. For example, talking with a mother of a young child about the family's potential move from the central city to a suburb for a cul-de-sac location, we informed the mother that, for several reasons, cul-de-sacs also can be dangerous. The mother burst out, without waiting for an explanation, "I'm so glad to hear that. I thought it was my moral responsibility to move to a cul-de-sac." If parents believe other parents are making this calculation, then potential buyers also will consider whether any location other than a cul-de-sac will provide as much security for their financial investment.

This chapter sketches the historical path of arguments and actions that contributed to the cul-de-sac becoming the dominant element in the post-World War II pattern of land development. Then we explore why cul-de-sac street networks may be as, or more, dangerous than grid street systems. In doing this, we will emphasize the risk of death and serious injuries in traffic accidents rather than the number of traffic accidents.

HISTORY

Rectangular street networks dominated early settlements. Christopher Tunnard wrote in *The Modern American City* that ". . . there was one national characteristic of cities making for an almost standardized product. This was the right-angled or orthogonal plan. There is something recognizable and persistent in American use of the gridiron plan, which was employed from the very beginning in Anglo-America. The little mercantile towns were built on grids, exceptions like New Amsterdam (now the lower part of Manhattan), Boston, and Annapolis being rare. Later Thomas Jefferson thought that the grid was the best method of laying out a city, and it was he who enshrined it in the national settlement pattern by the Land Ordinance of 1785."[8]

As early as 1841, landscape architects, such as Andrew Jackson Downing, had criticized gridiron street networks, which then were omnipresent in cities and towns. These writings, predating the automobile by several decades, were not addressed to safety issues. They had aesthetic interests in mind. Downing believed that "all sensible men gladly escape, earlier or later, . . . from the turmoil of cities."[9] In designing his ideal suburb, Downing advocated single-family dwellings with street frontages of 100 feet or more and curvilinear roads rather than roads crossing at right angles. Downing's partner, Calvert Vaux, also disdained the grid pattern, bemoaning that "the plans of country towns and villages are so formal and unpicturesque. They generally consist of square blocks of houses, each facing the other with conventional regularity; . . . in many new villages that are being erected the same dull, uninteresting method is still predominant."[10]

The best-known landscape architect in the years following the Civil War was Frederick Law Olmsted, designer of Central Park in New York City. Olmsted designed 16 suburbs with Vaux as his partner. The first was Riverside, outside Chicago, in 1868. In Riverside, wrote Kenneth Jackson, "Curved roadways were adopted to 'suggest and imply leisure, contemplativeness, and happy tranquility;' the grid, according to Olmsted, was 'too still and formal for such adornment and rusticity as should be combined in a model suburb.'"[11]

These opinions constituted a ready-in-waiting tradition when the opportune moment arrived to combine aesthetic arguments with other concerns. Concern for quiet and tranquility was one linking opportunity. Raymond Unwin, for example, sought to change a law in Great Britain that prevented construction of cul-de-sacs. "This action," he wrote, "has, no doubt, been taken to avoid unwholesome yards; but for residential purposes, particularly since the development of the motor-car, the cul de sac roads, far from being undesirable, are especially to be desired for those who like quiet for their dwellings."[12]

Stein and Perry

The ominous aspect of automobiles threatening the safety of children presented an additional opportunity to argue for adopting cul-de-sacs. Clarence S. Stein, reflecting later on the concepts that guided the planning of Radburn, New Jersey, in the late 1920s, wrote: "The flood of motors [in 1928] had already made the gridiron street pattern, which had formed the framework for urban real estate over a century, as obsolete as a fortified town wall. Pedestrians risked a dangerous motor street crossing 20 times a mile . . . Every year there were more Americans killed or injured in automobile accidents than the total of American war casualties in any year. The checkerboard pattern made all streets equally inviting to through traffic . . . Porches faced bedlam of motor throughways with blocked traffic, honking horns, noxious gases."[13]

In Radburn, Stein had sought a network of cul-de-sacs, pedestrian pathways, and interior natural areas so that walking and driving were facilitated but separated. In 1930, the *American Architect* complimented Radburn, saying it "represents the first scientific effort that has ever been made to establish a community designed exclusively to minimize the danger of automobile accidents. Yet there were other things to consider too . . . it was the desire of the builders to create not only a (safe) community . . . but also one . . . of beauty in appearance and the utmost in modern efficiency."[14] Planning historian Eugenie Ladner Birch noted that "transferable aspects of the [Radburn] plan such as the superblock, transportation system, and park arrangements cropped up repeatedly in designs for federal settlements [in the 1930s]."[15] While most residences were on cul-de-sacs in Radburn, the cul-de-sacs were narrow, and an intricate network of pathways and public open spaces facilitated walking throughout the development.

Cul-de-sacs were welcomed by Clarence Perry and Thomas Adams in the guidelines they suggested for neighborhood development as part of the Regional Plan of New York in 1929. As reported by Michael Southworth and Eran Ben-Joseph: "For the local streets, a pavement width of 18 to 20 feet is sufficient, and the balance of the right-of-way should be devoted to sidewalks and planting. . . . Staggered cross streets, dead-end streets, and cul-de-sacs contribute to safety, attractiveness, and variety. Cul-de-sacs and dead-end streets should be used only as part of a complete subdivision plan integrating both pedestrian and vehicular circulation. If long blocks are used, pedestrian footpaths should offer shortcuts."[16] Thus, Stein, Perry, and Adams recommended narrow streets, pathways, and a complete circulation plan, which could include cul-de-sacs. However, the cul-de-sac was not elevated either to the position of the most important ingredient nor was it a plan element that was advocated in the absence of supporting street and pathway connections.

Federal Housing Administration

The Federal Housing Administration (FHA) was established in 1934. The low down payments for purchasing owner-occupied housing and the mortgages that it insured against nonpayment were intended to revive housing markets during the Great

Depression. The FHA was not a planning or development organization, but it proposed development standards which, it said, were rational principles of development. Although the FHA's first plan guidance in 1935 retained flexibility in street conditions, the first signs of potential impediments to functional pedestrian activity appeared. The FHA proposed 10 feet for each traffic lane and 8 feet for two parking lanes, with blocks 600 to 1,000 feet long, and lots at least 50 feet wide containing 6,000 square feet or more.[17]

If parking was permitted on both sides of a street, the street width would be 36 feet, using these guidelines. Lots of 6,000 square feet yield only seven units per acre. Blocks 600 feet or longer impede walking by making it less convenient. When combined with single-use, residential-only districts, these guidelines set land development on a course in the 1930s of reducing the feasibility of walking.

In its 1936 bulletin, *Planning Neighborhoods for Small Houses*, the FHA first rejected the grid pattern for residential streets: "The gridiron plan ... creates waste by providing a greater paved area than necessarily adequate to serve a residential community. Secondly, it ... creates an increased traffic hazard. In addition to these disadvantages it creates a monotonous uninteresting architectural effect ..."[18] The standards went on to say that "cul de sacs are the most attractive street layout for family dwellings ..."[19]

The weight of its design suggestions was increased by a practice that the FHA added in 1938. The FHA offered to review plans and layouts before they were submitted for formal approval. The FHA said: "The FHA is interested in cooperating with real estate developers, builders, and their technical consultants in obtaining high standards of land development. The opportunity is welcomed to analyze proposed subdivisions and to make suggestions which, ... will create more marketable, attractive, and stable residential patterns."[20] This presubmission review and comment function helped establish a planning and design orthodoxy in subdivisions throughout the United States.

Marc Weiss observed that the FHA intended from the beginning to influence subdivision designs, as its *First Annual Report* in 1935 indicated: "Once the plan comes into wide-spread operation, the following results may reasonably be anticipated: ... Improvement in subdivision layouts—subdivisions that are regarded as specially good by the Federal Housing Administration will receive a more favorable loan rating."[21] In 1939, the FHA went farther in endorsing cul-de-sacs in *Planning Neighborhoods for Small Houses*: "Homes located on cul de sacs ... offer distinct advantages especially to families with small children."[22] In its 1940 *Annual Report*, the FHA said: "The steadily increasing reliance of the home building industry upon the neighborhood-planning principles fostered by the Administration since the start of the FHA program was reflected during 1940 by the fact that in some cities approximately 70 percent of the new homes financed under the FHA plans were located in new subdivisions planned and developed from the beginning in cooperation with the FHA."[23] The FHA also noted that of 2,680 subdivisions it analyzed in 1940, 98 percent contained nothing but single-family, detached houses.[24]

FHA standards also influenced local public planning processes. By 1941, 32 states had passed legislation assigning local elected planning commissions the power to approve subdivisions. The Public Administration Service's review of more than 200 cities' subdivision requirements found them to be similar, according to Southworth and Ben-Joseph, who also concluded: "Local planning commissions, once authorized and empowered by the community, adopted rules and regulations governing subdivision procedures largely based on federal criteria, in particular those of the FHA."[25] During the 1950s, cul-de-sacs and pedestrian pathways were promoted in publications of the American Society of Planning Officials.[26]

Urban Land Institute, American Public Health Association, and Institute of Transportation Engineers

Land developers also embraced cul-de-sacs. In the *Community Developers Handbook*, cul-de-sacs were referred to as "one of the best street types to use in single family development."[27] The 1960 handbook published by the Urban Land Institute (ULI) recommended that cul-de-sacs be no more than 500 feet long.[28] The 1968 edition accepted cul-de-sacs as long as 1,200 feet.[29] Whereas the 1960 *Handbook* editors had been concerned about overburdening collector streets with long cul-de-sacs, the 1968 *Handbook* editors had dropped references to this concern. Long cul-de-sacs, as well as stressing collector streets, also inhibit walking by requiring walkers to reach the open end of the cul-de-sac street before other pedestrian options are available.

The American Public Health Association (APHA) in its publication, *Planning the Neighborhood*, retained its traditional interest in walking as an important aspect of access,[30] recommending in 1960: "Walks from all dwellings should provide convenient and safe access to elementary schools, shops, playgrounds, and other chief pedestrian objectives."[31] However, the APHA also adopted the goal that "There should be no through traffic within the neighborhood. To discourage through traffic within the neighborhood, streets should be so laid out that no streets within the neighborhood can be used as a short cut between two points outside it . . . If dead-end streets (culs de sac) are used, their length should be limited and they should have adequate width and turning diameter at the end . . ."[32]

The APHA also recommended lot sizes and street frontage that made walking difficult, noting that "Lots narrower that 50 feet will usually not permit a layout in accordance with the principles [adequate light, air, and privacy] outlined above . . . Sixty-foot lot width would seem a reasonable requirement for detached one-family houses, and 75 feet is a desirable goal."[33] These lot sizes (with 100 feet or more in depth) would produce dwelling densities of five to eight units per acre at most, a density that would be inconsistent with the APHA goal of encouraging walking.

The Institute of Transportation Engineers (ITE) in its 1965 publication, *Recommended Practice for Subdivision Streets*, stated: "The primary objective of subdivision design is to provide maximum livability. This requires a safe and efficient access and circulation system, connecting homes, schools, playgrounds, shops and other subdivision activities for both pedestrians and vehicles."[34] This goal was inconsistent with the development practice observed as long ago as 1940 by the FHA that 98 percent of the subdivisions it analyzed contained nothing but single-family, detached residences. Even though it recommended variety and experimentation in design of neighborhood street systems, the ITE nevertheless recommended rigid standards, including street pavement width of 32 to 34 feet and cul-de-sacs with a 50-foot radius (100-foot diameter) at the end and a maximum length of 1,000 feet.[35] The 18- to 20-

foot streets recommended in 1929 by Perry and Adams had widened and lengthened, increasing again the obstacles that cul-de-sac systems impose on pedestrians.

Access preferences of fire departments also have contributed to the large widths of streets and diameters of cul-de-sac turnarounds. The cul-de-sac terminating bulb dimensions have been influenced, as Duany, Plater-Zyberk, and Speck observe, "in order that a large truck can turn around without shifting into reverse . . . The avoidance of reverse purportedly derives from the fact, now irrelevant, that the earliest fire trucks powered their pumping mechanisms with the reverse gear, rendering it inoperable."[36]

Safety

Source documents and commentaries about the history of land planning did not yield significant analyses about why cul-de-sac-based street networks are relatively safe. The cul-de-sac safety myth seems to be based on a geographically limited view of the obvious: If motor vehicles are blocked from traveling through residential streets, fewer accidents will occur there. This perspective was made more sophisticated by a study from 1951 to 1956 in Los Angeles that compared traffic accidents in residential grid patterns with accidents in residential, curvilinear, cul-de-sac patterns. The study covered 86 subdivision tracts with 53,000 residents, 108 miles of residential streets, and 660 intersections. The conclusion was that the grid pattern had eight times more accidents. This study, according to Southworth and Ben-Joseph,[37] became the basis for the ITE recommendations for residential streets.

This study had two serious flaws. The most serious flaw was that it did not measure what it purported to measure: danger to people. Number of accidents is relevant to danger to motor vehicles, although it is not as useful an indicator as value of damages. However, it did not measure danger to people, because the number of accidents is inversely related to the severity of accidents in some settings. The relevant measures of danger to people are traffic fatalities and serious injuries. The Los Angeles study did not cover either fatalities or serious injuries. Therefore, it bore little relevance to the subject of danger to people. Second, the study did not measure accidents within the network on which people traveled from their residences to their destinations and their return trips.

Few trips started and ended on residential streets in the neighborhood of origin. The significant comparison, therefore, would have been the network deaths and serious injuries on the larger street and highway system of which the grid and curvilinear, cul-de-sac subdivisions were parts. This larger network study was not conducted. The larger networks would have been significant, in particular, if the connections from local streets to collectors to arterials were influenced by the characteristics of the residential street patterns. These connecting intersections also were excluded from the study.

Reliance on accident rates to evaluate safety persisted into the 1990s. Reid Ewing in *Best Development Practices* cited several studies about traffic accidents in concluding, based on the existing literature, that "by keeping through-traffic out of neighborhoods, contemporary networks keep accident rates down and property values up."[38] Our findings about decline in middle-aged, post-World War II neighborhoods often applied to cul-de-sac neighborhoods, although we have not addressed that subject directly.

Clarence Stein claimed in *Toward New Towns for America* that his faith in the safety of cul-de-sac networks had been demonstrated by 20 years of experience in Radburn where "there have been only two road deaths. Both were on main highways, not in lanes. . . . That the small proportion of auto fatalities is due to the physical plan is indicated by the record of other towns that have followed in general the Radburn scheme. In 1949, when Greenbelt, Maryland, Greendale, Wisconsin, and Greenhills, Ohio, were all over ten years old, only one pedestrian had been killed by a car. . . . That is quite a good record for four towns of 2,500 to 7,500 population, compared with other towns of similar size."[39] Stein, however, did not compare those findings to other towns of similar size.

On the other hand, we discovered that Virginia keeps records of towns that have avoided traffic fatalities for 25 years or more. In checking the street maps of towns with 25 years free of traffic fatalities, we discovered that all of them had grid street systems or variations on them. These records did not prove that grids are safer than cul-de-sac networks, but they provide evidence more pertinent to the safety of street grids than Stein's evidence, which he mistakenly claimed supports the safety of cul-de-sacs.

EFFECTS OF STREET NETWORKS ON SAFETY

Several issues need attention in considering safety effects. One issue concerns whether people are more at risk in automobiles or by walking. Street network patterns influence the amount of walking that occurs and the frequency of automobile use. A second issue concerns situations of greater and lesser danger that occur in a street network. Some situations, especially certain types of intersections, are especially dangerous. A third issue concerns whether cul-de-sacs themselves contribute to behavior children learn there that is particularly dangerous if it occurs in other settings.

More Driving Equals More Danger

Single-family dwellings on large lots and separation of land uses inevitably make walking difficult by creating time-consuming distances between different land uses and activities. Cul-de-sac street networks add to impediments created by large lots and single-use, residential districts. Cul-de-sac systems interrupt through vehicular traffic intentionally. They also usually prevent pedestrian movement by channeling it along streets. Shortcuts often are prevented by physical obstacles, like ravines and fences. Mutual deference among neighbors also inhibits shortcuts, as neighbors avoid walking through each other's property. Pedestrian paths occasionally encourage movement through cul-de-sacs, but effective pathway systems are rare. In consequence, longer distances required in cul-de-sac systems than in grid networks impede walking to reach most routine destinations.

Safety is influenced by a street system, not a single street element such as a cul-de-sac. The street in front of a dwelling—whether on a cul-de-sac, a grid, or a variation on these systems—rarely is the most dangerous location in a street system. Residents leave their dwellings and streets for work, school, shopping, recreation, and worship for themselves, and also connect dependents, usually children, with their activities and friends. In most traffic generation studies, analysts assume 10 or more auto trips per household. The number of actual trips is related to proximity of residences to employment and other nonresidential activities. Cul-de-sacs exaggerate travel distances by imposing numerous closed streets. As a result, more people are in cars more often for more purposes on cul-de-sac networks than on grid networks. Not only are children driven farther and more often for their activities, but parents must bring small children with them when they drive farther and more often in carrying out daily and weekly errands.

Mean Streets 2000, a report by the Surface Transportation Policy Project, claims that walking is less likely near new schools and housing developments than near older schools and older neighborhoods, according to studies in Seattle and South Carolina. It also claimed that, in 20 years, the number of pedestrian trips declined by 42 percent, according to the *Nationwide Personal Transportation Survey*.[40] Noting that the 10 metropolitan areas with the highest death rates for pedestrians are in the South and Southwest, and have had substantial to very strong population growth rates, the authors of *Mean Streets 2000* blame post-World War II development patterns "dominated by subdivisions, office parks, and high-speed roads that are designed for fast automobile travel."[41] In another study summarizing findings in the literature, Howard Frumkin found that, "The most dangerous stretches of road were those built in the style that typifies sprawl: multiple lanes, high speeds, no sidewalks, long distances between intersections or crosswalks, and roadways lined with large commercial establishments and apartment blocks."[42]

Thus, typical suburban development patterns increase the frequency and distance of driving motor vehicles; reduce the amount of walking to achieve routine, everyday functions; and increase the danger of walking for such purposes.

Dangerous Intersections

A grid network has regular four-way intersections that require stop signs or stop lights. These intersections slow traffic. Some streets are arterial and collector streets, which are assigned higher speed limits and have longer distances between stops. Drivers wishing to turn onto these higher-speed streets can use the grid network parallel to it to get on a collector street, which has a traffic light at the intersection with the arterial street. The effects of the grid street system include slower average speeds, more stops, and more turn opportunities. The large number of intersections creates potential for more collisions. The relatively slow speeds, and the exclusion of most trucks from most streets, results in few maiming injuries or deaths. Instead, the grid creates "fender bender" intersections.

Cul-de-sac streets often are not laid out within a planned, large-scale network. The street system may emerge ad hoc in response to decentralized, episodic, and unpredictable decisions by land owners and developers. The planners and review boards responsible for regulating development usually permit diverse connections to the main traffic-bearing roads. Some of these connections occur close to each other, and some connections serve short cul-de-sacs with few residents. The roads to which the cul-de-sac systems connect often carry traffic at rather high speeds. The largest cul-de-sac networks usually will be granted stop-light intersections with the main road.

Sometimes even those cul-de-sac systems will be denied stop lights because they are too close to a nearby crossroads intersection. The lesser cul-de-sac streets with low traffic loads nearly always will be denied traffic lights.

The result is that numerous intersections occur where drivers must start from side streets and cut into fast-moving traffic for left turns. When traffic is heaviest, drivers are most likely to take chances and cut into a congested, fast-moving lane of traffic. In addition, drivers on the fast traffic road who wish to make left turns onto intersecting streets must stop in traffic to wait for a turn opportunity, creating risks of rear-end collisions. The faster the traffic and the less predictable the probability of left turns, the greater the danger. These intersections are most dangerous because the high speeds and low predictability increase the potential for broadside collisions near the driver's side of the vehicle, as well as high-speed, rear-end collisions.

Pitfalls of Parents' Overconfidence

Another problem with cul-de-sacs is that they lull some parents to sleep. Being tired of what may seem like perpetual requirements to limit and direct the activities of young children, many parents feel relieved to put their children in safe outdoor spaces where they can move about with little guidance. Because few strangers drive into cul-de-sacs, and those that do usually have enough wit to drive slowly, some parents relax their vigilance and let children play untended in cul-de-sacs at a young age. Parents may even teach their children to walk in streets by doing so themselves, sometimes by taking their children for walks on which everyone uses the street.

Cul-de-sacs convey ambiguous messages and create confusion in adults about what constitutes proper behavior for drivers, supervisors of children, and children. For example, these are events we observed during a mere 20 minutes on a 200-foot-long cul-de-sac with six dwellings in Columbus, Ohio, when three children—ages three, five, and seven—were playing in and near the street while being observed closely by adults. A van backed out of a driveway into the street, and the adults yelled and ran to warn the children to get out of the street. A man drove a car into, around, and out of the cul-de-sac, lost temporarily, looking for a through street, and the adults yelled, "don't move" to the children who were playing near the curb. The seven-year-old, who was well trained from living on a through street in another city, quickly forgot his prior training, following the lead of the younger children familiar with norms of playing in the cul-de-sac, and dashed into the street several times without looking. Later, the supervising adults discussed their anger at another incident: a driver who sped into the cul-de-sac, dropped off a passenger, and sped back out—a driver who, according to the adults, did not recognize the reality that the street had become a playfield and who concluded that the driver, not the supervising adults or the children, was acting improperly.[43]

The parental guidance problem is complicated by children needing to learn other behavior norms for through streets with more traffic. The ability of children to make wise distinctions between dangerous and safe streets is delayed by this process. It seems likely that some children are injured and killed because of their lower skill in making choices about appropriate behavior in streets. In addition, some dangers occur on cul-de-sacs, for example, from trash collectors backing up and from residents backing out of driveways.[44] Vehicles equipped with back-up warning alarms may not reduce dangers significantly to young children. In an experiment with 33 children, ages three to five years, none of the children responded to an alarm with avoidance behavior.[45] These dangers are more severe on cul-de-sacs because children are more likely to be in harm's way while they are playing in the streets.

The most common cause of pedestrian fatalities to children less than five years old in a study in Washington State was not from darting into traffic; it was from children being backed over both in the street and in driveways. The most common perpetrators were not speeders or drunk drivers; they were family members, most often the parents.[46] Several studies have shown that parents backing in sports utility vehicles, vans, and light trucks are the most frequent perpetrators of driveway injuries and fatalities to children under five years old.[47] According to the advocacy group Kids and Cars, about 100 children under four years old were backed over in driveways and parking lots, usually by family members or family friends in 2003 and 2004.[48] A study of 1998 death certificates by the National Highway Traffic Safety Administration estimated that 120 people per year, mainly small children and the very old, die in back-over collisions.[49] On the other hand, with children ages five to 12, sudden-appearance events, such as darting into traffic, constitute a majority of pedestrian injuries.[50] Pedestrian injuries also are most likely to take place close to home, usually on the residence's block.[51] The question of how the process of learning about street dangers affects child pedestrian injuries is not sufficiently understood.

Ironically, pedestrian deaths of small children (ages zero to four) constitute a tiny proportion of pedestrian deaths (152 of 4,739—3.2 percent in 2000) and traffic fatalities (152 of 41,945—0.4 percent in 2000). For children ages five to nine, a similarly low number of pedestrian deaths (164) occurred in 2000.[52] In addition, the darting-into-traffic type of accident, which is more common with older children, may be augmented by the delayed and intermittent vigilance by children and parents who grew up on cul-de-sacs. Given these small numbers, designing so much of urban and suburban America to mitigate these rare fatalities, while creating physical conditions that may be more dangerous to children and adults, seems another instance of mythical beliefs having powerful and ill-advised effects.

We have not found any direct evidence about the relative safety of grid and cul-de-sac street networks. Most traffic fatalities kill vehicle occupants, not pedestrians. Vehicle fatalities have increased steadily since 1940. Pedestrian deaths have not changed much since 1940. Vehicle use per capita has increased. Pedestrian activity per capita may have decreased. Cul-de-sac street networks have contributed to these vehicle and pedestrian trends. Analysts of accidents on roads with speed limits exceeding 30 miles per hour, where most fatalities occur, have not distinguished carefully between fatalities influenced by their proximity to grid or cul-de-sac street networks. Consequently, theories about the relative safety of street networks and settlement patterns must be derived from reasoned inferences and circumstantial evidence.

Undesirable Consequences

The cul-de-sac movement has culminated in a settlement pattern in which automobiles are required for nearly every activity for which people leave their residences. This pattern has contributed to a number of undesirable consequences. Driving distances are too long and waste time and energy. Drivers have too few options. Collector and arterial roadways often are jammed. Rush hour has turned into rush day and rush evening and even to rush weekend in some metropolitan areas. In some suburbs in the most congested metropolitan areas, more than 20 percent of commuters take more than one hour each way to get from home to work and back.

Cul-de-sacs create problems for public service vehicles. In a report for the Planning Advisory Service of the American Planning Association, Susan Handy, Robert G. Paterson, and Kent Butler wrote: "Emergency medical service, trash collectors, police and other municipal service providers have been strong supporters of greater connectivity. One issue in particular binds the group: the cul de sac . . . All service providers find the discontinuous transportation networks difficult to navigate, adding time, cost and inefficiency to their service."[53]

The sprawl settlement pattern, which cul-de-sacs aggravate, is costly to build and service with public infrastructure. Mass transit cannot be supported adequately with fares because housing densities are too low. People without cars cannot find housing close to work because work sites are too disbursed. High costs of time, energy, and infrastructure must be borne by businesses as well as by residents. Metropolitan suburbs, as well as central cities, are vulnerable to losing their competitive advantages versus small cities, villages, and rural areas because of high costs, transportation straight jackets, and high frustration levels with living conditions. Leap-frog development on the edges of metropolitan areas is encouraged as people try to escape congestion and find affordable housing. Government structure is fragmented; local governments are small and weak in the face of metropolitan and larger markets.

Once cul-de-sacs are in place, connecting them for through traffic—and through pedestrian passage—is murderous politically. Most current residents foresee big losses to their quality of life as well as the dangers of uncertainty. Gainers from changes that improve auto access are unidentified. They will exist in the future, if through streets are established in the place of cul-de-sacs, but they are not present to lobby and vote. For elected officials, fighting for individual cul-de-sac connections are no-win situations. Explanations of negative consequences from too many cul-de-sacs, therefore, are not likely to be sufficiently persuasive to lead to more connections in current residential street networks.

While the FHA, the ITE, the ULI, and local planning commissions were united in supporting cul-de-sac street networks and single-use residential districts, some individuals and organizations like Perry, Adams, and the New York Regional Plan Association were advocating connected residential street networks. The National Municipal League still was arguing for connections in its 1929 handbook, *City Planning*, in which Edward Bouton was the spokesman in a passage as convoluted as the cul-de-sac networks he was arguing against: "While, wherever possible, reasonably convenient communication with neighboring thoroughfares must be provided, the highly desirable object of preserving the local street from invasion of through traffic will often require that this communication should not be too direct, or at least too obvious, . . ."[54]

Besides creating somewhat obscure street connections, as Bouton, Perry, and Adams recommended, alternatives to cul-de-sacs include one-way networks with abrupt terminations, speed bumps and speed humps, narrow streets, low speed limits, parking on streets, narrow intersections, obstacles at midblock, and combinations of such methods as in the Netherlands' woonerf system. Bouton's reserve about, rather than rejection of, through streets seems a more appropriate attitude, with the benefit of hindsight, than the wholesale condemnation of grid street networks and other systems of streets connected within and without the areas of residential settlement.

Connections

Michael Poulton has argued, before the rise of interest in the new urbanism and more connected residential streets, that several variations on grid networks can be combined "to have excellent travel conditions and a fine physical environment in residential neighborhoods."[55] If a positive attitude toward vehicles is adopted, he said, "then good road layouts can be obtained from existing grid systems and the streets not needed for travel can be designed to assimilate moving and parked vehicles without being dominated by them."[56]

Grid and modified grid networks provide ample paths for pedestrians. Because walking and place making are companions, alternatives to grid-based systems will work well only if they are laid down at large scale with intricate pedestrian ways and open-space systems. These concepts were integral to Clarence Stein's Radburn system before Stein himself contributed to the excessive use of cul-de-sacs piecemeal through his influence on FHA street standards.

Cul-de-sacs for motor vehicles can contribute to walking, if the walking routes are important and adequately intricate. In Virginia, Charlottesville's downtown auto-free district with a pedestrian mall functions that way. Sometimes cul-de-sacs lead to greater density by accessing difficult terrain. Pedestrian paths in cul-de-sac neighborhoods can work, but if the densities are too low, they may be dangerous from limited use.

Large scale and intricate development of mixed land uses with excellent pedestrian access via separated walking pathways are rare. Therefore, critics of typical suburban development, like Randall Arendt, suggest requiring connections and discouraging cul-de-sacs: "Because they interrupt the pattern of connecting streets, thereby decreasing accessibility between adjacent neighborhoods (for residents, mail vehicles, rubbish trucks, school buses, etc.), cul de sacs should be strongly discouraged. In fact, it would help stem the further erosion of interneighborhood accessibility if all future residential streets were simply required to connect with other streets, . . . In areas lacking any existing or planned streets with which to connect, the cul de sac should include stubs extending to adjoining parcels in locations where future connections appear to be feasible."[57]

Besides being advocated by persuasive critics, like Arendt, the virtues of the grid can also be found in contemporary, mainstream site planning advice. In the third edition of *Site Planning*, for example, Kevin Lynch and Gary Hack wrote: "Grids are useful where flows are shifting and broadly distributed. They are clear and easy to follow, . . . The grid can be curved to fit topography. The essence of a grid system is its regularity of interconnection. It need not be composed of geometrically straight lines, nor must it enclose blocks of equal size and shape . . . Superblocks and dead-end streets impose a more and more circuitous path on local traffic as their size increases. . . . To facilitate circulation and social intercourse, there are distinct advantages in keeping block lengths short, . . ."[58]

In *Best Development Practices*, Ewing advocated either a grid or a network of comparable quality for pedestrians: "If we expect people to walk at all, we must provide a network for them as good as for motorists . . . it means that the same places must be reachable on foot or bike without jeopardizing life and limb."[59]

Convenient connectivity and mixed use are hallmarks of new urbanism. In Longmont, Colorado, new urbanist planning concepts have taken root and influenced street patterns. Advocates of this approach, feeling a responsibility to support their belief that connected streets could be safer as well as more convenient, studied 20,000 police accident reports to find correlates of street design characteristics in accidents that involved injuries. The study concluded: "The most significant relationships to injury accidents were found to be street width and street curvature. As street width widens, accidents per mile per year increases [sic] exponentially, and the safest residential street width is 24 feet (curb face)."[60]

Duany, Plater-Zyberk, and Speck describe how new neighborhoods and old neighborhoods should connect: "In order to avoid the inefficient hierarchical street pattern of sprawl, in which virtually every trip uses the same few collector roads, the new neighborhood must connect wherever practical to everything around it, even if its neighbors are nothing but single-use pods."[61]

Consumers' difficulty in distinguishing "front of dwelling" from network effects continues to influence their perspectives. Duany, Plater-Zyberk, and Speck describe responses to a survey question that lost them a potential client: "Home buyers will almost always choose a cul de sac over a through street when asked. But if you show them . . . how the cul de sac's very existence presupposes a high-volume collector road nearby—they tend to prefer the pedestrian-friendly network of through streets."[62]

Although new urbanists and others have moderated the appeal of cul-de-sac developments, the myth of safety on cul-de-sacs continues to influence consumer preferences, developers' practices, and regulators' rules. The evidence for traffic safety being greater on grid street systems is slim, but it is at least as defensible as arguments that cul-de-sac networks are safer. This much, however, is clear: Cul-de-sacs and single-use residential districts have reduced multipurpose walking, and walking is healthier and safer than driving.[63] The cul-de-sac safety myth, therefore, continues to be an obstacle to making places and combating sprawl, limiting income disparities, reducing concentrated poverty, and increasing reinvestment in old and middle-aged neighborhoods.

NOTES

1. Robert Cervero, *Suburban Gridlock* (New Brunswick, NJ: Rutgers University Center for Urban Policy Research, 1986); Anthony Downs, *New Visions for Metropolitan America* (Washington, DC: The Brookings Institution, 1994); Robert Puentes and Myron Orfield, *Valuing America's First Suburbs: A Policy Agenda for Older Suburbs in the Midwest* (Washington, DC: The Brookings Institution, 2002).

2. Douglas Porter, *Managing Growth in America's Communities* (Washington, DC: Island Press, 1997).

3. Ivonne Audirac, Ann H. Shermyen, and Marc T. Smith, "Ideal Urban Form and Visions of the Good Life: Florida's Growth Management Dilemma," *Journal of the American Planning Association* 56, no. 4 (1990), pp. 470-482; Peter Gordon and Harry W. Richardson, "Are Compact Cities a Desirable Planning Goal?," *Journal of the American Planning Association* 63, no. 1 (1997), pp. 95-106.

4. Andres Duany, Elizabeth Plater-Zyberk, and Jeff Speck, *Suburban Nation* (New York: North Point Press, 2000).

5. Judith I. De Neufville and Stephen E. Barton, "Myths and the Definition of Policy Problems: An Exploration of Home Ownership and Public-Private Partnerships," *Policy Sciences* (1987), p. 1.

6. Leo Marx, *The Machine in the Garden: Technology and the Pastoral Ideal in America,* 2d ed. (New York: Oxford University Press, 2000); Lewis Mumford, *The City in History: Its Origins, Its Transformations, and Its Prospects* (New York: Harcourt, Brace & World, 1961).

7. Brian R. Ball, "Developers Forge Ahead with TND Zoning," *Columbus Business First,* June 8, 2001.

8. Christopher Tunnard, *The Modern American City* (New York: Van Nostrand Reinhold Company, 1968), p. 17.

9. Kenneth T. Jackson, *Crabgrass Frontier* (New York, Oxford University Press, 1985), pp. 64-65.

10. Ibid., p. 67.

11. Ibid., p. 80.

12. Raymond Unwin, *Town Planning in Practice* (Princeton: Princeton Architectural Press, 1994 reprint of 1909 original), p. 393.

13. Clarence S. Stein, *Toward New Towns for America* (New York: Reinhold Publishing Corporation, 1957), p. 41.

14. Eugenie Ladner Birch, "Radburn and the American Planning Movement: The Persistence of an Idea," *Journal of the American Planning Association* 46 (October 1980), p. 427.

15. Ibid., p. 429.

16. Michael Southworth and Eran Ben-Joseph, *Streets and the Shaping of Towns and Cities* (New York: McGraw-Hill, 1997), p. 70.

17. Ibid., p. 83.

18. Ibid., p. 84.

19. Ibid.

20. Ibid., p. 85.

21. Marc A. Weiss, *The Rise of the Community Builders* (New York: Columbia University Press, 1987), p. 215.

22. U.S. Federal Housing Administration, *Planning Neighborhoods for Small Houses* (Washington, DC: U.S. Government Printing Office, 1939), p. 31.

23. Marc A. Weiss, *The Rise of the Community Builders* (New York: Columbia University Press, 1987), p. 155.

24. Ibid.

25. Michael Southworth and Eran Ben-Joseph, *Streets and the Shaping of Towns and Cities* (New York: McGraw-Hill, 1997), p. 88.

26. Eugenie Ladner Birch, "Radburn and the American Planning Movement: The Persistence of an Idea," *Journal of the American Planning Association* 46 (October 1980), p. 430.

27. Urban Land Institute, *Community Developers Handbook* (Washington, DC: Urban Land Institute, 1960), pp. 131-132.

28. Ibid., p. 132.

29. Urban Land Institute, *Community Developers Handbook* (Washington, DC: Urban Land Institute, 1968), p. 154.

30. American Public Health Association, *Planning the Neighborhood* (Chicago: Public Administration Service, 1948).

31. American Public Health Association, *Planning the Neighborhood* (Chicago: Public Administration Service, 1960), p. 57.

32. Ibid., p. 55.

33. Ibid., p. 35.

34. Michael Southworth and Eran Ben-Joseph, *Streets and the Shaping of Towns and Cities* (New York: McGraw-Hill, 1997), p. 93.

35. Ibid., pp. 94-95.

36. Andres Duany, Elizabeth Plater-Zyberk, and Jeff Speck, *Suburban Nation* (New York: North Point Press, 2000), p. 66.

37. Michael Southworth and Eran Ben-Joseph, *Streets and the Shaping of Towns and Cities* (New York: McGraw-Hill, 1997), p. 92.

38. Reid Ewing, *Best Development Practices* (Chicago: American Planning Association, 1996), p. IV. 4.

39. Clarence S. Stein, *Toward New Towns for America* (New York: Reinhold Publishing Corporation, 1957), pp. 51-52.

40. Barbara McCann, Bianca DeLille, and Michelle Garland, *Mean Streets 2000* (Washington, DC: Surface Transportation Policy Project, 2000), p. 6.

41. Ibid., p. 11.

42. Howard Frumkin, "Urban Sprawl and Public Health," *Public Health Reports* 117 (May-June 2002), p. 204.

43. William H. Lucy, observations of behavior on a cul-de-sac in Columbus, Ohio, July 3, 1990.

44. Peter Baker and Neil Henderson, "Dunn Loring Girl Killed by Trash Truck Backing Up," *The Washington Post*, March 25, 1990.

45. R.E. Sapien, J. Widman Roux, and L. Fullerton-Gleason, "Children's Response to a Commercial Back-Up Warning Device," *Injury Prevention* 9 (2003), pp. 87-88.

46. Robert J. Brison, Kristine Wicklund, and Beth A. Mueller, "Fatal Pedestrian Injuries to Young Children: A Different Pattern of Injury," *American Journal of Public Health* 78 (July 1988), pp. 793-795.

47. Evan P. Nadler, Anita Courcoulas, Mary J. Gardner, and Henri R. Ford, "Driveway Injuries in Children: Risk Factors, Morbidity, and Mortality," *Pediatrics* 108, no. 2 (2001), pp. 326-328.

48. Greg Schneider, "Safety Advocates Decry Back-Over Deaths," *The Washington Post*, April 28, 2005.

49. Ibid.

50. Joseph L. Schofer, Katherine Kaufer Christoffel, Mark Donovan, John V. Lavigne, Robert R. Tanz, and Karen E. Wills, "Child Pedestrian Injury Taxonomy Based on Visibility and Action," *Accident Analysis and Prevention* 27, no. 1 (1995), pp. 317-333.

51. M. Stevenson, "Analytical Approach to the Investigation of Child Pedestrian Injuries: A Review of the Literature," *Journal of Safety Research* 212 (1991), pp. 123-132.

52. U.S. Department of Transportation, National Highway Traffic Safety Administration, *Fatality Analysis Reporting System Web-Based Encyclopedia* (2002), www-fars.nhtsa.dot.gov.

53. Susan Handy, Robert G. Paterson, and Kent Butler, *Can't Get There from Here: Planning for Street Connectivity* (Chicago: American Planning Association, 2002), p. 15.

54. Edward H. Bouton, "Local and Minor Streets," in John Nolen, ed., *City Planning* (New York: D. Appleton and Company, 1929), p. 96.

55. Michael C. Poulton, "The Best Pattern of Residential Streets," *Journal of the American Planning Association* 48 (Autumn 1982), p. 480.

56. Ibid.

57. Randall Arendt, *Rural by Design* (Chicago: American Planning Association, 1994), pp. 24-25.

58. Kevin Lynch and Gary Hack, *Site Planning*, 3d ed. (Cambridge, MA: MIT Press, 1984), pp. 195, 200.

59. Reid Ewing, *Best Development Practices* (Chicago: American Planning Association, 1996), p. IV. 9.

60. Alan B. Cohen, *Narrow Streets Database* (1997), www.sonic.net/abcaia/narrow.htm.

61. Andres Duany, Elizabeth Plater-Zyberk, and Jeff Speck, *Suburban Nation* (New York: North Point Press, 2000), p. 192.

62. Ibid.

63. Reid Ewing, Tom Schmid, Richard Killingsworth, Amy Zlot, and Stephen Raudenbush, "Relationship Between Urban Sprawl and Physical Activity, Obesity, and Morbidity," *American Journal of Health Promotion* 5 (September/October 2003), pp: 47-57; Howard Frumkin, "Healthy Places: Exploring the Evidence," *American Journal of Public Health* 93, no. 9 (September/October 2003), pp. 1451-1456.

CHAPTER

11

The Myth of Exurban Safety and Rational Location Decisions

For cities and older suburbs to be stabilized or revived, middle- and upper-income households must remain in or move to cities and older suburbs in proportions similar to their proportions in newer suburbs and exurbs. If images of physical danger affect location decisions adversely for cities and older suburbs, then reducing the gap in dangerous conditions between cities, suburbs, and exurbs should be one of the goals of public policy makers. That goal is important. Part of the apparent gap in dangerous conditions, however, is perceived but is not real. Perceptions that central cities and older suburbs are relatively dangerous occur from exaggerating some dangers while ignoring others.

Rationality is an ambiguous concept—so ambiguous that it may not be useful—yet it is used. Economists often have claimed that people make rational decisions. A rational relationship between a government decision, an action, and a result has been used by courts in considering whether certain actions are constitutional. A rational relationship, in this legal context, is considered a modest rather than a rigorous standard.

Presumably, rational refers to a reasonable or plausible connection between objective conditions and decisions that take conditions into account. Interpretations of information link conditions and decisions, but information needed for reasonable decisions in market situations, as in government decision making, often is not available or the cost of acquiring and interpreting information is too large. Frameworks for interpreting information are not full blown, ready made, and everywhere available to everyone. Satisfactory interpretive frameworks are not available for many phenomena of urbanization. Interpretive frameworks evolve gradually and slowly through formulating theories, conducting research, and experimenting with alternatives. In the absence of effective interpretive frameworks, information—even if available—is unlikely to be interpreted appropriately to help markets or governments function efficiently.

Metropolitan housing markets probably malfunction, we believe, because of misinformation about dangerous residential locations. Misinformation concerning dangers of travel from residences to nonresidential activities is even greater. Information about safety is scarce, frameworks for analyzing safety are incomplete, and interpretations frequently are misguided.

Sprawl patterns of development are consistent with common judgments about safety. That is, low-density sprawl is the typical metropolitan development pattern. Presumably, residents of sprawling settlements believe such patterns are relatively safe or at least not excessively dangerous. However, these judgments often are mistaken about which development patterns promote safety. Safety is the condition that more often influences location preferences than any other neighborhood characteristic, according to some research about home-buying preferences.[1]

COMPARATIVE DANGER

Some aspects of danger are well known, especially crime; other aspects are more obscure, such as where traffic fatalities occur. Little information about traffic fatality locations is analyzed routinely, but it is relevant—in fact, essential—to a realistic interpretation of the relative safety of cities, suburbs, and exurbs. In 2000, for example, there were 41,821 traffic fatalities in the United States compared with 15,517 homicides. Locations of these traffic fatalities and homicides matter. They may have a major impact on where danger is greater.

Ironically, based on data we have discovered, realistic fear of the combination of traffic fatalities and homicides should be higher in exurbia and outer suburbs than in either central cities or older suburbs. The information about danger that most people in the United States think they know concerns crime, including homicides. Information that rarely is known concerns traffic fatalities and serious injuries from traffic accidents. In this chapter, we will examine some facts about dangers from traffic fatalities and homicides, and consider why danger of homicides is feared and the danger of traffic fatalities is rarely recognized. We will explore how greater attention to geographic concentrations of traffic fatalities and serious traffic injuries and homicides by strangers might lead to more accurate estimates of dangers associated with residential location decisions.

Are cities more dangerous than suburbs? Most people would say, "Of course." They probably also believe that exurbs are safer than either cities or suburbs. A non-random survey by the *Atlanta Journal-Constitution* may approximate common beliefs. Asked "Which area do you consider safest?," the respondents said: city, 21 percent; suburbs, 33 percent; and rural areas, 46 percent.[2] A decade earlier, a random poll for *Time* magazine and CNN of 500 respondents revealed that 10 times more people thought they were less likely to be victims of crime if they lived in small towns or suburbs rather than in big cities—69 percent said less likely and 6 percent said more likely.[3] It also is commonly believed that fear of crime has contributed to the flight of many middle- and upper-income households from cities to suburbs. Exodus of too many middle- and upper-income residents, and their replacement with lower-income persons, is one cause of too much sprawl and too intense poverty concentrations.

HOMICIDES, VIOLENT CRIME, AND TRAFFIC FATALITIES

Violent and property crime rates have been higher in cities than in suburbs or exurbs. In 2000, for example, in the 68 cities with more than 250,000 residents, 1,093 violent crimes, including 13.1 homicides and manslaughters, occurred per 100,000 residents. In suburban counties, according to the Federal Bureau of Investigation (FBI), there were 361 violent crimes, including 3.8 homicides and manslaughters, per 100,000 residents. On the other hand, in small cities of 10,000 to 100,000 residents, violent crime rates were not much different than in suburban counties, ranging from 323 to 494 per 100,000 residents in cities.[4] The belief that cities have more crime than suburbs, therefore, should be focused on large cities rather than all cities.

Regional differences in city and suburban crime rates were striking. The Northeast, which has the largest income gaps between cities and suburbs, has the lowest city property crime rates in the nation. Moreover, the property crime rate in Northeast cities (196 per 1,000 households) was less than the property crime rate in suburbs (239 per 1,000 households) and nonmetropolitan areas (214 per 1,000 households) in the West. The city rate in the Northeast (196 per 1,000 households) was only slightly higher than the suburban property crime rates in the South (177 per 1,000 households) and Midwest (178 per 1,000 households). It seems unlikely that many residents of suburbs in the Midwest, South, and West would predict that their areas are about as dangerous in terms of property crime as relatively deteriorated central cities in the Northeast.[5]

Traffic, however, is more likely than violent crime to cause deaths and injuries. For several years, traffic fatalities have been at least twice as numerous as homicides. As the number of homicides diminished during the 1990s, the gap between traffic fatalities and homicides increased. In 1991 there were 41,508 traffic fatalities and 24,700 homicides—a ratio of 1.7 to 1. In 1996, there were 42,065 traffic fatalities and 19,650 homicides—a ratio of 2.1 to 1. In 2001, there were 42,216 traffic fatalities and 15,980 homicides—a ratio of 2.6 to 1.[6] In 1991, there were 114 traffic fatalities and 68 homicides per day; by 1999, there still were 116 traffic fatalities per day compared with only 44 homicides (Table 11.1).

Whereas the homicide rate has varied greatly, falling rapidly in the 1990s after large increases in the 1970s and 1980s, traffic fatalities have been much more stable. This stability has been particularly evident in the 1990s, during the same period when homicides were declining.[7]

From the consistency in the traffic fatality data, one could infer that the causes of traffic fatalities have been stable but vehicle conditions changed in the 1990s. Air bags became standard for drivers and front-seat passengers. Vehicles became bigger, as sports utility vehicles, light trucks, and minivans captured more than 50 percent of new vehicle sales by 2000. Although the net safety effect of these changes is not clear, presumably the design engineers of air bags and the purchasers of large vehicles believed they were enhancing their safety. However, the number of miles driven per household increased, partly due to sprawling settlement patterns. Therefore, it is plausible that the steady number of fatalities is related to the settlement patterns within which people travel in motor vehicles.

Another perspective, emphasizing the relationship of age, experience, and danger, came from Phil Berardelli in an opinion column in *The Washington Post*: "Every day,

110 of us are slaughtered on the highways—a World Trade Center's worth of casualties every 3 and 1/2 weeks. Teenage drivers account for one-sixth of that figure, and as far as highway fatalities are concerned, age 16 is Ground Zero. Sixteen-year-olds are three times more likely to die in a crash than 17-year-olds, who are in turn four times more likely to die than everyone else . . . The risks grow . . . when speed, alcohol or drugs are involved. About one in 20 teens is injured in a crash each year."[8]

Therefore, one can infer that sprawl settlement patterns that increase the number of teenage drivers driving far, fast, and at late hours are more dangerous than settlement patterns that provide more transportation alternatives—walking, bicycling, public transportation, and short driving distances.

Traffic accidents and crimes also cause injuries, but the severity of injuries that occur is difficult to determine. Injuries may be minor or incapacitating, but traffic injuries are more than three times as numerous (3,189,000 in 2000) as aggravated assaults (910,774 in 2000)[9]—that is 8,866 traffic injuries per day compared with 2,495 aggravated assaults. Data about the severity of injuries are difficult to find. In Kentucky, however, the Department of Motor Vehicles reported that in 1999 there were 819 traffic fatalities, 8,359 incapacitating injuries, 19,809 nonincapacitating injuries, and 26,783 possible injuries. Incapacitating injuries were 10 times more numerous than traffic fatalities.

Table 11.1
Traffic Fatalities, Murders, and
Nonnegligent Manslaughters
in the United States

	Traffic Fatalities	Murders and Manslaughters
1991	41,508	24,700
1992	39,250	23,760
1993	40,150	24,530
1994	40,716	23,330
1995	41,817	21,610
1996	42,065	19,650
1997	42,013	18,210
1998	41,501	16,970
1999	41,717	15,530
2000	41,945	15,517
2001	42,216	15,980

Source: U.S. Department of Transportation, National Highway Traffic Safety Administration, *Traffic Safety Facts Book* (Washington, DC: U.S. Government Printing Office, 2002); U.S. Bureau of Justice Statistics, *Sourcebook of Criminal Justice Statistics 2001* (Washington, DC: U.S. Government Printing Office, 2002).

LOW DENSITY, SPEED, AND TRAFFIC DEATHS

One of the most striking facts about traffic fatalities is the proportion that involve single vehicles. In a two-vehicle crash, blame is uncertain; in a one-vehicle crash, either the vehicle malfunctioned, road conditions were beyond the driver's ability to manage the vehicle, or, more likely, driver error caused the fatal crash. The victim and the perpetrator in single-vehicle crashes are identical. One can imagine that the most frightening aspect of traffic could be that thousands of people can kill themselves inadvertently while going about their routine daily activities. In Virginia, for example, 29 to 31 percent of fatal accidents annually have been in single-vehicle crashes.[10] Thirty percent may seem high, but actually it is much lower than in some states. In Michigan, 46 percent of fatal crashes in 1999 involved one vehicle, as did 51 percent in Ohio.[11]

News articles like this one illustrate the danger: A truck driver "was killed Thursday morning in Nelson County, Virginia when the tractor-trailer he was driving veered off the road and smashed into trees. . . ."[12] A three-year study by the Virginia Transportation Safety Training Center's Crash Investigation Team concluded that distractions from driving were the most common cause of traffic fatalities, but the researchers were unable to determine which types of distractions were most often involved.[13]

Some believe that high traffic death rates are associated with high traffic volume and high population density; however, state traffic fatality rates suggest the opposite. In 1996, the highest traffic fatality rates per 100,000 residents were in states with relatively low population densities: Mississippi, Wyoming, New Mexico, Alabama, and South Carolina. The lowest traffic fatality rates were in highly urbanized states: Massachusetts, Rhode Island, New York, Connecticut, and New Jersey. Their death rates were two and one-half to four times lower than in the low-density states with the highest traffic fatality rates.

Danger to pedestrians followed a similar pattern. High pedestrian death rates were associated with low state and metropolitan population densities. The 10 highest child pedestrian death rates in 1997 and 1998 were in southern and western states: South Carolina, Mississippi, Utah, North Carolina, Alabama, Arizona, Florida, Alaska, Louisiana, and Kentucky.[14] The 10 metropolitan areas with the highest pedestrian death rates were in the South and Southwest, according to *Mean Streets 2000*: Tampa–St. Petersburg, Atlanta, Miami–Fort Lauderdale, Orlando, Jacksonville, Phoenix, West Palm Beach–Boca Raton, Memphis, Dallas–Fort Worth, and New Orleans.[15]

Excessive speed often is associated with traffic fatalities, in the numerous instances in which driver error contributes to accidents. Research has confirmed that people who drive farther, such as long-distance commuters, also drive faster.[16] The highest speed traffic occurs on interstate highways in rural and exurban areas, but traffic fatality rates there are not affected substantially by interstate highway traffic, since approximately 11 percent of fatalities occur on interstates. In contrast, 28,653 out of 37,280 fatal crashes in 1997 occurred on two-lane roads. The effect of speed is seen in that of 37,280 fatal crashes—only 3,132 were in urban areas on streets with speed limits of 30 miles per hour or less.[17]

Most fatal accidents are in exurban and rural areas. In 2000, 21,521 fatal crashes were in rural areas, 14,667 were in urban areas, and 1,221 were in unassigned locations.[18] In 1999 in Ohio, 1,027 fatal accidents were in rural areas compared with 403 in urban areas. In Wisconsin, 615 of 744 traffic fatalities in 1999 were in rural areas. Dane County Sheriff's Sgt. Gordon Disch attributed traffic deaths in his county to "people (who) travel much faster than the road is designed for. I think there's a large influx of people who have migrated to the rural areas and as a result those roads are becoming obsolete for the volume of traffic."[19]

Bad weather has counterintuitive effects on traffic dangers because of slower speeds. During the first six months of 2001, Nebraska and Iowa had the fewest traffic deaths in 50 years. The cause, according to state highway safety officials, was "the long and unrelenting winter on the Great Plains this year. There usually are more accidents on slick and icy roads, but because drivers tend to drive at slower speeds in such conditions, the crashes are less severe."[20]

Pedestrian deaths also are related to development patterns common in low-density states and metropolitan areas. For example, of pedestrian deaths for which location information was recorded in 2000 and 2001, "45 percent were killed where no crosswalk was available."[21] Highways, roads, and streets with no crosswalks typically are in areas developed since the 1950s where moving motor vehicle traffic quickly was the primary development and design goal. "The deadliest roads tend to be high-speed arterials, with few accommodations or protections for pedestrians," according to *Mean Streets 2002*.[22] Reid Ewing, Richard Schieber, and Charles Zegeer also found that pedestrian fatality rates, and overall traffic fatality rates, were higher in sprawling counties.[23]

Speed is related to risks to pedestrians as well as to drivers, according to a 1997 study in Great Britain: "Speed is also a major factor in whether a pedestrian accident proves to be fatal. A ten-mile per hour increase in speed, from 20 mph to 30 mph, increases the risk of death for a pedestrian in a collision nine-fold. If a car going 20 mph hits a person, there is a 95 percent chance that the person will survive. If that same car is traveling 30 mph, the person has slightly better than a 50/50 chance of survival. At 40 mph, the picture is bleaker still—only fifteen percent of people struck at this speed can be expected to survive."[24]

HOMICIDES BY FAMILY MEMBERS, ACQUAINTANCES, AND STRANGERS

Murders clearly indicate danger, but most murders are not related to travel or to the location of one's residence. Murders usually involve people who know each other. They are not random. Most murders are committed by family members, current and former lovers, friends, neighbors, co-workers, and business associates—especially by dealers in the illegal drug trade. The FBI estimate was that 20 to 23 percent of homicides from 1997 to 2003 were committed by strangers. For example, among the 57.3 percent of homicides for which a relationship between the perpetrators and victims was identified, 13 percent were committed by strangers in 2000. Extrapolating those percentage equivalents to a 100 percent total, 22.7 percent of homicides would be committed by strangers.[25]

Considerable variation exists among states in the percentage of homicides committed by strangers among the known perpetrator/victim relationships. For example, in Minnesota, it was 13 percent; Virginia, 15 percent; Pennsylvania, 18 percent; and New Jersey, 22 percent. If homicides are committed infrequently by strangers, who are the perpetrators? Nationally, 12.5 percent of victims were related to the offenders in 2003 and 30.5 percent were acquainted with them, 12.5 percent were by strangers, and 44.5 percent involved unknown relationships.[26]

The preponderance of homicides by family, friends, and acquaintances means that relatively few homicides grow out of what are referred to as "felony circumstances"— homicides that occurred in relation to another crime. According to the FBI's national data for 1999, 17 percent of total homicides grew out of felony circumstances, of which about half were robberies and one-fourth were drug law violations.[27] The large majority of homicides occur from conflicts between people who know each other, often intimately. Most homicides are not related to random violence or other crimes, or to travel from home to daily activities, or to the choice of a residential location. In addition, many nonfatal violent crimes are committed against victims known to the perpetrator, including 72 percent of rapes and 55 percent of assaults in 2001.[28]

The locations of nonfatal violent crimes also are revealing about dangers of leaving home. Of 6,723,930 violent crimes in 1999, 5,601,630 were assaults (of which 4,311,270 were simple assaults), 740,890 were robberies, and 381,400 were rapes and other sexual assaults. Of these, only 3.6 percent were on the street near the victim's residence, with another 8.7 percent occurring somewhere near the victim's residence. The most frequent location, 17.4 percent, was on a street other than near the victim's residence.[29] As for violent crimes related to transportation, 0.8 percent were on public transportation or in a station, while 7.2 percent were in a parking lot or parking garage.[30]

TRAFFIC FATALITY RATES IN CITIES, SUBURBS, AND EXURBS

The location and frequency of traffic fatalities should affect beliefs about whether danger is greater in exurbs, suburbs, or cities. William Lucy analyzed traffic fatalities, murders, and murders by strangers in seven metropolitan areas in Virginia from 1988 through 1997. He found that exurban counties had the highest combined traffic fatality and homicide-by-stranger rates in each metropolitan area for each five-year period. Similar results occurred from 1978 through 1982.[31]

Richmond, Virginia, whose homicide rate frequently was in the top 10 during the 1990s, was less dangerous than eight nearby exurban and outer suburban counties, measuring danger by traffic fatalities and homicides by strangers from 1993 to 1997. The most dangerous counties (Charles City, New Kent, and Prince George) were exurban counties with population densities of 34, 50, and 103 persons per square mile compared with Richmond's more than 3,000 persons per square mile (Table 11.2). Rapidly growing suburban and exurban Hanover County had a combined traffic fatality and homicide-by-stranger rate that was 30 percent higher than Richmond's.[32]

In the Washington, D.C., metropolitan area, combined traffic fatality and homicide-by-strangers death rates in the District of Columbia were exceeded by several exurban counties (Clark, Fauquier, Frederick, and Stafford), with exurban Fauquier County having the highest combined rate from 1993 to 1997.[33] These exurban counties were more dangerous despite Washington, D.C., ranking in the top 10 in the nation in its homicide rate in the 1990s.

Combined traffic fatality and homicide-by-stranger rates also were higher in suburban counties than in central cities in each of Virginia's small metropolitan areas: Charlottesville, Danville, Lynchburg, and Roanoke. The largest difference occurred

Table 11.2
Danger Ranking Based on Combined Fatality
Rates and Population Density in Seven
Metropolitan Areas in Virginia, 1988-1997

Rank from Most to Least Dangerous[c]	Counties and Cities	Combined Fatality Rate[a] (1988–1997)	Population Density[b] (1990)
1	Charles City	11.5	0.1
2	New Kent	9.9	0.1
3	Dinwiddie	8.1	0.1
4	Prince George	7.8	0.2
5	Botetourt	6.7	0.1
5	Fauquier	6.7	0.1
7	Goochland	6.4	0.1
7	Greene	6.4	0.1
9	Pittsylvania	6.3	0.1
10	Clarke	6.0	0.1
11	Suffolk	5.7	0.2
12	Frederick	5.3	0.2
13	Fluvanna	5.2	0.1
14	Spotsylvania	4.9	0.2
15	Powhatan	4.6	0.1
16	Hanover	4.5	0.2
16	Albemarle	4.5	0.1
18	Washington, DC	4.3	13.5
19	Amherst	4.1	0.1
20	Petersburg	4.0	2.6
21	Richmond	3.7	5.7
21	York	3.7	0.6
23	Stafford	3.6	0.1
24	Campbell	3.3	0.1
25	Danville	2.8	1.9
25	Norfolk	2.8	7.6
27	Gloucester	2.7	0.2
27	Loudoun	2.7	0.3
27	James City	2.7	0.4
30	Prince William	2.5	1.0
31	Chesapeake	2.3	0.7
32	Portsmouth	2.2	4.9
32	Lynchburg	2.2	2.1
34	Roanoke	2.1	0.5
34	Newport News	2.1	3.9
36	Henrico	2.0	1.4
36	Chesterfield	2.0	0.8
38	Roanoke (city)	1.9	3.5
39	Hampton (city)	1.5	4.0
39	Virginia Beach	1.5	2.5
39	Fairfax (county)	1.5	3.2

Table 11.2 (cont.)
Danger Ranking Based on Combined Fatality
Rates and Population Density in Seven
Metropolitan Areas in Virginia, 1988-1997

Rank from Most to Least Dangerous[c]	Counties and Cities	Combined Fatality Rate[a] (1988–1997)	Population Density[b] (1990)
42	Charlottesville	1.3	6.1
42	Hopewell	1.3	3.5
44	Arlington	1.2	10.3
45	Falls Church	1.0	7.5
45	Colonial Heights	1.0	3.3
45	Manassas	1.0	4.4
45	Alexandria	1.0	11.4
49	Fairfax (city)	0.7	4.9
50	Manassas Park	0.0	5.8

[a] Combined traffic fatality and stranger homicide rates, per 10,000 residents.
[b] Persons per acre.
[c] Where ties occurred, the same number is applied to all counties and cities sharing that ranking.

Sources: Virginia Department of Motor Vehicles, *Crash Facts 1997* (Richmond: Virginia Department of Motor Vehicles, 1998); Virginia Department of Motor Vehicles, *Crash Facts 1988-1996* (Richmond: Virginia Department of Motor Vehicles, 1989-1997); Virginia State Police, *Crime in Virginia 1997* (Richmond: Virginia State Police, 1998); Virginia State Police, *Crime in Virginia 1988-1996* (Richmond: Virginia State Police, 1989-1997).

in the Charlottesville area, where Greene County's rate was more than six times higher than Charlottesville's.[34]

We have been researching combined rates of traffic fatalities and homicides by strangers in 10 major metropolitan areas in other parts of the United States. In each instance thus far, danger in central cities has been less different than expected from their close-in suburbs. In each instance, in addition, some suburban and exurban counties have had the highest combined rates.

Combined traffic fatality and stranger homicide rates were higher in 44 of 78 counties than the average in their central cities during 1999, 2000, and 2001. The highest fatality rate counties were five or six times more dangerous than the cities with the lowest rates (Minneapolis and St. Paul). Eighteen counties were more dangerous than Dallas, the most dangerous city (Table 11.3).[35]

In the Chicago metropolitan area, the combined traffic fatality and homicide-by-strangers death rates were higher in three of nine counties (DeKalb, Grundy, and Kendall) than in Chicago. In the Cincinnati area, fatality rates were higher than in the central city in 10 of 12 counties (Boone, Campbell, Gallatin, Grant, and Pendleton in

Table 11.3

Average Traffic Fatality and Homicide Rates in 10 U.S. Metropolitan Areas (1999-2001)

Jursidictions in Each MSA Ordered by Population Density	Population	Persons Per Acre	Rates per 10,000 Population				
			Traffic Fatalities	Total Homicides	Homicides by Strangers	Traffic Fatalities and Homicides	Traffic Fatalities and Homicides by Strangers
Baltimore, MD PMSA	2,552,994						
Queen Anne's County	40,563	0.2	2.8	0.2	0.1	3.0	2.9
Carroll County	150,897	0.5	1.0	0.2	0.0	1.2	1.0
Harford County	218,590	0.8	1.3	0.2	0.0	1.6	1.3
Howard County	247,842	1.5	1.0	0.2	0.0	1.2	1.0
Anne Arundel County	489,656	1.8	1.0	0.2	0.0	1.3	1.1
Baltimore County	754,292	2.0	1.0	0.2	0.1	1.3	1.1
Baltimore City	651,154	12.6	0.8	0.2	0.8	1.0	1.6
Chicago, IL PMSA	8,272,768						
Grundy County	37,535	0.1	2.3	0.2	0.2	2.5	2.5
DeKalb County	88,969	0.2	1.5	0.2	0.1	1.7	1.6
Kendall County	54,544	0.3	2.0	0.1	0.2	2.0	2.1
McHenry County	260,077	0.7	1.2	0.1	0.0	1.2	1.2
Will County	502,266	0.9	1.2	0.3	0.0	1.5	1.2
Kane County	404,119	1.2	1.0	0.5	0.1	1.5	1.1
Lake County	644,356	2.2	0.9	0.2	0.0	1.1	0.9
DuPage County	904,161	4.2	0.6	0.1	0.0	0.7	0.6
Cook excluding Chicago City	2,480,727	5.4	0.7	0.3	0.0	1.0	0.7
Cook County	5,376,741	8.9	0.8	1.3	0.2	2.1	1.0
Chicago City	2,896,016	19.9	0.9	2.2	0.4	3.1	1.3

Table 11.3 (cont.)
Average Traffic Fatality and Homicide Rates in 10 U.S. Metropolitan Areas (1999-2001)

Jursidictions in Each MSA Ordered by Population Density	Population	Persons Per Acre	Rates per 10,000 Population				
			Traffic Fatalities	Total Homicides	Homicides by Strangers	Traffic Fatalities and Homicides	Traffic Fatalities and Homicides by Strangers
Cincinnati,OH– KY-IN PMSA	1,646,395						
Pendleton County, KY	14,390	0.1	2.5	0.7	0.1	3.2	2.7
Ohio County, IN	5,623	0.1	1.2	0.0	0.0	1.2	1.2
Gallatin County, KY	7,870	0.1	1.7	0.4	0.1	2.1	1.8
Brown County, OH	42,285	0.1	1.3	0.1	0.0	1.4	1.4
Grant County, KY	22,384	0.1	2.5	0.6	0.1	3.1	2.7
Dearborn County, IN	46,109	0.2	2.5	0.1	0.0	2.5	2.5
Boone County, KY	85,991	0.5	1.2	0.2	0.0	1.3	1.2
Clermont County, OH	177,977	0.6	1.5	0.1	0.0	1.6	1.5
Warren County, OH	158,383	0.6	1.4	0.1	0.0	1.5	1.4
Campbell County, KY	88,616	0.9	0.9	0.3	0.1	1.2	0.9
Kenton County, KY	151,464	1.5	0.7	0.4	0.1	1.1	0.8
Hamilton excluding Cincinnati	514,018	2.4	0.7	0.2	0.0	0.9	0.8
Hamilton County, OH	845,303	3.2	0.7	0.5	0.1	1.2	0.8
Cincinnati City	331,285	6.7	0.7	1.0	0.2	1.7	0.9

Table 11.3 (cont.)

Average Traffic Fatality and Homicide Rates in 10 U.S. Metropolitan Areas (1999-2001)

Jurisdictions in Each MSA Ordered by Population Density	Population	Persons Per Acre	Traffic Fatalities	Total Homicides	Homicides by Strangers	Traffic Fatalities and Homicides	Traffic Fatalities and Homicides by Strangers
						Rates per 10,000 Population	
Cleveland–Lorain –Elyria, OH PMSA	2,250,871						
Ashtabula County	102,728	0.2	2.0	0.0	0.0	2.0	2.0
Geauga County	90,895	0.4	1.5	0.0	0.0	1.5	1.5
Medina County	151,095	0.6	1.5	0.0	0.0	1.5	1.5
Lorain County	284,664	0.9	0.9	0.1	0.0	1.0	0.9
Lake County	227,511	1.6	0.5	0.0	0.0	0.6	0.5
Cuyahoga excluding Cleveland	915,575	3.8	0.5	0.1	0.0	0.6	0.5
Cuyahoga County	1,393,978	4.8	0.6	0.6	0.1	1.2	0.7
Cleveland City	478,403	9.7	0.8	1.6	0.3	2.3	1.1
Dallas, TX PMSA[a]	3,519,176						
Henderson County	73,277	0.1	2.5	0.6	0.1	3.1	2.6
Kaufman County	71,313	0.1	3.9	0.9	0.2	4.8	4.1
Hunt County	76,596	0.1	3.6	0.3	0.1	3.9	3.6
Ellis County	111,360	0.2	2.6	0.4	0.1	3.0	2.7
Rockwall County	43,080	0.5	1.3	0.0	0.0	1.3	1.3
Denton County	432,976	0.8	1.1	0.1	0.0	1.2	1.1
Collin County	491,675	0.9	1.0	0.1	0.0	1.1	1.0
Dallas County	2,218,899	3.9	1.2	1.2	0.2	2.3	1.4
Dallas City	1,188,580	5.7	1.4	1.9	0.4	3.3	1.8
Dallas Cnty excluding Dallas city	1,097,768		0.8	0.3	0.1	1.2	0.9

Table 11.3 (cont.)

Average Traffic Fatality and Homicide Rates in 10 U.S. Metropolitan Areas (1999-2001)

Jurisdictions in Each MSA Ordered by Population Density	Population	Persons Per Acre	Rates per 10,000 Population				
			Traffic Fatalities	Total Homicides	Homicides by Strangers	Traffic Fatalities and Homicides	Traffic Fatalities and Homicides by Strangers
Houston, TX PMSA[b]	4,177,646						
Chambers County	26,031	0.1	5.1	0.4	0.1	5.5	5.2
Liberty County	70,154	0.1	3.4	0.4	0.1	3.8	3.5
Waller County	32,663	0.1	3.3	0.6	0.1	3.9	3.4
Montgomery County	293,768	0.4	2.2	0.5	0.1	2.6	2.3
Fort Bend County	354,452	0.6	0.9	0.3	0.1	1.2	1.0
Harris County	3,400,578	3.1	1.2	0.9	0.2	2.1	1.4
Houston City	1,953,631	5.7	1.2	1.3	0.3	2.5	1.5
Harris excluding Houston	1,480,789		1.1	0.4	0.1	1.4	1.1
Milwaukee—Waukesha, WI PMSA	1,500,741						
Washington County	117,493	0.4	1.6	0.1	0.0	1.6	1.6
Ozaukee County	82,317	0.6	0.9	0.0	0.0	0.9	0.9
Waukesha County	360,767	1.0	0.7	0.0	0.0	0.8	0.7
Milwaukee County	343,190	3.7	0.3	0.1	0.0	0.4	0.3
Milwaukee County	940,164	6.1	0.5	1.4	0.3	1.9	0.8
Milwaukee City	596,974	9.7	0.6	2.1	0.4	2.7	1.1

Table 11.3 (cont.)
Average Traffic Fatality and Homicide Rates in 10 U.S. Metropolitan Areas (1999-2001)

Jursidictions in Each MSA Ordered by Population Density	Population	Persons Per Acre	Rates per 10,000 Population				
			Traffic Fatalities	Total Homicides	Homicides by Strangers	Traffic Fatalities and Homicides	Traffic Fatalities and Homicides by Strangers
Minneapolis–St. Paul, MN–WI MSA	2,968,806						
Pierce County, WI	36,804	0.1	2.0	0.1	0.0	2.1	2.0
Isanti County, MN	31,287	0.1	1.4	0.1	0.0	1.5	1.4
St. Croix County, WI	63,155	0.1	2.6	0.0	0.0	2.6	2.6
Chisago County, MN	41,101	0.2	1.8	0.2	0.0	1.9	1.8
Wright County, MN	89,986	0.2	1.2	0.1	0.0	1.3	1.2
Sherburne County, MN	64,417	0.2	1.1	0.1	0.0	1.1	1.1
Carver County, MN	70,205	0.3	1.7	0.2	0.0	1.9	1.7
Scott County, MN	89,498	0.4	1.5	0.1	0.0	1.5	1.5
Washington County, MN	201,130	0.8	0.7	0.0	0.0	0.7	0.7
Dakota County, MN	355,904	1.0	0.8	0.1	0.0	0.9	0.8
Anoka County, MN	298,084	1.1	0.8	0.2	0.0	1.1	0.9
Hennepin excluding Minneapolis	733,582	2.3	0.5	0.3	0.0	0.7	0.5
Hennepin County, MN	1,116,200	3.1	0.5	0.5	0.1	1.0	0.5
Ramsey excluding St. Paul	223,884	3.4	0.5	0.2	0.0	0.7	0.5
Ramsey County, MN	511,035	5.1	0.6	0.4	0.1	0.9	0.6
St. Paul City	287,151	8.5	0.7	0.5	0.1	1.2	0.7

Table 11.3 (cont.)
Average Traffic Fatality and Homicide Rates in 10 U.S. Metropolitan Areas (1999-2001)

Jurisdictions in Each MSA Ordered by Population Density	Population	Persons Per Acre	Traffic Fatalities	Rates per 10,000 Population				
				Total Homicides	Homicides by Strangers	Traffic Fatalities and Homicides	Traffic Fatalities and Homicides by Strangers
Philadelphia, PA– NJ PMSA	5,100,931						
Salem County, NJ	64,285	0.3	2.9	0.3	0.0	3.2	2.9
Burlington County, NJ	423,394	0.8	1.2	0.2	0.0	1.3	1.2
Chester County, PA	433,501	0.9	1.3	0.2	0.0	1.4	1.3
Gloucester County, NJ	254,673	1.2	1.5	0.1	0.0	1.7	1.5
Bucks County, PA	597,635	1.5	1.1	0.1	0.0	1.2	1.1
Montgomery County, PA	750,097	2.4	0.8	0.1	0.0	0.9	0.8
Camden County, NJ	508,932	3.6	0.9	0.6	0.1	1.5	1.0
Delaware County, PA	550,864	4.7	0.6	0.4	0.1	1.0	0.7
Philadelphia County/ City, PA	1,517,550	17.6	0.8	2.0	0.3	2.8	1.1

Table 11.3 (cont.)
Average Traffic Fatality and Homicide Rates in 10 U.S. Metropolitan Areas (1999-2001)

Jurisdictions in Each MSA Ordered by Population Density	Population	Persons Per Acre	Rates per 10,000 Population				
			Traffic Fatalities	Total Homicides	Homicides by Strangers	Traffic Fatalities and Homicides	Traffic Fatalities and Homicides by Strangers
Pittsburgh, PA MSA	2,358,695						
Fayette County	148,644	0.3	1.3	0.1	0.0	1.4	1.3
Butler County	174,083	0.3	1.3	0.1	0.0	1.4	1.3
Washington County	202,897	0.4	1.3	0.1	0.0	1.4	1.4
Westmoreland County	369,993	0.6	1.2	0.1	0.0	1.3	1.2
Beaver County	181,412	0.7	1.2	0.1	0.0	1.3	1.2
Allegheny excluding Pittsburgh	947,103	2.2	0.7	0.0	0.0	0.7	0.7
Allegheny County	1,281,666	2.7	0.7	0.0	0.1	0.7	0.8
Pittsburgh City	334,563	10.0	0.8	0.1	0.2	0.8	1.0

MSA = Metropolitan Statistical Area; PMSA = Primary Metropolitan Statistical Area

[a]Although small portions of the City of Dallas lie within Collin, Denton, and Rockwall Counties, all homicides and traffic fatalities within the City of Dallas were attributed to the much larger portion of the city within Dallas County.

[b]Although small parts of Houston lie within Fort Bend and Montgomery Counties, homicides and traffic fatalities within the City of Houston were attributed to that part of the city within Harris County.

Sources: All population data: U.S. Census Bureau, *Census of Population and Housing 2000.* Data on acreage for each jurisdiction from 1990 census for certain cities, www.census.gov/population/censusdata/places, from 2000 census, www.census.gov, and from packet "Population Density of Central Cities and Counties and Metropolitan Areas." County fatality data from Fatality Analysis Reporting System Web site, query function, www.fars.nhtsa.dot.gov. Traffic fatality data are from the National Highway Traffic Safety Administration, Traffic Safety Facts, www-nrd.nhtsa.dot.gov/pdf/nrd-30/NCSA/TSFAnn/TSF1999.pdf, and 2000 and 2001; Uniform Crime Reports County Data. Retrieved November 2001-April 2003, from the University of Virginia, Geospatial and Statistical Data Center, http://fisher.lib.virginia.edu/collections/stats/crime. City Homicide data from Federal Bureau of Investigation Uniform Crime Reports, www.fbi.gov/ucr/ucr.htm (1999, 2000, 2001). Uniform Crime Reports by some states as Pennsylvania, http://ucr.psp.state.pa.us/UCR/Reporting/Monthly/Summary/MonthlySumHomiUI.asp.

Kentucky; Brown, Clermont, and Warren in Ohio; and Dearborn and Ohio in Indiana). In Cleveland, three of six counties had higher combined fatality rates than the city (Ashtabula, Geauga, and Medina). In the Dallas area, the traffic and stranger homicide death rate was higher in Ellis, Henderson, Hunt, and Kaufman Counties than in the City of Dallas. In the Houston area, the combined death rate was higher in Chambers, Liberty, Montgomery, and Waller Counties than in the City of Houston. In the Minneapolis–St. Paul metropolitan area, the combined rate was higher in the counties of Anoka, Carver, Chisago, Dakota, Isanti, Pierce, Scott, Sherburne, St. Croix, and Wright than in the central cities. In the Philadelphia area, Chester, Gloucester, and Salem Counties had higher fatality rates than Philadelphia. In the Pittsburgh metropolitan area, the combined rate was higher in the counties of Beaver, Butler, Fayette, Washington, and Westmoreland than in the central city.[36] In the Baltimore and Milwaukee areas, only one county in each had higher combined rates than the central cities.

The relationship between low population density and danger becomes evident when all the metropolitan counties and cities are arrayed for the entire state of Virginia (Table 11.2). For the 14 jurisdictions with the highest combined rate of traffic fatalities and homicides by strangers, the highest population density was 0.2 persons per acre (143 persons or less per square mile). The jurisdiction with the highest population density, Alexandria, with 11.4 persons per acre, was the second safest jurisdiction in Virginia.[37]

The common belief, of course, is the opposite—that danger and high density go together, and safety and low density are companions. This is not true in Virginia. For 27 counties with population densities from 0.1 to 0.9 persons per acre, the mean traffic fatalities and homicides by strangers was 5.2 per 10,000 residents (the median was 4.9). For the 23 cities and counties with population densities of 1.0 to 11.4 persons per acre, the mean was 1.9 (the median was 1.5).[38]

Similar findings occurred in our study of traffic fatalities and homicides by strangers in 78 counties and 11 cities in 10 metropolitan areas (Baltimore, Chicago, Cincinnati, Cleveland, Dallas, Houston, Milwaukee, Minneapolis–St. Paul, Philadelphia, and Pittsburgh). The 18 most dangerous jurisdictions were outer suburban counties with population densities of 0.1 to 0.4 persons per acre, with 11 of them at densities of 0.1 person per acre. The City of Dallas was next, the 19th most dangerous jurisdiction; it tied Houston as the lowest density central city, with 5.7 persons per acre (Table 11.3). In these 10 metropolitan areas, inner suburbs consistently were the least dangerous areas. One or more outer suburban counties consistently were the most dangerous areas, with outer suburban areas being particularly dangerous compared with inner areas in the Minneapolis–St. Paul, Pittsburgh, and Houston metropolitan areas. In the 39 counties with population densities from 0.1 to 0.9 persons per acre, the mean traffic fatalities and homicides by strangers were 1.9 (the median was 1.6), while for 30 cities and counties with densities from 1.0 to 19.9 persons per acre, the mean of fatalities was 1.3 (the median was 1.0).[39]

Higher traffic fatality and stranger homicide dangers also occurred in the exurban counties of Baltimore and Philadelphia, in one-year samples for 2000, according to journalists for metropolitan publications. In January 2001, *The Baltimore Sun* reported findings for traffic fatalities and homicides by strangers in 2000: "[Baltimore] had a combined rate of 13.9 per 100,000 people (traffic fatalities and homicides by strangers), only slightly higher than Prince George's 13.8 and Harford at 13.3. Howard County's was 11.9, Baltimore County's 11.6 and Anne Arundel County's 10.8. Queen Anne's, Charles and Frederick counties—fast-growing exurban areas that recorded a handful of homicides but high traffic death rates—all have combined rates that exceed those of Baltimore."[40] The most surprising aspect of the Maryland data was the small difference between the City of Baltimore, which had one of the five highest homicide rates in the nation in 2000,[41] and the large suburban counties—Anne Arundel, Baltimore, Howard, and Prince George. The large number of traffic fatalities in those counties caused the small differences in overall safety.

In the Philadelphia area, *Philadelphia* magazine reported similar results: "Crunch the numbers, and it adds up to an average annual rate of about four homicides by stranger per 100,000 population in [Philadelphia], versus about nine auto fatalities per 100,000 in the four suburban counties. . . . a Chester County resident is now nearly four times more likely to die in a car crash than the average Philadelphian is to die at the hands of a violent criminal."[42] Quoting Chester County Coroner Rodger Rothenberger, Noel Weyrich wrote: "Most of us in Chester County are in a vehicle at some point during each day, and it's probably the riskiest activity that we do."[43] Describing the outrage of Scott Piersol, town manager of East Brandywine, Weyrich noted that Piersol said: "Some of these people basically feel invulnerable . . . People put their makeup on driving down the road. I've seen that, and it just drives me nuts. These people might as well have a gun in their hand, shooting at people. They can do the same damage with their vehicle."[44]

NARROW ROADS AND AGGRESSIVE DRIVING

A news article in the *Richmond Times-Dispatch* about traffic fatalities in suburban Chesterfield County reported that drivers' errors and substandard road conditions create a dangerous brew: "Forty-six percent of Chesterfield's nearly 1,400 miles of undivided two-lane roads, . . . have a width of 24 feet or more. That's the optimum standard for a new two-lane road carrying more than 2,000 cars per day, according to the Virginia Department of Transportation. . . . In Chesterfield, 8 percent of the miles on two-lane roads are 22 feet wide, while 30 percent are 20 feet, 11 percent are 18 feet and 5 percent are 16 feet or less. . . . Randy Green, a spokesman for AAA Mid-Atlantic . . . pinned the county's accidents on a lack of parental attention to teen drivers, smooth-riding SUVs and a kind of cul-de-sac mentality. 'People turn onto the main street and gun it.'"[45]

Another clue to traffic dangers in exurbia emerged from an analysis by the *Buffalo Evening News* about time of day and location of fatalities. It found that night fatalities had declined dramatically, from 300 between midnight and 4 AM from 1979 to 1983, to 131 from 1994 to 1998. The number of fatalities between 2 and 6 PM, however, had increased slightly, from 211 to 226.[46] The *Buffalo Evening News* concluded: "Driving home from work has replaced driving home from a night out as the most deadly time to be on the road."[47] Three of every four fatalities occurred on county roads where two-way roads were not physically divided.

An article in *The Washington Post* captured the problem: "Commuters hurrying to jobs in Fairfax and Loudoun [Counties] encounter slower trucks and local farm traffic, tempting them to pass on the double, yellow lines . . . Narrow shoulders and sharp curves leave little room for error, and hills cut visibility . . . In the last three weeks, five people have died in two head-on collisions on the two-lane part of Route 28 which stretches 21 miles from Manassas in Prince William [County] through Fauquier [County]."[48]

The worrisome rise in aggressive driving also has been related to stressful commuting conditions by Ricardo Martinez, director of the National Highway Traffic Safety Administration: "If a driver expects a trip to take 10 minutes and it takes more than 30 minutes, frustration grows. Many drivers respond by acting and driving aggressively. . . ."[49]

Ironically, gated subdivisions may house some of the most vulnerable metropolitan residents because of their use of dangerous exurban roads. Tracts of land large enough for developing gated subdivisions often are located on the metropolitan fringe. Gated subdivisions cannot avoid some dangers faced by exurban residents, especially traffic fatalities and serious traffic injuries. Residents of exurbia commonly drive in the most vulnerable areas—two-lane roads where motorists are driving farther and faster—and at dangerous times, commuting hours or late at night.

In general, security is a primary issue for residents of gated communities. In a survey, "nearly 70 percent indicated that security was a very important issue in their decision to live in their gated communities . . . More than two-thirds of the respondents believed there was less crime in their developments than in the surrounding areas. Of those, a full 80 percent attributed the difference to the gates."[50] Security is viewed as a matter internal to the residential neighborhood, not a matter of risks associated with going to and from the neighborhood.

Commenting in Lynchburg's *The News & Advance* on findings for the Lynchburg, Virginia, area that showed a suburban county to be more dangerous than the central city, Lynchburg Police Chief Charles Bennett said he was sure the statistics were accurate. "Most people think city traffic is more dangerous than rural traffic," Chief Bennett said, "but higher speeds on rural roads result in more fatalities." He added that most rural roads aren't built to handle the traffic that now travels them. He also noted that the ability to survive a traffic accident may depend on how quickly rescue personnel can get victims to hospitals.[51] According to National Highway Traffic Safety Administration data, out of 20,767 fatal crashes in which emergency vehicles drove victims to hospitals, deaths occurred in only 747 instances when they arrived at hospitals in less than 20 minutes. The average emergency vehicle travel time to hospitals in fatal rural crashes, however, was almost 50 minutes.[52]

AWARENESS OF DANGERS

The news media are an important instrument through which the public's images of reality are formed. How media report the news matters. Declining crime rates in the 1990s—and before that, rising crime rates in the 1970s and 1980s—were reported regularly in the news media, as were crimes that are particularly dramatic or grisly, especially murders. Television coverage of crime increased in the 1990s even as crime rates declined.[53] By the 1990s, television was the main source of news for a majority of Americans. Orfield cited a study by the Rocky Mountain Media Watch to demonstrate the prominence of crime coverage: "[It] analyzed 50 television news programs in 29 cities, all recorded on the evening of January 11, 1995. An average of 28.5 percent of total news time was devoted to crime alone, and 53.8 percent covered stories of crime, war, or disaster—collectively known as the 'mayhem index.'"[54] Michael

Medved cited a 1998 survey in *USA Today* that found 78 percent of local television news led with natural disasters, murders, and fires. There is a saying, he observed, that "if it bleeds, it leads."[55] Usually crime reports have location implications, conveying an impression that cities are more dangerous than suburbs, although sometimes an horrific event indicates that suburbia is not immune.

The cataclysmic events at Columbine High School in 1999 may have contributed to awareness that outer suburbia and exurbia are not safe havens from sudden disasters. The murders of 12 students and a teacher by two students at Columbine in an outer suburban area near Denver have been treated by some suburbanites as a wake-up call. A multitude of "what should be done" discussions ensued, even though the National School Safety Center reported that incidents of school violence have declined since 1994. For some people, the Columbine High School tragedy ended beliefs in an era of suburban and exurban isolation from unanticipated violence.

Dramatic events, such as transcontinental plane crashes, reported by news media may penetrate consciousness in contrast to common occurrences, such as the more than 100 persons killed in traffic fatalities on an average day. If the news media reported current trends about traffic danger, such as the fact that there were 4.8 traffic fatalities per hour in 1999 and 6.2 traffic injuries per minute, then traffic dangers might penetrate consciousness. Instead, it takes dramatic or ironic circumstances to generate news coverage.

Routine traffic deaths, like this one in Albemarle County outside Charlottesville, Virginia, are put on an inside page, given a small headline, and reported in their entirety in 96 words: "A 33-year-old Charlottesville man was killed early Thursday morning after his car ran off the road and struck a tree, Albemarle County police said. According to police reports, officers responded to the 3700 block of Stony Point Road at 12:43 AM to find Landon Morris of Charlottesville dead at the scene. His car was traveling north when it left the road, went airborne, crossed a private driveway and struck a tree, police said. No other passengers were in the car. Morris' car, a 1985 Dodge Omni, was destroyed. The crash is still under investigation."[56] End of story.

On the other hand, dramatic events occasionally are reported and may lead to perspective analyses, like the following one that began on the front page of *The Washington Post*: A 21-year-old male driver "learned a terrible lesson about the dangers of illegal drag racing . . . just before Christmas . . . [He] had been racing . . . on a road . . ., hitting speeds over 100 mph, police said, when he suddenly slammed into the rear of a Chevrolet Cavalier . . . What he realized next will no doubt haunt (him) for the rest of his life. 'It's Momma! I've killed Momma!' (he) said in a cell phone call . . . to his father, . . . (His) mother, . . . was killed in the . . . crash, along with her passenger, . . . The two women had been riding around . . . looking at Christmas lights."[57]

Traffic fatality and injury trends rarely are traced to geographic and local government locations the way that crime rates are. Comparisons between traffic fatality rates with murder rates, or with murder rates by strangers, are virtually absent. The findings that have emerged from Lucy's studies have seemed so unusual, even bizarre, to the news media that when they were released every two or three years, they generated a drumbeat of news coverage. Newspaper headlines like these appeared: "Suburban Living Can Kill or Maim You: Safety in Numbers,"[58] "Study Finds Suburbs Have More Danger than Cities,"[59] and "Fredericksburg-Area Living Can Be Hazardous to Your Health."[60] Reporters have called for elaboration; columnists have written about the implications. The analyses in *The Baltimore Sun* and *Philadelphia* magazine also followed release of data about Virginia. Then the subject disappeared again.

William Morris, sheriff of Greene County, which is 10 miles north of Charlottesville, Virginia, developed the only instance of public policy response to these studies as far as we are aware. By 1997, the Greene County Sheriff's Department was writing 15 times more speeding tickets than in 1992. The county's crackdown on speeders came after Lucy's 1994 study rated Greene the second most dangerous county in Virginia. "I saw that study and it really bothered me a lot," said Sheriff Morris. "I didn't want Greene developing a reputation as a place to speed."[61]

Sometimes media that report traffic fatalities configure the data as though dramatic reductions in traffic injuries have occurred. *USA Today,* in a front-page Snapshot displayed this headline: "Traffic injury rate drops in USA."[62] The fine print said there were fewer injuries per 100 million miles traveled. It did not state how many injuries or deaths occurred or how these numbers compared with population. The rate of traffic fatalities per 100,000 persons actually had declined dramatically from 1973 (25.5 fatalities per 100,000 persons) through 1992 (15.4 per 100,000). Thereafter, the rate increased to 15.9 in 1995 and 1996, and then dropped to 15.2 in 2000. After 20 years of declines in the 1970s and 1980s, the fatality rate was relatively flat through the 1990s, rather different than the *USA Today* graph, which showed traffic injuries declining from 169 per 100 million miles traveled in 1988 to 103 in 2002.[63] The *USA Today* interpretation could be applied to traffic fatality data and turned upside down, namely because more people were driving farther in the 1990s and early 21st century, and the traffic fatality rate per 100,000 persons had changed little since 1992, despite improvements in vehicle safety design. The *TDM Encyclopedia* about traffic safety concluded: "... reduced crashes per vehicle mile are largely offset by increased vehicle mileage."[64]

More people driving farther increases certain types of hazards. Crashes with animals, especially deer, are examples. In 2003, 210 fatalities occurred from crashes with animals—75 percent of them with deer—more than doubling the 101 animal crash fatalities that occurred in 1993. More than 1.5 million vehicle crashes with deer occurred in 2003, in which 13,713 people were injured and which caused $1.1 billion in vehicle damage.[65] Deer crashes are most likely on rural roads with speed limits of 55 miles per hour or more. People choosing exurban residential locations are most likely to increase their risk of severe crashes with deer.

MISINFORMATION, MISCALCULATIONS, AND MISDIRECTED EMOTIONS

Residential location decision making includes three geographic dimensions. The first is the commuting-to-work territory. Except for people who insist on walking to work, it has a radius of several or many miles. Second, numerous neighborhoods are possible residential locations within these commuting radii. Possible locations will be screened by criteria such as quality of structures and maintenance, investment potential, quality of schools, visible signs of public disorder, reputation for crime, access to shopping and recreation, open spaces nearby, and transportation alternatives. Third, dwelling issues—cost, size, quality, configuration, aesthetic attributes, and electrical and mechanical features—will determine which neighborhoods include structures currently for sale or rent that are satisfactory.

These subjects are complex. Understanding them depends upon attention to present conditions. Some of these conditions are visible; others, such as crime, schools, transportation, and neighbors, require research about local settings before their implications can be interpreted. Wise choices also require calculations about the future. How well will the dwelling hold up? Is the neighborhood changing? Will a purchase investment be secure? Will the neighborhood be hospitable for children (a concern for young parents) or for the elderly (a concern for retirees)?

Public order is the first task of governance, and personal security is the most vivid dimension of public order. Bandits, gangs, and private militias rule where governance is weak. Without order, a state cannot have a viable economy. Similarly, making a place where people want to be depends on adequate public order and personal security.

Attachments to any place, therefore, will be influenced by beliefs about personal security. Risks from crime on the routes used to conduct regular activities, or even from intruders into one's residence, are potential dangers. The potential for crime typically is on people's minds when they make location decisions. Consequently, crime may be overestimated. Risks associated with transportation vehicles used in conducting routine activities are a second type of danger, but these risks are much less likely to be recognized. In fact, many people associate motor vehicles with safety because they empower drivers with speeds many times greater than foot speeds with which they may believe they can escape from danger. Yet this very potential for high speeds is what causes greater dangers from driving motor vehicles than from being a pedestrian.

Fear is related to danger. To be feared, danger must be perceived. People vary in what they believe is dangerous and in how severe they believe a given danger is. In choosing a residence, the decision involves consequences during numerous months for renters and, on average, eight years for home buyers. Therefore, calculations of danger should be more weighty than voluntary decisions about short-term events.

Evaluations of current conditions and predictions about the future are influenced by information, calculations, and emotions. Evaluations and predictions, therefore, also can be influenced by misinformation, miscalculations, and misdirected emotions about safety. The relative danger of homicides and traffic fatalities is the subject of this chapter. The purpose of comparing the relative danger of homicides and traffic fatalities is to explore potential effects of perceptions about crime and traffic on residential location patterns. We believe misinformation, miscalculations, and misdirected emotions have influenced residential locations. Corrective action, therefore, should address misjudgments in addition to reducing dangerous conditions.

DANGER OF LEAVING HOME

Traffic dangers may warrant anxiety, but what evidence exists that danger from crime or traffic influences choices of residential locations? In casual conversation, concern about crime can be expected to come up as a screening issue when people rule out certain neighborhoods or even entire local government jurisdictions because of anxiety about crime. Journalists' accounts of city neighborhoods in transition include uneasiness about safety—whether from crime, racial change, or housing deterioration—as a key motivation for people moving to suburbs.[66]

It is somewhat surprising, therefore, that academic research about reasons for moving usually has not emphasized crime. Some prominent studies of reasons for moving in the 1950s and 1960s either did not discuss crime as a reason for moving[67] or they lumped crime in with neighborhood conditions, obscuring whether crime is an important neighborhood component.[68] Thomas Guterbock was unusual in focusing on crime and white flight. He found that, despite their prominence in journalists' interpretations of motivation, evidence to support the importance of either crime or white flight was lacking in his study of suburban deconcentration in the 1950s and 1960s in 39 metropolitan areas.[69] That is, Guterbock found similar rates of suburban deconcentration where crime and minority presence were relatively low as when they were high.

In the *Annual Housing Survey* of 1975, attitudes toward neighborhood conditions were surveyed. Crime was not cited as a problem in suburbs. In central cities, crime ranked third, both among home owners and renters. Street noise and heavy traffic ranked first and second and, with airplane noise ranked fourth, one suspects these were considered relatively minor problems. On the other hand, owners and renters who wished to move listed crime as a reason. When inadequate public services were mentioned, a similar relationship occurred. Public transportation and shopping were more serious neighborhood deficiencies than police protection, except for those who wished to move. Then police protection was ranked first and, for owners, schools were ranked second.[70]

In a 1991 survey of neighborhood characteristics important to buyers, less crime was combined with better neighborhood as a possible response. Fifty-seven percent gave it the most or next most important neighborhood factor on a five-point scale, virtually identical to good schools, which was chosen by 56 percent. Traffic dangers, or other characteristics of traffic, were not referred to explicitly.[71] When respondents in a second 1991 survey were asked their reasons for buying a home in a particular neighborhood, they consistently cited "better neighborhood" as the most important reason. Better neighborhood was not defined. By a process of elimination, one might infer that crime was an important component of the definition because schools, shopping, transportation, work, taxes, and proximity to relatives were listed separately.[72] In addition, Beth Milroy reported that "studies about women as housing consumers, . . . show that they combine a number of considerations and often rank personal safety for self and children above all others."[73]

Real estate consultant Christopher Leinberger claimed paramount importance for fear related to crime as the motivation for outer suburban development in the 1990s: ". . . the underlying reason for the growth of fourth-generation metro cores is undoubtedly fear. In spite of the fact that violent crime has remained stable over the past 20 years . . ., the perception persists that crime has become significantly worse. . . . The majority white population moving to the residential districts serving fourth generation metro cores sees the move as a way to ensure safety."[74] In Great Britain, Tim Heath reported that a majority of the persons who would not consider living in Britain's city centers were dissuaded "primarily by the busyness and the noise associated with the location as well as the perception of crime levels and personal safety."[75]

These views by Leinberger, in an article published in 1996, and Heath, based on interviews in 1998, seem in the same spirit as concern about crime expressed 30 years earlier. In 1968, during the period of the urban riots, 68 to 74 percent of respondents in cities said control of crime was a very serious problem, including 70 percent of respondents in nonriot cities.[76]

According to Gallup polls, concern about crime has declined through the 1990s. When a national sample of more than 1,000 respondents were surveyed about their perceptions, the percentage saying cities were safe increased as follows, from 1990 to 2001: Atlanta, from 45 to 62 percent; Chicago, from 26 to 53 percent; Los Angeles, from 26 to 39 percent; Philadelphia, from 40 to 60 percent; San Francisco, from 44 to 64 percent; and Washington, D.C., from 22 to 36 percent.[77] In Gallup polls conducted in 2001 and 2002, respondents were asked the most important problem facing the United States. In each of four surveys from November 8, 2001 to March 4, 2002, only 1 or 2 percent identified crime and violence as being the most important problem.[78]

The declining crime rate of the 1990s may open opportunities for cities and older suburbs to be perceived less fearfully, and other aspects of danger—such as danger in motor vehicles—may become more apparent.

FEAR OF CRIME

A clear identification of the importance of crime pertinent to location decisions appeared in a survey conducted by the National Association of Home Builders in 1999. Respondents were asked which factors would be very important if they were buying a home today. Percentages from 5 to 33 percent selected public transportation, highway access, and location of shopping. More than 50 percent of respondents between ages 25 and 44 said the school district was very important. The most important factor, however, was crime. In every age group, more than 80 percent said the crime rate was very important.[79]

These results were similar to what some of our students at the University of Virginia found when they asked their parents in February 2002 why they chose their current residence. As for issues of location, rather than characteristics of the residence itself, 73 percent said that safety was very important and 18 percent said it had some importance. Asked what influenced their perceptions of safety, 64 percent said danger from crime nearby and 52 percent cited danger from people hanging out on the streets. To our surprise, 64 percent also cited danger from passing cars on their street and 48 percent referred to high-speed traffic on highways or roads they would use. It is noteworthy, however, that passing cars on residential streets pose relatively little actual danger, and high-speed traffic on highways is less dangerous than somewhat less high-speed traffic on two-lane roads. The questions were not sufficiently precise to learn why these traffic conditions were feared and whether respondents had accurate impressions of greater and lesser traffic dangers.

A survey in the Philadelphia area captured some of the distinction between fear of crime and fear of traffic. Fear of traffic barely registered in comparison to crime. In *Philadelphia* magazine, Noel Weyrich described the following opinions about perceived dangers: "A far-ranging regional health survey in 1996 asked 10,000 people in the five-county [Philadelphia] area to note the 'most serious problems your community faces.' About 62 percent of city residents checked off the entries for property crime, violent crime and drug abuse. Among suburban respondents, 35 percent marked those same three categories. Just five percent of the suburban respondents checked the box for 'traffic/speeding.'"[80]

Mark Moore suggests that neighbors' "reactions to the threat of crime are similar to those they have to environmental and health risks. They can tolerate a great deal of risk if the risks they face are familiar and seemingly controllable."[81] Whatever the objective risks of harm, the feeling of insecurity is subjective. Fear of crime may be triggered more by environmental conditions associated with crime—graffiti, broken street lights, abandoned cars, and noisy youth—than by actual victimization rates.[82] Each of these conditions is more visible, and seemingly less subject to an individual or household's control, than the risks involved with automobile travel. Risks involved with automobile travel are seemingly controllable and, perhaps for that reason, are feared less.

In fact, some research about risks and behavior finds that "in very familiar activities there is a tendency to minimize the probability of bad outcomes. Apparently, people underestimate risks which are supposed to be under their control . . . More than half of the respondents to a 2002 Institute survey said they believe they can, through their own behavior, 'control risks on the highway' and, presumably, avoid crashing."[83]

That explanation is similar to the distinction between being vulnerable to unknown others face to face versus the abstract risk of traffic accidents while riding in a 3,000-pound vehicle that has the capacity to escape from dangerous people. Alan Durning argued that "because of strong psychological reactions to what criminologists call 'stranger danger'—fear of random, malicious acts—people tend to overestimate the risks of crime while dramatically underestimating the risks of driving."[84]

Our expectation is the same as Durning's report in 1996. Yet, one year later, in the 1997 *Customer Satisfaction Survey* of about 4,000 people by the National Highway Traffic Safety Administration, 72 percent of the respondents said "they are more likely to be a victim of a serious motor vehicle crash than a victim of a violent crime."[85] Thus, it is possible that people, on average, have a fairly accurate impression of the relative dangers of traffic injuries and violent crime, but they may not relate that awareness to actions they might take, such as deciding where to live. Other findings in the 1997 *Customer Satisfaction Survey* indicate a latent possibility that connection could be made in the future because 60 percent of Americans "think that compared to ten years ago, people today drive less safely." Moreover, "an overwhelming majority [95 percent] believe that most crashes are caused by driver error, rather than by vehicle failures [2 percent]."[86] Thus, vehicle occupants are perceived as vulnerable to driver errors, presumably including their own errors, and driving shorter distances and less frequently would reduce their danger.

SEX, INSURANCE, AND TRAFFIC INFORMATION

Greater awareness of the number, severity, and frequency of traffic deaths and injuries could influence location decisions. Perhaps more subtle but pervasive dangers eventually will register either in rational consciousness or in the subconscious. For example, subtle dangers, including high blood pressure and depression, are associated with long commutes, wrote Phillip Longman, who quoted a marriage counselor on commuter-related stress: "They come in having only a dim awareness that commuting is the problem. Instead, they say we're quarreling too much, and the affection's gone, and so is the sex."[87] Perhaps the twin dangers—less affection and more risk of serious injury and death—eventually will penetrate the consciousness of home buyers considering where it is sufficiently safe to live.

High blood pressure, depression, quarreling, and lack of sex may be stressful, but perhaps they do not link directly to a residential location decision. A policy innovation by the State of Oregon may provide a noticeable link. In July 2003, an incentive program to persuade insurance companies to offer pay-as-you-drive auto insurance was signed into law. Insurers were offered a limited tax credit for establishing a system in which the number of miles driven annually is factored into insurance rates.[88] If the insured and insurers both save money with this program, it might spread to other states. Benefits, besides increased safety, could include less sprawl, less air pollution, and less global warming. That would be a rational location outcome based on a reasonable assessment of the available information.

Based on the information and arguments presented here, changes in perceptions of danger in cities, suburbs, and exurbs seem possible, but can facts and arguments penetrate long-held beliefs, whether they are factual, habitual, or mythical? Perceptions do change. As noted in this chapter and in Chapter 9, perceptions of dangers of crime in cities diminished in the 1990s. Risky behavior can change, based on new information. Smoking is an example. With smoking prevention, long-term and massive national campaigns and lawsuits contributed to behavior changes. The number of overweight Americans of all ages has increased, and concern by medical personnel has risen with Americans' weight gain. A modest campaign to increase information about settlement conditions, such as sprawl, that contribute to weight gain was launched in 2003 and 2004. Any effects on behavior, location decisions, and settlement patterns will depend on how persuasive this information and argument effort becomes. Can concern about traffic dangers contribute to changing overall perceptions of how good communities, good neighborhoods, and good regions are structured? With enough effort, why not?

NOTES

1. Dowell Myers and Elizabeth Gearin, "Current Preferences and Future Demand for Denser Residential Environments," *Housing Policy Debate* 12, no. 4 (2001), pp. 633-659.
2. Janita Poe, "Fatality Risk Rated Highest in Exurbs; Closer-In Areas Safer, Study Says," *Atlanta Journal-Constitution*, June 17, 2002.
3. Yankelovich Partners, *Survey by Time and Cable News Network* (Storrs, CT: Roper Center for Public Opinion Research, University of Connecticut, August 12, 1993).
4. U.S. Department of Justice, Federal Bureau of Investigation, *Crime in the United States 2000*, Uniform Crime Reports (Washington, DC: U.S. Government Printing Office, 2001), pp. 195-196.
5. U.S. Department of Justice, Federal Bureau of Investigation, *Crime in the United States 2000*, Uniform Crime Reports (Washington, DC: U.S. Government Printing Office, 2001).
6. U.S. Bureau of Justice Statistics, *Criminal Victimization 1999* (Washington, DC: U.S. Government Printing Office, 2000); U.S. Census Bureau, *Statistical Abstract of the United States 2001* (Washington, DC: U.S. Government Printing Office, 2002).
7. U.S. Department of Transportation, National Highway Traffic Safety Administration, *Traffic Safety Facts Book* (Washington, DC: U.S. Government Printing Office, 2002), p. 15; U.S. Bureau of Justice Statistics, *Sourcebook of Criminal Justice Statistics 2001* (Washington, DC: U.S. Government Printing Office, 2002).
8. Phil Berardelli, "When the Road Kill Is Our Kids," *The Washington Post*, March 24, 2002.

9. U.S. Census Bureau, *Statistical Abstract of the United States 2001* (Washington, DC: U.S. Government Printing Office, 2002).

10. Virginia Department of Motor Vehicles, *Crash Facts 2001* (Richmond: Virginia Department of Motor Vehicles, 2001), p. 2.

11. Michigan State Police, *Michigan Traffic Crash Facts* (Lansing: Michigan State Police, 2002); Ohio Department of Public Safety, *1999 Ohio Traffic Crash Facts* (Columbus: Ohio Department of Public Safety, 2001).

12. *Charlottesville Daily Progress*, March 14, 1997.

13. Associated Press, "Distraction Key Cause of Wrecks, Report Indicates," *Charlottesville Daily Progress*, December 27, 2001.

14. Barbara McCann, Bianca DeLille, Michelle Garland, *Mean Streets 2000* (Washington, DC: Surface Transportation Policy Project, 2000), p. 12.

15. Ibid., p. 5.

16. Judy S. Davis, Arthur C. Nelson, and Kenneth J. Dueker, "The New 'Burbs: The Exurbs and Their Implications for Planning Policy," *Journal of the American Planning Association* 60, no.1 (1994), pp. 45-59.

17. U.S. Department of Transportation, *Traffic Tech*, Technology Transfer Series No. 200 (Washington, DC: U.S. Department of Transportation, National Highway Traffic Safety Administration, May 1999), www.nhtsa.gov/people/outreach/traftech/pub/tt200.html.

18. U.S. Department of Transportation, National Highway Traffic Safety Administration, *Traffic Safety Facts Book* (Washington, DC: U.S. Government Printing Office, 2002), p. 52, Table 30.

19. Barry Adams, "Rural Roads are Definitely Biggest Highway Death Traps," *Wisconsin State Journal*, August 17, 2001.

20. Henry J. Cordes, "Good News on the Highways: Harsh Winter Weather Credited," *Omaha World-Herald*, July 3, 2001.

21. Michelle Ernst and Barbara McCann, *Mean Streets 2002* (Washington, DC: Surface Transportation Policy Project, 2002), p. 11.

22. Ibid., p. 5.

23. Reid Ewing, Richard A. Schieber, and Charles V. Zegeer, "Urban Sprawl as a Risk Factor in Motor Vehicle Occupant and Pedestrian Fatalities," *American Journal of Public Health* 93, no. 9 (2003), pp. 1541-1545.

24. Barbara McCann, Bianca DeLille, Michelle Garland, *Mean Streets 2000* (Washington, DC: Surface Transportation Policy Project, 2000).

25. U.S. Department of Justice, Federal Bureau of Investigation, *Crime in the United States 2000*, Uniform Crime Reports (Washington, DC: U.S. Government Printing Office, 2001), p. 21; U.S. Department of Justice, Federal Bureau of Investigation, *Crime in the United States 2003*, Uniform Crime Reports (Washington, DC: U.S. Government Printing Office, 2004), p. 21.

26. U.S. Department of Justice, Federal Bureau of Investigation, *Crime in the United States 2003*, Uniform Crime Reports (Washington, DC: U.S. Government Printing Office, 2004), p. 21.

27. U.S. Department of Justice, Federal Bureau of Investigation, *Crime in the United States 2000*, Uniform Crime Reports (Washington, DC: U.S. Government Printing Office, 2001), p. 20.

28. U.S. Bureau of Justice Statistics, *Sourcebook of Criminal Justice Statistics—2002* (Washington, DC: U.S. Government Printing Office, 2003), p. 199.

29. U.S. Bureau of Justice Statistics, *Sourcebook of Criminal Justice Statistics 2000* (Washington, DC: U.S. Government Printing Office, 2001).

30. Ibid.

31. William H. Lucy, *Death in Exurbia: The Most Dangerous Cities and Counties in Virginia, 1993-1997* (Charlottesville: University of Virginia, School of Architecture, 1999).

32. Ibid.

33. Ibid.

34. Ibid.
35. William H. Lucy and Matthew Robbie, *Traffic Fatalities and Homicides by Strangers in 10 Metropolitan Areas* (Charlottesville: University of Virginia School of Architecture, May 2004); data for eight of these metropolitan areas also appeared in William H. Lucy, "Mortality Risk Associated with Leaving Home: Recognizing the Relevance of the Built Environment," *American Journal of Public Health* 93, no. 9 (2003), pp. 1564-1569.
36. William H. Lucy and Raphael Rabalais, *Traffic Fatalities and Homicides by Strangers: Danger of Leaving Home in Cities, Inner Suburbs, and Outer Suburbs* (Charlottesville: University of Virginia School of Architecture, April 29, 2002); William H. Lucy and Matthew Robbie, *Traffic Fatalities and Homicides by Strangers in 10 Metropolitan Areas* (Charlottesville: University of Virginia School of Architecture, May 2004).
37. William H. Lucy, *Death in Exurbia: The Most Dangerous Cities and Counties in Virginia, 1993-1997* (Charlottesville: University of Virginia, School of Architecture, 1999).
38. Ibid.
39. William H. Lucy and Matthew Robbie, *Traffic Fatalities and Homicides by Strangers in 10 Metropolitan Areas* (Charlottesville: University of Virginia School of Architecture, May 2004).
40. Eric Siegel, "Not as Dangerous as You Think," *The Baltimore Sun*, January 25, 2001.
41. Scott Morgan, *City Crime Rankings* (Lawrence, KS: Morgan Quitno Press, 2001).
42. Noel Weyrich, "Those Mean Suburban Streets," *Philadelphia*, August 2001, p. 23.
43. Ibid.
44. Ibid., p. 24.
45. Meredith Fischer and Will Jones, "Some Roads Are Deadly: Deficient Design, Driver Inattention Can Be Fatal Mix," *Richmond Times-Dispatch*, February 6, 2001.
46. *Buffalo Evening News*, June 4, 2000.
47. Ibid.
48. *The Washington Post*, March 23, 1997.
49. *Los Angeles Times*, July 18, 1997.
50. Edward J. Blakely and Mary G. Snyder, *Fortress America: Gated Communities in the United States* (Washington, DC: The Brookings Institution, 1997), pp. 126-127.
51. *The News & Advance*, April 29, 1999.
52. U.S. Department of Transportation, National Highway Traffic Safety Administration, *Traffic Safety Facts 2000* (Washington, DC: U.S. Government Printing Office, 2002), p. 48, Table 26.
53. Michael Medved, *Media Seduction, Adolescent Destruction* (Chautauqua, NY: Chautauqua Institution, 2000); Myron Orfield, *Metropolitics* (Washington, DC: The Brookings Institution, 1997).
54. Myron Orfield, *Metropolitics* (Washington, DC: The Brookings Institution, 1997), p. 23.
55. Michael Medved, *Media Seduction, Adolescent Destruction* (Chautauqua, NY: Chautauqua Institution, 2000).
56. "Man Killed After Car Hits Tree," *Charlottesville Daily Progress*, March 22, 2002.
57. Sue Anne Pressley, "The Fast and the Fatal: Drag Racing Resurges," *The Washington Post*, March 17, 2002.
58. Patrick Lackey, "Suburban Living Can Kill or Maim You: Safety in Numbers," *Virginian Pilot*, May 7, 1999.
59. Shannon Brennan, "Study Finds Suburbs Have More Danger than Cities," *The News & Advance*, April 29, 1999, p. A-1.
60. Larry Evans, "Fredericksburg-Area Living Can Be Hazardous to Your Health," *The Free Lance-Star*, April 30, 1999, p. C-1.
61. *Charlottesville Daily Progress*, August 8, 1997.
62. *USA Today*, Snapshot, June 17, 2003, p. 1.

63. Ibid.

64. *TDM Encyclopedia*, "Evaluating Safety and Health Impacts: TDM Impacts on Road Safety," Personal Security and Public Health (Victoria, Canada: Victoria Transport Policy Institute, June 4, 2004), p. 26, www.vtpi.org/tdm/tdm58.htm.

65. Insurance Institute for Highway Safety, *Vehicle Crashes with Animals* (2004), www.iihs.org.

66. Anthony Lukas, *Common Ground: A Turbulent Decade in the Lives of Three American Families* (New York: Knopf, 1986); Ray Suarez, *The Old Neighborhood* (New York: Free Press, 1999).

67. Peter H. Rossi, *Why Families Move* (Glencoe, IL: Free Press, 1955); Alden Speare, Jr., Sidney Goldstein, and William H. Frey, *Residential Mobility, Migration and Neighborhood Change* (Cambridge, MA: Ballinger, 1974).

68. John L. Goodman, "Reasons for Moves out of and into Large Cities," *Journal of the American Planning Association* 45, no. 4 (1979), pp. 407-416.

69. Thomas M. Guterbock, "The Push Hypothesis: Minority Presence, Crime, and Urban Deconcentration," in Barry Schwartz, ed., *The Changing Face of the Suburbs* (Chicago: University of Chicago Press, 1976).

70. U.S. Census Bureau, *Annual Housing Survey: 1975, Current Housing Reports Series H-150-75B, Indicators of Housing and Neighborhood Quality* (Washington, DC: U.S. Government Printing Office, 1976).

71. National Association of Realtors, *Survey of Home Buyers and Sellers 1991* (Washington, DC: National Association of Realtors, 1991).

72. National Association of Home Builders, *Housing Facts, Figures, and Trends* (Washington, DC: National Association of Home Builders, 1991).

73. Beth Moore Milroy, "Taking Stock of Planning, Space, and Gender," *Journal of Planning Literature* 6, no. 1 (1991), pp. 3-15.

74. David Rusk, *Inside Game Outside Game: Winning Strategies for Saving Urban America* (Washington, DC: The Brookings Institution, 1999), p. 99.

75. Tim Heath, "Revitalizing Cities: Attitudes Toward City-Center Living in the United Kingdom," *Journal of Planning Education and Research* 20, no. 4 (June 2001), p. 470.

76. Otto Kerner, *Supplemental Studies for the National Advisory Commission on Civil Disorders* (Washington, DC: U.S. Government Printing Office, 1968).

77. Gallup Organization, Gallup poll, "Do You Consider Cities Safe?" (Storrs, CT: Roper Center for Public Opinion Research, University of Connecticut, September 10-11, 1990); Gallup Organization, Gallup poll, "Do You Consider Cities Safe?" (Storrs, CT: Roper Center for Public Opinion Research, University of Connecticut, October 11-14, 2001).

78. Gallup Organization, Gallup poll, "What Do You Think Is the Most Important Problem Facing This Country Today?" (Storrs, CT: Roper Center for Public Opinion Research, University of Connecticut, November 8, 2001-March 4, 2002).

79. Dowell Myers and Elizabeth Gearin, "Current Preferences and Future Demand for Denser Residential Environments," *Housing Policy Debate* 12, no. 4 (2001), p. 642.

80. Noel Weyrich, "Those Mean Suburban Streets," *Philadelphia*, August 2001, p. 24.

81. Mark H. Moore, "Security and Community Development," in Ronald F. Ferguson and William T. Dickens, eds., *Urban Problems and Community Development* (Washington, DC: The Brookings Institution, 1999), p. 294.

82. Ibid.

83. Insurance Institute for Highway Safety, *Low Priority Assigned to Highway Safety,* Status Report 37, no. 10 (December 7, 2002), p. 5.

84. Alan T. Durning, *The Car and the City* (Seattle: Northwest Environment Watch, 1996).

85. U.S. Department of Transportation, *Traffic Tech,* Technology Transfer Series No. 200 (Washington, DC: U.S. Department of Transportation, National Highway Traffic Safety Administration, May 1999), p. 1, www.nhtsa.gov/people/outreach/traftech/pub/tt200.html.

86. Ibid., p. 2.

87. Phillip J. Longman, "Traffic: How It's Changing Life in America," *U.S. News & World Report*, May 28, 2001.

88. Elisa Murray, "Is That American? Oregon Posts Reward for Driving Less," (Beulah: Michigan Land Use Institute, October 17, 2003), www.mlui.org/growthmanagement/fullarticle.asp?fileid=16582.

CHAPTER

12

The Past and Future of Small House Neighborhoods

Myths about safety on cul-de-sacs and safety in exurbia have simplified and distorted reality with less than desirable consequences for metropolitan income patterns and for households' well-being. Next, we describe how beliefs about house size and location characteristics have interacted in much of suburbia to produce problematic neighborhood conditions in the 21st century. We explain why suburbs with a predominance of middle-aged, often small houses competed ineffectively in the 1990s for replacement in-movers of similar income status. We focus on Henrico County, adjacent to Richmond, Virginia—a county with large swaths of small, detached, middle-aged housing units. Incipient public policy responses to deterioration in Henrico County are instructive.

Some beliefs simplify reality in a positive sense. "I will be happy if I, and my family, can live in" a certain type of house in a certain type of neighborhood in a certain type of school district or local government is such a myth. Years of complex future lives of family members are collapsed into a single sentence. These are the beliefs that drive private sector home building and subdivision developments. This type of myth drove post-World War II suburban development, when only 14 percent of households in one survey preferred apartment or previously owned, rather than new, houses.[1]

Population growth and delayed family formation during World War II created a large group of potential home buyers. Public policies also contributed. Availability of low down payment mortgages guaranteed by the Federal Housing Administration and the Veterans Housing Administration prodded banks to lower their down payment requirements dramatically and to extend the length of mortgages. Although these terms required home buyers to pay huge amounts of interest over the life of 20- to 30-year mortgages, federal tax policies made these interest payments deductible from federal income taxes. The result of these conditions and policies was that the percentage of home owners increased from 44 percent in 1940 to 63 percent in 1970. In 1970, there were about 24,689,000 more home owners than in 1940.[2]

Because many of these new home buyers had modest incomes and small savings, many small houses were built in modest neighborhoods. In 1950, the median-size, new, single-unit residence had 1,100 square feet. In the most famous development of this era, Levittown on Long Island, New York, the standard house had 750 to 800 square feet. When built out, Levittown had 82,000 residents and 17,400 two-bedroom houses,[3] an average of 4.7 persons per household. These houses and neighborhoods met the test of the residential happiness myth in that era. It featured clean air, congenial neighbors of like-minded families, playmates for young children who were everywhere, safe if sometimes overcrowded schools, more room and more control than in rented city apartments, and possibilities of expanding while staying in place. True, it sometimes was difficult coping with one car—Dad was commuting and Mom was at home with the children. However, if no public transportation was available, car pooling often was feasible and, if necessary, errands requiring a car could be done after work and on weekends. Contrary to the deadening boredom that some critics attributed to these suburbs,[4] residents generally were pleased[5] and they kept coming—more suburbs, some with small houses and some not, and more people who found the myths accurate enough to keep developers building.

CONTEMPORARY "HAPPY" RESIDENCE BELIEFS

Fast forward 40 or 50 years to 1990 or 2000. Where do these "happy" suburbs fit in the residential location beliefs at the end of the 20th century? Public policies remained similar. Small down payment mortgages were available, and mortgage interest still was deductible from federal income taxes. Demography had changed. Families were smaller and fewer people were in two-parent families. More women were in the labor force. There were proportionately more immigrants, more elderly, more employed empty nesters, and more divorcees. There also was more affluence but increasingly skewed affluence.

This demographic mixture was producing a different house type and different settings in 1990 and 2000 than in 1950, 1960, and 1970. The most prominent physical pattern was more suburban and exurban sprawl and much larger houses, even though demographic changes, including household sizes, seemed to favor accessibility and convenience over more space to keep up and more time to commute and do errands. By 1990, the median-size new house had reached 1,905 square feet. By 2000, the median size was 2,057 square feet and, by 2002, it hit 2,114 square feet—nearly twice the 1950 median of 1,100 square feet.[6]

The residential happiness belief at the end of the 20th century apparently included more people who thought bigger was better. More flexible and diverse interior space—larger rooms, more family rooms, more entertainment rooms, more home offices, more extra bedrooms, and more bathrooms—was reflected in the size data.

For many people, the minimum requirement in a house became four bedrooms and a big yard. A column in the *St. Louis Post-Dispatch* captured this typical house-searcher's dilemma: "When my friends decided to move to St. Louis last year, I tried to help them find a home. They wanted four bedrooms and a big yard . . . I asked their real estate agent to restrict the search to the city of St. Louis and St. Louis

County. He found nothing that matched their vision . . . Next day, their agent took them straight to the home of their dreams, . . . Suddenly I saw the outer suburbs in a new light. I had believed, . . . that racist motives pushed families to choose homes in the outer suburbs. At last I understood that for a typical family, the market offers no other choice."[7]

NEW HOUSE PROFILES

Our focus in this chapter is on the viability of middle-aged neighborhoods composed of houses built between 1945 and 1970. Differences between middle-aged houses and the typical new 2000 house illustrate obstacles to middle-aged areas attracting residents, buyers, and investors able to maintain them.

Size was the most encompassing and therefore the clearest difference between the typical new houses built in 2000 compared with earlier decades. However, there were numerous other major differences. For single-unit, new houses, the comparisons between 1970 and 2000 are given in Table 12.1.[8]

Styles and configurations also changed. After World War II, the one-and-one-half-story Cape Cod house was most popular.[9] One-story ranchers (73 percent of new houses in 1970) and split levels (10 percent of new houses) succeeded the Cape Cod in popularity. In 2000, 52 percent of new houses had two stories, 47 percent were one story, and 1 percent were split levels.[10]

Smaller houses were built before 1970, and their mechanical and electrical equipment was less modern than in 1970. In 1950, the median-size new house was 1,100 square feet. In 1952, only 1.3 percent of residences even had window air conditioners, and central air was not recorded in the 1950 census.[11]

Table 12.1
Characteristics of New, Single-
Unit Houses in 1970 and 2000

	Percent of Total New Single Units	
	1970	2000
Living Area		
Under 1,200 Square Feet	36	6
Over 2,000 Square Feet	21	53
4 or More Bedrooms	24	35
2 or More Bathrooms	48	93
Two Stories	17	52
Central Air Conditioning	34	85

Sources: U.S. Census Bureau, *Statistical Abstract of the U.S. 2003* (Washington DC: U.S. Government Printing Office, 2004); U.S. Census Bureau, *Statistical Abstract of the U.S. 1973* (Washington DC: U.S. Government Printing Office, 1974).

Whatever the reasons for home buyers preferring larger houses in 2000 than in 1950 or 1970, changes in housing markets have transformed many cities and suburbs. Because housing markets changed, neighborhoods dominated or overwhelmed with these small, typical houses of 1950, 1960, and 1970 often experienced major decline in relative income and sometimes major physical deterioration (see Chapter 8). The more extensive these small house areas, the more at risk such neighborhoods were to deterioration by 2000.

WHY SMALL HOUSE EXPANSION AND ADAPTATION IS DIFFICULT

The reasons for substantial, sometimes severe, neighborhood deterioration are not obvious. These houses and neighborhoods could have been settings for major upgrades and expansions.[12] Just as cities developed where there were location advantages, so did suburbs that developed after 1945. The automobile expanded the territory and number of good locations. However, in a general sense, areas closer to the traditional center, or closer to subcenters that emerged throughout the 20th century, had location advantages over more remote areas that were less accessible. Therefore, the same people who bought new 2,000-square-foot houses farther out could have bought expanded 2,000-square-foot houses—houses that originally were 1,000 or 1,375 square feet—closer in. Sometimes that has happened but, in 2000, the value of additions to residences was 8 percent of the value of new residences.[13] As a percentage of 2,000-square-foot houses, the share that grew by expansions of small houses is quite small, a relationship that decision-making costs help to explain.

Aging of housing is accompanied by higher maintenance costs. "Push factors" contribute to neighborhood deterioration. Changing demographics may lead to more crime and lower performance in public schools. The real property tax base may not increase as much as public sector costs. Public services may deteriorate or property taxes may increase. Reinvestment therefore looks riskier to home owners than some alternative investments in housing.

Additional influences on small house neighborhood stagnation, decline, and deterioration are the decision-making costs of remodeling. Expansion is a difficult process, starting with time-consuming and nerve-wracking issues about whether to consider expansion. Furthermore, lenders, architects, builders, local regulatory officials, and temporary housing suppliers are not organized to facilitate expansion of small houses.

Many pre-1940 neighborhoods have housing that is larger and superior in interior and exterior details and structural strength. This housing is located in neighborhoods that are more convenient, with more commercial and entertainment activities within walking distance and near public transportation. If old neighborhoods also have moderate housing prices, price attraction may overcome negative neighborhood social conditions. If housing prices are high, that will indicate neighborhood social problems have been overcome.

Old neighborhoods, however, may have detached housing that is too densely concentrated on small lots or in row houses, which make expansion difficult. Old neighborhoods also may have considerable multifamily rental housing that is not amenable to ownership—a severe deterrent to middle-income home buyers.

WHY THE SUBURBS' MID-LIFE CRISIS MAY GET WORSE

Decision-making obstacles to upgrading and expanding small, middle-aged houses is at the heart of suburban problems, in addition to contributing to cities' problems. Consider the expansion challenges from the perspective of owners and buyers:

- Design options are puzzling, exploring them is time consuming, and a decision not to proceed is more likely than proceeding.
- If the design phase looks promising, finding a capable, willing, and affordable builder is challenging. Builders may ask a premium for taking on small projects with uncertain obstacles awaiting them. The result may be higher per-square-foot costs for remodeling than for new construction.
- New zoning regulations and updated building codes must be considered and mastered. Public meetings, professional drawings, and discussions with administrators take time and money.
- Financing is needed. Home equity loans may not be available if the house was purchased recently. Home equity loans may not be sufficient if the expansion is major, especially if 800- to 1,200-square-foot houses are being expanded by 50 percent or more.
- For buyers, two homes must be financed during construction. Owner occupants must find temporary housing—without disrupting family members excessively. Most rentals come with year leases. Finding a suitable apartment or house for a family with children—in the same school district—may be difficult.

Even if these hurdles can be surmounted, another challenge lurks. Because most suburban developments contained a narrow range of housing sizes, quality, and prices, major expansions risk losing part of one's reinvestment, especially if one goes first as a major remodeler in a neighborhood—and someone must play that role.

For developers, the challenge may be equally daunting. To get economies of scale, a large tract with some combination of tear-downs and expansions may be needed, but private acquisitions will take years. Intervention by a local government exercising eminent domain is unlikely. While renovation and expansion can proceed one unit at a time, the operating costs are excessive. The developer faces the same risks of excessive reinvestment as the home owner in the leadership role. Why should a developer prefer this challenge to others that are more familiar?

INSTITUTIONS AND FINANCE

The financial obstacles to major expansion in small houses—especially where these districts extend for blocks or even miles—are daunting. Local government initiative to solve these obstacles is likely to be slow in coming. Individuals with resources to tackle these problems usually will decide to invest where the problems are fewer. Nonprofits are focused on more severely distressed areas and on lower-income households. The second mortgage market is not geared to offering construction loans or welcoming these mortgages after construction is completed—given the high cost of significantly expanded residences relative to the norm in small house neighborhoods.

Suburban governments are unlikely to tackle problems stemming from too many small houses. Suburban county governments typically will lack a sense of urgency, or awareness, about problems stemming from too many small houses. The lack of urgency will stem in part from the potential of suburban county governments to extract property tax and sales tax revenue from higher income, expanding districts, especially newer shopping centers and office parks. Taxes from still-prosperous areas may be sufficient to keep taxes low, permitting elected officials to defer the problems of deteriorated small house neighborhoods.

To the extent that deterioration is perceived to be a problem, commercial districts are more likely to get priority attention than residential districts. Counties may have abandoned shopping centers and office parks for which new uses have not been found. New urbanist planners typically advocate converting discarded shopping centers into mixed-use districts with interior streets laid over previous parking lots. These discarded shopping centers are on commercial strip streets that still have abundant traffic. Few of these first-generation shopping centers are so well located that they compete effectively for development investment against greenfield areas that are farther out and redevelopment sites that are closer to the old downtown center.

Besides, if local governments decide to tackle the reinvestment challenges in small house neighborhoods, where would they start and by what means? Suburbs that developed one subdivision at a time—without mixed use and with no center—lack a rationale for tackling specific districts ahead of others. There is no district comparable to downtown in a central city; downtowns usually become the focus of major reinvestments because of their historic and continuing multipurpose and high-value functions. However, if local governments, and the nonprofit and private sectors, do not increase small house expansions, a significant contributor to sprawl will continue. Middle-class households with a new child or growing children who seek more space have a choice, as they see it, to expand or to move, usually farther out, and often farther out beyond the boundary of the county in which they have lived. Usually they choose to move rather than expand.

Small suburbs have bigger problems than large counties with many outmoded houses. While the need for action is clearer in small suburbs than in large counties, the resources with which to take action are fewer. In addition, social problems may be greater—as in deterioration of public schools—with fewer options for investing in buildings, paying teachers well, and shifting attendance zones to cope with racial imbalances and household income disparities. Finding jurisdictions where these problems have been tackled vigorously, and perhaps overcome, and studying useful local policies is a major research need of the next decade.

A CASE STUDY OF PROBLEMS, OPPORTUNITIES, AND POLICIES

The Richmond–Petersburg, Virginia, metropolitan area provides a setting to observe problems involving too many small houses in suburbs. What are the future prospects of the City of Richmond, Virginia, and Henrico and Chesterfield Counties that surround the city? Although several small cities and developing counties were included in the Richmond metropolitan area in 2000, Richmond (20 percent), Henrico (26 percent), and Chesterfield (26 percent) contained 72 percent of the total metropolitan population of 996,512 (Map 12.1).

We will look at relative income in 2000 and in earlier decades for the 65 census tracts in Richmond, and at Henrico's 60 and Chesterfield's 59 census tracts. Richmond's tracts averaged about 3,000 residents, while Henrico and Chesterfield had about 4,000 residents per tract. When the income of residents of census tracts is com-

Map 12.1
Cities and Counties of the Richmond–Petersburg, VA Metropolitan Statistical Area

Source: U.S. Census Bureau, Cartographic Boundary Files, www.census.gov/geo/www/cob/bdy_files.html.

pared to metropolitan average income over time, that comparison will tell us which neighborhoods have been more attractive than others and how their ability to attract residents has changed over time. By looking at these trends comparatively, we can get a sense of future challenges and opportunities in Richmond, Henrico, and Chesterfield. Trends in census tracts between decades were facilitated by using the Neighborhood Change Database by GeoLytics, Inc., developed in association with the Urban Institute.

From population data, it appears that Richmond nearly collapsed in the 1970s and continued to fade in the 1980s and 1990s at a slower pace of decline. A better test of the city's trend comes from looking at supply and demand for housing. If population was a guide to changes in housing, Richmond would have had 10,000 less occupied housing units in 1980 than in 1970 and 17,000 less occupied units in 2000 than in 1970. Instead, Richmond actually added 3,000 units in the 1970s, while losing 30,000 residents. In 2000, Richmond had 1,700 more units than in 1970, but nearly 52,000 fewer residents.

The explanation is that average household size (AHS) dropped dramatically—by 15 percent in Richmond in the 1970s alone. That made it appear that Richmond was emptying out when it actually was adding housing.

RELATIVE INCOME AND FAMILY POVERTY

On the other hand, Richmond was getting poorer relative to Henrico, Chesterfield, and the balance of the metropolitan area. By 1990, Richmond had much lower median family incomes relative to the metropolitan family median, and Chesterfield's families were well above the median, with Henrico slightly above the metropolitan median. Here again, one can exaggerate Richmond's deterioration because Richmond did much better in per capita income than median family income. In 2000, Richmond's per capita income was 22 percent below Chesterfield's and 26 percent below Henrico's, but that relationship was heavily influenced by the racial distribution, with Richmond being a black majority city. Among whites alone, however, Richmond in 2000 had per capita income 6 percent above Henrico's and 17 percent above Chesterfield's. Richmond white's median family income ($63,154) was only slightly below Henrico's ($65,097) and Chesterfield's ($67,387), but black's median family income in Richmond ($28,536) was much below Henrico's ($44,759) and Chesterfield's ($55,153). It appeared that the black middle class had fled from Richmond.

Looking at the citywide and countywide trends in relative income between 1990 and 2000, the first hints of decline in Henrico and Chesterfield appear—slight declines in income relative to the metropolitan area—but overall they appear to be flourishing. Richmond clearly has far more poverty families, but perhaps the slight upturn in family poverty in Henrico and Chesterfield between 1990 and 2000 was another clue that something in those counties had changed.

REVERSAL OF NEIGHBORHOOD TRENDS AND AGE OF HOUSING

Census tract changes reveal dramatic reversals of neighborhood fortunes. In the 1970s, relative average family income in most of Richmond's neighborhoods was going down, often by more than 10 percent. In the 1980s, the differences were small between Richmond, Henrico, and Chesterfield. In the 1990s, a substantial reversal occurred. Decline in relative income was much more common in Henrico and Chesterfield's census tracts than in Richmond's (Table 12.2).

An important cause of these shifting fortunes of Richmond, Henrico, and Chesterfield is related to their housing and neighborhood conditions. For the metropolitan area overall, most housing was built in the 1970s, 1980s, and 1990s, with significant amounts constructed in the 1950s and 1960s. In Richmond, more housing was constructed before 1940, with one-third of its housing built during the 1950s and 1960s. In Richmond, the fairly small number of census tracts that were above the metropolitan income average usually was in census tracts that specialized in older housing. By

Table 12.2
Declining Relative Average Family Income
in Richmond and Neighboring Counties

		Census Tracts Decreasing in Relative Average Family Income					
By 2.5 Percent or More	*Total Tracts*	Number—Percent					
		1970-80		**1980-90**		**1990-2000**	
Richmond City	65	40	62%	42	65%	29	45%
Chesterfield County	59	11	19%	38	64%	40	68%
Henrico County	60	34	57%	40	67%	42	70%

By 10 Percent or More	*Total Tracts*	Number—Percent					
		1970-80		**1980-90**		**1990-2000**	
Richmond City	65	26	40%	33	51%	21	32%
Chesterfield County	59	6	10%	23	39%	27	46%
Henrico County	60	14	23%	28	47%	23	38%

Source: Neighborhood Change Database (NCDB) Tract Data from 1970-2000
(East Brunswick, NJ: GeoLytics, Inc., 2003).

Figure 12.1
Percent of Occupied Housing Units Built in Each Decade, Richmond, VA

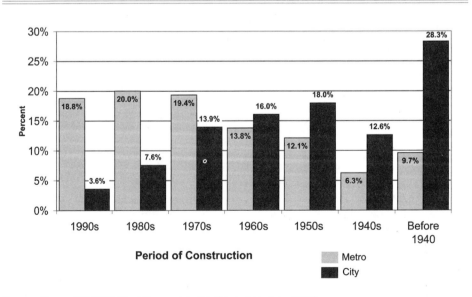

Source: CensusCD 2000 (East Brunswick, NJ: GeoLytics, Inc., 2002).

specialized, we mean that a given census tract had more than the metropolitan average of its housing built during that time period (Figure 12.1).

In Henrico, in contrast, far more census tracts were above the metropolitan average, but they tended to be in census tracts with new housing—housing built in the 1980s and 1990s. Few census tracts with considerable housing built before the 1980s were above the metropolitan average income. A similar pattern of above average income in census tracts with new housing occurred in Chesterfield.

In the 1980s, Richmond showed some signs of revival, as a considerable number of census tracts with old housing went up in relative income (Table 12.3). The rise of Richmond's census tracts was much stronger in the 1990s, again with areas with old housing leading the way (Table 12.3). Three-fourths of census tracts (nine or 12) with 40 percent or more of their housing built before 1940 went up in relative income by 10 percent or more from 1990 to 2000 in Richmond. Richmond's census tracts with less old housing were more likely to decrease than increase in relative income.

The contrast between Richmond, Henrico, and Chesterfield was dramatic. In Henrico, a significant number of census tracts with new and old housing increased in relative income, but hardly any census tracts increased where middle-aged housing was prominent. In Chesterfield, a similar pattern occurred, but there, even neighborhoods dominated by housing built in the 1980s were unlikely to increase in relative income.

These trends also can be seen in maps about income changes in the 1980s and 1990s. The biggest surprise occurs in the map describing relative average family income levels in 1999. In it, census tracts in Henrico with relative incomes less than 80 percent of metropolitan averages extend in an uninterrupted swath for 15 miles (Map 12.2).

Large variations in the size of housing units occurred among Richmond, Henrico, and Chesterfield. Henrico's housing characteristics approximated those of the metropolitan area; Richmond's housing was smaller, older, and with less owner occupancy; and Chesterfield's housing was newest, largest, and most frequently owner occupied (Table 12.4).

HENRICO'S 60 CENSUS TRACTS

Henrico's 60 census tracts varied in median age of all housing from 1953 to 1996. The median age of owner-occupied housing varied slightly more, from 1946 to 1996. A slight majority of tracts (31 of 60) had median age of owner-occupied housing in the 1950s (17) or 1960s (14). Decade of housing construction and changes in average family income in the 1990s were closely associated in Henrico. Census tracts specializing in housing built between 1950 and 1980 were least likely to increase in relative income (Table 12.3).

We hypothesize that four main factors account for the limited ability of middle-aged neighborhoods to attract replacement in-movers of equal or greater income than the metropolitan norm compared with newer and older neighborhoods. These four factors are the size of middle-aged housing, the characteristics of housing, the deterioration of this housing, and the neighborhood settings of housing. Of these four factors, only size of housing can be accessed readily with census data. Although square footage is not available, the number of rooms or number of bedrooms approx-

Table 12.3
Percent of Census Tracts Specialized by Decade of Housing
Construction Showing Increase in Relative Average Family Income,
City of Richmond, and Henrico and Chesterfield Counties

	Total Tracts	Decade of Construction of 2000 Housing Stock						
		Pre-1940	1940s	1950s	1960s	1970s	1980s	1990s
CITY OF RICHMOND								
Number of Tracts	65							
Number of Specialized Tracts		51	53	49	31	15	2	0
Increased in Relative Average Family Income 1980-1990								
Percent of Specialized Tracts Increased		37%	34%	33%	19%	13%	—	—
Increased in Relative Average Family Income 1990-2000								
Percent of Specialized Tracts Increased		55%	55%	43%	42%	33%	—	—
HENRICO COUNTY								
Number of Tracts	60							
Number of Specialized Tracts		7	22	35	29	29	24	21
Increased in Relative Average Family Income 1990-2000								
Percent of Specialized Tracts Increased		43%	32%	14%	7%	7%	33%	48%
CHESTERFIELD COUNTY								
Number of Tracts	59							
Number of Specialized Tracts		0	8	8	16	36	41	27
Increased in Relative Average Family Income 1990-2000								
Percent of Specialized Tracts Increased		—	38%	25%	13%	14%	22%	44%

Census Tracts are "Specialized" if they have more than their share of metropolitan housing built in a particular decade. Richmond had 65 Census Tracts in 2000.

Source: Neighborhood Change Database (NCDB) Tract Data from 1970-2000 and CensusCD 2000 (East Brunswick, NJ: GeoLytics, Inc., 2003).

Map 12.2
Relative Mean Family Income 1999 Inner Counties—
Richmond–Petersburg, VA Metropolitan Statistical Area

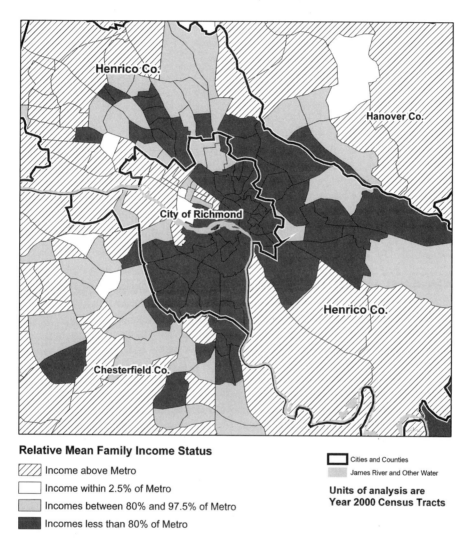

Relative Mean Family Income Status

▨ Income above Metro

☐ Income within 2.5% of Metro

▧ Incomes between 80% and 97.5% of Metro

■ Incomes less than 80% of Metro

☐ Cities and Counties

▨ James River and Other Water

Units of analysis are
Year 2000 Census Tracts

Sources: U.S. Census Bureau, Cartographic Boundary Files, www.census.gov/geo/www/cob/
bdy_files.html; Neighborhood Change Database (NCDB) from 1970-2000 and CensusCD 2000
(East Brunswick, NJ: GeoLytics, Inc., 2003).

Table 12.4
Housing Characteristics of Richmond City,
and Henrico and Chesterfield Counties in 2000

	Percent of Housing with 4 or More Bedrooms	Percent of Housing with 6 or Fewer Rooms	Percent of Owner-Occupied Housing	Median Age of Owner-Occupied Housing
Richmond	14%	74%	46%	1950
Chesterfield	37%	49%	81%	1983
Henrico	26%	61%	66%	1976
Metropolitan Area	25%	61%	68%	1976

Source: U.S. Census Bureau, *Census 2000, Summary File 3*, generated by David Phillips, using American FactFinder, http://factfinder.census.gov, June 13, 2003.

imates housing size. In the analysis that follows, we identified census tracts with relatively small amounts of housing with seven or more rooms (Table 12.4).

To examine changes in census tracts dominated by small houses, we focused on 15 of Henrico's tracts with more than 70 percent of their housing units with six or less rooms. Of 19 such tracts, we eliminated four (leaving 15) because of their high proportion (78 to 95 percent) of their housing stock in multiunit structures. We expected these 15 tracts to be middle aged and to have relative incomes below the Henrico and metropolitan norms.

WHAT HAPPENED IN SMALL HOUSE NEIGHBORHOODS?

By 2000, all 15 census tracts characterized by small dwellings were below the Henrico County level for relative median family income and relative per capita income. For relative median family income, these 15 tracts averaged 72.8 percent of the metropolitan income, while Henrico overall was at 105.3 percent. For relative per capita income, these 15 tracts averaged 74.9 percent of metropolitan income compared with Henrico's overall level of 111.5 percent. These and other characteristics are described in Table 12.5.

These 15 census tracts on the average were older than the Henrico County median age for owner-occupied housing—1962 compared with 1976. They had somewhat less single-unit structures than the county—63 percent of total dwellings compared with 72 percent for the county. They also had more renters—50 percent compared with the county average of 34 percent. The black population was considerably higher in these 15 tracts—45 percent compared with the county average of 25 percent.

Therefore, characteristics of these 15 census tracts with small dwellings in 2000 are consistent with our expectations that areas with small, middle-aged housing would be lagging in relative income. From these relative income conditions in 2000, one can imagine plausible decision-making sequences by the occupants of these dwellings and neighborhoods that led to these results.

Table 12.5
Size, Age, Renters, Single Units, Race and
Relative Income in Selected Tracts of Henrico County

Selected Henrico County 2000 Census Tracts	Percent of Total Housing with 6 or Fewer Rooms	Median Year Owner-Occupied Housing Built	Percent of Total Housing in Single Units	Percent of Renter-Occupied Housing	Percent of Population Black Only	Median Family Income as Percent of MSA	Per Capita Income as Percent of MSA
Henrico County	60.9	1976	72.0	34.3	24.6	105.3	111.5
2008.04	91.4	1967	30.6	77.1	80.6	53.8	61.8
2003.03	90.8	1955	73.9	51.9	10.7	68.1	68.0
2004.11	89.6	1988	47.8	50.4	30.0	92.1	94.5
2004.04	84.9	1959	58.8	46.2	25.6	78.2	79.5
2011.01	82.7	1983	47.1	57.7	79.4	65.4	74.3
2008.05	82.0	1954	55.2	60.0	92.7	39.1	50.1
2012.02	81.8	1977	70.7	41.8	57.6	73.5	68.0
2010.02	81.5	1958	81.1	33.8	71.9	66.0	65.2
2005.01	81.2	1957	53.0	60.1	21.9	74.3	68.4
2011.02	80.2	1958	71.0	42.9	49.2	84.7	82.9
2010.03	79.7	1962	90.8	20.1	92.3	69.2	65.5
2014.05	79.7	1954	55.4	78.7	24.5	82.7	77.4
2007	76.5	1946	58.3	44.4	3.1	85.8	107.8
2004.09	76.3	1959	60.5	49.0	28.6	76.4	65.6
2006	71.7	1949	75.0	39.8	12.5	82.9	94.0
Unweighted Average of the 15 selected tracts	82.0	1962	62.6	50.3	45.4	72.8	74.9

MSA = Metropolitan Statistical Area

Source: U.S. Census Bureau, *Census 2000, Summary File 3*, generated by William Lucy, using American FactFinder, http://factfinder.census.gov, June 13, 2003.

New residents in these neighborhoods in the 25 years after World War II tended to be middle income or higher because then, as now, new housing was not affordable by most low- and moderate-income households. Their level of affluence varied, with small houses occupied by households approximating median incomes for the region. Houses often had three bedrooms, but two-bedroom houses also were common and more frequent than four-bedroom houses.

Henrico County had been almost entirely white. In 1960, only 5 percent of county residents were black. The black share increased to 15 percent in 1980 and jumped to almost 25 percent in 2000.

One can speculate about general location decision sequences that would lead to these relative income patterns in small house neighborhoods in 2000. As the housing aged, some families could afford larger houses. As they decided whether to maintain, upgrade, or expand their houses, more often those who desired larger or newer quarters moved rather than reinvested. As the black population increased, some residents were anxious about what racial change would mean for the schools, crime, and property values. Compared with blacks who remained in Richmond, new black residents of Henrico were considerably more affluent. However, because blacks on average had much lower incomes than whites, the effect over time was to lower relative incomes in these Henrico neighborhoods relative to metropolitan income. Consequently, as houses needed more maintenance and repair as they aged, some of their occupants were less able to reinvest adequately to keep up their quality because the structures required more reinvestment than in previous years. In-movers were not all black, and out-movers were not all white, but both white and black in-movers averaged somewhat lower relative incomes than those who left. As average incomes declined and housing aged, owner occupancy declined and renters increased. Moreover, much of the new housing built in these areas was multiunit housing for rent.

These post-World War II census tracts were developed when lenders, developers, planners, and buyers preferred single-use residential districts. They were inconvenient by design, making through traffic rare because of distance from commercial areas and due to cul-de-sac street patterns. Schools adopted single-story layouts with large play areas. Many neighborhoods lacked reasons for walking or biking except to visit friends. As these neighborhoods aged, the closest commercial strips fell on hard times, with numerous shopping centers having less patronage and more vacancies. Eventually schools also declined in physical quality. Some closed from low demand; others became seedy as the local governments either concentrated on building new schools in rapidly growing areas or lacked the resources to maintain schools in their previous quality as the number of students declined.

As these trends unfolded, a smaller percentage of residents were willing to reinvest to maintain their houses. As norms for housing sizes increased dramatically in the 1970s, 1980s, and 1990s, these neighborhoods looked risky as options for expanding houses. Few households chose expansion of old or middle-aged houses over buying new houses built to contemporary size, quality, and design tastes. Consequently, neighborhoods dominated by small houses were more likely to decline in relative income than neighborhoods of similar ages with larger houses where the reinvestment and upgrade challenges were less daunting.

In these 15 census tracts in Henrico County, six tracts had a majority of black residents in 2000, and two-thirds exceeded the 24.6 percent black share of county population. Median family income in these tracts was only 61.1 percent—less than the average 72.8 percent in all 15 tracts. Renter occupancy averaged 50 percent in the 15 tracts but was highly varied. In one tract (2010.03), the renter share was only 20 percent, despite 92 percent black population and 69 percent relative median family income. The unique characteristic of this tract was that 91 percent of the housing was in single units compared with the 63 percent average in the 15 tracts. Single-unit dominance had helped maintain a high ownership rate, but relative income was not higher than the norm among these 15 tracts.

The two oldest tracts, 2006 and 2007, with median owner-occupied housing ages of 1949 and 1946, had maintained their income levels better than all but one other tract (which had a median housing age of 1988) among these 15 tracts. They also had small black percentages, indicating that something about the neighborhood had induced white in-movers to replace white out-movers. Perhaps their age had given them a different architectural ambiance and greater accessibility than some other tracts.

HENRICO'S PUBLIC POLICY RESPONSES

In May 2004, Henrico County's Board of Supervisors reacted to concerns about deterioration by creating a new Department of Community Revitalization. Henrico County first began addressing issues of deterioration in the mid-1990s by creating a community maintenance planner position in the Department of Planning. Creating a department with a staff of 24 in 2004 reflected more emphasis on revitalization. The veteran director of planning, John Marlles, was named the first department head.

During the mid- and late 1990s, the community maintenance planner had been tasked to deal with problems of housing and building code violations and abandoned cars and white goods (e.g., refrigerators and washing machines). A *Critical Issues Report* in 2000 highlighted the need for revitalization. The new Department of Community Revitalization in 2004 was given an expanded assignment. Its emphasis was on older commercial corridors for which land-use plans will be developed, with zoning changes considered, and zoning enforcement increased. Public-private partnerships with business owners to improve street landscaping, store fronts, and sidewalks were envisioned,[14] and free design assistance and façade improvement grants up to $30,000 were provided.

These program components implemented a general change in attitude. According to John Marlles, the Board of Supervisors had been grappling for almost 10 years with conceiving of Henrico "as an urban rather than as a suburban county."[15] This attitude change meant accepting greater density and being less concerned about height limits. The attitude change crystallized in the Urban Mixed Use District addition in 2002 to the zoning ordinance. It amended a strict "separation of land use zoning code that had been in effect since 1962."[16] The 2002 zoning ordinance permitted residential and commercial uses within the same building. It also permitted new urbanist developments. Two mixed-use developments (Rockets Landing along the James River near Richmond and one at Innsbrook in western Henrico) had begun by 2004.[17]

The emphasis in these plans is understandable. Commercial corridors involve property and sales tax losses, and successes may lead to revenue gains. They focus on areas visible to neighbors, users, and passers-by. Potential collaborators—the business owners and managers—are easily identified. They have clear motivation to see conditions improve. Thus, public officials have some hope of being efficient in allocating their time and resources, and the areas of potential gains are limited, making priority decisions manageable although less obvious than the usefulness of reinvesting in a downtown.

Residential areas are another matter. Assigning staff time to alleviate the most grievous violations of housing, building, and sanitary codes is one thing. Improving some infrastructure is manageable, but coping with generalized, large scale, block after block and even mile after mile of housing and neighborhood deterioration raises immense questions of feasibility, partnerships, and policies. In the next chapter, we will address some policies that are promising and that can cope with some of these decentralized obstacles. The hurdles, however, are imposing. According to Marlles, neighborhood planning should be on the county's agenda soon.[18]

CENTRAL CITY VERSUS SUBURBAN PROSPECTS

James Bacon, former editor of *Virginia Business*, and editor of a Web site called Bacon's Rebellion, summarized his view of the potential for the City of Richmond to revive and the probability that many suburbs would decline in this way: Richmond "has character, monuments and statues, developable waterfront along the James River, and neighborhoods with history and distinctive architecture. It has institutional anchors, like the state capitol complex, Virginia Commonwealth University and a host of museums. All the suburbs offer is vacant land and new houses, new malls and new office complexes. Much of the commercial space, financed with 20-year depreciation schedules, is designed for planned obsolescence. Once the newness wears off, there's nothing left to hold customers or businesses, who migrate to the latest and newest product."[19]

Many suburbs are worn, not new. Everything is worn—houses, schools, streets, and commercial districts. Some infrastructure, like sidewalks, was never built. Many residents experience these conditions and leave. Many prospective residents anticipate them getting worse and they don't buy.

Richmond has numerous problems. Its homicide rate has declined, but it was one of the nation's highest in the 1990s. Its politics has featured symbolic racial conflicts over a statue to Arthur Ashe and one memorializing the Confederacy. Several city councilors have been arrested, convicted, and jailed, with vote bribery among the charges. Improved governance would improve Richmond's prospects.

Richmond also has some missed housing opportunities. The city's home ownership rate was only 46 percent in 2000 compared with a metropolitan rate of 68 percent. In 2000, 24 percent of the city's single-unit structures was rented rather than owned. They provided an increased ownership potential for nearly 12,000 households, which, at a 2.5 AHS rate, would put 30,000 more home-owning family members in the city population of less than 200,000. Some jurisdictions in Virginia, including Arlington and Alexandria, had more owner occupants than single-unit structures in 2000. The difference is many condominiums in Arlington and Alexandria.

The paucity of condominiums is another opportunity for Richmond. According to the census, only 80 condominium units were built in Richmond during the 1980s and 1990s. Condominium sales took off nationally in 2003 and 2004, spurred partly by low mortgage interest rates. Finally, several condominium projects came to Richmond. Overlook Townhouses in Richmond's Oregon Hill neighborhood alone would create 82 condominiums, exceeding total construction over two decades.[20] A 122-unit apartment building was converted to condominiums while under construction in 2004 in downtown Richmond on the James River.[21]

If Richmond continues to revive, as many neighborhoods did in the 1980s and 1990s, the potential for middle-class family additions will increase. In 2000, the per capita incomes of whites were higher in Richmond than in Henrico and Chesterfield Counties. Median family incomes of whites in the city nearly matched Henrico and Chesterfield's white incomes. The large city-suburban income gap was driven by exodus of the black middle class and by the larger black proportions of the city than the suburban population. These relationships have been shifting rapidly, however, and the potential for more racial balance between city and suburbs, and more income balance, was increasing. The combination of relocation of the races, more home ownership opportunities in Richmond, and an accumulation of middle-aged housing ills in the suburbs contains elements for a major change in city and suburban prospects by 2020 and perhaps earlier.

NOTES

1. Kenneth T. Jackson, *Crabgrass Frontier* (New York: Oxford University Press, 1985), p. 240.
2. U.S. Census Bureau, *Statistical Abstract of the United States 1973* (Washington, DC: U.S. Government Printing Office, 1974).
3. Kenneth T. Jackson, *Crabgrass Frontier* (New York: Oxford University Press, 1985), p. 235.
4. John Keats, *The Crack in the Picture Window* (New York: Houghton Mifflin, 1957); William H. Whyte, *The Organization Man* (New York: Simon & Schuster, 1956).
5. Herbert J. Gans, *The Levittowners: Ways of Life and Politics in a New Suburban Community* (New York: Pantheon Books, 1967).
6. U.S. Census Bureau, *Statistical Abstract of the United States 2003* (Washington, DC: U.S. Government Printing Office, 2004).
7. Steven Korris, "Don't Tell Us Where We Can Live," *St. Louis Post-Dispatch*, December 6, 2001.
8. U.S. Census Bureau, *Statistical Abstract of the United States 1973* (Washington, DC: U.S. Government Printing Office, 1974); U.S. Census Bureau, *Statistical Abstract of the United States 2003* (Washington, DC: U.S. Government Printing Office, 2004).
9. Kenneth T. Jackson, *Crabgrass Frontier* (New York: Oxford University Press, 1985), p. 240.
10. U.S. Census Bureau, *Statistical Abstract of the United States 1973* (Washington, DC: U.S. Government Printing Office, 1974); U.S. Census Bureau, *Statistical Abstract of the United States 2003* (Washington, DC: U.S. Government Printing Office, 2004).
11. U.S. Census Bureau, *Statistical Abstract of the United States 1973* (Washington, DC: U.S. Government Printing Office, 1974).
12. Alan M. Hay, "The Economic Basis of Spontaneous Home Improvement: a Graphical Analysis," *Urban Studies* 18 (1981), pp. 359-364.
13. U.S. Census Bureau, *Statistical Abstract of the United States 2003* (Washington, DC: U.S. Government Printing Office, 2004).
14. Nicole Johnson, "Henrico Agency Plans to Revitalize Older Areas," *Richmond Times-Dispatch*, May 14, 2004.
15. John Marlles, interview, July 26, 2004.
16. Ibid.
17. Ibid.
18. Ibid.
19. James A. Bacon, *Inflection Point*, Bacon's Rebellion: The Op/Ed Page for Virginia's New Economy (2004), www.baconsrebellion.com/Issues04/01-19/Inflection_point.htm.
20. Jeffrey G. Kelley, "At Home Atop the Hill," *Richmond Times-Dispatch*, June 13, 2004.
21. Carol Hazard, "Awaiting Life Downtown," *Richmond Times-Dispatch*, June 20, 2004.

13

Can Local Policies
Make a Difference?

For many years, advocates for cities have bemoaned the impetus that federal policies have given to suburban sprawl.[1] Even more than federal policies, state policies may have encouraged sprawl.[2] Inner suburbs have suffered from outer ring sprawl, and they have received fewer targeted federal program benefits than cities.[3]

Sprawl driven by middle- and upper-income households leads to concentrated poverty in central cities and inner suburbs, as well as too little reinvestment in older areas.[4] New regionalists tend to think that regional reforms, such as tax-base sharing, are indispensable to correct these imbalances.[5]

While we support regional reforms, we believe recent changes in beliefs by many home buyers and renters provide raw material that have revived substantial parts of cities and inner suburbs. Evidence about relative income increases in city and suburban neighborhoods leads us to be optimistic about prospects for continuing their revival. At the same time, we have become pessimistic about the prospects of many of the suburbs that were developed between 1945 and 1970. The small house problem, in particular, will haunt these middle-aged suburbs. The middle-aged, small house problem also exists in cities. In the central cities in six metropolitan areas in Virginia, for example, 48 percent of the housing was constructed from 1940 to 1969.[6]

Raw material expressed by citizens' preferences in housing markets can be capitalized upon by well-designed public policies. While federal and state policies should bear most of the burden of redressing income and financial inequities, local policies can be effective to some extent, even when federal and state policies are misdirected.

Numerous local policies can nurture the positive trends that have been generated by greater interest in accessible and walkable residential locations. Some local policies require financial support from higher levels, such as mass transit investments. Other local policies can be created independently of federal and state support, except for delegated legal authority. Here, we introduce several types of policies, with brief examples, for which local action is essential and feasible. They involve community design; transit-oriented development; small house expansion; condominium creation; and attention to vacant land, abandoned buildings, rehabilitation codes, bank reinvestment requirements, brownfield redevelopment, and preservation rules.

DOWNTOWN REVIVAL DESPITE SPRAWL

Greater interest in mixed use, convenience, walking, culture, and entertainment may have accompanied, or caused, the revival of some downtowns in central cities. If central cities and older suburbs are going to revive, their historic downtowns probably will lead the revival. Downtowns usually contain more assets than any other part of a city or older suburb. Exceptions to this statement occur, principally around colleges and universities. However, where downtowns have many economic and cultural assets, revival of their jurisdictions is unlikely unless the historic center succeeds.

While the significance of downtown revival seems obvious, its probability seems doubtful. The deleterious effects of suburbanization on cities often became apparent first in cities' downtowns in the 1950s and 1960s. Vacant retail buildings, empty streets after 5:30 PM, and minimal comparison shopping testify to downtowns' deterioration across the nation. As residential sprawl continued, outward movement of retailing chasing customers accelerated, and it continues to the present.

On the other hand, numerous traditional strengths of downtowns have persisted. While varying greatly, and being affected by a city's population size, downtowns often have retained their central role in finance, law, courts, government, education, and culture, and many have added entertainment, conventions, modernized hotels, theaters, and restaurants, sometimes by reclaiming waterfronts for pedestrians. Moreover, 50 years of post-World War II development and planning modeled on separation of land uses produced few places in suburbs where residents can walk to nonresidential activities. Thus, even as downtowns have faltered across the nation, competitors have produced flawed settings that are vulnerable to losing ground to attractive mixed-use downtowns with convenient opportunities for pedestrians.

Population increases in numerous big-city downtowns were described in Chapter 3. We believe that desires to walk to numerous activities, in addition to convenient access to employment, have motivated many movers to downtowns. If our hypothesis is correct, then small cities in small metropolitan areas might experience downtown residential growth, even though commuting times are very short and not nearly as inconvenient as in large metropolitan areas. We offer Charlottesville, Virginia, population about 40,000 in a metropolitan area of about 160,000 in 2000, to illustrate this potential.

CHARLOTTESVILLE'S DOWNTOWN REVIVAL AND BEYOND

When Charlottesville confronted downtown decline in the late 1960s, the usual coalition of bankers, businessmen, and local government officials considered and rejected one typical remedy of that era—the short pedestrian mall near the main shopping street, adorned with small- to medium-sized ornamental trees with some street furniture and sculptures to add visual interest—the type of remedy that has been judged unsuccessful and removed in cities across the nation.

Instead, on its main business street, Charlottesville opted for the longest pedestrian-only mall in the United States relative to the size of its downtown. Charlottesville built a brick mall eight blocks long with no vehicles permitted on or across it. In doing so, the city created placid side streets one block on each side of the pedestrian mall, with the effect that one-half of the downtown area became a virtual car-free district. Thus, the pedestrian mall was an urban design strategy for transforming the character of downtown for pedestrians, rather than being a trivial pedestrian ornament added to an auto-dominated downtown.

Equally important, Charlottesville planted 63 shade-producing willow oak and maple trees in the pedestrian mall rather than the ornamental Bradford pear trees that had been recommended. The willow oaks grew within 15 years after planting to 50-foot heights with canopies that shaded virtually the full 66-foot width of the mall, achieving 50 percent shade of the entire mall during the moderate, warm, and hot months from April through October. The shade attracted outdoor restaurants, which attracted people, which attracted people to watch and visit with other people. The trees themselves were beautiful, in effect creating a city park in the main shopping, dining, and business street. In adjacent blocks, the city tried to improve traffic flow with signals and one-ways. The tight traditional street grid was retained, with major streets 36 feet wide, connecting streets 21 to 24 feet wide, and small blocks only 200 feet long, which enhanced a convenient walking context for pedestrians.

Within five years of the mall's installation in 1976, owners had renovated nearly 50 percent of the downtown buildings. Public investments occurred during the next 10 years in parking garages, government offices, courts, and libraries, with private investments in specialty shops, restaurants and residences, and a public-private partnership in a new hotel. These investments sustained downtown when department stores moved to the suburbs in the early 1980s. Downtown gradually picked up steam, adding more restaurants, comparison antique shopping, and special events. Then, from 1995 to 2005, a six-screen movie theater, an ice skating rink, a community theater building, and a renovated 1931 movie palace serving as a chic theater and music venue, seating more than 1,000 patrons, were added.

Having recreated a downtown that attracted patrons and residents by its new worth, supplementing much traditional strength, the attractive power of downtown spilled into more neighborhoods. From its launch in 1976, the revival of the downtown business and government core had been matched by revival of the north downtown residential area—the previous high-end portion of downtown's surroundings. From 2000 forward, the spillover attractions reached the working-class Belmont neighborhood, the African-American Starr Hill and Fifeville neighborhoods, and even the mixed-use warehouse, industrial, and low-income housing neighborhood south of the railroad tracks, which began to attract market-rate housing in apartments and condominiums as well as shops, light manufacturing, and athletic clubs. The effect of this transformation was to make residences more valuable per square foot than office and commercial properties. In north downtown, residences routinely sold for $250 per square foot and up, with some exceeding $300 per square foot. Housing market success brought with it growing concern about affordable housing, as real estate assessments in the working-class Belmont neighborhood increased by 40 percent in a single year in 2004.

This transformation of downtown, and neighborhoods near downtown, had several causes. The car-free downtown district strategy created a successful balance between pedestrians and motor vehicles, similar to limitations on motor vehicles found in many European cities. Charlottesville's city officials had kept their eye on the ball, adopting a consistent emphasis on the same downtown strategy for 35 years, rather than scattering attention on diverse claimants for public investments. The large tree-park strategy on the downtown mall had worked better than anyone anticipated in creating a uniquely attractive environment. The restaurant, entertainment, and culture evolution downtown had caught the wave of changing consumer preferences in a timely fashion—first benefiting from the increase in dining out, and then from an increase in the number of households who want to do functional walking to work, shop, dine, relax, and socialize.

Charlottesville's downtown illustrates benefits of effective planning, persistent management, innovative concepts, and aggressive taming of motor vehicle dominance. Charlottesville also demonstrates that even a small city in a rapidly sprawling region can, under some circumstances, stage a revival. One more observation: Downtown's revival was only marginally related to its presence in a university town. The University of Virginia was located between 1.5 and 3 miles west of downtown, bordered by its own retail, restaurant, commercial, and office districts. These districts competed with downtown more than they supported it. Consequently, as Charlottesville contemplated the future, the growing together of two areas of strength—downtown and the university—identified additional potential areas for rejuvenation.

Downtown's appeal has grown so strong in the metropolitan area that public officials of Albemarle County, which surrounds Charlottesville and has twice the city's population, have adopted downtown Charlottesville as their model for preferred development. If ideas about good places evolve in the direction of mixed use and greater density, then another major potential influence favoring reinvestment in existing settlements will have been unleashed.[7]

TRANSIT-ORIENTED DEVELOPMENT

Relationships between transportation and land use are integral to many redevelopment strategies. That was true in Charlottesville, although pedestrian access may not occur to many policy makers as a transportation strategy. Mass-transit enhancement is a more likely path to redevelopment success. The period from 1956 to 1970 was dominated by beliefs that expressways from suburbs to cities could bring shoppers back downtown. After nearly 50 years of failure of that strategy, most policy makers realize that expressways sped suburbanization without equal benefit to cities or downtowns. The balance between sprawl and compact development will be influenced considerably by how much transit-oriented development occurs.

Many older suburbs in large metropolitan areas have declined with symptoms similar to declining cities. They too have experienced population losses, relative income declines, and some poverty increases. Mass transit sometimes has been available as a revitalization strategy in older suburbs, albeit with massive federal financial assistance. Suburban political cultures often are not hospitable to increasing density, however, including near transit stations. Although federal or state financial assistance can make available transit-oriented development options, local government actions are required to capitalize on them. Interesting examples of successful use of transit-oriented development strategies are illustrated by the policies of Arlington County and the City of Alexandria in northern Virginia, adjacent to Washington, D.C.

ARLINGTON AND ALEXANDRIA

From 1960 to 2000, Washington, D.C.'s population dropped 25 percent. Outer suburban counties grew rapidly: Prince William County doubled between 1980 and 2000, while Loudoun County tripled in population. Forces stimulating residential sprawl were strong, and middle- and outer-suburban employment also increased dramatically, especially in Fairfax County. In addition, the inner suburbs of Arlington and Alexandria appeared in the 1970s to be declining rapidly, losing 10 percent of their population. Population loss was somewhat deceiving because occupied housing actually increased, as in many cities, with smaller household size accounting for their entire population decline.

Arlington and Alexandria planned in the 1960s and 1970s to locate stations on the 103-mile, heavy-rail transit system (known as METRO), financed substantially with federal funds, where dense development would be welcomed. Integrated office, shopping, and residential districts were planned. In contrast to outer suburbs, where park and ride with little adjacent development were planned, Arlington and Alexandria limited parking and promoted intense development for people who would work, shop, and recreate near residences.

Transit stations opened beginning in 1980. Arlington and Alexandria's population increased 24 percent in the 1980s and 1990s. Both jurisdictions were maintaining their prosperity. Housing values made their success most apparent, especially in contrast with Fairfax County, next in line heading toward the outer suburbs. Fairfax, one of the most affluent suburbs in the U.S., had median, owner-occupied housing that was 126 percent of the metropolitan median in 1970 compared with 105 percent in Arlington and 95 percent in Alexandria. By 2000, Fairfax's relative housing value had barely moved, at 130 percent of the metropolitan median value. Arlington's relative median, owner-occupied housing value had jumped to 147 percent, and Alexandria's rose to 141 percent, bringing them to the top of the housing value list in the metropolitan area. On a per-square-foot basis, Arlington and Alexandria fared even better because their housing units averaged considerably less than Fairfax's. In addition, Arlington had the lowest real property tax rate in northern Virginia, and its relative per capita income increased in 20 of 39 census tracts between 1990 and 2000.

Business Opportunities Director Terry Holzheimer said that Arlington had mainly used special permit processes to obtain the type of development it wanted near transit stations.[8] Only one parking garage was built in conjunction with a major department store. Arlington did not even create a redevelopment authority to invest in projects. Instead, it granted density bonuses, required ground-level retail, and insisted on residential development in conjunction with office development, which for nearly two decades was developers' preferred occupancy mode. However, by 2000 and thereafter, residential property sales per square foot were exceeding the values of office building sales at the two most intensely developed METRO station areas—Virginia Square and Court House. In Holzheimer's opinion, development in the early years would have been entirely office and retail if the county had not required residential development.[9]

Arlington and Alexandria benefited from growing comfort with condominium ownership. In 1970, the owner occupancy rate was 34 percent in Arlington and 26 percent in Alexandria. By 2000, single units' share of total residential structures was

41 percent in Arlington and 36 percent in Alexandria—less than owner occupancy, which had increased to 43 percent in Arlington and 40 percent in Alexandria. Desires for home ownership were being satisfied, even as density increased.

What are the lessons for aging suburbs in these trends? Fixed-rail transit investments and effective land development planning can facilitate mixed-use development. Rampant sprawl on the metropolitan fringe need not kill all city and inner-suburb redevelopment. Inner suburbs that exploit access advantages can increase population, relative incomes, home ownership, and property values, while limiting property tax rates. Most development can be concentrated near transit stations. Achieving a balance between walking, mass transit, motor vehicles, and a variety of private and public activities close to transit stations is the key to redevelopment success. Local governments must plan for what they want to achieve. Transit-oriented development will not happen based merely on private developers and residents' preferences.

MIDDLE-CLASS LOCATION DECISIONS AND SMALL HOUSES

Small house suburbs, and small house districts in cities, are more prevalent settings for reinvestment than downtowns and transit station areas. Their geographic scope creates huge opportunities for, as well as major obstacles to, reinvestment.

The median size of houses built in 1950 was 1,100 square feet. By 1970, the median size still, despite growing affluence, was only 1,375 square feet. In 2000, the median size reached 2,000 square feet, and the average exceeded 2,200 square feet—testimony to affluence, housing as investments, home offices, guest rooms, and home entertainment—as average household size plummeted during this same 50 years from 3.4 persons in 1950 to 2.6 persons in 2000.

Whatever the reasons for home buyers preferring larger houses in 2000 than in 1950 or 1970, changes in housing markets have transformed many cities and suburbs. Because housing markets changed, neighborhoods dominated or overwhelmed with these small, typical houses of 1950, 1960, and 1970 often experienced major decline in relative income and sometimes major physical deterioration as well. The more extensive these small house areas, the more at risk these neighborhoods were to deterioration.

The reasons for substantial, sometimes severe, deterioration are not obvious. Just as cities developed where there were location advantages, so did suburbs that developed after 1945. The automobile expanded the territory and number of good locations. In a general sense, however, areas closer to the traditional center, or closer to subcenters that emerged throughout the 20th century, had location advantages over more remote areas that were less accessible. Therefore, the same people who bought new 2,000-square-foot houses farther out could have bought expanded 2,000-square-foot houses—from houses that were 1,000 or 1,375 square feet—closer in. Sometimes that has happened but, as a percentage of such houses, the share of expansions is quite small.

At the heart of suburban problems are the decision-making obstacles to significant expansion of small, middle-aged houses to bring them to currently popular sizes and quality, as was discussed in Chapter 12.

- Design options are puzzling.
- If the design phase looks promising, finding a builder also is challenging.
- Zoning regulations must be mastered.

- Financing is complicated.
- For buyers, two homes must be financed during construction, and owners must find temporary housing—without disrupting family members excessively.

For developers, the challenge may be equally daunting. The developer faces the same risks of excessive reinvestment as the home owner in the leadership role.

Local governments usually are not organized to help with small house expansions. Why? The significance of the small house problem as an obstacle to reinvestment and relative income stability is not obvious. Therefore, it may not be a high enough priority. If the problem gets on a local government's agenda, specific locations in which to target assistance may be difficult to discern. One key question is: What makes one small house neighborhood rank higher than another for local government attention?

The answer to these dilemmas probably is to craft assistance that can help decentralized and dispersed owners and buyers make decisions. Design guidebooks can illustrate options for expanding standard house configurations. Architectural computer programs for remodeling in local government planning or housing offices can demonstrate implications of alternative designs. Lists of interested architects and contractors, and guides to references and projects, can shorten searches for assistance. Training for local government staffs and coordination among them, and user-friendly guides to navigating zoning and site plan processes, can aid owners and buyers who are trying to determine whether design options are feasible. Fees for applications and building permits can be waived or reduced. Focus group discussions with lenders may help them create shortcuts to satisfactory financing. Financing can be facilitated for construction periods long enough to cope with uncertainties. Construction loans can flow smoothly into long-term mortgages, even at the long-term mortgage rate.

A design guidebook has been developed by First Suburbs Coalition of the Mid-America Regional Council in Kansas City, Missouri, "to assist owners and potential buyers of homes in the region's first suburbs with renovations to post-WWII housing ... The First Suburbs Coalition Idea Book examines four of the most common housing types found in these suburbs—Ranch, Split Level, Two Story, and Cape Cod—and provides dozens of ideas for appropriate ways to update and make additions to them."[10] This guidebook project illustrates how a regional council of governments can help its constituent members with small house adaptations.

Sometimes publicly supported neighborhood planning can help. If neighbors are aware of mutual interests in expanding and upgrading, cooperation in timing can reduce risks associated with being the first expander or upgrader in the neighborhood. Perhaps a nonprofit local housing trust fund will be needed to provide some gap financing. Furthermore, if a nonprofit developer takes the lead with several upgrades, expansions, or new construction, private owners also may be encouraged to upgrade or expand.

Short-term rental housing is the most difficult problem. Perhaps a local government redevelopment authority or a nonprofit housing trust fund can own, rent, and manage small houses in target neighborhoods as temporary replacement housing. Temporary housing probably can be provided at minimal cost or even at an operating profit and, upon resale and if the neighborhood has been upgraded, the houses eventually can be resold at a profit.

The easiest local government policy to implement is for tax abatements for expansions and improvements in quality. Tax abatements will tend to be less useful than the other policies described here because the benefits occur at the end of the process and the amount of the tax savings is small compared with the required investment. The tax abatement is more likely to influence the amount of reinvestment, encouraging reinvestment sufficient to qualify for the tax abatement, rather than influencing initial decisions to upgrade.

Each of these policy steps is low cost and technically feasible. In sum, they amount to a considerable administrative effort. Engaging in all of them requires a major organizational commitment. Such engagement will occur only if the importance of the subject is clearly perceived. This necessity returns public officials to the original problem. If public officials are not educated to be aware of how small houses have become a cause of relative income and property value decline in neighborhoods and jurisdictions, then the policy steps will not be taken. The front-end burden, therefore, lies with the internal educators of a local government who, more often than not, will be the planners, redevelopers, budgeters, and finance officials.

Major policy and administrative efforts to upgrade and expand small houses are more feasible but less likely for large counties than for small suburbs. Large counties have potential to extract property tax and sales tax revenue from higher income and expanding districts, especially newer shopping centers and office parks. Large counties also have abandoned shopping centers and office parks for which new uses have not been found. Andres Duany and Peter Calthorpe have argued that the design challenges to converting old shopping centers to mixed-use developments with streets and blocks are not difficult.[11] Moreover, political obstacles are limited in that neighbors usually will not object to redevelopment of derelict commercial properties. The political will to tackle these expensive redevelopment projects may be lacking, however, and financial incentives for developers to adopt these sites may be inadequate to persuade them. Moreover, the property and sales taxes from still-prosperous commercial areas in large counties usually are sufficient to permit elected officials to defer these problems.

CHICAGO'S HISTORIC BUNGALOWS

Cities have variations on the problem of too many small houses. Sometimes the construction and design virtues of older housing can strengthen desires to rehabilitate and expand attractive housing. Baltimore and Norfolk have started programs to provide design assistance, recruit house expanders and rehabbers, and guide potential reinvestors to financing options. Baltimore's Healthy Neighborhoods Initiative puts these market-enhancing elements in a neighborhood context. Announcing this program in 2005, the program Web site said that the five or six neighborhoods selected in the first year should "have no or very little vacant housing, relatively stable real estate values with potential for an increase, active resident involvement and a workable set of target blocks with strong anchors . . . selecting a doable area where the impact is apparent and will leverage other investments is important."[12] The goal is to give market demand a boost rather than to create a market where demand was meager.

Chicago launched a variation on the theme of stimulating latent market demand in 2000 with The Historic Chicago Bungalow Initiative. Chicago's most common single-family, detached house type is the bungalow style. These 80,000 one-and-one-half-story brick houses account for nearly one-third of the city's single-family residences. Due to their age, typically 80 years, Chicago has combined historic preservation, rehabilitation, green building, and expansion goals.[13] The historic character of these resources constituted a promotion opportunity that the city government has exploited as a special asset, in addition to location and sound-structure aspects of the houses.

Besides extensive education and promotion, tangible assistance is provided to owners, buyers, and renovators in many forms. Although not required to be followed, the city's design guidelines provide extensive education and helpful hints about how rehabilitation should be conducted. When owners have their residences certified as Historic Chicago Bungalows, they are eligible for free permit assistance from the Chicago Department of Buildings, and qualify for discounts from the list of vendors who participate in expositions of designs, products, and services. Four Pattern Drawings can be purchased, each of which has 12 to 15 pages of architectural drawings, a floor plan, a site plan, and a demolition plan. Guides for cost estimating are included. Pattern Drawings are for a rear addition, dormer addition, kitchen, and bathroom. They include sections, plans, elevations, details, materials inventories, and cost worksheets. Guidance is provided about how to work with an architect.

Financial assistance is available. Energy Savers grants, with a $1,000 limit and a 50 percent match, are available for windows, doors, and insulation. A $2,000 limit and a 50 percent match apply to furnaces, water heaters, air conditioning, and solar heat. A $500 energy-efficient appliance voucher is available. Low- and moderate-income households may qualify for grants of $3,000 to $5,000. Mortgage financing also is available. For low- and moderate-income households, down payment grants and partial exemptions from federal income taxes may be available. For traditional financing, rehabilitation can be financed at the same time and at the same interest rate as the mortgage, and the mortgage amount can be based on the appraised value of the residence after rehabilitation, rather than on the purchase price of the unimproved residence.

Because the bungalow style is so prevalent, the historic bungalow program constitutes much of a neighborhood rehabilitation plan. It is a rebuilding and expansion program that discourages demolition. While special benefits are provided for low-income applicants, the basic education, free permitting, permit assistance, design alternatives, and mortgage financing opportunities are available to everyone.

SINGLE-UNIT DWELLINGS

Other opportunities for reinvestment and revival of cities and older suburbs are the conversion of single-unit rental housing to owner occupancy and the construction or conversion of residential condominiums. These are the main opportunities to increase home ownership in central cities and in middle-aged suburbs. Home ownership is desired by such a large percentage of the middle class—about 90 percent of persons in their 50s and 60s were living in residences that they or their spouses owned in 1980 and 1990.[14] Home ownership is a necessity if neighborhoods and jurisdictions are to recover from the draining of the middle class from local residency to outer suburbs in larger houses.

Rented single-unit houses occur mainly due to local and regional housing market conditions. Often rentals occur because the housing market for ownership has been weak. If household formation is static or declining, then some existing houses will not find buyers, because some new houses will be constructed and occupied by owners. If the economy is adding jobs and households are increasing, but average wages are low in the additional jobs, then many households will not be able to afford ownership unless mortgage interest rates are uncommonly low, as they were from 2002 to 2005.

The jurisdictions and neighborhoods that are less attractive than most alternatives will depend on a stronger regional market to maintain or increase their ownership rate. In these situations, some public sector or nonprofit housing trust fund encouragement may be needed to increase home ownership. Public sector encouragement may involve improvements in neighborhood infrastructure, shopping, education, public services, and aesthetics. Housing programs may help, such as programs to expand small houses, grant tax abatements for rehabilitation and expansion, assist with site assembly, and dedicate publicly owned properties to home ownership projects. Finding resources for these investments, and deciding which neighborhoods most merit these types of investments, are difficult hurdles. Prospects for success in increasing home ownership under these conditions are modest.

High percentages of rented single-unit structures also may occur because the local and regional rental market is strong. Strength in the rental market may occur either because of increases in household formation or because there is a sizable percentage of local residents who are present for a few years, perhaps with breaks in their presence. College and university students are the main category of such residents who have incomes and housing strategies that produce attractive rents for landlords. In these situations, investors may acquire single-unit structures to rent, especially near the magnet for renters, such as a university or perhaps a teaching hospital. These renters are an advantage to landlords and local governments in that their rents are sufficient to enable owners to maintain the property and pay taxes while having few school children, thereby limiting demand for public school resources.

This advantage also is a liability. Single-unit structures are the most likely housing type for middle-income families with children. Lacking sufficient middle-income children in public schools, the schools will deteriorate in performance or perception, or both. Deterioration of public schools then becomes an obstacle to retaining and attracting middle-class families. Consequently, programs to expand small houses and to provide multiunit rental housing near the magnet (universities and hospitals) may compensate for competition from renters for single-unit structures, returning more of these structures to owner occupancy.

CONDOMINIUMS INCREASE OWNERSHIP

Condominiums also are important, but they have a different clientele than single-unit structures. Condominiums are attractive owner-occupant options for many single people, couples without children, empty nesters, and retirees. Their relatively rare occupancy by families with children is a matter of taste rather than inherent size or location characteristics. Apartments with children are not likely, as a rule, to be better located for children than are condominiums. Many of the potential occupants of condominiums, however, live in single-unit structures, even though they do not prefer them. The single-unit structure, which usually comes with a yard, and may come with an inconvenient location, has disadvantages that many condominiums can overcome. Condominiums are a useful housing option for central cities, older suburbs, and perhaps middle-aged suburbs to retain and attract more middle-income households.

Between 2002 and 2003, comparing resales of housing units for the second quarter, single-unit houses increased in price by 7.4 percent and condominiums increased by 15.2 percent. In 2003, condominiums were 25 percent of multifamily housing units produced.[15] In the post-World War II period, home ownership increased nationwide from 45 percent of occupied housing in 1945 to 62 percent in 1960. The housing stock in central cities contained too much multifamily housing for an equivalent percent increase in ownership there. Consequently, much of the owner occupancy increase occurred in suburbs where detached, single-unit structures were the norm, and where the owner occupancy rate was 73 percent compared with a central city rate of 47 in 1960.[16] Condominiums during those 15 years from 1945 to 1960 were rare.

From the run-up in ownership nationwide, we infer that more of that ownership increase could have occurred in central cities if the legal framework, lending policies, public sector encouragement, and developer capacity for constructing or converting condominiums had existed in more cities. William Hudnut has observed that "the Levittowns of post-World War II America made the ideal of home ownership a reality. Critics of suburbia missed this point . . . For these middle-class Americans, home ownership in suburbia—in spite of the homogeneity, the architectural similarity, the low-density development, and all the other defects [Lewis] Mumford and others noted—represented an achievement, not a tragedy . . . Here, white, middle-income Americans invested in their future, . . ."[17] Renting, not owning, was required in most multiunit structures, however, and this condition contributed to relative income declines in most large American cities.

Why was supply still lagging behind demand for condominiums at the start of the 21st century? Part of the answer is that most buyers have preferred single-unit structures, both for the clarity and limited complications involved with such ownership and for the outdoor space and suburban locations that usually accompanied the construction of new housing. However, additional aspects of the answer lie in the incentive, legal, institutional, and public policy emphases on single-family, detached housing compared with condominium housing. Although those obstacles have been reduced, some of them persist.

For developers, almost any site that is practical for condominiums also will be feasible for apartments. Apartments are easier administratively and financially. If the apartment project can be rented profitably initially, tax benefits augment apartments' advantages. If the project is to be sold as condominiums, the developer must sell them promptly, face heavy carrying costs, or get into the rental business. With single-family projects, they can be staged and lots can be sold to numerous builders, spreading the risk over longer periods of time and among more investors.

Lenders, faced with similar issues, want many condominium units presold (reserved) before providing construction financing. Numerous buyers must be found before the project is built, before even a model unit can be examined. Lenders want more equity during the condominium construction process than in a single-unit structure project. Buyers also may face higher down payments if not enough units are sold to owner occupants and too many are bought by investors to rent. This can deter resales, slowing or eliminating the gain in unit values.

If there are problems with roofs, foundations, plumbing, paint, or mold, condominium developers are more vulnerable to lawsuits than in single-unit structure projects because more buyers will have the same complaint, and they are organized in a condominium association. These issues, cumulatively, make developers more sensitive to location issues. If a location is marginal, lacking clear comparability to previous condominium successes, then developers may defer development or construct apartments instead. For these reasons, local governments may need to impose mandates or offer density bonuses on desirable sites, and provide infrastructure or parking incentives for condominium development in marginal locations.

ENHANCING DECENTRALIZED DECISIONS

Each of these subjects—small house expansions, renter-to-owner transitions, and more condominiums—involve highly decentralized decisions by buyers and sellers, facilitated by government but not managed by government. Downtown redevelopment and transit-oriented development are decentralized to local governments and private investors, but at the local level they are more centralized than the other policy subjects discussed above because of their large scale. Another array of problems falls in the category of decentralized reinvestment decisions, which can confound the redevelopment potential of cities and suburbs.

Management of vacant land, abandoned buildings, tax-delinquent properties, rehabilitation codes, bank reinvestment requirements, brownfield and grayfield redevelopment, and preservation rules also are noteworthy for their decentralized effects on buyers and sellers in redevelopment markets. Each subject involves longevity. How long a life span should be expected from a building? How long can a building remain unused with taxes unpaid before it is claimed by the government and made available to investors? Should banks that accept deposits from neighborhood residents be required to reinvest some portion of those assets within the neighborhood? How much remediation of polluted land should be required before active reuses can begin? Which historic preservation rules will apply in which areas and by whom will they be interpreted?

Public-private partnerships have been advocated and in vogue for many years. Public-private partnerships are important, especially in downtown and transit-oriented development, because big projects require collaborations. However, the functioning of land and building markets in commonplace settings, as described above, is at least as important because many more properties, decision makers, and neighborhoods are involved. Beliefs about locations must be effectuated in land and building markets. If those land and building reinvestment markets create too many obstacles, then the tyranny of easy development decisions yields additional sprawl patterns.

These subjects need attention from local decision makers, but local action often will not be enough. State laws about tax lien enforcement systems can reduce average times for local governments acquiring tax-delinquent vacant properties from seven years, as in Philadelphia, to far fewer.[18] Michigan has reduced the time to develop a marketable title after a tax sale from six to three years.[19] State building codes often have been blamed for needlessly obstructing rehabilitation of buildings by imposing high costs, thus rendering buildings useless, constituting fire hazards, and blighting their surroundings. New Jersey's Rehabilitation Subcode won a government initiatives award in 1999 from Harvard's Kennedy School of Government.[20] Maryland adopted a similar rehabilitation code in 2001. State legislation can facilitate brownfield redevelopment, but the variation in laws in the 48 states with voluntary clean-up programs suggests there is much to learn about best practices.[21] Federal loan disclosure rules (Community Reinvestment Act of 1977 and Home Mortgage Disclosure Act of 1989) may affect loan frequencies beneficially by race and perhaps by neighborhood.[22]

Federal legislation recognizing problems of first suburbs was introduced in May 2005 by Senator Hillary Rodham Clinton (D–New York). The Suburban Core Opportunity, Restoration, and Enhancement (SCORE) Act of 2005 is a planning and project construction grant program for project areas having some of these characteristics: deteriorating properties, an average housing cost burden of at least 50 percent of gross income, a commercial property vacancy rate 30 percent above average, and an obsolescent regional mall. The planning process is intended to propose a mixed-use project, provide diverse housing types, preserve historic features, and increase open space.[23] The tone of the legislation is similar as in legislation focused on central city revival during the period from 1960 to 2000. The intent of SCORE seems to be to make suburbs eligible for attention that previously was directed mainly toward central cities.

INVESTMENT DECISIONS

If beliefs in households about where residents would like to live have been changing, and if they will change more in the future—toward potential revival of central cities and older suburbs—those beliefs need to be implemented through investment decisions for them to have meaningful impacts. Preferences are not enough. Willingness to invest is required. Willingness to invest brings on decisions, and decisions confront realities of current values and future prospects. Geographic proximity alone cannot overcome vacant land and abandoned buildings, unworkable rehabilitation codes, insufficient loan funds, and unrealistic reclamation requirements.

Federal and state laws that govern these subjects have a promising aspect. They can be modified without confronting intrametropolitan political calculations within specific metropolitan areas. Reducing obstacles to reform of foreclosing on vacant buildings does not threaten middle-income residents of new suburbs. Rehabilitation codes do not much concern representatives of exurban settlements. Neighborhood reinvestment requirements for lenders have a simple fairness aspect that is persuasive. Brownfields' abatement may be costly in dollars but it does not impose a geographic risk to bedroom suburbanites. Consequently, there is reason to hope that well-targeted legislative reform efforts at these subjects may survive many of the city-versus-suburb political battles, which doom much federal and state legislation that is advocated for central cities.

NOTES

1. Robert Fishman, "The American Metropolis at Century's End: Past and Future Influences," *Housing Policy Debate* 11 (2000), pp. 199-213; Norman J. Glickman, ed., *The Urban Impacts of Federal Policies* (Baltimore: Johns Hopkins University Press, 1980); Bruce Katz, ed., *Reflections on Regionalism* (Washington, DC: The Brookings Institution, 2000).
2. Myron Orfield, *American Metropolitics* (Washington, DC: The Brookings Institution, 2002).

3. William H. Hudnut III, *Halfway to Everywhere* (Washington, DC: Urban Land Institute, 2003); Robert Puentes and Myron Orfield, *Valuing America's First Suburbs: A Policy Agenda for Older Suburbs in the Midwest* (Washington, DC: The Brookings Institution, 2002).

4. Anthony Downs, *New Visions for Metropolitan America* (Washington, DC: The Brookings Institution, 1994); Peter Dreier, John Mollenkopf, and Todd Swanstrom, *Place Matters* (Lawrence: University Press of Kansas, 2001).

5. Myron Orfield, *American Metropolitics* (Washington, DC: The Brookings Institution, 2002); David Rusk, *Inside Game Outside Game: Winning Strategies for Saving Urban America* (Washington, DC: The Brookings Institution, 1999).

6. William H. Lucy, "Cities Emerging Opportunities and Suburban Problems" (Hampton: Virginia First Cities Coalition, May 18, 2005).

7. William H. Lucy, *Charlottesville's Downtown Revitalization* (Charlottesville, VA: City of Charlottesville, 2002).

8. Terry Holzheimer, interview, December 5, 2001.

9. Ibid.

10. Mid-America Regional Council (April 28, 2005), http://marc.org.

11. Andres Duany, Elizabeth Plater-Zyberk, and Jeff Speck, *Suburban Nation* (New York: North Point Press, 2000); Peter Calthorpe and William Fulton, *The Regional City* (Washington, DC: Island Press, 2001).

12. Mayor's Healthy Neighborhoods Initiative (May 11, 2005), www.baltimorecity.gov/neighborhoods/mhninitiative.html.

13. The Historic Chicago Bungalow Initiative (2005), www.chicagobungalow.org.

14. Dowell Myers and Jennifer R. Wolch, "The Polarization of Housing Status," in Reynolds Farley, ed., *State of the Union: America in the 1990s, Vol. 1* (New York: Russell Sage Foundation, 1995), p. 279.

15. David Seiders, *Condominiums: The Brightest Spot on the Horizon* (Las Vegas: International Builders Show, January 2004).

16. U.S. Census Bureau, *Metropolitan Housing, Volume 1* (Washington, DC: U.S. Government Printing Office, 1963).

17. William H. Hudnut III, *Halfway to Everywhere* (Washington, DC: Urban Land Institute, 2003), pp. 28-29.

18. Paul C. Brophy and Jennifer S. Vey, *Seizing City Assets: Ten Steps to Urban Land Reform* (Washington, DC: The Brookings Institution and CEOs for Cities, October 2002).

19. U.S. Department of Housing and Urban Development, Regulatory Barriers Clearinghouse, www.huduser.org/rbc.

20. New Jersey Department of Community Affairs, New Jersey's Rehabilitation Subcode (2004), www.state.nj.us/dca/codes/forms/rehab.htm.

21. Nancey Green Leigh, *The State Role in Urban Land Redevelopment* (Washington, DC: The Brookings Institution, April 2003).

22. Alex Schwartz, "The Impact of Community-Reinvestment Agreements on Mortgage Lending to Minority and Low-Income Households and Neighborhoods," in Fritz W. Wagner, Timothy E. Joder, and Anthony J. Mumphrey Jr., eds., *Human Capital Investment for Central City Revitalization* (New York: Routledge, 2003).

23. Senator Hillary Rodham Clinton, Suburban Core Opportunity, Restoration, and Enhancement (SCORE) Act of 2005 (S.1024), http://thomas.loc.gov/cgi-bin/query/query.

14

Prospects for
Stability and Revival

Major reinvestment has occurred in central cities throughout the second half of the 20th century, even in most northern industrial cities that have suffered the greatest declines in population, occupied housing, and relative income. Reinvestment sometimes has been ill conceived, as with some interstate highways. In most cities, reinvestment has been spotty, and sometimes it has been inconsequential compared with larger areas of disinvestment. The 1990s provided significant evidence that widespread reinvestment in residential areas in many of these northern central cities and older suburbs, as well as others throughout the nation, may be possible by attracting and retaining a larger share of middle-income households.

Trickle-down processes of neighborhood change became less predictable in the 1990s. In the 1980s, some old neighborhoods increased in relative income. Then, in the 1990s, many more old neighborhoods reversed the direction of the standard trickle-down processes of neighborhood change, with those neighborhoods rising rather than falling in relative income.

By 2000, the lowest income census tracts were those specializing in 1940s housing rather than pre-1940s housing. More pre-1940 than 1940 specialized census tracts had higher average family incomes than the metropolitan average. Almost as many pre-1940 as 1950s specialized tracts were above the metropolitan average. Moreover, the probability of income going up in pre-1940s census tracts was higher than in census tracts specializing in the housing of any decade except the 1990s. Consequently, if this trend continues between 2000 and 2010, more pre-1940s census tracts should be above average family metropolitan incomes by 2010 than census tracts where 1950s housing is prominent and should be closing the gap with 1960s tracts. This is the trend we predict.

We believe these changes have been nurtured by an altered distribution of beliefs by households about where they would like to live. These changes, we suspect, have been modest, although significant, to date. If consumer preferences have aided these neighborhood transformations, what might happen if consumers obtained and acted on more accurate information than heretofore, learning, for example, that relative dangers of leaving home are lower where walking is easier and public transportation is available? Would the trickle-down process of neighborhood change be reversed in more neighborhoods in many more cities and older suburbs?

Perhaps. It is remarkable that the turnaround in attractiveness of pre-1940 housing in many cities, many high-poverty census tracts, and in many older suburbs has occurred with little impetus from major or consistent public policy innovations or investments—or so it seems—but that is one of the questions not addressed here systematically. Grogan and Hudnut have claimed that local public policies have accomplished much.[1] Downs, Dreier, Katz, Orfield, and Rusk have argued that, with major innovations and new coalitions, much could be accomplished.[2] Duany and Calthorpe have stressed that the problems are within reach of public and private development projects executed sequentially and collaboratively.[3] However, these commentators have not provided evidence that gains have occurred.

Although we have provided evidence of gains in central cities, still there has been a continued downward trend in cities' relative median family income through the 2000 census. Even in Charlottesville, with its vivid property value escalation, only modest evidence has surfaced that relative income of city residents overall has halted its three-decade downward slide—although free lunch and reduced price eligibility of Charlottesville's public school children declined from 51 percent in 1998 to 49 percent in 2004. In Arlington and Alexandria, outside Washington, D.C., the trends and public policies (heavy-rail rapid transit, preservation, and urban design) interacted to produce stability and improvements. Relative per capita income has a brighter story nationwide for cities than relative median family income—perhaps for the same reasons that middle-income and affluent singles, and households without children, often have preferred cities to suburbs.

In sum, the overall trend during the 1990s continued to be declining relative incomes in cities compared with suburbs. These downward trends in central cities signal continuing stresses. If we had not discovered the surprising reversal of direction in incomes of residents in pre-1940 neighborhoods, we would have continued to be as pessimistic as other analysts about central cities' prospects based on trends from 1990 to 2000.

The relative income trend from 2000 to 2003 tells a different story. Based on data for 20 central cities in large metropolitan areas, the fortunes of cities improved dramatically after 2000 compared with the 1990s. As described in Chapter 4, only six out of 20 cities increased in relative per capita income in the 1990s; from 2000 to 2003, 15 cities increased. Only three of 20 cities increased in relative median family income in the 1990s; from 2000 to 2003, 11 cities increased. Because the improving cities are diverse regionally (north, south, east, and west) and economically (industrial, high tech, information processing, and balanced), we have some confidence that the apparent post-2000 improvements in large cities are real. These census data also match anecdotal and factual data about rapid residential sales prices and real property assessment increases in cities between 2000 and 2005.

VARIATION AND UNCERTAINTY

Because vulnerabilities of cities, older suburbs, and middle-aged suburbs are substantial, their prospects continue to be uncertain and highly varied. Central cities' assets usually are rich and diverse. Sometimes assets—more often in suburbs than cities—are few and unfocused. Weaknesses in middle-aged suburbs are predictable—weak fiscal bases; too many small, outmoded houses; ordinary rather than gracious older homes; too little preservation; and unattractive neighborhood and strip commercial areas. Cities and suburbs that historically were dependent on assembly-line manufacturing are adorned by empty hulks of factories or they have factories that will close eventually. Their heritage of brownfields, vacant lands, and abandoned buildings are among the challenges to overcome.

Race is another reason for uncertainty about prospects for cities and suburbs. African-Americans have made some income gains, especially when two-parent households are college educated. Poverty concentrations among blacks have fallen. Blacks are being supplanted by Hispanics as the largest minority group. Blacks suburbanized in the 1980s and 1990s, but segregation, though slightly less, still dominates residential patterns. All-black, or all-Hispanic, suburbs are more likely to occur than all-minority central cities. By 2000, some minority-dominated suburbs had become poorer than central cities that had majority black populations. Whereas the blacks who moved from the South in the 1950s and 1960s in search of work and opportunities fed white avoidance in those cities where the influx was heaviest, can it be said that avoidance of blacks is as evident in the 1980s and 1990s, when black population numbers have been stable and black suburbanization has been common?

Schools are another arena of immense uncertainty. Has outward movement of middle-class families been fueled each decade since 1950 by the search for better schools, and safe peer settings, as well as bigger houses, more space, and, in particular, ownership and the investment and control that accompany ownership? Much common knowledge—informal conversations and Realtor conventional wisdom—will say that schools are a major motivator of where to buy. The persistent downward trend of relative median family income in central cities from 1970 through 2000 provides reason to suspect that schools' images contribute to neighborhood and jurisdiction results. When Atlanta had a relative per capita income ratio in 2000 of 1.03 and a relative median family income ratio of only .63, shouldn't we expect that schools played a role in that difference? Those who worry about such trends, like Orfield and Rusk, and Grogan and Proscio who claim progress has been vivid, have been unable to identify school programs that show prospects of assisting a revival of interest in central cities by middle-income families with children.

REGIONALISM

Each of these subjects—small, outmoded houses; race and minority language barriers; schools; and safety—is a pertinent subject for public policy research about what has worked, is working, or may work. Each of these problems may be addressed by geographically broader public policies. This broader reach is the goal of regionalists. They argue that regional strategies must be implemented to reduce residential segregation and ongoing discrimination in housing, reduce unequal revenue capacities among local governments, augment capacities for sound investment in regional infrastructure, and diminish sprawl tendencies through effective regional planning and implementation of more compact development.

These goals are important, and well-structured regionalism could enhance pursuit of each one, but whether these regional approaches are essential or helpful is an important distinction. If they are as essential as some advocates claim, then the gains made in high-poverty census tracts, downtowns, transit-oriented development, old neighborhoods, and old suburbs would seem unlikely, even impossible.

Regionalism emerged before 2000 as a reinvigorated concept about how to improve conditions in metropolitan areas. Whereas regional governance attempts in the mid-20th century tended to emphasize how metropolitan governance could produce efficient and effective government and perhaps more equity, recent arguments have emphasized how regionalism can enhance equity in finance and service quality and contain suburban sprawl. Moreover, claims have been made that equity and sprawl containment are impossible without enhancing regional governance, however difficult such governance may be. Critics counter that regional governance is an even more utopian concept than revival of poverty areas through neighborhood self-help activities. While meaningful efforts at revival have occurred in hundreds of poverty neighborhoods by nonprofit agencies and some government programs, significant regional innovations, other than limited-purpose special districts, have been rare.

Data reported in Chapters 3 through 6 indicate that some metropolitan areas that have championed aspects of regionalism—like Portland, Seattle, Minneapolis–St. Paul, and Indianapolis—have made more gains than have been typical. Other data indicate that central cities, which include substantial portions of their metropolitan areas and which have been able to annex territory from time to time—Las Vegas, Charlotte, San Antonio, Phoenix, Houston, Columbus, and San Diego—have been more successful than the norm at retaining and attracting middle-income families as well as individuals. What is to be made of gains in cities where no significant regional governance changes occurred and which contain small shares of metropolitan population—Chicago, Los Angeles, Atlanta, San Francisco, and Richmond (and Arlington and Alexandria outside Washington, D.C.)? Other forces also are at work in some metropolitan areas that offer hope for central cities.

BELIEFS RELEVANT TO LOCATION DECISIONS

Prospects for less sprawl, less concentrated poverty, and more reinvestment will be facilitated by altered beliefs and more attractive settings as well as by sounder public policies. Relying on public policies alone is too fragile and therefore it is unrealistic, as we suggested in Chapter 2. A focus on public policy changes by critics of sprawl and social inequities is understandable because public policies seem more likely to change than beliefs are to be altered. Public policies also are more sweeping in their potential effects than creating more attractive settings as a way of altering beliefs about places. We argue, however, that beliefs have been changing in ways that augur well for comebacks in some central cities. Moreover, perceptions seem to have altered about whether city or suburban settings are more attractive. Therefore, more settings may be adapted in coming decades to attract middle-income households than occurred from 1950 to 1990.

One of the motivating beliefs impelling post–World War II development patterns—the belief that cul-de-sacs are safe, especially for small children—has been exaggerated and continues to be misguided. This belief about cul-de-sacs is an example of a cultural myth with potentially massive impact on behavior. If this cultural myth shifts moderately, the effect on residential location decisions may be significant. If this cultural myth shifts dramatically—even reversing direction so that cul-de-sacs are perceived as no safer than through streets, or are perceived as more dangerous and unhealthy because they lead to driving too much and walking too little—then major alterations in residential location patterns may occur. As concern about the dangers of obesity increase, the potential also increases that cul-de-sac residential street networks will be seen as dangerous to health by inhibiting walking.[4]

In the realm of behavior, beliefs about safety in outer suburban areas also affect residential location decisions. Exurban locations usually are more dangerous than central city, inner-suburban, and middle-suburban locations because of the frequency of traffic fatalities and serious traffic injuries. Awareness of these conditions seems meager. Neither residential location decisions nor survey responses reveal much concern about traffic dangers. The lack of such awareness is somewhat surprising from one perspective: the emphasis placed on traffic dangers by many protesters in public meetings about development proposals who oppose connecting streets through residential neighborhoods to external areas. Ironically, it is another array of small-scale dangers—dangers of walking and being robbed, assaulted, or murdered by strangers—that exceed concern about high-speed traffic dangers.

If differences in crime rates continue to narrow between central city and suburban areas, avoidance of cities by the crime-wary may diminish. If awareness of traffic dangers in outer suburbia increases, then the attractiveness of these areas may diminish. Little is known about how one influence on location decisions, such as safety, ranks versus others. However, surveys reveal that safety is cited more often in home buyer surveys than any other single subject as a concern in choosing residential locations. Therefore, a major change in perceptions of relative safety could have a meaningful effect on location decisions. Less faith by middle-income households in the myth of cul-de-sac safety and the myth of exurban safety could lead to significantly less motivation for sprawl and more desires to remodel existing housing.

BELIEFS, ROLES, AND POLICIES

In our perspective on metropolitan conditions, trends, and problems, we give substantial weight to citizens' beliefs, decision-making dynamics, and public policies. Decision-making dynamics are mechanisms that link the public and private sectors through markets and professional roles and norms. Giving substantial weight to each influence, we discern different determinants than analysts of metropolitan problems. For example, Robert Fishman compiled and commented on the results of a survey of members of the Society for American City and Regional Planning History who were asked to rank the "top 10 influences on the American metropolis of the past 50 years."[5] Fishman's experts came up with the following rank order with each point score in parentheses: Interstate Highway Act of 1956 (906 points), Federal Housing Administration mortgage guarantees (653), deindustrialization of central cities (584), urban renewal (441), Levittown-type suburban houses (439), racial segregation and job discrimination (436), enclosed shopping malls (261), suburban sprawl (242), air conditioning (234), and the urban riots of the 1960s (219).[6]

One can discern probable influences on location decisions by households and businesses in this set of causes. The list includes federal legislation, economic transition, behavior regarding race, technical innovations, physical aspects of suburbanization, and events. Each condition has been important. Interpreting the results, Fishman wrote: "The single most important message of this list is the overwhelming impact of the federal government on the American metropolis, especially through policies that intentionally or unintentionally promoted suburbanization and sprawl."[7]

Critiquing this federal government-centered interpretation of city decline, Robert Beauregard has argued that greater specificity about causal claims, awareness of sequencing of federal policies and city and suburban outcomes, and more comparison of differences among cities in regions of the U.S. and the U.S. versus Europe would lead to greater attention to the role of market decisions by investors and consumers. Concluding, Beauregard wrote that the federal government "commands vast resources and broad powers, can act nationally, and (purportedly) can influence private sector decisions. . . . In addition, the government seems open to public concerns. It is more difficult to influence the private sector; collective pressure is not as easy to deploy and less likely to be influential."[8]

Here we argue that the private sector has been influenced by stressful suburban conditions, by modified images of the "good neighborhood," and by evolving conditions of housing and neighborhoods in cities and suburbs. Our focus on beliefs, decision-making dynamics, and public policies interactively led to some variations from Fishman's list. If one thinks about beliefs, mistaken beliefs about safety in relation to residential locations, and beliefs about what constitutes a good neighborhood, they should be considered for a list of leading causes of suburbanization. State policies may have had more influence on metropolitan outcomes than federal policies. If one considers differences in cities' conditions among the states, one's attention is directed to state laws that increasingly limited annexation by cities of their suburbs, and the sweeping but uncertain effects of rural-dominated state legislatures nationwide, until the redistricting aftermath of the U.S. Supreme Court's one-person, one-vote decision in *Baker v. Carr* in 1962.[9] In *Governance and Opportunity in Metropolitan America*, the authors identify state policies as those most conducive to creating interjurisdictional inequalities: "The distinctively American political institutions that give rise to spatial patterns of residential location are local control of land use decisions, state laws permitting easy incorporation of municipalities, and a fiscal system that requires municipal governments to finance most of their local services from their local tax base."[10]

If one considers professional roles and their interaction with public policies, it was not necessary that architects practice and advocate the least appealing designs in history during the 1950s and 1960s when urban renewal was the public policy of choice. Aided by the arrival of preservation instincts and activism in the 1970s, the form and content of architecture gradually improved from 1970 through the end of the 20th century. It was not necessary that the tyranny of easy development decisions (easy development on the fringe, neighborhood opposition to infill, and absence of regional votes on development patterns) dominate land development processes. These decision-making forces also were the causes of sprawl. It was not necessary that cities would pay too little attention to the civic and neighborhood-stabilizing virtues of home ownership. Public policies were a result of some of these beliefs and decision practices. These citizen beliefs and development practices produced worse results than would have occurred from the influences of federal policies alone.

In our view, focusing on beliefs, influences on reinvestment decisions, and public policies interactively provides a more balanced target for remedial action. Public policies should not be the only arena in which action and results are sought.

MARKETS AND DECENTRALIZED DECISIONS

Consumer preferences expressed in housing markets have been credited or blamed for suburbanization. Federal policies have been implicated, especially interstate highways and low down payment mortgages with deductible interest on federal income taxes. State and local policies on school finance, property taxes, and land-use controls are relevant. "Push factors"—crime, drugs, disorder, race, and schools—have been involved. Ample geography and history that extol moving onward have shaped attitudes. These forces merge in individuals and communities. Ultimately, location decisions are expressed through housing markets because nearly all housing in the United States is provided through private markets.

Humorist Will Rogers recommended investing in land in the 1930s because no more land was being made. He was mistaken. More land was made that was reachable conveniently by automobiles and trucks. Because more land was accessible, it was valuable and worth investments, but accessible land can be badly managed. Good houses in dreary settlement patterns do not hold their value.

Markets relate supply and demand, but demand without supply is inarticulate and supply is not free. Physical, labor, and financial components are needed. Legal authorization and political support also are required. If political support is weak or absent or, in contrast, if political opposition is vigorous, then supply will be affected. Where people live, therefore, provides useful clues but not definitive answers about demand.

Prices of housing and incomes of residents provide better clues about demand. Here again, clarity is difficult. Trends may not be the same as current or recent conditions that have accumulated over decades. The trickle-down process of neighborhood change has been in play, but it has not dominated everywhere, and much less frequently in the 1990s than in the 1980s and less in the 1980s than in the 1970s. Demand seems to have shifted. At least to us, there seems more reason to credit shifts in demand than shifts in public policies, although some public policies have tapped into latent demand—as in Charlottesville, Arlington, and Alexandria—and provided places for demand to be expressed.

Markets are both conservative and radical. They are conservative in the sense that once consumer preferences have been met, the apparatus that meets them tries to perpetuate the preferences to maintain markets in which producers and suppliers are thriving. Markets also are radical because rapid changes occur. Inventions open possibilities. Technology gradually converts new ideas into salable products. Tastes evolve. Producers compete with each other. International trade has impacts. Risks are taken, and suddenly global giants of one year can be bankrupt the next—witness Enron, WorldCom, and United Airlines in 2002.

Joseph Schumpeter described this characteristic of capitalism as creative destruction.[11] Society can thrive as business firms succeed, grow, atrophy, and die. Society, however, is composed of settlements. Settlements produced by markets also can succeed, grow, atrophy, and die. The equation can be reversed. It is apparent that, as settlements rise and fall, business firms can either follow the same trajectory as settlements, if they are locked in place, or they can serve markets for the prosperous, moving on as needed to reach them.

The trends described here track the rise and fall and partial revival of neighborhoods and governmental jurisdictions. Some neighborhoods and jurisdictions are more successful and more resilient than others. Not much is known yet about what the resilience of suburbs will be. Cities, it seems, may have been demonstrating more resilience in the 1990s than many observers expected, but the forces that influence community trajectories are so numerous and complex that predictions rest on shaky foundations.

Still, we will hazard the general prediction that challenges to, and some reversals of, the trickle-down process of neighborhood change will become more common. We predict as well that at least a few positive breakthroughs in public policies will occur. These breakthroughs are much more likely by states than by the federal government. Ever more numerous advances by local governments will also occur, we predict with more confidence, because urban design ideas promoted by the new urbanism and smart growth advocates have taken root in land development professions and with substantial segments of housing consumers.

While these predictions have a positive tone, other predictions are gloomy. As an illustration of reasons for pessimism, we describe a visit to Henrico County, adjacent to Richmond, Virginia, where we were invited in 1998. A tour of a part of the county that had been developed in the 1950s conjured the impression that it was a future slum—1,000-square-foot houses, no sidewalks, nothing to walk to, no commerce, chain-link fences, no front porches, little landscaping—an aesthetic wasteland. It was a big area, block after block after block. We inquired of our tour guide whether he could think of any place in Henrico County where people might go because they like being there rather than because they have some functional task to perform. After a lengthy pause, he gave up: "I can't think of any," he said.

The county administrator had formed 10 task forces on the future of Henrico County. One dealt with suburban decline. Henrico County in recent decades has regarded itself as the elite governmental jurisdiction in the Richmond metropolitan area. We asked at one task force meeting whether anyone in Henrico County could imagine aspiring to be like the City of Richmond. No one could conceive of such an aspiration.

After the tour, I (Lucy) said, "I cannot not figure out what Henrico can do to avoid becoming a basket case. It seems inevitable, given your housing stock, and the lack of assets and any reason why someone would want to live in middle-aged parts of the county, if they had a choice. By 2020," I said, "I predict that the City of Richmond will be doing well, and much of Henrico will be regarded as an area with no future."

The trend revealed in the 2000 census seems as predicted, even though the west end of Henrico County is bustling with trendy, high-end shopping and office parks, and development conditions that delay fiscal problems and therefore forestall a sense of crisis. Key questions are: What will Henrico do about the downward relative income trend in a 15-mile downward swath of its residential areas? When will much of Henrico hit bottom where some neighborhoods already are at less than 50 percent of average metropolitan incomes? What possible rebounding path can be imagined?

We have grown accustomed to lamenting the condition and prospects of large central cities. The days of lamentation for central cities are not over, but signs of hope have emerged and some progress has occurred in some cities. The days of lamenting conditions in suburbs have begun. When suburban conditions deteriorate, so that relative income, for example, is well below the level of Detroit in relation to its metropolitan area, what path to revival is possible? This subject may seem filled with irony, perhaps even a sad humor amid decades of talk about whether the prosperous suburbs need cities anymore. It will not be pretty. The deluge for middle-aged suburbs has only begun.

WHERE NEXT?

What are the beliefs and goals that are rearranging socioeconomic status patterns? More people are seeking relief from motor vehicle dependency. Motor vehicle dependency is exhausting but unhealthy. With freedom from daily mobility by muscle power come overweight and atrophied bodies. With control of more private space comes deterioration of public space. With an acre of land for every middle-income suburbanite comes frustration with chauffeuring children to school, friends, lessons, movies, sports, church, and even babysitting. For people frustrated with this lifestyle, will the desire for more convenience be satisfied with mere safety, more travel options, and less wasted time? Will convenience be complemented with recreation variety, cultural alternatives, social diversity, and civic engagement—each of which is facilitated by more travel options and less wasted time?

Reviving cities and older suburbs in 2005 and beyond is not as straightforward as creating suburbs with separated land uses in the 1950s. Institutional, infrastructure, legal, and financial frameworks should be adapted to make revival more likely and to improve its quality. New regionalism has some virtues. New urbanism is helpful. Neighborhood civic and economic engagement is useful. Reinvestment opportunities downtown, near transit stations, and in small house districts should be seized. Owner occupancy of residences in compact settlements should be increased. Rules that inhibit revitalization should be challenged. Financing that facilitates rather than limits rehabilitation, expansion, preservation, and infill should be enhanced. Public policies can improve each of these subjects. Planning and design that create quality places where people want to be may be as or more important than public policies. Beliefs influence spatial patterns and public policies. Ultimately, people need to think rightly, believe in what is sensible and valuable, and take responsibility for cumulative social and political effects as well as individual economic benefits.

NOTES

1. Paul Grogan and Tony Proscio, *Comeback Cities* (Boulder, CO: Westview Press, 2000); William H. Hudnut III, *Halfway to Everywhere: A Portrait of America's First-Tier Suburbs* (Washington, DC: Urban Land Institute, 2003).

2. Anthony Downs, *New Visions for Metropolitan America* (Washington, DC: The Brookings Institution, 1994); Peter Dreier, John Mollenkopf, and Todd Swanstrom, *Place Matters* (Lawrence: University Press of Kansas, 2001); Bruce Katz, *Reflections on Regionalism* (Washington, DC: The Brookings Institution, 2000); Myron Orfield, *American Metropolitics* (Washington, DC: The Brookings Institution, 2002); David Rusk, *Inside Game Outside Game: Winning Strategies for Saving Urban America* (Washington, DC: The Brookings Institution, 1999).

3. Andres Duany, Elizabeth Plater-Zyberk, and Jeff Speck, *Suburban Nation* (New York: North Point Press, 2000); Peter Calthorpe and William Fulton, *The Regional City* (Washington, DC: Island Press, 2001).

4. Kenneth E. Powell, Linda M. Martin, and Pranesh P. Chowdhury, "Places to Walk: Convenience and Regular Physical Activity," *American Journal of Public Health* 93, no. 9 (2003), pp. 1519-1521.

5. Robert Fishman, "The American Metropolis at Century's End: Past and Future Influences," *Housing Policy Debate* 11 (2000), p. 199.

6. Ibid., p. 200.

7. Ibid., p. 201.

8. Robert A. Beauregard, "Federal Policy and Postwar Urban Decline: A Case of Government Complicity," *Housing Policy Debate* 12, no. 1 (2001), p. 147.

9. *Baker v. Carr*, 369 U.S. 186; 82 S.Ct. 691; 7 L.Ed.2d 663, 1962.

10. Alan Altshuler, William Morrill, Harold Wolman, and Faith Mitchell, eds., *Governance and Opportunity in Metropolitan America* (Washington, DC: National Academy Press, 1999), p. 29.

11. Joseph Schumpeter, *Capitalism, Socialism, and Democracy,* 6th ed. (London: Unwin Paperbacks, 1987).

Index

339